# MAKING VISIBLE THE INVISIBLE:

## an anthology of original essays on film acting

*edited by*
CAROLE ZUCKER

The Scarecrow Press, Inc.
Metuchen, N.J., & London
1990

British Library Cataloguing-in-Publication data available

**Library of Congress Cataloging-in-Publication Data**

Making visible the invisible : an anthology of original essays on film acting / edited by Carole Zucker.
p. cm.
ISBN 0-8108-2220-2 (alk. paper)
1. Motion picture acting. I. Zucker, Carole.
PN1995.9.A26M35 1990
791.43'028—dc20 89-36466


Manufactured in the United States of America

Printed on acid-free paper

For my parents,
Doris and Allyn

"On stage, you make all the decisions. In movies,
you say to yourself, 'It's not my fault!
It's not my fault!' "

—GERALDINE PAGE

# CONTENTS

# PREFACE

AT A FILM STUDIES CONFERENCE I chaired a workshop on screen acting. The experience confirmed the view I held concerning the state of acting theory and criticism: each of the nine workshop participants proposed a unique approach to the subject. The modes of examining film acting were varied; a semiological analysis of gesture, socio-historical interpretation of performer/spectator/industry relationships, a reading of narrative patterns in support of the development of the star persona, and observations on the "objectification/commodification of images of women"[1] were some of the methodologies and concepts presented. This polyvalence of critical positions is both salutary and commendable. It betokens a vigor, enthusiasm, and openness in a field or investigation that is in its inaugural stage. This anthology, in some measure, mirrors this salubrious plurality of thought.

In the last decade we have witnessed a pronounced increase in the number of texts concerning screen performance. This efflorescence began with the publication in 1979 of Richard Dyer's seminal book, *Stars,* and continues with the exploration of the subject in several major journals (*Screen,* 1985; *Wide Angle,* 1984; and others), plus the promise of book-length studies on the work of individual actors and performance theory in the near future.

While acclaim is in order for the recognition of film acting as an important area of study, one is nonetheless struck by the persistence of a phenomenon Dyer records in *Star*.

> While everyday critical talking about film tends to concentrate on performance (e.g., "What was so-and-so like in the film you just saw?"), an important tradition in film theory has tended to deny that performance has any expressive value: what you read into the performer, you read in by virtue of signs other than performance signs.[2]

It would seem that since the 1929 publication of Pudovkin's *Film Technique and Film Acting* there has been scant discussion of what actually occurs when an actor acts in a film, in spite of the fact that "a good deal of the meaning of the fiction film is borne by its actors and their performances."[3]

I would speculate that this disinclination to deal with performance is rooted in several issues. First, film studies is a comparatively youthful discipline, still searching, at times, for legitimacy. Ostensibly, to discuss acting is to align oneself with the "ordinary" (i.e., untrained) moviegoer or the "everyday critical talking" cited by Dyer. (Potentially even more deleterious is the association of this subject with "popular" television/radio style criticism.) While it seems like a natural part of the experience of moviegoing to pass judgment on an actor's performance, this emphasis on the evaluative process is anathema to many scholars. Second, it is mostly true that film acting is "impure" when compared to acting in the theater, where the performance is thrown into high relief. (As George Jean Nathan once wrote ". . . a screen performance bears the same relationship to a stage performance that a hiccup bears to Camille's tuberculosis."[4]) Critical analysis of film acting is muddied by numerous signs that are not "performance signs": mise-en-scène, framing, camera movement, the written text, the soundtrack, etc. But these elements indisputably bear an effect on our perception of the performance. Questions of authorship for the work of the screen actor present an untidy enigma, at best. Finally, when discussing the actor, we enter the awesome and perilous territory of the human presence. Interest circulates around the expressive qualities of an actor's voice and body; the project of describing and articulating an aural characteristic or a gestural trait can be daunting. This same presence is, moreover, a source of reflection, passion, and even revelation, uncommon conditions for scholarly labor.

The articles composing this anthology partake of numerous methodologies, in part a reflection of the polyvalence of contemporary film theory. The plurality of approaches also mirrors the newness of film acting as an area of study; it is a topic that calls forth a variety of responses and remains relatively untrammeled territory (which is not to claim that any of the methodologies employed in these articles represent "maiden" endeavors in theory, but rather that their application to the subject at hand brings some vivifying discourse to film studies).

The anthology is divided into two broad categories. Part I deals with film acting in a historical and generic context. Pearson's essay examines the changes from the histrionically to verisimilarly coded acting in Griffith Biographs from 1908 to 1913, while comparing the gestural system of the period to other coded systems. Like Pearson, Rothman deals with melodrama, explicating the role the actor and camera have in declaring a hero or villain's moral identity. In his essay on the musical, Delamater investigates the "ritualization of performance" and the relationship of "ritual" musical numbers to the narrative. He claims—using Gene Kelly as his primary example—that "performance exists within realist space but simultaneously exploits concepts of cinematic abstraction." Waugh discusses the performative aspects of documentary, foregrounding the shift between "presentational" and "representational" modes, and raising the issue of the accountability for the "performance" of the "social actor." Commencing with a look at the Doinel figure in Truffaut's work and continuing with analyses of key *nouvelle vague* works, Testa determines that in the films of this "school" there is a contestation of the various means by which an actor obtains star presence: through non-classical use of space; reinforcement of play-acting; and disruption of the integrity of human presence (e.g., disjunction between sound and image). Fischer's feminist reading of films about actresses playing actresses—with *Persona* and *The Girls* as the focus—develops the connection between the mother as willing, then unwilling object of a child's desire. This "rejection" is mis-read as deceit, or trickery, and the woman is forever consigned to be a player of roles, thus creating archetypal woman as actress.

The articles in Part II concentrate on case studies of individual actors, or on a director's work with actors. In her piece on John Barrymore, Keane speculates that Barrymore's thought about himself as an actor and about acting are incorporated into his performances, and—under the most fortuitous circumstances—

acknowledged by the camera and director. Carroll characterizes Keaton's acting as an "interaction with things in their physical dimension" and explores the structure of gags as a way in which we understand Keaton's character. The confluence of the written word and performance in French film of the 1930's is Gendron's topic. She concentrates on the main actors in *La Grande Illusion,* and how their association with certain objects, manner of dress, gesture and speech patterns are molded by the scenario and emerge from the individual qualities of the performers. My essay is a close analysis of the collaboration between Sternberg and Dietrich, centering on issues of stylization, theatricality and authorship.[5] The history of the Method and the enactment of a "method" performance by James Dean (and its conflict/contrast with other performance styles in *East of Eden*) is the subject of the article written by Larue with my assistance. Falsetto looks at two different Kubrick films, *Barry Lyndon* and *The Shining,* and reveals two radically dissimilar performance styles, each conceived with respect to the concept of the film as a whole. As Tomlinson avers in his study of *A Man Escaped,* Bresson inhibits processes of "projection" and "identification" with the actor through "flattening" the body, face and voice, disavowing access to emotional properties and the revelation of spiritual qualities. Dalle Vacche proposes definitions of representation, spectacle, and performance, and views the acting in *The Conformist*—in its dialectical shift between stasis and movement—as a process through which the site of the body becomes the body politic.

The articles in this anthology embody many of the divergent currents in performance analysis and theory as it now stands. It is my hope that the extraordinary richness of this area of study is revealed in this collection.

I would like to emphasize that this is a collection of original essays, and I thank my contributors for their collaboration. Thanks to the Conservatoire d'art cinématographique for the use of their prints, and to the Museum of Modern Art Stills Archive and the Harvard Theater Collection for the use of stills. My gratitude extends to Concordia Assistance to Scholarly Activity and the Aid-to-Publication Grant, the Faculty of Fine Arts, Dean Robert J.

Parker, and Barbara MacKay for their financial assistance. Thanks to Bart Testa and Francine Blais for their thoughtful criticism of the manuscript. I am obliged to Julie Corcoran for her careful and inventive graphics for the chart on method acting. I am indebted to Benny Chou for his excellent and exceedingly hard work on the frame enlargements. Kudos to Donna Lytle for her speedy proofing and Annie Ilkow for the index. *Je veux adresser mes remerciements, les plus sincères* to Johanne Larue, who worked as my research assistant, typist, collaborator, and who, through many long weekends and late nights, was always a model of enthusiasm, resourcefulness, and support. Most of all I would like to acknowledge my deepest gratitude to Mario Falsetto, who played the part of my champion in this endeavor. The frustrations and pleasures unique to compiling an anthology were shared by my husband; for his forbearance and support I am grateful.

CAROLE ZUCKER
Concordia University
Montreal, Quebec

## NOTES

1. Richard Lippe, "Kim Novak: A Resistance to Definition," *CinéAction!*, no. 7 (Dec. 1986), p. 7.
2. Richard Dyer, *Stars* (London: British Film Institute, 1979), p. 162.
3. John O. Thompson, "Screen Acting and the Commutation Test," *Screen* vol. 19, no. 2 (Sumnmer 1978), p. 55.
4. George Jean Nathan, cited by Alexander Knox, "Acting and Behaving," in *Film: A Montage of Theories*, ed. Richard Dyer McCann (New York: E.P. Dutton, 1966), p. 63.
5. This article is reprinted in a modified form from Carole Zucker, *The Idea of the Image: Josef von Sternberg's Dietrich Films* (Associated University Presses, 1988).

# 1. "O'ER STEP NOT THE MODESTY OF NATURE": A Semiotic Approach to Acting in the Griffith Biographs

Roberta E. Pearson

## I.

FILM CRITICS AND HISTORIANS find much that is admirable in D.W. Griffith's early Biographs, the less scholarly among them giving credit to the "Belasco of the Screen" for every technical advance in the second decade of cinema. Yet even the most devout acolyte of the "great dictator" harbors reservations about the acting in these films, characterizing it with such pejorative terms as overwrought, exaggerated, theatrical, and most damning of all, melodramatic. The latest addition to the rapidly growing Griffith bibliography, *D.W. Griffith: An American Life* by Richard Schickel, accepts this traditional view. Speaking of Griffith's first film, *The Adventures of Dollie*, Schickel says, "Despite the stylized pantomimic gestures employed by Linda (Arvidson) and Arthur Johnson ... , some small transcendence of types and situations was achieved."[1] Schickel might find *Dollie* laudable in all other respects, but to him the acting is on an equal, that is to say equally bad, footing with any other 1908 one reeler.

A few pages later, discussing the results of the 1909/10 California expedition, Schickel states, "There was still, even in Griffith's films, plenty of posturing, exaggeration, excessive movement ... , but in fact he was managing to tone down and sometimes ... to almost totally eliminate it."[2] Here again Schickel follows his predecessors, who see a steady progression from the posturing of the early Biographs to the restrained, yet powerful and affecting performances of Lillian Gish, Blanche Sweet, and Mae Marsh in the later one reelers and features. Given this teleological perspective, devotees can then add the development of cinematic acting to Griffith's list of credits.

Acting style undeniably changed drastically over the five years Griffith directed at Biograph. To take two well-known examples, consider *The Song of the Shirt* (October 1908) and *The Painted Lady* (October 1912), films featuring two of Griffith's leading ladies, Florence Lawrence and Blanche Sweet. By 1908 standards, Lawrence underplays, but her arm flailing and hyperbolic grief at her sister's deathbed invariably produce titters from a naive modern audience, which condemns her for "going over the top." By 1912 Sweet portrayed a mad woman with remarkable restraint, only at one point resorting to the "stylized, pantomimic gestures" which Lawrence had employed much more frequently in the earlier film. Her performance thus has much greater resonance for that same modern audience.

While we cannot expect the average viewer of a seventy-five-year-old film to respond in the same manner as the original audience, we can expect a film critic or scholar not to use the aesthetic standards of his or her own time and culture in judging an artifact from another time and culture. Those who ridicule the acting in the earlier Biographs commit this error, which they then compound by assuming a natural evolution to the more familiar and more modern style of 1913.

This annoying parochialism inspired me to study Biograph acting, trying to avoid both time-bound aesthetic standards and easy, yet ultimately meaningless contrasts such as "overwrought" versus "restrained." The goal was to develop some relatively objective way to describe and document the change in performance style between the first and last of the Biographs. The sparse and inadequate literature on cinematic acting proved of very little help in this endeavor. Since my project dealt with a system of signification (i.e., acting), I turned to the field of semiotics.

With the exception of intertitles (still infrequent during this period), the actor's movements conveyed most of the narrative information in silent film. Hence, that part of semiotics which focuses upon gestural signification looked promising. If verbal and gestural communication were similar enough so that the latter displayed the same characteristic regularities as the former, then the task of objectively describing and documenting Biograph acting would be greatly facilitated. In the hope of developing a widely applicable, synchronic, and ahistorical model of acting style, I began to investigate the parallels between speech and gesture.

Unfortunately, the preponderance of evidence suggests that gesture does not signify in the same way as speech. Gesture, as opposed to speech, lacks both double articulation and a limited lexicon and is analogical rather than digital in nature.

**(1) Double articulation.** Semioticians often begin their analysis of signifying systems by searching for a minimal unit which constitutes the basic building block, as it were, of that system. Eisenstein and Pudovkin, though not calling themselves semioticians, identified the shot as the minimal unit of cinema. The minimal unit of spoken and written communication is the smallest distinct articulated grouping of letters. These combine to form significant units, or monemes. Monemes constitute the first articulation and phonemes the second articulation.[3] No one has yet isolated minimal units of gesture which form larger units. There seem to be no gestural equivalents to phonemes and morphemes. As Metz argues about the shot, a gesture is not a word or a syllable but a whole phrase which cannot be further broken down. Eco labels this phenomenon a "super sign," defining it as a sign "whose content is not a content-unit but an entire proposition; this phenomenon does not occur in verbal language but it does occur in many other semiotic systems."[4]

**(2) Limited lexicon.** The resemblance of gestures to phrases or even whole sentences rather than words precludes a gestural dictionary. Just as there are an infinite number of possible shots, there are an infinite number of possible gestures. This distinguishes both cinema and gesture from natural language systems. As Metz says of cinema, " … one of the great differences between this language system [cinema] and natural language is due to the fact that, within the former, the diverse minimal signifying units … do not have a stable and universal signified. In a natural language each morpheme (moneme) has a fixed signified. … "[5]

The lack of double articulation and a limited lexicon would cause Juri Lotman to deny that gesture is a language system. "A system, in order to fit the classical definition of a language, must possess a finite number of repeating signs which at every level can be represented as bundles of a more limited number of differentiating factors."[6] The absence of a minimal gestural unit and presence of an infinite number of possible gestures also greatly complicates any possibility of a gestural semiotics. Gesture's analogic rather than digital character represents a further complication.

**(3) Analogic versus digital communication.** Digital communications, such as formal language systems, involve "discrete, discontinuous elements and gaps."[7] Barthes claims that this discontinuous character has in the past (i.e., before he wrote) been considered necessary for signification to occur at all.[8] Gesture is, however, an analog communication, involving "continuous quantities with no significant gaps."[9] This continuous flow of signifiers, along with the lack of a minimal unit, makes it extremely difficult for the analyst to segment gestural signification. "We define gesture as that which cannot be limited or isolated, as that which cannot be isolated from the flow of communication without damage resulting."[10]

Since gesture cannot be segmented, the one-to-one correspondence between signifier and signified of verbal communication does not exist. Greimas states that the semiosis of the gesture will consist "in the relation between a sequence of gestural figures, taken as the signifier, and the gestural project, considered as the signified."[11] The recipient understands this gestural project only by translating it into another sign system, that of verbal language.[12] Barthes points out that this sort of translation is common in the case of analogic systems. "These systems are almost always duplicated by articulated speech … which endows them with the discontinuous aspect which they do not have."[13]

The nature of gestural signification renders improbable a widely applicable, ahistorical, synchronic model of cinematic performance. This does not, however, totally invalidate a semiotic approach to Biograph acting style, since we have thus far limited ourselves to traditional Saussurean semiotics. Eco, in his *Theory of Semiotics,* argues that the problem with many previous semiotic studies has "been that the interpretation of various signs on the basis of the linguistic model, and thus the attempt to apply to them something metaphorically similar to the sound parameters or the model of double articulation, etc."[14] Later he continues in the same vein: "It is wrong to believe ... that every sign system act is based on a 'language' similar to the verbal one."[15]

Eco proves useful for my purposes not only because he jettisons the linguistic model, but because he introduces the diachronic element. Frederick Jameson warns us against "the dangers of an emergent *synchronic* thought, in which change and development are relegated to the marginalized category of the merely *diachronic*, the contingent or the rigorously nonmeaningful,"[16] a criticism which has rightfully been made of Saussurean semiotics. As an alternative to Saussure's linguistically based and strictly synchronic model, Eco offers a diachronic semiotics based on a theory of codes and taking into account the cultural and historical milieu in which signs are produced and received.

The difference between Saussure and Eco is like the difference between baseball rules and statistics and an actual baseball game. The rules and statistics, postulating an ideal and unchanging universe, govern every play by the same regulations and judge the players' performance against a consistent hypothetical standard of excellence. Saussurean semiotics, postulating an ideal and unchanging universe, imagines every signifying action to be governed by the same regulations and every communicator to possess the same hypothetical standard of linguistic competence. In actual practice, neither baseball nor signification works this way. Each time the pitcher winds up, a great many factors determine his pitch and his opponent's response: the player's condition, the score, the number of outs, the batting lineup, the mood of the crowd, the weather, etc. In baseball each play is a unique and singular event. Each time a signifying act occurs, a great many factors determine which signs the addressor produces and what interpretation the addressee gives them: culture, ideology, time, place, the linguistic competence of both parties, etc. In Eco's semiotics each signifying act is a unique and singular event.

It is unreasonable to demand that a semiotics account in detail for every single ramification of every single signifying act. Eco merely suggests that it is possible for the analyst to identify the various codes which broadly account for signification.

Critics who condemn the acting in 1908 Biographs unthinkingly apply their own aesthetic codes while making no effort to understand the contemporary codes at work. To reformulate my earlier question: How can we avoid the trap of applying the wrong codes in our analysis of these films? Let us consider again Lawrence and Sweet and their respective performances. A critic with some knowledge of theatrical history might characterize Lawrence's style as melodramatic, and Sweet's style as realistic or naturalistic. Such labels are marginally more useful than "overwrought" versus "restrained," but they involve their own theoretical difficulties. As our imaginary student of the theater should be aware, the concepts of realism and naturalism have had wide currency in dramatic criticism since Shakespeare's time at least. Remember Hamlet's advice to the players: "O'erstep not the modesty of nature; for anything so o'erdone is from the purpose of playing, whose end, both at the first and now, was and is to hold, as 'twere, the mirror up to nature." Nineteenth-century theatrical reviewers quoted this line almost as frequently as revivalist preachers invoked the Bible. Melodrama and its adjective, melodramatic, are of more recent origin, the dramatic form itself not appearing until the end of the eighteenth century. By the end of the following century, however, "melodramatic" had become a frequently used pejorative, and our present critics use the term to describe everything from the films of Douglas Sirk to the latest television miniseries.

The adjectives "melodramatic," "realistic," and "naturalistic" are so indiscriminately applied to such greatly diverse theatrical eras and performers that one begins to feel like Alice conversing with Humpty Dumpty. The egg rather scornfully remarked, "When I use a word it means just what I choose it to mean—neither more nor less."[17] To make matters worse, the use of these adjectives is not restricted to the drama: literary and other critics of the arts all too frequently abuse and misuse the terms.[18] Worse yet, by using the word "realism," one risks becoming mired in philosophical debates on the nature of reality, a subject far beyond the purview of a humble film scholar.

Fervently hoping to skirt the theoretical debates attendant upon the terms melodramatic and realistic (or naturalistic), I shall avoid the latter as much as possible and use the former only in a very strictly defined sense. Following Humpty Dumpty's advice to Alice, I shall invent my own terms for Biograph performance styles.

Is it feasible to claim simultaneously to apply contemporary codes to Biograph acting and yet want to create neologisms for these codes? Certainly, if one realizes that codes have no independent existence of their own but are a construct of the analyst. "Codes exist only because the analyst has created them with materials furnished by the message."[19] In this case, the codes are created not only from the message, that is the films themselves, but from a knowledge of the culture in which the films were made. "Code" is used here not in the strict sense of a set of rules by which the analyst elucidates the organizing principles of a system of signification. Rather, "code" refers to a shared frame of reference between the addressor and addressee based upon common knowledge of a certain body of texts—or, in other words, upon intertextuality. The texts can be literary, dramatic, or even common notions about the state of the world. As Culler tells us, "It is important to assert that a work's relation to other texts of a genre or to certain expectations about fictional worlds is a phenomenon of the same type … as its relation to the interpersonal world of ordinary discourse."[20]

Between 1908 and 1913 the shared frame of reference about performance style between the Biograph producers (in the broadest sense) and their audience gradually shifted. In 1908 the producers and audience derived the frame of reference primarily from their knowledge of culturally specific notions about the mimesis of everyday life. Performance was "verisimilarly" coded.

The *Oxford American Dictionary* defines "histrionic" as "theatrical in character or style, stagey."[21] Why not simplify matters by referring to 1908 acting as theatrically coded? Obviously, any code which figures in a theatrical (or cinematic) production can be dubbed theatrical, notwithstanding the frame of reference from which it is derived. "Histrionic" specifies the texts referenced: the melodrama.

Melodrama as a theatrical form originated in late eighteenth-century France and became extremely popular throughout the nineteenth century both in Britain and the United States. Though various sub-genres, such as the gothic and the domestic, emerged and disappeared over the years, certain elements remained constant. Plots centered around imperiled virtue, black villainy, and fantastic coincidences which allowed the former to triumph over the latter. Heightened emotion and exciting situations mattered far more than coherent narrative progression. Stock figures of no psychological depth inhabited these improbable plots: most importantly, the pure heroine, the gallant hero, and the dastardly villain. These characters, even the humblest among them, all possessed great verbal facility, their speech marked by rhetorical excess and bombast.

As they spoke actors gestured in an equally broad and overstated fashion—the villain twirling his mustache and flourishing his mandatory cloak, the heroine clasping her hands to her bosom in terror and pleading, the hero clenching his manly fists as he vowed to protect his beloved.[22] The actors selected their gestures from a repertoire of standard, conventional gestures kept alive not only through an "oral" tradition, but through descriptions and illustrations in acting manuals and handbooks. These handbooks, coupled with contemporary reviews, theatrical promptbooks, and close viewing of the Biographs themselves, facilitate a general analysis of the principles underlying the histrionic code.

The term "verisimilar" comes from Todorov's concept of verisimilitude. Todorov says that "we speak of the work's verisimilitude insofar as the work tries to convince us it conforms to reality and not its own laws. In other words, verisimilitude is the mask which is assumed by the laws of the text and which we are meant to take for a relation with reality."[23] Verisimilitude should not be equated with reality; rather, verisimilitude is what a particular culture takes for reality. Reality in this sense is a cultural construct, a matter of commonly held opinion, rather than a historical or philosophical concept.

Labeling performance as verisimilarly coded does not require determining how closely the Biograph actors' gestures approximated the gestures of their real counterparts in the America of 1913. Instead it requires determining how the Biograph producers and the audience believed the real counterparts behaved. It is possible, indeed probable, that madwomen in 1912 did not wander vaguely around draped in the shawl in which they had murdered their lover, as does Sweet in *The Painted Lady*. But if Sweet's acting corresponded to a 1912 audience's idea of how a madwoman might behave, we are justified in calling her acting verisimilar.

But how can we discover what people in 1913 thought of as everyday behavior? Theatrical promptbooks and acting manuals provide little assistance, so we must turn to evidence from the contemporary trade press. Though space limitations prevent my doing so, it is possible to trace in reviews of the Biographs, interviews, and other material the gradual application of such terms as "life-like," "realistic," etc., to Biograph acting. Contemporary written evidence indicates that later Biograph performance style was indeed considered more "realistic." Here is a representative statement from Griffith himself speaking in December 1913, a few months after his departure from Biograph. "It [film acting] does not require any training in the legitimate stage for the reason that that kind of acting is so bad, so far away from human life, and so unreal as to appear ridiculous in moving pictures. But it does require special training in naturalness, which we give ourselves."[24]

As this suggests, Griffith and the trade press were seeking to distance film acting from its melodramatic origins and had been doing so for quite some time prior to 1913. The ideological implications of such a strategy fall beyond the present scope of this paper. For the present, suffice it to say that Griffith, and at least that part of his audience which was the trade press, consciously contrasted the new verisimilarly coded acting with the old histrionically coded acting.

## II.

The first part of this paper established a theoretical approach to the changes in Biograph acting style. The second part will expand upon the notions of the histrionic and verisimilar codes. The goal is to elucidate the general principles as histrionic, verisimilar, or some mixture of both.

The histrionic style's derivation from theatrical melodramatic conventions necessitates a brief exploration of nineteenth-century acting. Though several different acting schools (in the loose sense of the word) flourished both simultaneously and consecutively throughout the century, only those which appear markedly similar to early Biograph acting need concern us at the moment. One of the most popular of these, which I shall use as emblematic of the others, was founded by François Delsarte, a Frenchman who headed a theatrical academy in Paris and died shortly after the Franco-Prussian War. Delsarte founded his system upon the observation of human behavior, assuming that emotions are mirrored in posture, a different posture corresponding to every shade of feeling. Delsarte devised exercises which taught his students to reproduce these postures, aiming for a style which might be dubbed "selectively verisimilar." As one of his American disciples, Genevieve Stebbins, put it, "The actor's art is to express in well known symbols what an individual man may be supposed to feel. ... But unless the actor follows nature sufficiently close to select symbols recognized as natural, he fails to touch us."[25] But Stebbins goes on to warn against a thoughtless and slavish reproduction of everyday behavior. "Strict fidelity to nature is nonsense. Art must always idealize nature, and when it fails to do this, it fails in its proper expression."[26]

The Delsarte system enjoyed an American vogue, largely due to the proselytizing of Steele McKaye, one of the period's great actor managers who also lectured widely and established the first dramatic school in New York City. Delsarte's enthusiastic proponents used his system for everything from dance to oratory, in the process perverting his original intentions, rendering the system mechanical and artificial, a mere cookbook of theatrical emotions. They disposed of both the theorizing and the observation, as well as any idea of verisimilitude, and devised "correct" poses for each emotion and state of mind. "Delsarte" instruction books illustrating these poses resembled others of the period, which also taught the amateur actor "correct" movements and gestures.[27]

Theatrical promptbooks and other sources show that these books do to some degree reflect actual theatrical practice. My viewing of the early Biographs has revealed strong resemblances between the "Delsarte" and other systems, and Biograph performance style.[28] The similarities among theatrical practice, the "Delsarte system" and Biograph performance substantiate the notion that histrionically coded acting referenced melodramatic texts. If one were so inclined, it would be possible to present numerous instances, complete with frame enlargements and plate reproductions, of poses found in both the films and the instructions manuals. Two reasons prevent my doing this. First, though strong similarities existed, one would not wish to overstate the case: Biograph performance style, as will be seen below, did not exactly duplicate contemporary melodramatic practice. Secondly, the interesting parallels between Biograph and melodramatic performance style lie not in specific poses but in the overall principles of histrionically coded acting. The presentation of massive amounts of data without interpretation would ignore these underlying principles in favor of a fruitless multiplication of examples. What follows is an analysis of the histrionic code predicated upon the semiotic terms introduced at the beginning of the paper.

Though it was stated above that the preponderance of evidence suggests that gesture does not signify in the same manner as speech, histrionically coded acting shares several characteristics with natural language, a fact which greatly facilitates verbal description both of the workings of the code and individual gestures.

**(1) Limited lexicon.** Though the Delsarte system encompasses a multitude of possible postures/emotions, it does not encompass an infinity of possibilities. Each emotion or state of mind must be represented by a particular, precise arrangement of the torso, limbs, and head. In actual practice, it is unlikely that any two actors could have faultlessly reproduced their teacher's exact pose; in this sense, an infinity of possible poses did exist. But this is akin to individual pronunciation of a standard vocabulary, which some semioticians have referred to as an idiolect. Nonetheless, the Delsarte system theoretically sanctioned a Platonically ideal pose for each emotion. In a lecture delivered in the early 1870s, Steele McKaye stated, "The actor who is a follower of Delsarte is taught to express an emotion according to the laws of the emotion—the use of the appropriate and most powerful physical presentation of the impassioned thought."[29]

Though McKaye's interpretation of Delsarte was more subtle and complex than the next generation of "Delsartians," this statement could be seen to countenance the publication of gestural lexicons giving students the "Delsarte" vocabulary.[30] The vocabulary, however, consisted not of words but of phrases. Eco's concept of the "super sign" corresponds to the way the "Delsartians" themselves thought of gesture. "But one gesture is needed for the expression of an entire thought, since it is not the word but the thought that the gesture must announce."[31]

Though it is not my intention to become the Dr. Johnson of gestural lexography, I shall give a few entries from the Biograph gestural lexicon.

> "Resolution or conviction": fist clenched in air, brought down sharply to side of body.
>
> "Despair, shame": hands covering face or head buried in arms.
>
> "Fear": arm extended, palm out toward fearful object, other hand perhaps clutching the throat.
>
> "Heaven help me!": arms fully extended above head, sometimes hands clasped.

> "Feminine distress": hand to cheek or hands on both side of face.
>
> "Honey, you and I are going to have a great future together": Gesture performed by a man, when he and his woman have finally transcended all obstacles to togetherness. The hand is raised as in the Fascist salute, palm down and fingers spread, and waved slowly from side to side.

**(2) Digital nature of histrionically coded acting.** Though Pavis asserts that gesture "cannot be isolated from the flow of communication without damage resulting," the histrionic style depended upon the isolation of gesture. Melodramatic actors deliberately struck attitudes, holding each gesture and abstracting it from the flow of motion until the audience had "read it." An author of one of the numerous Delsarte instruction manuals advises, "But one gesture is needed to express an entire thought. Consequently, the gesture must be held until the impression which caused it melts away, and gives place to another impression."[32] One need only look at the early Biographs to observe the holding of gestures, but a 1907 *Atlantic Monthly* article confirms that this attitude striking was also integral to melodramatic practice. The writer describes the heroine's actions as she declares her innocence: "For gesture, one hand may be slightly extended and upraised, the other pressed timidly upon the breast; and at the close of the word [innocent] the eyes should fall, the head drop forward with sweet submission. This position may be maintained for several seconds. Then the gallery will clap."[33]

Not only were aspiring actors told to "rest long enough in a gesture,"[34] they were urged to avoid excessive movement which might detract from attitude striking. Dion Boucicault, one of the leading names in theatrical melodrama, warned against superfluous gesture. "Let the gesture be exactly such as pertains to what you say ... and no more. Do not use *gesticules*—little gestures—that is fidgety."[35] The elimination of the small gestures brings about the physical equivalent of silence between the grand, posed gestures resulting in the "discrete, discontinuous elements and gaps" of digital communication.

**(3) Double articulation.** Histrionically coded acting might be said to possess a rudimentary double articulation. The Delsarte system, in its original and debased forms, instructed students to reflect the same emotion with all parts of their body, from the feet to the head. Having learned the correct positions for the head, hands, feet, legs, etc., they were then taught to combine them into an overall posture. Delsarte's daughter, in an 1892 American lecture tour, gave lessons on the hand, the arm (including elbow and shoulder), and then on "inflections of the hand" or combinations of the arm and the hand. A caress, for example, involves movement of the shoulder, elbow, and hand. "Raise the shoulder; bend the head; keep the elbow close to the side; raise the hand as high as the face and, with palm outward, bring it slowly down again as if stroking an object, at the same time raising the head."[36] This is perhaps more analogous to forming sentences from words than to forming morphemes from phonemes, but nonetheless, it is possible to identify some minimal units of signification combining to form larger units.

Another hallmark of natural language is opposition.[37] The presence or absence of phonemes in morphemes or of morphemes in sentences can entirely change the meaning of a word or sentence. Natural language often exhibits a perfect binary opposition: the distinction between dour and pour, for example, stems solely from the opposition between the *d* and the *p*. Opposition in histrionically coded acting is more a matter of degree. Actors had to decide (1) the length of time of the gesture, (2) the stress and speed of the gesture, (3) the direction of the gesture, all of which involve a whole range of choices.

**(1) Length of time.** Though actors might be told to "rest upon a gesture," the histrionic style did not demand that each gesture be held for precisely the same number of seconds. Instead, actors varied the time of gestures for dramatic effect. The emotional intensity of a particular scene and the scene's place within the narrative both determined the time for which a particular pose might be held. At the climax of each act, always an emotional highpoint, players in a melodrama often froze in place, forming a motionless tableau which might last for several seconds before the curtain fell.

**(2) Stress and speed.** The weight and speed of gestures also constituted significant oppositions. Generally, slow, languid movements connote resigned despair, pensiveness, calm content, quiet love, and similar states of mind. Fast, forceful movements connote fear, anger, unbearable misery, grief, and the other more active, and often negative, emotions. *The Actor's Art,* from 1882 (not a Delsarte handbook), tells us, "A calm thought will prompt a quiet action. The arm will move slowly without abruptness."[38] However, "should the sentiment be strong, the thought will prompt the arm to rise rapidly."[39] Once again, actors suited the stress and speed of the gesture to the progress of the narrative: early Biographs often begin with slow, languid gestures, climax with fast, forceful gestures, and resolve with slow, languid gestures.

**(3) Movement.** The final significant opposition concerns the direction of movement with regard to the actors' bodies: toward the feet or the head; toward or away from the body; parallel or perpendicular to the body. Movements directed upward may indicate acceptance, pleading, or an appeal to heaven, while movements downward indicate conviction, resolution, or rejection. Boucicault was quite insistent upon these distinctions. "Why in the attitude of appeal do you put your hands up *so*? You cannot appeal *that* way (the palms upwards)."[40] Movements close to the body may indicate pleading, acceptance, or shame, while movements away indicate rejection, fear, repulsion. Generally, the closer the movements to the center of the body, the calmer the emotion, while stronger emotions result in movements upward, downward, or outward. The greater the extension of the arm in these directions, the more intense the emotion. The author of *The Actor's Art* states, "So long as in their movement the hands do not rise above the waist, they express sentiments of a quiet nature, ... but soon as the hands are raised above the waist, and therefore reach the chest ... their expression assumes much greater force, much more intensity."[41]

To summarize, the three main oppositions in histrionically coded acting are (1) time of gesture, (2) stress and speed of gesture, and (3) direction of gesture. Using various combinations of these oppositions, an actor could suit his movements to the nature and intensity of his character's state of mind. Let us now focus specifically upon histrionically coded acting in the early Biographs and formulate some general principles (supported by examples from the films) about the actors' use of gesture at various points in the narrative. Most shots (a shot usually corresponding to an entire scene—that is, having unity of time and place) in these films fall into one of five categories: (1) tableau, (2) everyday activity, (3) conversations, (4) heightened emotions and action scenes, and (5) gestural soliloquies, in which a character emotes while alone in the frame.

**(1) Tableau.** Though Griffith took the tableau from the melodrama, he somewhat modified its usage. The strong emotions portrayed at the ends of acts meant that the actors often froze with arms fully extended outward, upward, or downward. A drawing of the end of the second act of *East Lynne* shows actors in poses of this sort. In the center a man sits in a chair, his hands clasping his head in an agony of despair. A young girl kneels at his feet, her right hand reaching up in supplication. To the left, an elderly gentleman has both hands raised high above his head in an appeal-to-heaven posture. To the right, a stern woman points at the girl with her left hand, while her right arm is half perpendicular to her body, the finger pointing to the door, in perhaps the most parodied of all melodramatic gestures.[42]

Griffith adopted the stillness of the tableau, but even in his early films, his actors expressed emotional intensity through lack of movement alone, keeping their arms close to the center of their bodies and eschewing extended movements. Perhaps the best known tableau in Griffith's work, and certainly one of the most effective occurs in *A Corner in Wheat* (1909) at the moment when the poor line up to buy the overpriced bread and become perfectly motionless, contrasting with the frenzied activity of the Wheat King's party (see the photographs on page 17).

Nor did the actors in the Biograph tableaux always remain totally still. Many of the Biographs end with the obligatory "reconstitution of the family" shot, in which the actors make small gestures. In the last shot of *The Drunkard's Reformation* (1909),

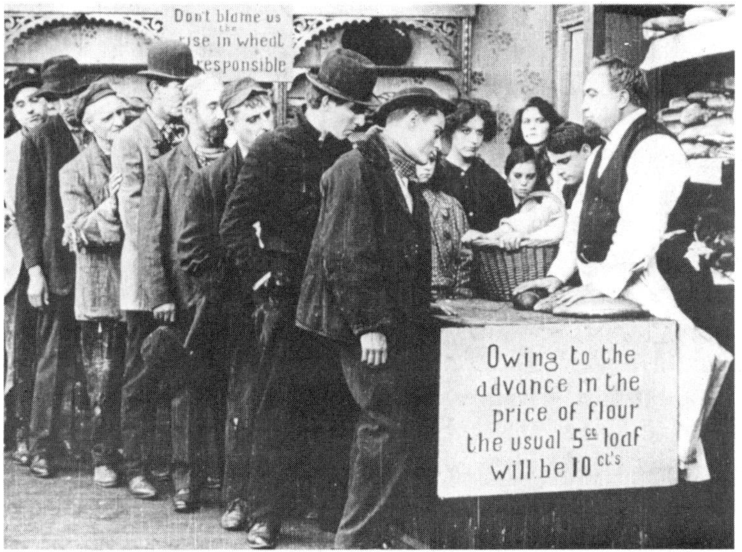

**Top: A *Corner in Wheat.* Bottom: *A Convict's Sacrifice.* (Photos courtesy of the Museum of Modern Art/Film Stills Archive)**

Arthur Johnson and Florence Lawrence sit in front of the fire with their little girl. The child sits on the floor before her father's chair, her mother sits on the arm of the chair. Lawrence has her arm around Johnson, and they hold hands. With his free hand, Johnson gestures to the girl, as if to credit her with his reformation.

**(2) Everyday activity.** Everyday activity refers to characters going about their normal routine prior to the introduction of narrative disequilibrium. They might be shown at work, as in the opening shot of *A Corner in Wheat,* or at home, as is the happy family at the beginning of *The Lonely Villa* (1909). In these shots, gesture helps to establish a character and his or her relation to other characters, rather than give narrative information. The characters often handle props, such as books or the tools of their trade, which prevent fully extended outward movements. Gestures tend to be close to the body, fairly slow and unstressed, and are not held for any significant time.

In the first shot of *Lady Helen's Escapade* (1909), Mary Pickford portrays a bored, upper-class woman. She sits on a chair beside a table, on which her arm rests, her hand dangling loosely over the front. A maid offers her food, which she refuses with a languid wave of the hand. Then she heaves a sigh, her shoulders moving visibly, and yawns. All her gestures are slow, and with the exception of the wave, her arms and hands stay close to her body.

**(3) Conversation.** To introduce yet another semiotic term, conversations in the early Biographs (and perhaps on the melodramatic stage, though I as yet have no evidence) contain a great many "diectic" or "anaphoric" gestures, the gestural equivalent of verbal "shifters": personal pronouns and words which indicate place, such as "here" and "there."[43] In the films, these meanings are expressed both by inward movements, indicating I, or here, and outward movements, indicating you, there, etc. In most conversations these diectic gestures are almost casually interjected, performed quickly and without stress. In *A Convict's Sacrifice* (1909), the released convict, James Kirkwood, talks to a laborer, Henry Walthall, who is eating his lunch. Kirkwood points to the food and himself and Walthall hands him the dinner pail. Then Walthall asks his boss to hire Kirkwood, pointing at himself and then the convict, as if to vouch for his behavior.

Conversational gestures usually fall somewhere between the contained stillness of the tableau and the frantic extended movement of the gestural soliloquy. In *A Summer's Idyll* (1909), Walthall proposes to a society woman who rejects him. He leans closer to her, his hand on his chest, then extends his other hand to her palm up (undoubtedly following Boucicault's advice). Then he takes her hand in both of his. She says no, and he pleads, with his right hand extended to her and his left hand on his chest, the fingers relaxed. All his motions are slow and graceful, and his arms are never fully extended in an outward direction.

**(4) Heightened emotions and action scenes.** It is in this category and the next that gesture begins to resemble the conventional stereotyped notions of melodramatic acting. In these shots, Richard Schickel could discover an abundance of "posturing, exaggeration, excessive movement," for the hands and arms are fully extended outward, downward, or upward, and the gestures tend to be held longer than in everyday or conversation shots and are heavily stressed and quickly performed.

In *The Call of the Wild* (1908), a woman rejects the proposal of a "civilized" Indian (he wears a suit and attends parties). The veneer of civilization immediately vanishes, and he leads an Indian band on the warpath, captures his beloved, and proceeds to work his will upon her. He kisses her and she falls to her knees, arms outstretched in supplication. Her left hand points to her chest and then to heaven, while her right hand points to him. He points to his Indian followers, as if to say, "I am one of them." She points to heaven again, her arm straight up and fully extended. Finally seeing the light, he raises both arms, sinks to his knees, lowers his head on his arms. She then points off screen right, as if to say, "Come back with me." Here we see a mixture of the diectic gesture, which gives most of the narrative information, and the fully extended, heavily stressed, quickly performed gestures characteristic of emotional high points.

**(5) Gestural soliloquies.** The most extreme form of histrionically coded acting appears in the gestural soliloquy. Often characters in this situation have only one simple point to make: "I am angry," "I am grief-stricken," or "I am desperate." Given both a lack of props and the absence of another performer with whom to interact, the actors resort to a series of gestures (sometimes even precisely repeating the same gestures), all of which express the same state of mind. While narratively redundant, these "variations upon a theme" gestures serve to emphasize emotional climaxes, allowing the characters to undergo an emotional catharsis.

Acting in the gestural soliloquies often violates injunctions against the "useless multiplication of gesture," though this runs counter to contemporary performance practice. Although I have no evidence on this point, the very nature of the melodramatic text would seem to license such emotional catharsis. Or perhaps this multiplication of gestures is another of Griffith's modifications of the histrionic code. Nonetheless, the multiplied gestures still remain distinctly separate, preserving the digital nature of histrionically coded acting.

*The Tavern Keeper's Daughter* (1908), like *The Call of the Wild,* relates a tale of lust, villainy, and redemption. This time the pursued virgin takes refuge in a cabin occupied only by a baby in a crib. The villain charges in, overlooks the girl, but spies the baby. The innocent child, in best melodramatic tradition, precipitates a change of heart, and the villain enacts a gestural soliloquy. He sinks to his knees by the crib, beats his breast, raises clenched fist in the air, puts bowed head in hands, spreads arms wide, looks up to heaven, crosses himself, and slumps forward, head in hands. Then he rises, puts his forearm to his eyes, and his other hand on his chest. All these gestures could be translated into one or two verbal phrases: "I'm sorry. Forgive me."

Given the shared characteristics between natural language and the histrionic code, the analysis and segmentation of histrionically coded acting presents no overwhelming theoretical difficulties. Unfortunately, segmentation and analysis of the verisimilar code do present theoretical difficulties, at least at this stage of the research. The verisimilar code, unlike the histrionic code but like most gestural signification, does not resemble a natural language. Moreover, the melodramatic texts referenced by the histrionic code can be fairly easily reconstructed through the evidence of acting manuals, promptbooks, reviews, etc. To what evidence does one turn when seeking the texts referenced by the verisimilar code—how does one determine the 1913 cultural construct of reality? The trade press can be used to prove that the performance style in the later films was perceived as more "lifelike." But precisely what did this "realism" consist of? What kinds of behavior, movement, gestures, etc., were thought to be "lifelike"? Barthes argues in *S/Z* that a great deal of the effect in realist literature derives from the inclusion of convincing details which remain largely unnoticed by the reader, yet serve a naturalizing effect. "There is a belief that great structures, serious symbols, grand meanings, are built upon an unimpressive foundation of ordinary acts that the discourse notes as a matter of form, 'to speak truly': all criticism therefore rests on the notion that *the text contains insignificant elements* or, in effect, nature ... "[44]

What were the insignificant elements which naturalized acting and made it appear verisimilar to a 1913 audience? Ultimately, this question will have to be addressed by once more invoking intertextuality. Other texts, such as plays and novels which referenced the same cultural construct of reality as the films, can be examined to arrive at an approximation of 1913 versimilitude.

With this research still to be done, for the moment we must define the verisimilar code mostly by contrasting it with the histrionic code.

(1) While the histrionic code is digital, the verisimilar code is analogic. The gestural isolation and the elimination of little gestures of the histrionic code gives way to a continuous flow of movement linked by little gestures. These little gestures may constitute the insignificant details of which Barthes spoke.

(2) Verisimilarly coded acting does not rely upon a standardized gestural repertory, which leaves room for greater individual interpretation of a part. It is often difficult to distinguish among the early Biograph actors on the basis of performance style alone, while the later actors developed distinctly individualized styles. This observation may be supported by introducing yet another semiotic term, "commutation." The commutation test,

strictly speaking, "simply involves trying out a sound change [in a word] and observing whether a meaning change is produced or not."[45] In "Screen Acting and the Commutation Test," John Thompson speculates about the changes in meaning which might result from substituting one actor for another, a mental exercise we might apply to the Biographs. The early Biograph actor's use of a limited lexicon means that the commutation test produces no great changes. It did not really matter whether Arthur Johnson or Owen Moore played the jealous lover; yet had Lillian Gish portrayed the painted lady, one can envision an entirely different film.

(3) Though opposition still operates in the verisimilar code, the oppositions are not so extreme as in the histrionic code. The verisimilar style abandoned the holding of gesture for dramatic effect and the fully extended upward, outward, or downward movements of heightened emotions. In the verisimilar style, the arms remain closer to the center of the body while the hands and face relay a good deal of information.

To sum up, players in the later Biographs used small gestures in which the hands and mouth were more important than the arms. This resulted in an accumulation of small details which almost imperceptibly flowed into each other. The actors seem to rely more upon their own instincts (and presumably those of the director) than upon pre-established gestures, resulting in more individualized performances.

Specific examples will aid in contrasting the histrionic and verisimilar codes. *Brutality* (December 1912), starring Walter Miller and Mae Marsh, is practically a remake of *The Drunkard's Reformation* (April 1909), starring Arthur Johnson and Florence Lawrence.

Why examine films from 1909 and 1912 instead of 1908 and 1913? To slip into social science jargon for a moment, the films were chosen in an effort to control as many variables as possible. It is almost impossible to consider one textual code, in this case performance, in isolation from other codes. Film "integrates several codes, cannot be reduced to any one of them and plays them one against the other. The system of the text is the process which *displaces* codes, deforming each of them by the presence of others, contaminating some by means of others and ... *placing* each code in a particular position in regard to overall structure. ... "[46]

With regard to both plot and editing, *Brutality* and *The Drunkard's Reformation* are fairly similar despite the four years that separate them. In both films a man takes to drink, mistreats his wife (and, in the earlier film, his child), and finally repents after seeing a stage play which parallels his own circumstances. In both films, Griffith used point-of-view editing during the climax to illustrate the characters' growing realization of their guilt. Though *Brutality* has almost twice as many shots (59) as does *The Drunkard's Reformation* (32), and the camera is farther away in the earlier film, the main difference between the two films is that performance style is histrionic in one and verisimilar in the other.

Consider the ways in which the female leads perform the gestural soliloquies in which they despair over their husbands' cruelty. After her child and husband leave for the theater, Lawrence walks slowly back to the dining room table, running her hands along the table and the backs of chairs in a manner characteristic of everyday activity shots. When she reaches the chair, she sinks into it, rests her head on her arms, which are extended straight out in front of her, then raises her head, sinks to her knees, and prays with arms fully extended and at about a forty-five degree angle to her body. Note that her gestures resemble those described above when discussing heightened emotions and gestural soliloquies.

Unlike Lawrence, Marsh eschews the extended gesture in her portrayal of misery. After her husband leaves to go to a bar, Marsh walks back to a dining room table covered with the debris of their meal. She sits down, bows her head, and begins to collect the dishes. She looks up, compresses her lips, pauses, then begins to gather the dishes again. Once more she pauses, raises her hand to her mouth, glances down to her side, and slumps a little in her chair. Slumping a little more, she begins to cry. What Lawrence accomplished through movement of her entire body and extended arm gestures, Marsh accomplishes with a hand gesture, a compression of the lips, and a slight slump. The verisimilar style required the actor to expend far less energy than the histrionic.

When the male leads in both films go to the theater, Griffith cuts between the action on the stage and reaction shots of the characters to reveal their mental processes. Like Marsh, Miller reveals his character's state of mind through slight body movements and small gestures of the hand. As the play progresses, Miller rubs his chin, plays with a newspaper, shifts lower in his seat, lowers his head, and glances at Marsh who is sitting next to him. Johnson is far more active, using a combination of diectic gestures and large body movements. He talks to his little girl, moves his hands from his lap and folds them across the chest, points to the girl and the stage to make clear the similarity between their lives and the theater piece. He takes the girl's hand, puts an arm around her shoulder and clutches the seat with his other hand as he becomes increasingly distressed, pulls the girl closer to him, then leans forward in his chair, eyes fixed on the stage, points a finger at his chest, hugs his daughter, lets her go, then slumps in his chair before hugging her again. Both actors tell the audience that they have guilty consciences and wish to reform, yet they do so in very different fashion.

## CONCLUSION

The concepts of histrionically and verisimilarly coded acting advanced in this paper enable a more rigorous approach to the problem of the change in Biograph performance style than has hitherto been possible. Yet a great many questions remain to be answered. One can confidently state that 1908 performance was primarily histrionically coded and 1913 performance verisimilarly coded. What of the years in between? Was there a single temporal point at which the actors seemed suddenly to adopt the new code? Or, as is far more likely, was there a subtle shift as one code gradually replaced the other? Is it possible to identify a transitional style that mingled the two codes?

Having dealt with these questions, one must then proceed to the interaction of cinematic codes referred to above. How do narrative and characterization affect performance style? Do actors vary performance style according to the role of the genre? What are the effects of changing patterns of editing, lighting, and camera movement?

To go beyond the confines of a formalist textual analysis, how did Griffith and his actors contribute to the shift to verisimilitude? What were their theatrical backgrounds and experiences? What were their ideas about film acting? To go beyond the confines of 11 East 14th Street, how might economic changes in the film industry between 1908 and 1913 have affected performance style? Is there a connection between the emerging middle-class audience which some have postulated and the change to verisimilarly coded acting? As this rather daunting list of questions makes clear, much remains to be discovered about acting in the Griffith Biographs.

## NOTES

1. Richard Schickel, *D.W. Griffith: An American Life* (New York: Simon and Schuster, 1984), p. 110.
2. Schickel, p. 154.
3. Roland Barthes, *Elements of Semiology* (New York: Hill and Wang, 1977), p. 3.
4. Umberto Eco, *A Theory of Semiotics* (Bloomington: Indiana University Press, 1979), p. 231.
5. Christian Metz, *Language and Cinema* (The Hague: Mouton, 1974), p. 131.
6. Juri Lotman, *Semiotics of the Cinema* (Ann Arbor: Slavic Contribution, Michigan. 1976), p. 35.
7. Bill Nichols, "Glossary" in Bill Nichols, ed., *Movies and Methods* (Berkeley: University of California Press, 1976), p. 629.
8. Barthes, p. 52.
9. Nichols, p. 629.
10. Patrice Pavis, "Problems of a Semiology of Theatrical Gesture," *Poetics Today*, 2:3, (Spring 1983) p. 71.
11. A. J. Greimas, quoted in Peter Brooks, *The Melodramatic Imagination* (New Haven: Yale University Press, 1976), p. 70.
12. Brooks, p. 71.
13. Barthes, p. 64. Eco however disputes the primacy of the verbal. "It is true that every content expressed by a verbal unit can be translated into another verbal unit; it is true that the greater part of the content expressed by non-verbal units can also be translated into verbal units; but it is likewise true that there are many contents expressed by complex non-verbal units which cannot be translated into one or more verbal units (other than by a very weak approximation)" (Eco, p. 173). I suspect that gestures can be much more readily translated into words than such other semiotic systems as music or

painting. Interestingly enough, however, Eco supports his point by referring to Wittgenstein's realization of the inadequacy of words to convey the "meaning" of "a certain Neapolitan gesture" (Eco, p. 173). It is of course possible that Wittgenstein was simply being overly polite.

14. Eco, p. 176.
15. Eco, p. 231.
16. Frederick Jameson, *The Political Unconscious* (Ithaca: Cornell University Press, 1981), p. 91.
17. Lewis Carroll, *Through the Looking Glass* (New York: Signet Classics Edition, New American Library, 1960), p. 186.
18. For a history of the use of "realism" and "naturalism" see Raymond Williams, *Keywords* (New York: Oxford University Press, 1976). For an article on the current misuse of the term melodrama see Russell Merritt, "Melodrama: Postmortem for a Phantom Genre," *Wide Angle* (5:3), p. 24.
19. Metz, p. 54.
20. Jonathan Culler, *Structuralist Poetics* (Ithaca: Cornell University Press, 1975), p. 139.
21. *Oxford American Dictionary* (New York: Avon Books, 1980), p. 415.
22. For a discussion of the suitability of melodramatic performance style to the plays' plots and characters see Brooks (supra).
23. Tzvetan Todorov, *The Poetics of Prose* (Ithaca: Cornell University Press, 1977), p. 83.
24. Colgate Barker, "David W. Griffith: The Genius of the Movies," *New York Review*, (8:7, Dec. 13, 1913). For further evidence on this point see Janet Staiger, "The Eyes Are Really the Focus: Photoplay Acting and Film Form and Style," *Wide Angle* (6:4), p. 14.
25. Genevieve Stebbins, *Delsarte System of Expression* (New York: Dance Horizons, 1977). This is a reprint of a 1901 book which was the sixth revised edition of Stebbins original 1885 text.
26. Stebbins, ibid.
27. The most extended, albeit atheoretical, discussion of melodramatic acting can be found in Michael Booth, *English Melodrama* (London: Herbert Jenkins, 1965). See also Gilbert B. Cross, *Next Week—East Lynne* (Lewisburg, PA: Bucknell University Press, 1977).
28. This is not to argue a cause and effect relationship: The Biograph actors were not themselves necessarily "Delsartians" or adherents of any other school. Yet, just as any present day actor would know something of the Method, the Biograph actors would have been familiar with Delsarte's basic principles and poses. Pragmatic considerations of text availability have led me to focus largely upon the Delsarte material. I use quotes (Delsarte) to refer to the system as practiced by Delsarte's American followers and not the original Delsarte material.
29. Steele McKaye, unpublished lecture, quoted in Virgina Elizabeth Morriss, "The Influence of Delsarte in America as Revealed through the Lectures of Steele McKaye," M.A. Thesis, Louisiana State University, Department of Speech, 1941, p. 35.
30. The New York publishing firm of Edgar S. Werne specialized in Delsartism, flooding the market with instruction books. See, for example, *Delsarte*

*Recitation Book and Directory*, edited by Elsie N. Wilbor, 2d edition, 1883. The book contains orations complete with suggested poses.

31. John W. Zorn, *The Essential Delsarte* (Metuchen, NJ: Scarecrow Press, 1968), p. 164.
32. Florence A. Fowle-Adams, *Gesture and Pantomimic Action* (New York: Edgar S. Werne, 1897, 4th edition), p. 43.
33. H. J. Smith, "The Melodrama," *Atlantic Monthly*, March 1907, p. 321.
34. Dion Boucicault, *The Art of Acting* (New York: Columbia University Press, 1926), p. 35. Lecture delivered at Lyceum Theatre, July 29, 1882 (emphasis in original).
35. Boucicault, p. 33.
36. Mme. Geraldy, lecture, reprinted in Zorn, p. 125.
37. See Barthes, pp. 73–86, on opposition in natural language.
38. Gustave Garcia, *The Actors Art* (London: Messrs. Simpkin, Marshall and Co., 1888), p. 51.
39. Garcia, p. 51.
40. Boucicault, p. 31.
41. Garcia, p. 60.
42. Cross, p. 135.
43. Kier Elam, *The Semiotics of Theatre and Drama* (New York: Methuen, 1980), pp. 72-75.
44. Roland Barthes, *S/Z* (New York: Hill and Wang, 1974), p. 51 (emphasis in original).
45. John O. Thompson, "Screen Acting and the Commutation Test," *Screen, 1978,* 9:2 (Summer 1979), p. 57.
46. Metz, p. 103.

# 2. VIRTUE AND VILLAINY IN THE FACE OF THE CAMERA

## William Rothman

IN THE THEATRICAL MELODRAMAS of the nineteenth century, Peter Brooks argues in *The Melodramatic Imagination*, the nightmare struggle for the liberation of virtue is won when innocence is publicly recognized in a "movement of astonishment" and evil—with its lesser power to astonish—is driven out. Melodrama is a drama of recognition, and what Brooks calls "acts of self-nomination" play an essential role. "The villain ... at some point always bursts forth in a statement of his evil nature and intentions."[1] The heroine too announces her moral identity by declaring "her continued identification with purity, despite contrary appearances."[2]

In melodrama, good and evil can and must declare themselves. How can good and evil be declared in films? This is the question I address in this essay. My motivation is to gain insight into the conditions under which, in movies, human beings are presented and present themselves. That is, to gain a deeper understanding of what becomes of human beings on film and of the role of the camera in effecting their transformation—a necessary prolegomenon to any serious study of film "acting" or "performance."

In *Double Indemnity*, there is a moment at which Barbara Stanwyck's evil is meant to be unambiguously declared. As Fred MacMurray is struggling to kill her husband, she sits silently in the front seat of the car. The camera frames her closely, capturing a clear view of the look on her face (fig. 2.1).

This is the one moment in the film when we are privileged to view the look that Stanwyck's stepdaughter saw years before, the look that stamped her stepmother as evil in her eyes. It is a serious weakness of the film that at this moment it offers no more definitive demonstration that this woman is evil. Stanwyck looks almost

**Fig. 2.1**

toward the camera, but her eyes are vacant, as if she were absorbed in a private reverie. It may not be nice that she is in a trance while her husband is being murdered in a plot she instigated, but this doesn't make her a villain. How could this look—how could any look the camera might capture—show that this woman (who we know as the noble heroine of *Stella Dallas*, the romantic lead of *The Lady Eve*, and a decidedly admirable woman from Brooklyn) is absolutely evil?

What is missing at this moment is an act of self-nomination. Stanwyck does not declare her moral nature here; indeed, she never does so in the film. An example that immediately springs to mind of a villain announcing his moral identity—and this is surely a moment of astonishment—occurs in *The Thirty-Nine Steps* when the villainous Professor raises his hand to reveal that the top joint of his little finger is missing.

Note that just before the moment of revelation, Hitchcock frames the Professor and Hannay in such a way that we see—and see that Hannay does not see—the Professor give a start on Hannay's words, "I believe she was coming to see you about some Air Ministry secrets." Hence, when the Professor turns to face Hannay and says, calmly, "Did she tell you what the foreign agent looked like?" we know he is dissimulating like a true villain.

But not only villains dissimulate. It is a running joke—and

more than a joke—in *The Thirty-Nine Steps* that the innocent Hannay must put on act after act, must slip into role after role, in order to protect his innocence. It is only at the moment he shows his hand—in effect, authoring a view and presenting it to Hannay—that the Professor unmasks himself. Then the astonishing view the Professor presents to Hannay is matched by an equally astonishing view Hitchcock presents us: the full-frame image of the Professor's pinky-less hand, viewed from Hannay's perspective (fig. 2.2).

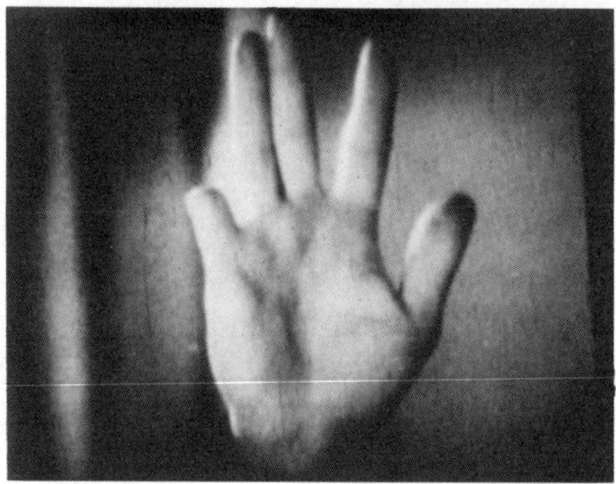

**Fig. 2.2**

The implication of these matched gestures is that there is a link between the villain and Hitchcock (both are authors of views) as there is a link between Hannay and us (both are viewers). We might also say that the gesture is the camera's. It is this view framed by the camera that shows Hitchcock's hand. The camera is revealed at this moment as an instrument of villainy.

In Hitchcock's films—and not just in films by Hitchcock—there are incessant suggestions that the camera is an instrument of villainy. This passage from *The Thirty-Nine Steps* exemplifies one form these suggestions take: the assertion of a link between the villain's gesture and a gesture of the film's author. Two passages from *The Lodger* exemplify a second form: the camera's assumption of the villain's place.

First is the film's opening shot, a view of a terrified woman from the perspective of her murderer, a villain we never get to view. Second is our introduction to the lodger (Ivor Novello), who may or may not be a murderer. Before we view his face, the camera assumes his perspective—one that has been, from the opening, associated with the villain—as he approaches the front door of the house and reaches his hand into the frame to grasp the knocker.

Closely related to these two examples are those passages in which Hitchcock frames a human figure in such a way as to make him a symbolic stand-in for the camera. This occurs, for example, when the lodger first enters the house and is framed in the entrance foyer, his back to the camera. In this frame, Novello is the camera's subject, but he also stares into the depths of the space, possessing it with his gaze.

When the Professor unmasks himself, he authors a view that declares his moral identity, and Hitchcock matches this with a view that reveals his bond with the villain. When the camera assumes the villain's place, by contrast, it is not the camera's status as an instrument of authorship but its passive aspect that is revealed. At such moments, villainy is invoked, certainly, but it is linked with the act of viewing, not with the authoring of views. Hence these moments are akin to the passages in Hitchcock's films—and again, not just in Hitchcock's films—that portray guilty acts of viewing. For example, the crofter in *The Thirty-Nine Steps* spying on his wife, or Norman Bates in *Psycho* viewing Marian Crane through his peephole. These have, as their ancestor, the extraordinary shot in *The Birth of a Nation* of Gus, the "renegade Negro," mad with lust, guiltily viewing the innocent Little Sister (Mae Marsh) as she in turn is absorbed in viewing a playful squirrel. These are not examples of a villain's self-nomination. At such moments, the human representative of evil within the world of the film stands revealed not by his own gesture but by the camera, which links his villainy to his guilty act of viewing.

There is a third general way of revealing the camera's link with villainy. I am thinking of those moments when a villain appears to unmask himself by looking directly into the camera. For example, at just the moment in *The Lodger* when our suspicion that

Ivor Novello is a murderer is at a height, he gives the camera a knowing look, complete with a villainous smile, that appears to confirm that he is guilty (fig. 2.3).

Fig. 2.3

When a villain meets the camera's gaze, he presents himself to be viewed by the camera. We view him without his "false face," to use Brooks' phrase, and we are astonished. He reveals himself to be an author of views, like the Professor; but the view whose authorship he claims is presented to us, not to someone within the world of the film—and it is our view of him.

Yet this gesture is also akin to the camera's suggestions that the act of viewing is villainous. Meeting the camera's gaze, the villain reveals his knowledge of our viewing; this look by which he unmasks himself denies our innocence. And what is perhaps most significant about this double-edged gesture is that it appears to be at once a gesture of the camera and a gesture of the camera's subject. Their gestures appear not only to match, but to coincide.

In speaking of a gesture that appears to be both the villain's and the camera's, I have in mind such passages as the ending of *Psycho*, when Norman Bates (Tony Perkins) raises his gaze directly to the camera and grins (fig. 2.4). Hitchcock and Bates appear to be conspirators of such intimate complicity that a distinction can hardly be made between them. In effect, the film's author has become one with the human subject of his camera. Bates has become a mask for Hitchcock, one of Hitchcock's stuffed birds; in turn, the grinning Bates has been impressed indelibly on our idea of who Hitchcock was.

**Fig. 2.4**

But consider a passage from *Beloved Rogue,* a silent film starring John Barrymore as François Villon and Conrad Veidt as the King of France.[3]

In this scene, Villon succeeds in taking the king in, convincing him that he has such magical powers that he dare not execute him. But Barrymore goes beyond the dramatic needs of the scene by presenting a knowing, villainous look to the camera. This look is astonishing, and it is easy to imagine that it equally astonished the film's director, Alan Crosland. Crosland's camera performs no gesture that matches Barrymore's suggestion here that the film's hero has a capacity for evil. Barrymore has appropriated—and undermined—the director's authority.

There are in turn cases in which the camera undermines the authority of a figure who appears to nominate himself as a villain. For example, when the lodger looks at the camera in the moment earlier cited, he appears to be unmasking himself, but this is followed by a shot from his point of view that places him within the audience at a fashion show. Here a look we took to be a villain's self-nomination is given an innocent explanation: this is only a spectator, this is only a spectator's look. (Then again, perhaps a spectator—or this spectator—is not innocent.) Thus a view that seemed clearly legible has turned ambiguous and enigmatic. Indeed, the sequence leaves us only with a question about the camera's motivation coupled with a demonstration that for all we know this human being—and perhaps any human being—may be a villain. That is, the passage confronts us with the limits of our access to the world of a film: we cannot take for granted that the camera will reveal to us—even that it can reveal to us—innocence or guilt. The role of the camera undermines the very basis of melodrama.

At the end of *Psycho*, as we've seen, Norman Bates fixes the camera in his gaze and grins: again, a villain appears to be unmasking himself, with the camera's complicity. But then "mother's" mummified face is momentarily superimposed over—or surfaces from under?—his living face. Whoever or whatever we take Norman Bates to be, this extraordinary gesture declares, he is no villain of melodrama. In *Hitchcock—The Murderous Gaze*, I interpret this composite figure, this being possessed by death, as emblematic of the condition of all human beings on film.

> The camera fixes its human subjects, possesses their life. They are reborn on the screen, creatures of the film's author and of ourselves. But life is not fully breathed back into them. They are immortal but they are always already dead. The beings projected on the screen are condemned to a condition of death-in-life from which they can never escape. What lures us into the world of a film may be a dream of triumphing over death, holding death forever at bay. But ... the world of a film is not a private island where we may escape the conditions of our existence. At the heart of every film is a truth we already know: we have been born into the world and we are fated to die.[4]

For Hitchcock, film ultimately turns out to be not a medium of melodrama but the medium perfectly suited to express a vision of human existence as an imprisonment from which there is no imaginable escape. Hitchcock's films are no more tragedies or comedies than melodramas are, but they are also not melodramas. Their underlying vision undermines melodrama, for there are no villainous human beings responsible for creating what it is that film lays bare that is intolerable in the human condition.

Villainy is integral to Hitchcock's vision, but it emerges from and expresses a perfectly human dream of escaping from the real conditions of human existence. The camera can "nominate" a villain only by nominating itself. The camera becomes evil's only real exemplar, but melodrama requires that evil manifest itself perfectly in human form. Villains in melodrama are the creation of an occult force; in films they are, in part, the creation of the camera. Perfect human representatives of evil are not real; human beings wish for them and create them, and melodrama is motivated in part by that wish. But the camera reveals that human beings are—only human. When they appear inhuman, as they often do in films, the camera—which human beings also wished for and created—participates in creating that inhumanity. Evil, understood as an occult force that exists apart from human beings and their creations, has no reality in the face of the camera.

What I'm suggesting, as I wade through deep waters, is that film not only undermines melodrama but provides a particular way of understanding melodrama's motivation. Of course, melodrama has its opposing vision, which provides in turn its own interpretation of film. Its interpretation, that is, not of film's motivation but its nature: film is evil.

But now it is time to turn to virtue or innocence and how it might be declared—or declare itself—in films.

* * *

In *Pursuits of Happiness*, Stanley Cavell invokes Matthew Arnold in elucidating the claim that in remarriage comedies like *The Philadelphia Story* film has found one of its great subjects. Cavell writes:

> There is a visual equivalent or analogue of what Arnold means by

> distinguishing the best self from the ordinary self and by saying that in the best self class yields to humanity. He is witnessing a possibility or potential in the human self not normally open to view, or not open to the normal view. Call this one's invisible self; it is what the movie camera would make visible.[5]

Cavell argues that films like *The Philadelphia Story* stake themselves on the claim that the camera has the power to reveal virtue or innocence in any human subject—to participate in making it visible. In the comedies Cavell studies, the camera's power to reveal the "invisible self" enables romance to contain the threat of melodrama. The remarriage comedies, like the Hitchcock thrillers, discover in the camera—film's instrument of villainy—the means to undermine melodrama. For melodrama demands the conviction that there are persons whose exemplification of good or evil is absolute; human beings who know their moral identity and have the power of naming it.

We have seen that the camera can single out a human subject as a villain, an exemplar of evil, but only by revealing in the same gesture that this figure's villainy cannot be separated from the camera's bond with him. But can the camera also compellingly single out a human exemplar of virtue and, if so, what does this reveal about the camera?

Let us return to *The Birth of a Nation.* In the sequence that culminates in the view of Gus viewing, Griffith cuts from a long shot of Mae Marsh, amused by a squirrel in a tree, to an iris insert of the squirrel. (This is not, strictly speaking, a point-of-view shot, but our view and hers do not essentially differ.) We cut back to the delighted and unsuspecting girl, then to a shot, remarkable for its expressionism, of Gus coming into the foreground to get a better view of something off-screen (figs. 2.5–2.7). The shot of Mae Marsh that follows is closer than the preceding view of her, registering the menace of Gus' gaze, although again this is not literally a shot from Gus' point of view. Griffith cuts again to the playful squirrel and then back to Marsh, delectable and frighteningly vulnerable in her unselfconscious absorption.

In this context, the cut to the expressionistically-composed tight close-up of Gus, viewing guiltily, is deeply disquieting. Gus' guilty viewing is contrasted within this sequence with the Little Sister's innocent viewing. Her absorption in her views of the squirrel reveals her girlish innocence, her guiltlessness; but it hardly makes her the astonishing heroine of melodrama who knows and declares her moral identity. What the sequence establishes, rather, is her vulnerability. She is vulnerable to Gus and vulnerable to the camera. But is the camera in this sequence innocent like the Little Sister or guilty like Gus? True, the camera does not exactly assume Gus' point of view, does not exactly present to us his guilty views, as it presents to us views of the squirrel that are effectively indistinguishable from Little Sister's girlish views. In this sequence, the camera frames no views that are fully charged with Gus' desire. When it frames Gus' staring eyes, the camera links villainy with the act of viewing, as I've argued, but not with its own viewing. Griffith's camera attempts to disavow its implication in villainy, yet to us this implication—this connection between Gus and the camera—is manifest.

In passages like this, "virtue" is really vulnerability, or we might call it "virginity." The camera's revelations of Mae Marsh's innocence are also violations of that innocence. It is a small step from such violations to the pornography of those Griffith passages in which the camera, in effect, acts as the very instrument of a woman's terrorization (for example, the famous scenes in *Broken Blossoms* in which Lillian Gish, framed closely, hysterical from fear of her brutal father, appears brutalized by the camera itself). Then it is another small step to films like *Back Street* or *Stella Dallas*. In such films, there is ordinarily no human figure responsible for the noble heroine's suffering. They are often called "melodramas," and this always seemed to be a misnomer, since melodramas have villains; but maybe it is the right name after all. Perhaps they are examples of what becomes of melodrama on film, with the camera appropriating the villain's role, serving as agent—as well as observer—of the heroine's anguish.[6]

In general, it seems clear to me that when the camera designates a heroine as virtuous in the same gesture by which it manifests yet disavows its own implication in villainy, this

Fig. 2.5

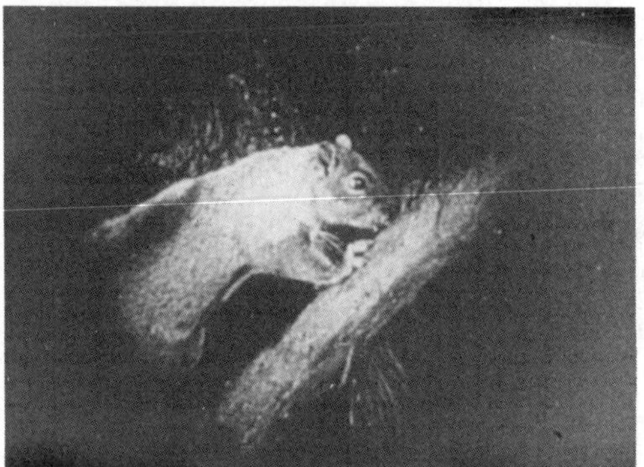

Fig. 2.6

Fig. 2.7

declaration has no real authority. The woman designated, however "noble," is not a heroine but a victim. As in *Double Indemnity,* what is missing is an act of self-nomination, in this case performed by the heroine.

There is a problem, however, in conceiving of such acts on film. A heroine cannot unmask herself, because she wears no mask. How then can she declare herself to the camera? What can she do, in the face of the camera, that would reveal her virtue other than to endure the camera's gaze?

"Enduring the camera's gaze" is how I think of our final poignant vision of Margaret (Peggy Ashcroft), the crofter's wife in *The Thirty-Nine Steps*, after she gives Hannay her husband's overcoat and he disappears into the night. She knows that with this stranger's departure all hope for her own escape from her private hell has also vanished, just as she knows that her husband will beat her when he learns that she gave away his Sunday best coat. In the framing that closes out this sequence, she doesn't confront the camera, and indeed she gives no outward signs that she knows she is being viewed. Yet she is not absorbed like Mae Marsh nor oblivious; I view her as knowingly bearing the burden of the camera's gaze, the way she knowingly bears the burden of her husband's brutality (fig. 2.8).

**Fig. 2.8**

A less inhumane way the camera can declare an exemplar of virtue is by designating representative human beings as "judges" and letting these representatives' judgments stand as conclusive. In such a case, the camera need not claim the authority to recognize perfect virtue; all it need claim is the power to nominate qualified witnesses. To be qualified, one need not be a hero or heroine; all one need be is manifestly human. To declare its subject human, in this scene, all the camera need do is make visible that subject's invisible self, and this is something the camera does have the power to do.

A textbook example of this strategy occurs in the James Whale *Show Boat*. In the sequence I have in mind, the Helen Morgan character, now pathetically reduced in station, is auditioning. As she begins the song "Bill," the camera frames her squarely and holds this framing, compelling her to endure its gaze for a painfully long time. At last there is a cut to the impresario, who nods approval—to our great satisfaction—to someone off-screen, and a cut to the piano accompanist, who firmly nods his agreement. The tension broken, we cut to an "objective" three shot. When we return to the original frontal framing of Helen Morgan, its effect is completely transformed. We are now this woman's appreciative audience, not her judge; the verdict is in. For the remainder of the song, Whale cuts back and forth between ever closer and more ravishing views of Helen Morgan and shots of all the people in the theater, from janitors to dancers, gathering around the singer one by one—a community joined in astonishment at the beauty of her performance, sign of the beauty of her soul.

There is a second relatively humane way the camera can declare an exemplar of virtue. It can pay its respects by withdrawing its gaze. Films abound in gestures of this kind. For example, the camera's withdrawing to satisfy Thomas Mitchell's wish to die alone in *Only Angels Have Wings*; the camera's cutting away from Emil Jannings at the climax of his humiliation in *The Blue Angel*; the camera's respecting the privacy of Frank Morgan's suicide in *Shop Around the Corner*; the camera's withdrawal from the heroine at the end of Carl Dreyer's *Gertrud*.

Can an exemplar of virtue declare himself or herself by

meeting the camera's gaze? Here I think of the moment near the end of *Dinner at Eight* when Marie Dressler, hearing the news of John Barrymore's suicide, looks right into the camera. It's not that Dressler presents herself to George Cukor's camera, like a villain; at this moment, she endures the camera's gaze, like a heroine. She is not in a trance but perfectly clear-eyed. Then what does she see in the face of the camera? What she sees, I take it, is essentially what we see when we view Tony Perkins at the end of *Psycho.* We are viewing no perfect exemplar of an occult moral force here, no villain or heroine of melodrama; we are viewing a human being mindful of a mortality we can see all too clearly stamped on that human being's face. This moment of Marie Dressler's recognition of her humanity is also the moment of our recognition of it. It is a moment exemplary of the camera' s capacity to render the invisible self visible. Like the ending of *Psycho,* then, this moment undermines the basis of melodrama.

Perhaps the most astonishing of all examples of this power of the camera to render the invisible self visible, thereby undermining melodrama, is the passage from Jean Renoir's *La Grande Illusion* in which the nice old German prison guard gives a harmonica to Jean Gabin, who is near the breaking point from solitary confinement. In the course of this brief sequence, Renoir's camera employs all the strategies available to it for rendering respect for its human subjects without falsely denying the camera's capacity for inhumanity.

This sequence opens with the camera framing only the wall of Gabin's cell. The camera tilts up and pans left until it holds on Gabin's face, which reveals a look of anguish and despair such as belonged, in the films of the thirties, only to this beloved star. *

Having demonstrated this man's capacity to endure its gaze, the camera humanely withdraws, reframing to take in the entrance of the guard, who immediately reveals his humanity, proving that he is qualified as a judge. Seeing the haunted look on Gabin's face, he vainly tries to offer solace, settling on the gesture of giving the

---

*Ed. note: see Sylvie Gendron's "The Actor and His Text: *La Grande Illusion*, fig. 9.2.

prisoner a harmonica on the outside chance he might comfort himself with music.

In the face of the guard's efforts, however, Gabin bursts into a violent rage. The guard is stunned; when the camera reframes to exclude him, this underscores the fact that he has momentarily become a horrified spectator, and Gabin a spectacle. At the same time, the camera's gesture reveals that it has the calm assurance to wait the storm out. When the guard quietly leaves, he passes through the frame on his way to the door, and the camera does not even mark his exit. Has this human being simply been forgotten? It is unimaginably satisfying when Renoir's camera withdraws from Gabin and cuts to the guard outside the door, awaiting a sign. And it can make life seem worthwhile that the camera now reveals that the guard—starving for music—is immediately transported by the music Gabin plays. When he recognizes the tune ("Frou-frou"), he knows that Gabin has come back to life. The guard is satisfied—satisfied that his own capacity for happiness is still alive and that he has lightened this stranger's burden. And Renoir shows how much he respects this human judge by allowing him to speak for the film when he says, to another guard who was wondering what was going on, "The war has gone too long."

* * *

Film's massive appropriation of nineteenth-century theatrical forms, most importantly melodrama, must not blind us to its fundamental break with theater. Movies owe almost everything to melodrama, yet they are not melodramas. Indeed, they undermine melodrama by placing the viewer in an intimate relationship, unavailable to a theater audience, with human beings who inhabit a world and hence cannot in themselves be pure exemplars of virtue or villainy. And they also bring to the fore the encounters between the camera and the human subjects whose privacy it penetrates, encounters for which melodrama knows no equivalent. The human subjects of the camera alternate tensely and hesitantly between acting and viewing as they prepare their entrances onto the world's stage, perform, and withdraw again into a privacy to which only the camera has access.

It was D.W. Griffith who discovered and explored the disquieting implications of the capacity for villainy that is an inescapable consequence of the camera's role. Following Griffith, the most serious filmmakers have understood their enterprise as he did: their task is to reveal from within that capacity for villainy, the camera's astonishing capacity for humanity.

## NOTES

1. Peter Brooks, *The Melodramatic Imagination* (New Haven: Yale University Press, 1976), p. 37.
2. Brooks, p. 38.
3. For introducing this passage to me and showing me how to think about it, I am grateful to Marian Keane, who has been studying this film in the context of her dissertation on John Barrymore.
4. William Rothman, *Hitchcock—The Murderous Gaze* (Cambridge: Harvard University Press, 1982), p. 341.
5. Stanley Cavell, *Pursuits of Happiness: The Hollywood Comedy of Remarriage* (Cambridge: Harvard University Press, 1981), p. 158.
6. In "In the Face of the Camera," *Raritan*, 4:3 (Winter 1984), pp. 116-135, I give a detailed reading of several sequences from *Stella Dallas*. The present essay complements that one, whose aim was to elucidate the ways the camera presents heroines like Stella.

# 3. RITUAL, REALISM, AND ABSTRACTION: Performance in the Musical

**Jerome Delamater**

AS AN ASPECT OF FILM HISTORY, film acting represents the major stylistic shift in all areas of film. The close-ups of Mae Marsh's hands in *Intolerance* contrast with the full-figured agony of, for example, Anne Mayen (as Jackie, Christine's niece) at the end of *Rules of the Game*, but to judge one style by the standards of the other is to misunderstand and misinterpret, for the acting is as much a part of the film text as the editing or the camera movement. Indeed, I believe that in the acting of a film text "... the medium intrinsically forces actor and role to coalesce utterly...."[1] If one considers the acting to be an essential textual element, then it is possible—maybe necessary—to include it in any discussion of theory. Pudovkin's discussion of the Kuleshov experiments, of course, suggests the dependence of acting on the editing process. The techniques of Renoir, Ophuls, or Minnelli, however, deny the supremacy of montage, and the result is clearly a different relationship between the acting and the other elements of film—if not a totally different kind of acting. Ultimately, film acting manifests a constant interplay of theoretical principles; as part of the text—but a part having a particularly mimetic relationship to the pro-filmic world—acting raises major questions about the nature of film realism.

The situation becomes especially complex with the musical, since most musicals operate on different performance planes. The characters function both hermetically, confined to the world of the diegesis, and presentationally, as if aware of the audience watching the film. Jim Collins's application of the concepts of *histoire* and *discours* to the genre seems instructive as a way of distinguishing among the complexities of acting within the musical.[2] Any given musical has frequent shifts from the traditional, hermetic, third-person *histoire* of the diegesis to the interactive, presentational, first- and second-person *discours* of the numbers. The distinction is not always that discrete, however, for there are often numbers that operate solely within the usual limits of *histoire;* the Kelly and Reynolds characters sing and dance exclusively for each other in "You Were Meant for Me" from *Singin' in the Rain,* for example. Not infrequently there are moments when the seamless *histoire* is ruptured by a nonmusical *discours,* as when Maurice Chevalier breaks out of character to address the audience in *Gigi.* In addition, musical numbers will sometimes begin with characters singing and dancing to each other but then continue by performing for an audience—the *histoire* becomes *discours* when, in *Born to Dance,* Eleanor Powell and Jimmy Stewart first proclaim being "Nuts about You" to each other, then with their fellow characters, and finally to the film's audience. Singing and dancing become part of acting in the musical, and the forces that influence styles of performance in narrative cinema must expand to include a broader definition of acting.

Laleen Jayamanne insists on the term *performing* in preference to *acting* in order to enlarge the context within which the act of performing operates: "I think of Performing as having to do with the relationship of bodies and texts. Texts would include not only verbal language but also sound, light, objects. These relationships are those of spaces, textures, absences and presence."[3] Performance suggests more than acting (which is only one kind of performance)—particularly, in the case of the musical, singing and dancing. Harriet and Irving Deer suggest that "the basic myth underlying all musical comedy [is] the myth of discovering meaning through performance."[4] Musicals, in other words, are about performance, and in the genre performance becomes ritual condensation, "the material representation of abstract ideas."[5] Performance in its ritualized form often functions as *discours;* the characters are no longer just characters whose existence is restricted to the text, but they are performers *as* characters who frequently invite the audience to participate in the ritual with them.

It is the ritualization of performance that truly distinguishes the musical from other genres, and it is the relationship of the ritual musical numbers to the narrative that most often elicits inquiry into the genre. Understanding musical performance, therefore, suggests application of ideas of ritual and investigation of the contexts in which ritual operates. Certain studies[6] illuminate a variety of approaches to ritual; by extension, those ideas reveal that the musical embodies significant form. Rituals, for our purposes, can be defined as sequences of actions, often stylized and repetitive, that give ceremonial form to ideas and abstractions; rituals simplify complexities and make them comprehensible, primarily through metaphoric structures. "At the very least, any ritual activity has visual, verbal, spatial and temporal dimensions … ,"[7] and one could easily add terms like musical and rhythmic that would also be appropriate. Although there are many different purposes for which rituals are enacted, those involved with rites of passage are among the most lucid and consistent, generally following a three-phase pattern, as Edmund Leach has pointed out[8]: "Initial 'normal' condition"; "Abnormal condition. Initiate without status, outside society, outside time"; "Final 'normal' condition." (The three phases are separated by transitional stages that become especially significant in applying this schema to an analysis of performance in the musical.) Rites of passage symbolically prepare both the initiate and the society for one's acceptance of adult responsibilities; what Anthony Wallace calls "rituals of salvation are, in a sense, similar to rites of passage because they seek to effect a change in the career line of their subject…."[9] The character is returned to the world transformed. Although occasionally musical numbers may be rites of passage (e.g., John Travolta/Tony's disco dances in *Saturday Night Fever*), more frequently they serve multiple functions; nevertheless, they follow that ritual pattern and, perhaps most importantly, are a means either for effecting change in the narrative or for fulfillment of some earlier narrative promise. In spite of the criticism sometimes leveled by those hostile to the genre that the musical numbers interrupt the narrative, musical numbers as ritual "ceremonies … have the double function of proclaiming the change of status and of magically bringing it about.

From another point of view they are the internal markers in the progression of social time."[10]

Historically, the move toward the so-called integrated musical complicated the relationship between the musical numbers and the narrative. In general, the numbers in early musicals were narratively and stylistically distinct from the rest of the film; they were often community rituals and fulfilled goals for the group.[11] In the integrated musical of the forties and fifties, narrative and stylistic continuity was the aim, and rituals of individual characters predominated.[12] Performed on a stage, usually as part of the show the characters had been preparing throughout the film, the numbers in Busby Berkeley's films, for example, were the ritual culmination of the narrative. The repetitive images, designs, and patterns associated with Berkeley's choreography were, however, essentially rituals for the audience of the film; the illusion of performing for a diegetic audience was generally abandoned except through some conventional transition as the camera, initially and finally, observed the action from the viewpoint of a theater seat. By contrast, one aspect of integration was that the characters seemed to perform spontaneously,[13] primarily for their fellow characters and only incidentally for the film's audience. The cues that the performance was functioning on a different plane, however, were often the same as in the backstage musical: cameras dollying in and excluding the diegetic audience, full-figured frontal photographing of the dancer or singer, a climactic ending to signal that the performance was over, and cutting to return the character to his/her other, nonperforming world.

Transitional stages help identify when ritual is about to occur and create boundaries between the formalized, stereotyped action of ritual and the less formalized, unstereotyped action of its social (or narrative) context. "When we use symbols (either verbal or non-verbal) to distinguish one class of things or actions from another we are creating artificial boundaries in a field which is 'naturally' continuous in both space and time."[14] Acting in the musical is epitomized by the boundaries of ritual, for it is precisely in the transition, the demarcation between the numbers and the narrative, that theoretical principles conflict. In language similar to that Leach uses when emphasizing life as a spatial and temporal continuum, Dudley Andrew distinguishes between André Bazin's concepts of film realism and more traditional, montage-oriented theories.

> Perceptual reality is, for Bazin, spatial reality: that is, visible phenomena and the spaces which separate them. A realistic style of editing, at the most basic level, is a style which would show an event developing in an integral space. Specifically the realistic film style is that style which preserves the autonomy of objects within ... the undifferentiated *homogeneity of space*. In general, spatial realism is destroyed by montage and preserved by the so-called *shot-in-depth,* where universal focus pays tribute to the space between objects. The long take and depth-of-field emphasize that primary fact of cinema, its relation ... to perceptual reality and specifically to space. Montage, on the other hand, substitutes for this an abstract time and a differentiated space seeking to create a mental continuity at the expense of perceptual continuity.[15]

The musical is not ordinarily associated with aspects of film realism (certainly not in the sense of striving for verisimilitude), but the principle of integrated musicals has generally meant that the song and dance numbers grew "naturally" from the narrative, that the films adhered in one sense to the Bazinian theory of realism because the numbers were not set off but made to seem as "real" as the rest of the film. This reality has usually meant narrative continuity, but one aspect of the integration of number and narrative must also imply that the cinematic boundaries are de-emphasized: the ritual song-and-dance space and time are part of the narrative space and time through the cinematic processes of perceptual continuity.

Gene Kelly's work seems particularly valuable as an example to explore the complexities of performing in the musical. Kelly's work is eclectic; he has worked with many different directors but has also directed himself (i.e., co-directed with Stanley Donen). He has operated—often self-consciously—in a variety of film styles, at times fulfilling aspects of Bazin's criteria for film realism, at times working in levels of abstraction that seem to go against everything Bazin preferred. Leo Braudy refers to the "interplay between formal style and disruptive realism" in Gene Kelly's work,[16] and the essence of Kelly as a performer exists within that interplay; he turns disruptive realism into a formal style. The Kelly persona is a recognizable popular culture figure, but the persona exists in a stylized world. The sailor in *On the Town* exists within a stylized abstraction that suggests "New Yorkness" (and dances in a ritual abstraction of the abstraction in "A Day in New York")—that "New Yorkness" itself suggested by both locations and studio sets. Moreover, that identifiable Kelly persona often plays its roles in spatial contexts generally associated with film realism. The realist aesthetic of long shot, long take, and moving camera becomes a formal stylistic feature for Kelly. Finally, within a broad array of roles and dance styles, Kelly embodied the ritualization of performance crucial to an understanding of the musical.

Whatever the possible metonymic connections that may exist (post-World War II New York in *On the Town,* late 1920s Hollywood in *Singin' in the Rain*), any given film presents a self-contained, metaphoric fictional world; in the musical, ritual helps to reveal that world. "The content of human ritual communication is a twofold message: first, it is a statement of an intention; second, it is a statement of the nature of the world in which the intention is to be realized."[17] The musical numbers of *Singin' in the Rain,* for example, connect the film's major narrative and thematic elements: a group's overcoming obstacles in putting on a show (i.e. making a film); Don and Kathy's courtship and romance; the fulfillment of the performance tradition in the musical; Don and Cosmo's friendship; the coming of sound to Hollywood; the Lina Lamont parody of the star system; the good-natured, self-reflexive satire of the film industry. The numbers have individual functions but contribute to the gestalt of the film. Moreover, several of the ritual musical numbers from *Singin' in the Rain* (particularly by comparison with similar ones in other films) display the logical relationships,[18] ordinarily unobserved, that can be seen in all musical performances.

*"Make 'em Laugh"*

> " ... ritual performances ..., being dynamic, are to be regarded as *signals* which automatically trigger off a change in the (metaphysical) state of the world" (Leach, p. 52).

"Make 'Em Laugh," like almost all musical numbers, has multiple functions. Diegetically, its ritual function is therapeutic: Don Lockwood, unhappy about "losing" Kathy Selden, needs to be cheered up. Thematically, the song and the routine are a paean to the glories of show business, particularly vaudeville performance. The lead-in to the song connects these two functions, because Cosmo reminds Don of his responsibility as an actor: "Come on, now—snap out of it. You can't let a little thing like this get you down. Why, you're Don Lockwood, aren't you? And Don Lockwood's an actor, isn't he? Well, what's the first thing an actor learns? The show must go on." The characters don't yet know that they're going to be faced with another obstacle—making sound films—but the ritual is preparing them to carry on later as well. However, Cosmo's performance for Don is also Donald O'Connor's performance for us. "Make 'Em Laugh," like "Be a Clown" in *The Pirate* and "That's Entertainment" in *The Band Wagon,* for example, epitomizes the ritual reaffirmation of the virtues of popular entertainment; we may not need to be convinced of those virtues, but like religious or national/political ritual, the repeated presentation on a regular basis satisfies on the screen as it does at Christmas in church or on the Fourth of July in one's home town.

In the musical the performer foregrounds his own abilities in order to fulfill the function of the character he plays. Cosmo Brown is trying to cheer up Don Lockwood; Donald O'Connor starts to play the piano and sing, walks across the keys, jumps down, and does a series of movements (including knee slides and jumps and kicks), all specifically directed at Lockwood. With the cut to the third shot of the number, however, as the two workers lift O'Connor on the board, Don Lockwood is eliminated from the sequence. The performance is no longer for Don but for the film audience, and O'Connor evokes his own vaudeville roots and other film roles in a series of facial and bodily tricks, slapstick gags, and athletic stunts of the kind that only he (and one or two others) could do. The lyrics of the song signal his general (and several specific) actions:

> "Be an actor ... But be a comical one!"
>
> " ... those old honky-tonk monkeyshines."
>
> "Just slip on a banana peel, the world's at your feet."
>
> "Take a fall, butt a wall, split a seam."
>
> [Copyright Robbins Music Corp.]

O'Connor moves into new areas of space, away from his fellow characters, and therein enacts material from the traditions that the group will need to emphasize in order to be successful filmmakers. Culminating in his backflips off two walls (one a *trompe-l'oeil* hallway) and a crash through a third, the number ends as O'Connor directly addresses the camera, as he has throughout the number, repeating, "Make 'em laugh, make 'em laugh, make 'em laugh!" As Cosmo cheers up Don and as the two of them prepare themselves for their immediate job of making a film (the next scene is the filming of *The Dueling Cavalier),* O'Connor—in the process—performs for us and invites us to participate with him in the joys of praising show business; the *histoire* becomes ritual *discours.*

### *"You Were Meant for Me"*

> "The crossing of frontiers and thresholds is always hedged about with ritual, so also is the transition from one social status to another." (Leach, p. 35)

In the musical, courtship rituals are usually presented as song and dance numbers. Fred Astaire and Ginger Rogers worked out their mutual attraction/repulsion in "Night and Day" *(The Gay Divorcee)* or "Cheek to Cheek" *(Top Hat)* with corresponding dance movements toward and away from each other. Ultimately, of course, they established their partnership with simultaneous movements like the kick and bend with which they leave the frame at the end of "Let's Face the Music and Dance" *(Follow the Fleet)*. "You Were Meant for Me" is Don Lockwood's and Kathy Selden's courtship in *Singin' in the Rain*. Having finally found her, Don can express his feelings for her only through a performance in, as he puts it, "the proper setting," a film production stage. (The pivotal ritual in their relationship, it is not, however, the only one. When Kathy sings "All I Do Is Dream of You" as part of the entertainment provided by the Coconut Grove troupe, the words represent what will become Don's obsession; at the end, almost having lost her again, he confirms their personal and professional partnership with "You Are My Lucky Star," sung, significantly, on a stage in front of a moviegoing audience.) The number becomes the means of their working out a previous antagonism, of Don's revealing his true character (the Kelly persona often being that of a brash and aggressive egotist hiding a more lovable song-and-dance man),[19] and of Kathy Selden's (Debbie Reynolds's) beginning her movie career. The number follows a three-part pattern that is certainly akin to Leach's ritual schema. Setting the scene, Don consciously exploits the artificiality of the backdrop; he turns his normal world into a stage for ritual. Singing to Kathy as she stands on a ladder, he begins with a lyric that is similarly tentative and self-reflexive:

> Life was a song. You came along.
> I lay awake the whole night through.
> If I'd but dare to think you'd care,
> This is what I'd say to you.
>
> [Copyright Robbins Music Corp.]

When he has finished singing, there is a cut; they begin to walk and, with a barely perceptible change, to dance. Although the cut opens up the space available for their dance, no cut separates the walking from the dancing; the natural movement leads into the abstraction of performing movement with continuity of space and time. Their dancing becomes their courtship. Separated from their normal world, the characters become oblivious to the artificial set they have created and oblivious to the camera and audience; ritually they become transformed. At the end of the number they have changed status; they have become a couple.

"You Were Meant for Me" is primarily a diegetic ritual in which Don sings for Kathy and the two dance only for each other. It is important to remember, however, that ritual is a social action even when the initiates enact it alone; on film that becomes especially significant. Although they do not acknowledge the camera as they would in a more discursive number (in fact, they assiduously avoid looking into the camera), Kelly and Reynolds nevertheless do perform for the audience in that ambiguous state that combines performer and character. Kelly continues the persona established in other films. His characters sing and dance in courtship rituals only after abandoning their brash facade. (For example, in "Main Street" from *On the Town,* a number similar in form and identical in function to "You Were Meant for Me," he woos Vera-Ellen only after he apologizes to her for the way in which he initially pursued her.) "You Were Meant for Me" is, moreover, identifiably a Kelly number, a combination of soft shoe, elaborated ballroom dance, and some balletic movements with a strong relationship between the music (particularly the orchestral arrangement) and the camera work; this integration of camera, dance, and performance space is crucial in all of Kelly's films. Although there are only five shots in the whole number (beginning with the close-up on Debbie Reynolds's face as Kelly poses her before he sings), the constant camera movement and the cuts serve to reposition the performers' movement within their ritual space and to provide the audience with multiple perspectives. This particular narrative ritual suggests that in the musical, performance exists within realist space but simultaneously exploits concepts of cinematic abstraction.

*"Good Morning"*

> "Social rituals ... arouse in the participants a state of readiness and an intention to perform the consummatory action...." (Wallace, p. 223)

The metaphor of a new day, the participants ready to cast off self-doubt and to assume new challenges, informs the ritual of "Good Morning." Like "Fit as a Fiddle" and "Moses Supposes," also from *Singin' in the Rain,* "O'Brien to Ryan to Goldberg" from *Take Me Out to the Ballgame,* and "New York, New York" from *On the Town,* the number embodies the group's values, inspires them to achieve, and provides them with another "stage" for performance. "Good Morning" is situated between two important discoveries the characters make about their professional dilemma (one, that they can turn *The Dueling Cavalier* into a musical and, two, that Kelly can dub Kathy's voice for Lina's), thereby overcoming the "impaired identity"[20] Don has suffered at that night's preview: "I'm no actor, I never was. Just a lot of dumb show. I know that now." As they realize that a literal and figurative new day has arrived, they celebrate their good fortune by experimenting with varieties of performance. They don costumes (the raincoats), perform in different styles (ballet, tap, soft shoe), adopt conscious roles (Kathy does a Hawaiian number, Don a flamenco, and Cosmo a Charleston), and exploit Don's house for alternate performing spaces. At the end of the number, as a result of their participation in the ritual and having surveyed and glorified the options available to a musical performer (while performing them), they can discover the new option, dubbing, when reminded of one final obstacle—Lina's shrill voice.

As is often the case with certain musical rituals, the lyrics signal aspects of their function. "Good Morning" becomes a discursive number partially because the lyrics "ask" the performers to address themselves "to you and you and you." Kelly, Reynolds, and O'Connor entertain the film's audience while their characters rejoice in solving a problem (and thereby lead to solving another). A direct reference in the song to the characters' plight and the metaphoric solution suggests something too of the film's ritual nature.

> When we left the movie show,
> The future wasn't bright.
> But came the dawn,
> The show goes on
> And I don't want to say, "Good Night."
>
> (Copyright Chappell & Co., Inc.)

Wallace says, "... if the effort [to restore identity] is supported and guided by others and if some sort of model of the transformation process is provided by the culture, the effort is successful."[21] The cultural model provided within the film is performance; the characters, as a result, make a successful sound film. The cultural model provided *by* the film is also performance; the diegetic situation, the characters' dilemma, provides the reason for the ritual, and the ritual, in turn, becomes the means by which Kelly, O'Connor, and Reynolds entertain the audience.

*"Singin' in the Rain"*

> "Solitary rituals ... seem useful principally in reducing anxiety in situations of ambiguity with respect to learning or discrimination." (Wallace, p. 223)

The film's title number, unlike most soliloquy/solitary rituals in Kelly's work, is jubilant rather than pensive and melancholy. In the Alter Ego dance from *Cover Girl* or the Squeaky Board number from *Summer Stock,* the character withdraws; he wants to overcome his anxiety alone. "Singin' in the Rain," on the other hand, is a celebration because ambiguity has been resolved.[22] Nevertheless, it does share some formal and functional qualities with Kelly's other solitary rituals: its use of space, its combination of theoretical principles, its self-affirming discourse on the joys of putting on a show and falling in love. The number is a reversion to childhood actions and a purification; following hard upon the "Good Morning" ritual, "Singin' " is the final washing away of Don's single, silent-movie-star state and his emergence as loving and loved sound film singing and dancing star.

"Singin' in the Rain" begins and ends without major preparation or climactic showmanship. There has been a change in the character's personal and professional life, and he celebrates that change by putting on a show/performance. Every object and configuration of the street becomes part of Kelly's ritual stage: he jumps onto the lamp post, strums his umbrella like a guitar, splashes in puddles. The camera views him almost exclusively in medium and long shot, allowing him to perform within identifiable space. Each cut of the number (there are nine shots) is to a long shot that reidentifies his milieu while broadening the space for his performance (figs. 3.1–3.2). At the end he is reintegrated into the community by contact with a policeman and a passerby. To the cop he explains, "I'm dancin' and singin' in the rain"; what else should one do under these circumstances but perform? And he gives the passerby his umbrella; he is a new person now and no longer needs it. The number concludes simply: he walks away down the street, jubilantly swinging his arms.

Gene Kelly used a number of different dance styles, but each one had a conventional association. Ballet tended to be associated with dream, for example, whereas *joie-de-vivre* was usually expressed through tap dancing. "Singin' in the Rain" follows that somewhat oversimplified pattern. Kelly uses a number of different tap combinations early in the number, but as the dance progresses he becomes more athletic in his movements. For Kelly almost any kind of action can be performed as part of a musical number. Here, for instance, splashing in puddles, whirling with an umbrella, and balancing on a curb while mimicking a tightrope walker are choreographed into his dance. Don Lockwood's ability to sing and dance is explained early in the film. (But Kelly did not always feel that necessity: Gaby in *On the Town* is a sailor; his ability to dance is never explained—it's just natural for him, an integral part of his being. By contrast, Eddie O'Brien in *Take Me Out to the Ballgame* is a baseball player who is also a vaudeville hoofer.) As a result, it is only logical that his professional salvation should lie with making *The Dueling Cavalier* into a musical. Kelly's own ability to dance, however, had come to include every possible kind of ritual movement, even the camera movement into a close-up of his smiling face (which occurs twice in this number). Kelly does not document his performances with a disinterested observer-camera. Instead he and the camera perform together. Indeed, "Singin' in the Rain" demonstrates that all the elements of cinema work together to present musical performance.

**Fig. 3.1**

**Fig. 3.2**

*"The Broadway Ballet"*

> " … ritual, no matter whether it takes place at a wayside shrine temporarily erected for the purpose or in a permanent setting such as the sanctuary of a cathedral, is performed within the confines of a stage, the boundaries and segments of which are artificial." (Leach, p. 85)

"The Broadway Ballet" is spectacle—*Singin' in the Rain*'s equilvalent of *On the Town*'s "A Day in New York" or the title ballet for *An American in Paris.* The latter numbers, however, are recapitulation rituals in which the hero relives the events in his imagination in order to conclude them successfully—for Gaby to find Miss Turnstiles, for Jerry to be reunited with Lise. "The Broadway Ballet" is ironic, however, in contrast to those numbers. Presented as if on a screen in Don's imagination, supposedly the number is to be the modern section of *The Dancing Cavalier* but it can be no such thing. As Cosmo outlined it, the modern portion was to be "realistic" and the costume sequences (already shot for the disastrous *Dueling Cavalier*) were to be the hero's dream. Unlike the other numbers of the film, which generally attempt to suppress the artificiality of their ritual state, this one foregrounds its own spectacle. Leach suggests that one "purpose of ritual activity … is to bring about a transition from normal to abnormal time at the beginning of the ceremony and another transition from abnormal to normal time at the end of it."[23] This seems particularly true of most spectacle numbers, which operate in an abnormal time of dream or imagination or on the separate stage of a show within the film. In addition, they are often stylistically distinct (abnormal) in contrast to other numbers. The abstraction of the set gives "The Broadway Ballet" a totally different quality from the film's normal diegetic milieu. The agents' offices are suggested by a series of doors in an obviously painted wall (fig. 3.3); a night club is a few tables and a dance floor (fig. 3.4); the dancer's career path is a song phrase ("When I hear that happy beat—Feel like dancing down the street") repeated three times, each before a more sophisticated chorus line. Moreover, the number ends with a looming close-up of Gene Kelly smiling to make the transition back to "normal time" and the studio (where the producer says of the completely visualized number we have just seen, "I can't quite visualize it. I'll have to see it on film, first") (fig. 3.5).

"The Broadway Ballet" is a highly stylized performance in a completely artificial world designed to showcase Gene Kelly and an entire show business tradition. Indeed, the number recapitulates the genre, not just an individual film. This is what musicals are about: hoofers going to Broadway (the term being metonymic for the theater district and a metaphor for show business in general), striving for success and stardom, being disillusioned (often about love but also having doubts about themselves), but ultimately finding salvation in performing. Kelly's performance moreover encompasses the world of show business. The hoofer's career path is equivalent to changes in theatrical respectability: he goes from a baggy pants burlesque buffoon to a more refined vaudeville dancer to a Ziegfeld star in top hat and tails. As a performer who's "gotta dance," he does so in a variety of styles highlighted by his ethereal modern dance/dream with Cyd Charisse. The cyclical nature of show business is also emphasized when, at the end, a new young hoofer who's also "gotta dance" startles Kelly into seeing a younger version of himself, someone who is bound to replace him eventually. The spectacle of "The Broadway Ballet" restates the essential nature of performance as ritual.

* * *

One of Edmund Leach's most important points in *Culture and Communication* is that all communication—and ritual, in particular—is both metaphoric and metonymic.[24] His distinction is especially cogent here because it allows for the possibility of the blurring of character and performer that is inevitable in the musical. There is surely an intrinsic (metonymic) relationship between the figure we see on the screen and the actor-performer Gene Kelly, but there is an arbitrary (metaphoric) relationship between Don Lockwood and Kelly. The two do coalesce, however, and although this may be true of all screen performance, in other respects

Fig. 3.3

Fig. 3.4

Fig. 3.5

performance in the musical is different. It is more ritualistic since the musical numbers move the narrative on to different stylistic planes, often within different spatial contexts. Kelly, particularly, exploited the spaces and textures (that Jayamanne referred to) for the presentation of his ritual dances. He was always aware of the relationship between the camera and the performer, primarily because, as a choreographer, he was constantly arranging dancers (including himself) and making them part of the narrative/performing space. Kelly operated within the general attributes of realist style, but he also did so while sometimes emphasizing the abstraction of his character's milieu. For Kelly the dancing performer needed the space allowed by long shot and long take, even if that space included an artificial *mise-en-scène*. Other musical performers may have operated differently (Astaire's preference for single-take dances when he was working at RKO emphasized the pro-filmic integrity of the number), but Kelly was always concerned about the inalterable coalescence of character and performer, of performance and medium, of ritual number and narrative progression. Acting in the musical includes a kind of performance that is not just an impersonation of fictional characters but is a presentation of the performer's singing and dancing abilities. The characters go through a narrative ceremony that sets them apart from the rest of the film, but it is one in which the performer sings and dances primarily for the audience of the film. The transition from diegesis to ritual may occur within the same space and time as the narrative or it may occur by means of editing; but in either case the ritual functions "abnormally," irrespective of the excuse for the number's diegetic possibilities. Even when the character's ability to dance and sing was not explained as part of his show business role, the rituals glorify the performer's innate show business roots while furthering the character's immediate narrative end. In one sense, the performer is just a medium for the narrative ritual, yet, as Kelly's work suggests, the medium becomes the essence of the ritual; in a genre that is about the necessity of performance, performance becomes the means of its own ritual fulfillment.

## NOTES

1. John O. Thompson, "Screen Acting and the Commutation Test," *Screen* 19 (Summer 1978), p. 57.
2. "Toward Defining a Matrix of the Musical Comedy: The Place of the Spectator within the Textual Mechanisms," *Genre: The Musical,* ed. Rick Altman (London: British Film Institute, 1981), pp. 134-45. Collins derived his ideas from Christian Metz who, in turn, appropriated them from Emile Benveniste.
3. "Modes of Performing: Bodies & Texts (some thoughts on fe/male performances)," *Australian Journal of Screen Theory,* no. 9/10 (1981), p. 126. The author is not referring specifically to musicals, however.
4. "Musical Comedy: From Performer to Performance," *Journal of Popular Culture,* vol. 12, no. 3 (1978–79), p. 420.
5. Edmund Leach, *Culture and Communication: The Logic by which Symbols Are Connected* (New York: Cambridge University Press, 1976), p. 37.
6. For this analysis Edmund Leach's book, cited above, and Anthony F.C. Wallace, *Religion: An Anthropological View* (New York: Random House, 1966), are crucial. Others include: Evelyn Underhill, *Worship* (London: Nisbet, 1936), whose primary focus is a particular religious tradition, but who recognizes the importance of "speech, gesture, rhythm and agreed ceremonial" (p. 37) as part of ritual (she would, however, hate the idea of secularized ritual being important); Kenneth Burke, Attitudes toward History, 2d ed. (Los Altos: Hermes Publications, 1959) whose literary investigation of "General Nature of Ritual" (pp. 179–215) was of general interest but was less specifically important than Leach's and Wallace's anthropological approaches.
7. Leach, p. 81.
8. Leach, pp. 77–79. Wallace, after Arnold van Gennep, calls them separation, transition, incorporation, p. 105.
9. Wallace, p. 206.
10. Leach, p. 77.
11. Mark Roth's study of Busby Berkeley's films in terms of Roosevelt's New Deal seems the perfect analysis of this kind of ritual: "Some Warner's Musicals and the Spirit of the New Deal," reprinted in Altman, pp. 41–56.
12. Wallace makes the distinction as social (allo-communicative) and solitary (auto-communicative) rituals, p. 223.
13. The Deers discuss this illusion of spontaneity as does Jane Feuer, *The Hollywood Musical* (Bloomington: University of Indiana Press, 1982).
14. Leach, pp. 33–34.
15. Dudley Andrew in *Major Film Theories: An Introduction* (New York: Oxford University Press, 1976), pp. 157–8.
16. Leo Braudy, *The World in a Frame: What We See in Films* (Garden City: Anchor Press, 1976), p. 148.
17. Wallace, p. 237. I am primarily interested in understanding how ritual operates within the fictional world, but one could, of course, use these ideas to explore how any given film—itself a ritual—serves as a "statement of the [real] world" in which the film is an artifact.
18. Leach, p. 27.

19. I have elaborated on this in *Dance in the Hollywood Musical* (Ann Arbor, MI: UMI Research Press, 1981), pp. 142–151.
20. "When identity is seriously impaired..., we can expect that the experience will call for strenuous efforts to understand and repair the damage to self-esteem...." Wallace, p. 140.
21. Wallace, p. 140.
22. "I Like Myself" from *It's Always Fair Weather* is one other similarly jubilant soliloquy.
23. Leach, p. 83.
24. Leach, pp. 69–70. The parallel distinctions Leach sets up, (pp. 12–15) are metaphor/metonymy, arbitrary/intrinsic, symbol/sign.

# 4. "ACTING TO PLAY ONESELF": Notes on Performance in Documentary

Thomas Waugh

IN 1940, JORIS IVENS, IN THE MIDST of finishing *Power and the Land* for Pare Lorentz's U.S. Film Service, wrote an essay on "Collaboration in Documentary." It was time to summarize much of what he had learned in the first fifteen years of his career. Much of the resulting manual of the classical documentary concerns the challenge of working with nonprofessional subjects in "re-enactment," one of documentary's "wide variety of styles." As a lead-in to my reflection on the presence of performance within the documentary film tradition, it is worth excerpting this text at length:

> ... We come to the problem that has attracted and sometimes baffled us for many years: the handling of non-actors. In re-enacting a situation with a group of extremely pleasant persons, who for your purposes have become actors, the danger of letting them do what they like, of falling back on pleasant, easy naturalism, is even greater. And as your location work progresses, the non-actors become the central figures in your group, creating problems that temporarily force all the other problems out of your consciousness....
>
> Our farm film presented material that seemed to demand re-enactments .... In choosing the people who were to play the roles (of themselves—the farmer as the farmer, his sons as the farmer's sons, etc.), the first visual impression is very important. Casting has its own difficulties too. A father and a son may work well separately, but not at all well when they're together in a scene. To get close enough to these people, to work with them, the director must be sensitive to these relationships. In general, I feel a knowledge of psychology is demanded of every member of the group, for all must watch and sense delicate situations.
>
> The writer must employ his imagination to manipulate the real personal characteristics of the new actors—searching them with seemingly careless observations. He must learn thereby, for exam-

ple that the farmer takes a special pride in the sharpness of his tool blades, and therefore suggest a toolshed scene which will make use of that fact. The key to this approach, I think, is that a real person, acting to play himself, will be more expressive if his actions are based on his real characteristics.

My experience has been that directives to non-actors who are playing together would usually be given them separately, so that a certain amount of unrehearsed reaction can be counted upon. To get natural reactions we played tricks similar to those Pudovkin has recorded, and some of them worked. For example: the father was filmed receiving a notification from the dairy that his milk is sour; he expected to unfold and pretend to read a blank piece of paper. But he read instead a startling message from me, complaining about his sour milk in no uncertain terms.

In general my method was to give precise directions to these non-actors but not to do it for them—simply to tell them what has to be done.... The farmer will have his special way of doing it, whether it is entering a room or moving a chair, and it is usually a very good way.

I have come to believe it is best to have as few retakes as possible. Repetition seems to have a deadening effect on the non-actor. If rehearsals are necessary, allow some time to elapse between rehearsals, and shooting. Use yourself or anybody as stand-ins—to keep the non-actor from exhaustion or self-consciousness. On the other hand, if the period of filming a re-enactment is short or very rushed, there can be less care in humoring him, depending more on the camera's ability to break up the action into useful close-ups.

The cameraman has to understand the special difficulties in working with non-actors ("What good is all this fooling with lights?") to render the length of time during light and camera adjustment tolerable to the non-actor. I don't believe in having long conferences before takes, while the non-actor waits. Keep discussions away from him. He begins to feel that these long, visible, but inaudible conversations are about himself and his acting—and he is usually right. We learned to use a code. Whenever a cameraman said, after a shot, "Very good" I knew he meant, "It's not so hot, try some other way."...

The surest way to avoid loss of time with re-takes is to know and anticipate the real movements of the man, to catch the regular rhythm of his normal action (which is far from re-enactment). The whole action should be watched (away from the camera) before breaking it up for filming. And the breaking up, and covering shots, should absolutely include beginnings of an action, endings of an

> action, and the places where the worker rests—not just other angles of the most exciting sections of his movement. Thus you get material for good human editing....
>
> Overcoming self-consciousness is of course the greatest problem with the non-actor, no matter what his background. If you work for months with the same group of persons, you can gradually expect to find more consciousness of themselves as actors. They become more flexible and adaptable and greater demands can be made of them. They can even be taught something of the film's technique. When the father in the farm film couldn't understand why he had to repeat an action more than once while the camera was shifted about, I took him to see a Cagney movie at the local theatre and pointed out how an action in a finished film was made out of long shots, medium shots and close-ups. From then on he understood our continuity problems and gave very useful assistance in this way. But I don't think it wise to show them their own rushes. I waited until the last few days before showing our farm family themselves on the screen.
>
> I advise not to fool with a man's professional pride. Don't ask a farmer to milk an empty cow, even though it's just for a close-up of the farmer's face. He fights such an idea because to him it is false—until he has been with the film group for a long time.
>
> Even as simple a rule as "Don't look at the camera" is bound up with the man himself. But this is such a basic necessity for the quality of your film that you must enforce the rule even though it hurts you to.[1]

Ivens goes on to illustrate this last point with an anecdote from his Chinese shoot a few years earlier *(The Four Hundred Million)* where he had had to force himself to impose the rule of not looking at the camera on traumatized stretcher-bearers in a battle scene.

## ACTING NATURALLY IN THE CLASSICAL DOCUMENTARY

Documentary film, in everyday commonsense parlance, implies the absence of elements of performance, acting, staging, directing, etc., criteria which presumably distinguish the documentary form from the narrative fiction film. Ivens' text helps focus a discussion of performance in documentary because it challenges the common understanding. It reveals how basic the ingredients of performance and direction are within the documentary tradition—certainly within the classical documentary as reflected in this 1940 document, but also, as I will argue, in the modern vérité and post-vérité documentary as well.

For Ivens and his generation, the notion of performance as an element of documentary filmmaking was something to be taken for granted. Towards the end of the thirties, as documentarists yearned to get out of the basements and into the theaters, semi-fictive characterization, or "personalization," as Ivens called it, seemed to be the means for the documentary to attain artistic maturity and mass audiences. Social actors,[2] real people, became documentary film performers, playing themselves and their social roles before the camera.

The decade's prevailing notion of documentary performance is reflected most in Ivens' terminology with its echoes of narrative studio-based filmmaking: "roles," "re-take," "continuity," "covering shots," "rehearsals," "casting," etc. His directing techniques, significantly, are borrowed from Pudovkin, a director notable for his work with professional dramatic actors. Documentary performers "act" in much the same way as their dramatic counterparts except that they are cast for their social representativity as well as for their cinematic qualities, and their roles are composites of their own social roles and the dramatic requirements of the film.

Ivens' term "natural" indicates a problematical concept and practice for the classical (pre-vérité) documentarist. By "naturalism" Ivens means a cinematography characterized not by "content value" (a concept he uses elsewhere in the article) but by a spontaneous textural or behavioral quality, a quality which the later vérité generation would transform into an aesthetic gospel. But he also refers to "acting naturally," in reference to not looking at the camera, the code of illusion by which both extras, such as the Chinese stretcher bearers, and principal (non-) actors should "perform" unawareness of the camera. This clearly artificial code of acting naturally is so rooted in our cinematic culture, then as now, that Ivens posits it unquestioningly as a basic axiom of "quality" cinema. The vérité school, in its American observational incarnation (Leacock, Wiseman), would share this axiom with Ivens and his generation however much they would repudiate the didacticism of the principle of "content value."

But the concept and the practice of acting naturally are far more complex than either generation realized, and the familiar concepts of "representational" and "presentational" discourse are of some help. Let us use **"representational"** to refer to Ivens' "acting naturally," the documentary code of narrative illusion borrowed from the dominant fiction cinema. When subjects perform "not looking at the camera," when they represent their lives or roles, the image looks natural, as if the camera were invisible, as if the subject were unaware of being filmed. This performance convention is by no means inherent in the documentary mode. Certainly, in documentary still photography it is considerably less unanimous, for from August Sander to the Farm Security Administration to Diane Arbus, from Wilhelm von Gloeden to Robert Mapplethorpe, the convention of posing is much more the dominant tradition. In contrast, the convention of representation as found in, say, Henri Cartier-Bresson, (whose influence on the cinema-vérité is of course not without interest), informs a vigorous but secondary counter-current. The convention of performing an awareness of the camera rather than a nonawareness, of presenting oneself explicitly for the camera—the convention the documentary cinema absorbed from its elder sibling photography—we shall call **"presentational"** performance.

Although posing, the presentational convention of acknowledging the camera, never became the standard convention in classical documentary cinema, it did become an important secondary variant of documentary cinematic practice, particularly in the sound era. Whereas Flaherty's silent Nanook was depicted performing presentationally a few times—posing for the camera with a grin or a look—he for the most part performed naturalistically, "acting" or representing his daily life for the camera without explicitly acknowledging its presence. *Moana* similarly displayed some engaging moments of presentation—a subject displaying a captured tortoise to the camera, for example—but by and large Flaherty succeeded in getting his Samoan social actors to perform according to the codes of representation. By the time of his later features, *Man of Aran* and *Louisiana Story,* Flaherty was following the codes of representation obsessively—to the extent that they become abstract mytho-narrative meditations on exotic landscapes rather than social narratives rooted in the daily cultural contexts of those landscapes' inhabitants. These latter films are no longer able to bear, for contemporary eyes at least, the slightest pretension to ethnographic veracity, nor even, my students would say, the least claim to the documentary mantle at all—a point whose significance I will take up later.

Not all sound documentarists followed Flaherty's lead. During the sound era, the countercurrent of presentational performance in fact became quite visible—or rather audible. Inspired in part by radio, aural presentational conventions like the interview, the monologue, even choral speech, were experimented with in the thirties by Vertov, by Grierson's British school, by Frontier Films, and even by Flaherty himself in his project for the U.S. Film Service (slightly later than Ivens'), *The Land.* Traumatized by the devastation he "discovered" in his own backyard on this latter project, Flaherty somehow let go of the representational style he'd perfected on Aran. Prominent in the film are curious silent/non-sync variations of aural presentational performances as well as several moments of silent presentational posing clearly inspired by Flaherty's fellow Federal employees in the still photography business. For his part, Ivens was accustomed of course to "representing" far more traumatic devastation than nonelectrified farming in Ohio, as his Chinese anecdote reminds us. In *Power and the Land,* then, his representational skills were thus honed to their finest point, and the performances that spurred the writings excerpted at the outset of this article became milestones in documentary representation.

It is interesting that the two traditions intersect in the career of a single editor, Helen van Dongen. Ivens' long-time collaborator and a principal pioneer in the perfection of representational documentary editing, Van Dongen edited both *The Land* and *Power and the Land.* I have always found odd her complaint about the staged quality of Flaherty's most intricate representational scene, in which a black farmhand moves about a deserted plantation and rings the plantation bell. In practice, Van Dongen sculpted this scene with all the representational precision and smoothness which she had just brought to *Power and the Land* and would later bring to *Louisiana Story.*[3] Flaherty's uncharacteristic posing shots, however, were never brought up in her published notes about the editing, though they clearly disturbed the seamless continuum that was Van Dongen's professional pride. The FSA-style posing shots she treated with an anomalous awkwardness, cutting them off with abrupt, haunting fadeouts before the intrinsic rhythm of the shot and the dynamic of the spectator's encounter with the performers are fulfilled.

As for Flaherty's and Ivens' British contemporaries (and admirers), they pushed the cumbersome sound technology of the day much further than the Americans in the direction of both presentational and representational performances, achieving unintentional self-parody with the latter in *Night Mail* and groundbreaking revelation with the former in the legendary interviews and monologues of *Housing Problems.* In the Soviet context, such experimentation appeared even earlier. As early as 1931, the only Soviet documentarist of the sound period whose work is available in the West, Dziga Vertov, incorporated short production pledges delivered as monologues by shock workers in *Enthusiasm,* the film that must be considered his manifesto of the possibilities of documentary sound, despite the stilted and self-conscious effect of these first attempts. Three years later, *Three Songs of Lenin* offered vivid and personalized portraits of Soviet citizens by virtue of a more developed use of monologue performances: two of the portraits feature a woman shock worker who shyly describes how she averted an accident with some concrete tubs in a construction project, and a woman Kolkhoz worker who chats with amazing informality and dramatic gestures about the role of women on her farm. The possibility of Vertov's influence on his Western European counterparts is a strong one since the Grierson group knew his work.

Yet, despite the inspiration occasioned by Grierson's rat-plagued housewife holding forth to the camera, and by Vertov's vivid portraits, the presentational style predominated only in the documentary vernacular of the commercial newsreel (as later in its descendent, television journalism), or in specialized forms like the still rare campaign film (such as Renoir's *La Vie est à Nous,* which incorporates Party oratory along with a range of representational sketches). Ivens' representational style of naturalistic acting and *mise-en-scène* was never edged from its hegemony within the hybrid repertory of the so-called artistic documentary of the period.

In summary, now that we have returned to Ivens, performance—the self-expression of documentary subjects for the camera in collaboration with filmmaker/director—was the basic ingredient of the classical documentary. Most directors relied principally on naturalistic, representational performance style borrowed from fiction, which some varied from time to time with presentational elements akin to the conventions of still photography and radio. The difference between representation and presentation is not that one uses performance and the other doesn't, but that the former disavows and hides its performance components through such conventions as not looking at the camera, whereas the latter openly acknowledges and exploits its performance components. This difference must be explored.

## PRESENTING VERSUS REPRESENTING

The distinction between representational and presentational performance is a very useful one for looking diachronically at documentary history. The pendulum of fashion and usage has swung back and forth between the two conventions, from one period to another, from one culture to another, and from the margin to the mainstream within one particular period and culture. I have already mentioned, for example, that presentational performance became visible, though not predominant, during the latter half of the thirties, during the first maturity of the sound documentary. At the same time proponents of the predominant representational element of the period's hybrid form often went even further than Ivens in availing themselves of the resources of fictional cinema: the use of studio sets *(Night Mail)* and professional actors *(Native Land)* during the thirties as a means of both overcoming technological difficulties and deepening social perspective did not attract any notice at the time, but would become anathema thirty years later during the heyday of vérité. During the Second World War *(Fires Were Started),* and especially during the postwar decade, the representational convention evolved so much that the resulting "docudrama" format *(Quiet One, Strange Victory, Mental Mechanisms Series)* seemed the unanimous style on the eve of the vérité breakthrough, although voiceover narrations by subjects sometimes superimposed a presentational patina *(Paul Tomkowicz Street-Railway Switchman, All My Babies)* on representational films from those years.

The first wave of vérité or direct technology, cresting in the early sixties, continued the representational mode of performance. At the same time, vérité radically revised its execution. The new technology was often able to dispense with *mise-en-scène,* though not with performance, to follow an event or performance without "setting it up." While much of the studio paraphernalia of rehearsals and retakes, etc. was no longer necessary, the code of not looking at the camera, whether implicit or explicit, was still in force—at least in the United States. The classical American vérité filmmakers systematically snipped out all looks at the camera in order to preserve the representational illusion. It didn't matter that even the most noninterventionist camera instigated palpable performance on the part of subjects, tacitly understood and enacted as part of the representational code: has anyone seen hospital workers or high school teachers as conscientious, flamboyant, and downright cinematic as those who performed their daily jobs for Wiseman? The subject in a Wiseman film, consenting to continue daily activity, to act naturally, and to perform the pretense that there is no camera or crew, consenting to show the putative audience his or her life, is performing at a most basic level. The pretense, the disavowal of performance on the part of filmmakers, editors, and subjects is at the heart of the basic contradiction of cinéma-vérité—the contradiction between the aspiration to observational objectivity and its actual subjectively representational artifice. Small wonder that the best moments in Wiseman often involve highly histrionic individuals such as *Hospital's* black "schizophrenic" hustler, fighting the system for his self-reliance while flirting with the camera operator, or the bad-tripping art student, who waxes melodramatic indeed ("I don't want to die") amid the floods of vomit and the most attentive audience he has ever had. These social actors become such memorable film actors because their clearly inscribed awareness of the camera amplifies their performance and transcends the representational pretense of vérité observation.

Small wonder also that two important genres of vérité have outshone Wiseman's cold observational eye in the marketplace to this day, genres that by their subject matter bypass and compensate for vérité's disavowal of performance:

(1) films whose crews have or establish intimate relationships with subjects, such as *Warrendale, Grey Gardens, Harlan County U.S.A., Best Boy, Soldier Girls, Seventeen,* leading to on-camera performances that are clearly enabled by, addressed to, and improvised enactments of that relationship, despite token adherence to the "don't look at the camera" code; and

(2) films about subjects whose extra-filmic social role consists of public performance, including entertainers *(Jane, Burroughs, Comedian, Eye of the Mask),* musicians (from *Lonely Boy* to *Woodstock* and *Stop Making Sense* via *Antonia: A Portrait of the Woman*), prostitutes *(Chicken Ranch, Hookers on Davie),* politicians *(Primary, Milhouse, The Right Candidate for Rosedale), transsexual people (The Queens, What Sex Am I?, Hookers on Davie),* sexual performers *(Not a Love Story, Striptease),* guerillas *(Underground, When the Mountains Tremble),* bodybuilders *(Pumping Iron I* and *II),* artists *(Painters Painting, Portrait of the Artist—As an Old Lady),* teachers *(High School),* street kids *(Streetwise),* salespeople *(Salesman, The Store),* crusaders *(If You Love This Planet),* and clergy *(Marjoe).* In this group of films, special scrutiny is usually given to the dialectic of public and private, the subject's identity expressed by

means of an onstage-offstage intercutting. The genre offers as one of the pleasures of the text the deciphering of borders between social performance, film performance, and so-called private behavior, and the discovery that the borders are both culturally encoded and imaginary.

## INTERVIEWS AND BEYOND

Now, of course, within North American documentary, we have been back in a phase since the early seventies where presentational forms of performance are very much in vogue. The seventies revived the interview in the documentary, thanks largely to the feminists, the New Left, and such individual pioneers as Emile de Antonio. The eighties have witnessed a flourishing wave of hybrid experimentation with these presentational modes as well as with stylizations of representational modes, including dramatization, a wave that has been termed, not surprisingly, "post-documentary."[4] The current repertory includes a whole spectrum of performance elements, usually incorporated within hybrid works, as often as not alongside vestiges of earlier styles, from voice-of-God direct address narration, to observational vérité, to interview/compilation conventions of the seventies. The following is a brief tabulation, offered simply as a suggestion of the richness and range of the evolving performance vocabulary since the sixties.

---

### TABLE

#### I. Presentational

Social actor performs formal oral narrative, fiction *(Storytelling)*, and nonfiction *(When the Mountains Tremble)*

Social actors perform daily life presentationally *(Rate It X, 24 Heures ou Plus)*

Social actors explore geographical setting of their past at instigation of filmmaker *(Burroughs, The Life and Times of Rosie the Riveter)*

Social actors present musical performances *(La Turlute Des Années Dures, Before Stonewall, Silent Pioneers, Bombay, Our City)*

Interviews: social actors analyzing present *(Not a Love Story, Dark Circle);* remembering past in archival/historical format *(Union Maids, The Times of Harvey Milk);* marathon autobiographical format *(Word Is Out, Portrait of Jason)*

Social actors present monologues *(The Life and Times of Rosie the Riveter, Rate It X)*

## II. Representational

Social actors role-play or dramatize improvisationally real-life situation *(A Bigger Splash, Michael a Gay Son)*

Social actors perform/improvise fictive or "mise-en-presence" situation created by filmmaker *(Waiting for Fidel)*

Social actors perform daily lives, representationally *(Seventeen, Streetwise, Quebéc-Haiti, Mother Tongue)*

Representational group discussions by social actors *(Rape, Pink Triangles)*

Indecipherable mixture of real and professional actors in scripted improvisational situation *(Prostitute)*

Professional actors in real life situation *(Dernier Glacier)*

Professional actors reconstruct event *(In the King of Prussia)* with help of social actors and transcript

Professional actors in scripted historical reconstruction employing simulated documentary codes *(Edvard Munch)*

Representational autobiographical personae in investigative documentary format *(Not a Love Story, Dark Lullabies, Rate It X)*

**III. Hybrids**

Social actors dramatize representationally their own social conditions, contextualized presentationally *(Quel Numéro, What Number?, Not Crazy Like You Think)*

Social actors dramatize representationally their collective history, contextualized presentationally *(Two Laws)*

Composite documentary characterizations performed presentationally by actors *(What You Take For Granted)*

Pseudo-vérité docudrama plus autobiographical voice of filmmaker *(Daughter Rite)*

Professional and nonprofessional performers construct intertextual essay on socio-political situation, including elements as diverse as transcript-based dramatization and semifictional autobiographical improvisation *(Far From Poland).*

---

A timely intervention by Bill Nichols has pointed out a central problem of authority and voice arising from the seventies current of interview films, namely those mostly historiographical projects reacting against vérité discourses, building on the de Antonio model, and addressing Feminist or New Left constituencies.[5] The model is very familiar: representative subjects offer interview performances of personal reminiscences or present experiences that figure large in a documentary investigation of a politically apt topic. Nichols' criticism is directed at those documentaries in which the authority of the filmmaker is diffused through, or uncritically hidden behind, the voices of the subjects. The best known example of this risk is New Day Films' *Union Maids,* in which the evasions and nostalgias of the subjects' oral histories become the liabilities of the film as a whole. "Interviews diffuse authority." Nichols argues,

> A gap remains between the voice of a social actor recruited to the film and the voice of the film .... The greatest problem has been to retain that sense of a gap between the voice of interviewees and the voice of the text as a whole ... [In *The Day After Trinity,*] the text not only appears to lack a voice or perspective of its own, the perspective of its character-witnesses is patently inadequate ... the voice of the text disappears behind characters who speak to us ... we no longer sense that a governing voice actively provides or withholds the imprimatur of veracity according to its own purposes and assumptions, its own canons of validation ... the film becomes a rubber stamp. ... The sense of hierarchy of voices becomes lost.

The problem of the disappearing voice, however, is not intrinsic to the interview performance mode—it may just as well be a condition of state funding for most of the films in question. In any case, it would be extremely foolish to disparage the tremendous advances in popular social history and the political enfranchisement enabled by the interview genre, nor to disallow filmmakers' choices to mute their individual voices in favor of providing a forum for voices that have been suppressed, forgotten, or denied media access. Nichols points to several films—such as *Rosie the Riveter* and de Antonio's works—in which the self-reflexive contextualization of interviews allows the filmmaker's analytic perspective to complement and coexist with, without drowning out, the voices of subjects. The disappearance of the voice derives less from the interview format than from a lack of focus in conceptualization, research, and goals, or from a self-censorship triggered by Public Broadcasting or NFB or NEH funding. It has also derived from a fuzzy and sentimental populism leading to what Jeffrey Youdelman has described as an abdication of political leadership on the part of media intellectuals, and to the absence of historical contextualization with which both

Youdelman and Chuck Kleinhans have taxed *The War at Home*.[6] Ethics also enters into the picture, whether it is a question of responsibility to the subject or to the spectator. The latter is certainly not served by the camouflage of the terms of the construction of the discourse: does the spectator not have the right to know who is speaking, what the author's political relationship to the speaker is, and how, to whom, and to what end the film is addressed?

Nichols diagnoses this latter problem by focusing on corrective self-reflexive tendencies in some of the best recent films. However, it is more pertinent to this article to focus on evolving performance styles in the same work, particularly on the very promising excursions into the presentational mode (which in any case have much in common with Nichols' prescription of self-reflexivity). For the most visible and innovative pattern in the current decade is in fact the expansion of performance input by social actors which goes beyond the oral history format of the seventies to experiment with dramatic performance modes, both presentational and representational. The new visibility of dramatized and semifictional performance components constitutes a reaction against the "string-of-interview" orthodoxy. Dramatization is clearly a useful means of fleshing out the gaps left by the interview format, gaps of a technical or ideological nature, or gaps due simply to uncontrollable factors (as in *Michael a Gay Son,* in which a very tense "coming out" encounter with the protagonist's hostile family is conveyed through fictionalized role-playing). It is not surprising that the new "dramatized" documentaries, (or "docudramas," as they are called in some quarters, misleadingly I think, since the term is used most commonly and aptly for fictionalized reconstructions like the United States television films *The Missiles of October* or *The Atlanta Child Murders*)[7] may be divided like all their forebears into: (a) those whose emphasis or context is presentational *(In the King of Prussia, Far from Poland, The Kid Who Couldn't Miss, Two Laws, Not Crazy Like You Think, Quel Numéro What Number*—in fact films Nichols would call self-reflexive) and (b) those whose primary address is representational *(Michael a Gay Son, What You Take for Granted, Journal Inachevé, Democracy on Trial,* the historical episodes of *When the Mountains Tremble, Le Dernier Glacier, Caffé Italia, The Masculine Mystique).* Needless to say, the new expansion of the repertory into the terrain of dramatization has greatly multiplied the importance of performance in documentary as a whole and greatly expanded the opportunities for social actors to "perform" their lives in every format from semifictional improvisation to didactic sketches.

The eclecticism of the expanded hybrid repertory sharpens our sense of our bearings in relation to our documentary past. One useful observation is that the more presentational of these new formats is most in keeping with the traditional documentary genius for incorporating the presence and performance of social actors into the cinematic text. The more representational films seem inclined more towards a long tradition of "docu-flavoured" fiction (de Sica/Rossellini, Cassavetes, McBride, Loach/Garnett). From another point of view, the new repertory removes us yet another step away from the sixties: the small amount of work still appearing in an unadulterated vérité style *(Middletown, The Store)* seems purist indeed, even classical, and reminds us that the sixties are no longer the definitive crucible for today's documentarists, but more and more just another period style available for postmodern recycling. On the other hand, the new work looks back in a very vivid way to the years of the Popular Front, in particular to the "wide variety of styles" that characterized such late-thirties hybrid films as *Spanish Earth* and *Native Land.*

It is not surprising that the thirties are evoked more than any other period by the present work. For Ivens and his contemporaries were no strangers to several contextual conditions that have influenced today's alignment of a hybrid performance-based documentary style with an atmosphere of increasing political polarization and crisis, and of cultural attrition:

(1) Economic factors may have been predominant: after the late seventies and the arts funding crisis of the Reagan-Thatcher-Mulroney era, very few independents other than Wiseman, the National Film Board, and a handful of TV-funded artists have been able to afford the high-ratio budget of representational vérité (except perhaps in video). Sustaining

representational illusion is too expensive for the austerity of the eighties, and presentational elements offer filmmakers and subjects alike more control over the pro-filmic event and the budget. In the pre-war period, for similar reasons, it was no accident that it was with the (relatively) luxurious state-supplied budget of *Power and the Land* that Ivens left behind the off-the-cuff hybridity of his earlier films for the graceful representational coherence of that film.

(2) The fact that the new presentational performance modes were pioneered by political filmmakers, whether feminists or other progressives, is highly pertinent. In this regard, we've arrived once more back at Ivens, the Old Left grandfather of New Left political documentarists and their contemporaries. For Ivens, the proto-vérité style that he called "easy naturalism" precluded the organized communication of "content value," that is, the psychological dynamic or atmospheric texturing obscured the social text. Social documentarists generations later came independently to the same conclusion: pure representational vérité was often a medium of aestheticist psychologism that by itself often precluded the political explorations that such filmmakers sought to produce.

(3) Other factors in the post-vérité configuration must not be discounted, though they are decidedly minor. First, the critical acceptance of the presentational performance style was encouraged by the currency of Brechtian theory in film culture persisting since 1968. There may also have occurred a certain cross-fertilization with a presentational counter-tradition outside of Anglo-Saxon culture that predates the current phenomenon by a whole generation. This tradition, originating in France (Rouch and Marker) and in Quebec (Pierre Perrault and a national documentary tradition known as "le direct"), has never had any commitment to representational illusion. Since the late fifties, this tradition has accumulated a rich repertory of presentational elements, elevating verbal and interactional performances to a degree of exceptional expressiveness. Although Rouch is a household word among documentarists (and Perrault would be were he from Paris rather than Montreal), this possible cross-fertilization remains a subject for future research since the cross-linguistic circulation of this

cinema has been greatly hampered by its privileging of speech and oral culture. Finally, the post-modernist absorption and recycling of the presentational television vernacular is surely as important as it is hard to quantify as an element of the new post-documentary performance style.

## PERFORMANCE AND COLLABORATION

"Collaboration in Documentary": Ivens' title is more than just a literal description of the relationship engendered by the *mise-en-scène* of subject performance by filmmaker. "Collaboration" also embodies a perennial ideal of the documentary tradition, the goal of a changed, democratized relationship between artist and subject. The subject's performance for the camera becomes a collaboration, a stake in and a contribution to the authorship of the work of art. Performance becomes a gauge of the ethical and political accountability of the filmmaker's relationship with subject.

Although Ivens' respect for the integrity of his cast is obvious, his distance from the democratic ideal of collaborative performance is problematical. He admits quite openly to manipulating and tricking his "performers" into performing, and of keeping them in the dark as to film techniques and as to the results of their own performance. These less-than-egalitarian terms of the collaboration were necessary, he claims (not unlike some Method director who has terrorized his leading lady) to preserve elements of freshness in the performance. Unwittingly, Ivens points to an ethical liability of the representational mode during its classical phase, a problem which surfaces perhaps even more acutely in the work of Ivens' contemporary, Flaherty.

I mentioned earlier the dichotomy in Flaherty's work between his two silent ethnographic features with their presentational elements and his later mytho-narrative features based exclusively on representational performances. The issue of collaboration seems to be the crux of this dichotomy. The absence of presentational elements in *Man of Aran* and *Louisiana Story* is surely an index of the films' minimization of the input of the subjects and of their virtual embargo on the cultural textures and social realities of the Aran (West Irish) and Cajun communities respectively. It is true that in both films rudimentary voice-tracks gently ruffle the surface of the seamless representational unity: in the former, the performers improvise semi-synchronized dialogue-commentary over the edited film, and in the latter, Flaherty's voice-over commentary is interpolated by a few awkward and static direct sound sequences of an expository nature. But the verbal performances of the actors in either case do not constitute a qualitative heightening of their collaborative input—especially in *Louisiana,* with the heavily scripted and heavily rehearsed feel of the dialogue. The representational web is ultimately as intact as the hegemony of authorial vision and control over ethnographic mission and subject input. The legendary contribution of "Nanook" to the film that bears his name is by now a distant memory and inoperative ideal.

A decade after *Louisiana,* the introduction of direct sound technology into the documentary arena transformed the potential for subject collaboration as surely as it transformed the nature of subject performance. Vérité, as I have stated, failed to push this potential as far as it would go by retaining the representational mode of documentary performance. By the time the vérité movement had consolidated direct sound as the everyday vocabulary of the documentary, grassroots political movements were beginning to arise to profit from the hitherto untapped political potential of the new apparatus. The New Left of the late sixties, and especially the women's movement a few years later, embraced speech and intercommunication as a political process, favored participatory and collaborative cultural forms, and privileged oral history as an essential means of political and cultural empowerment. It is not surprising then that their documentary cinema featured presentational performance elements ranging from the simple interview and group discussion formats[8] of the early years to the more complex formats I have listed. Incorporating vocal performances into a film was a crucial strategy for an artist who wished to share creative and political control with subjects/social actors. Whereas vérité had by and large retained the Flahertian mystique of authorial control, the presentational modes of the New Left and the women's movement dissipated that mystique and permitted varying degrees of subject input into the finished documentary, of subject responsibility for his or her image and speech. The ideal to which such filmmakers subscribed, to greater or lesser degree, was of the documentarist as resource person, technician or facilitator, and of the subject-performer as real steward of creative responsibility.

Such a prescriptive distinction between the political and ethical advantages of a specific formal strategy of course runs the risk of aesthetic idealism and political naivete, not to mention a technological fallacy: the power of the filmmaker is such that ultimately no strategy is the automatic guarantee of collaborative process. Even the most presentational, collaborative performance is subject to ethical abuse in the editing room or exhibition context. Ultimately, the creative and political accountability of the artist is clearly the final guarantor against political and ethical abuses. However, this caveat having been registered, a concluding glimpse at two recent Canadian documentaries that focus on a similar subject clarifies the political dimension of the distinction between presentational and representational modes that I would like to insist on as a general guideline to the artist's accountability to subject performance and collaboration.

Bonnie Klein's National Film Board of Canada feature, *Not a Love Story, A Film about Pornography,* and Kay Armatage's independent short, *Striptease,* consider aspects of the sex industry through predominantly representational and presentational approaches respectively. With *Not a Love Story,* the relationship between the on-screen filmmaker persona, embarked on her voyage of discovery of the pornographic night, and her guide, ex-stripper Linda Lee Tracy, is conveyed representationally through traditional vérité. Much of the criticism of the film centered on the manipulative appearance of this relationship between artist and collaborator. The narrative thread of the relationship includes two sex performance interludes set in representational frames (Tracy as stripper on location in a Montreal club, Tracy as centerfold model in the studio of a *Hustler* photographer) and an ultimate conversion denouement, in which filmmaker and stripper discuss the latter's re(-)formed vision of her past and future. This thread is intercut with interviews with feminist authorities on the subject. Caught up in the emotional charge of the subject, the audience may not notice that the distribution of representational and presentational roles in the film follows a certain hierarchy. The sex worker, Tracy, is caught in a representational role, performing her ongoing life in the service of the film, while the recruited intellectuals perform their role of analysis and polemics within the presentational interview formats. It is not difficult to conclude that the democratic ideals of feminism are being sacrificed in the process—are sex workers themselves less entitled than intellectuals to verbalize directly about the sex industry? Furthermore, the specter of voyeurism and visual pleasure is unavoidably raised by the strong construction of observational discourse in Tracy's two principal scenes of sexual performance, with their assault on conventional notions of tact and their inescapable flirtation with the "pornographic" discourse that is the target of the film. To compare the *Hustler* posing session, for example, with its scandalous aura of brutality and complicity (the female photographer applies "pussy juice" before the take), with, say, the similar scenes from the improvised but fictional *Prostitute,* where the sexual performance scenes are lucid, controlled, and self-reflexive, demonstrates the clear shortcomings of representational vérité in the domain of sexual politics.

Armatage's *Striptease* has surprisingly more clarity and complexity than *Not a Love Story* despite its infinitely more modest means: strippers and other sex industry workers present themselves in interviews and monologues, and present their work in erotic dance-performances constructed solely for the camera (in *Prostitute,* at the other end of the scale, they perform semifictional dramatizations within a self-reflexive narrative, collaboratively scripted, to a similar effect). In *Striptease,* the sex industry is not validated, but its workers are: subject-generated performance, sharpened by its presentational mode, ensures that the dignity and subjectivity of the subjects are respected along with their right to present themselves, to define their images and their lives. As for the problem of voyeurism, I suspect that the visual pleasure of the spectator is compromised by the explicit aura of control that characterizes the sexual performance. It is no coincidence that Armatage enables glimpses of a collective political solution (unionization) that makes Klein's ambiguous individual moral solution all the more superficial.

## VOICE AND FIRST-PERSON PERFORMANCE

*Not a Love Story* has been criticized also for the autobiographical presence within the diegesis of author Bonnie Klein. The first-person performance seemed ineffectual in terms of cinematic charisma presumably, but more importantly in terms also of the issue of authorial voice. As Nichols puts it, such authorial presence lacks both the "self-validating, authoritative tone of a previous [voice-of-god] tradition" and "seem[s] to refuse a privileged position in relation to other characters."[9] Submitting both to the authoritative testimony of the stellar lineup of expert witnesses and to the grandstanding of her representational protagonist Tracy, the diegetic Klein serves rather as a timid, inconclusive, perhaps *faux-naif* guide throughout the pornographic nightmare. Similar problems are arguably posed by the whole tradition of autobiographical performance, from the first-person narrations of Flaherty *(The Land)* and John Huston *(The Battle of San Pietro)* in the forties to the Me-Decade's self-presentations of everyone from Werner Herzog *(La Soufrière)* to Michael Rubbo *(Waiting for Fidel, etc.).* It seems to me that the first-person format too often limits social-issue documentary to the exploratory phase, pegs it at the level of political evasion, bewildering empiricism, and individual moral or metaphysical floundering. Even where it is rigorously self-reflexive, as with Jill Godmilow, the personal is perhaps shown to be political, but the political often fails to rise above the personal level. While the first-person performance does undeniably provide a manageable dramatic entry to the enormously complex subjects of pornography, Solidarity *(Far from Poland),* and the Holocaust *(Dark Lullabies, Shoah),* it does not necessarily serve the political dissection of these subjects. It may be argued that the strategy seems best suited for properly individual, autobiographical subjects such as intrafamily relationships *(Best Boy, Coming Home),* or for the feminist genre that connects individual socialization to broader political forces *(Daughter Rite, Joyce at 34, Home Movie).*

Ultimately, while the problems of authorial voice can be addressed in part by the strategy of first-person performance, and while authorial presence can signal a refreshingly self-reflexive honesty, more often than not the authorial performance—whether representational in such films as *Not a Love Story,* or presentational and self-reflexive in such films as *Far from Poland*—raises as many issues as it solves. In any case, a whole range of other questions are raised by autobiographical performance in documentary—from ethics to narcissism to the demographic representativity of the media worker—but these are beyond the scope of this paper and are receiving due critical attention.[10]

## CONCLUSION: THE RIGHT TO PLAY ONESELF

I have offered a historical overview of the presence of performance in documentary. I have discerned alternating and simultaneous impulses toward presentational and representational performance throughout the documentary tradition, then briefly engaged the current debate about voice in political documentary, and finally only touched on the distinct subcategory of autobiographical performance. All of this has led to a global assertion of the special aptness of the presentational mode in the present context, alongside both an insistence on the continuing relevance of the interview format of oral history popularized in the seventies and an enthusiastic welcoming of the current experimentation with hybrid performance modes, including dramatization. Subject performance, affirmed and enriched as a presentational element of documentary film, remains a means by which the most committed of documentary filmmakers can aspire to the realization of their democratic ideals. Collaboration between artist and subject, as elaborated by Joris Ivens at the end of the thirties, remains a meaningful political ideal as well as an artistic strategy, but the terms he set out have been somewhat transformed. "Acting to play oneself" is still the key, but, "Don't look at the camera" is replaced by, "Look at the camera" as a "basic necessity" of documentary collaboration. In the same decade, Walter Benjamin spoke of "modern man's legitimate claim to be reproduced";[11] might we not add that the individual has now established the claim also to construct that reproduction, the right to play oneself?

## NOTES

1. This text excerpted from the periodical *Films,* vol. 1, no. 2 (Spring 1940), pp. 30–42, appears in a later modified form in Ivens' autobiographical *The Camera and I* (New York and Berlin: International Publishers, 1968), pp. 187–206.
2. The term "social actors" designating real-life characters playing their own social roles in nonfiction film and presumably having an extratextual autonomy has been standard usage in documentary studies since Bill Nichols' influential *Ideology and the Image: Social Representation in the Cinema and other Media* (Bloomington, IN., 1981) cf., pp. 181–85.
3. Helen van Dongen, "Robert J. Flaherty, 1884–1951," *Film Quarterly,* vol. XVIII, no. 4 (Summer 1965), p. 4.
4. See for example Geoff Pevere, "Projections: Assessing Canada's Films of '85," *The Canadian Forum,* vol. LXV, no. 755 (March 1986), p. 39.
5. Bill Nichols, "The Voice of Documentary," *Film Quarterly,* vol. 36, no. 3 (Spring 1983); rpt. in Nichols, ed., *Movies and Methods, Volume 11* (Berkeley, 1985), pp. 265–6.
6. Jeffrey Youdelman, "Narration, Invention, and History: a Documentary Dilemma," *Cineaste,* vol. XII, no. 2, 1982, pp. 8–15; Chuck Kleinhans, "Forms, Politics, Makers, and Contexts: Basic Issues for a Theory of Radical Political Documentary," in Thomas Waugh, ed., *Show Us Life: Toward a History and Aesthetics of the Committed Documentary* (Metuchen, N.J.: Scarecrow Press, 1984), pp. 318–42.
7. For example, the scope of a 1986 McGill University symposium on docudrama included a range of NFB productions: a TV-movie style fictionalized reconstruction *(Canada's Sweetheart: The Saga of Hal C. Banks)* an archival compilation interpolated with cabaret-style theatrical sketches *(The Kid Who Couldn't Miss),* several documentaries incorporating fictional episodes *(Mourir A Tue-Tete, Le Dernier Glacier, Passiflora),* and a scripted fiction feature constructed on improvisational performances by nonprofessional actors *(Ninety Days).* Cf., the author's "Thunder over the Docudrama:

Symposium Highlights NFB's World-Class Role," *Cinema Canada*, no. 128 (March 1986), p. 26.

8. Julia Lesage has often discussed the importance of consciousness raising as a deep structure of feminist discourse in documentary, most recently in "*Feminist Documentary: Aesthetics and Politics*," in Waugh, op. cit., pp. 223–51.
9. Nichols, op. cit., p. 265.
10. See for example a recent installment of the ongoing discussion of autobiographical documentary: David Schwartz, "First Person Singular: Autobiography in Film," *The Independent*, vol. 9, no. 4, pp. 12–15. The author of one of the most elaborate studies of documentary autobiography is John Stuart Katz, e.g., Katz, ed., *Autobiography: Film/Video/Photography* (Toronto: Art Gallery of Ontario, 1978). Katz's more recent work and much other material relevant to this article appears in Larry Gross and Jay Ruby, eds., *Image Ethics: The Moral and Legal Rights of Subjects in Documentary Film and Television* (Philadelphia, 1988).
11. Walter Benjamin, "The Work of Art in the Age of Mechanical Reproduction," in Hannah Arendt, ed., *Illuminations* (New York: 1969), p. 232.

## List of Films Mentioned

*A Bigger Splash*, Jack Hazan, U.K., 1974

*All My Babies*, George Stoney, U.S.A., 1953

*Best Boy*, Ira Wohl, U.S.A., 1980

*Before Stonewall: The Making of a Gay and Lesbian Community*, Greta Schiller, U.S.A., 1985

*Bombay, Our City*, Anand Patwardhan, India, 1985

*Burroughs*, Howard Brookner, U.S.A. 1983

*Canada's Sweetheart: The Saga of Hal C. Banks*, Donald Brittain (NFB/CBC), Canada, 1985

*Caffe Italia*, Paul Tana, Quebec, 1986

*Chicken Ranch*, Nick Broomfield, U.S.A., 1982

*Comedienne*, Katherine Matheson, U.S.A., 1983

*Coming Home*, Bill Reid (NFB), Canada, 1973

*Dark Circle*, Judy Irving, Chris Beaver, Ruth Landy, U.S.A., 1972

*Dark Lullabies*, Irene Angelico and Abbey Neidik (NFB), Canada, 1985

*Daughter Rite*, Michelle Citron, U.S.A., 1978

*Day After Trinity, The*, John Else, U.S.A., 1980

*Democracy on Trial: The Morgentaler Affair*, Paul Cowan (NFB), Canada, 1984

*Dernier Glacier, Le*, Roger Frappier and Jacques Leduc (NFB), Quebec, 1984

*Edvard Munch,* Peter Watkins, Norway, 1974
*Enthusiasm,* Dziga Vertov, U.S.S.R., 1931
*Eye of the Mask,* Judith Doyle, Canada, 1985
*Far from Poland,* Jill Godmilow, U.S.A., 1984
*Fires Were Started,* Humphrey Jennings, U.K., 1943
*Four Hundred Million, The,* Joris Ivens, U.S.A., 1938
*Grey Gardens,* David and Albert Maysles and Ellen Hovde, U.S.A., 1976
*Harlan County, U.S.A.,* Barbara Kopple, U.S.A., 1976
*High School,* Frederick Wiseman, U.S.A., 1969
*Hookers on Davie,* Holly Dale and Janis Cole, Canada, 1984
*Home Movie,* Jan Oxenberg, U.S.A., 1972
*Housing Problems,* Edgar Anstey and Arthur Elton, (John Grierson, producer), U.K., 1935
*If You Love This Planet,* Terri Nash (NFB), Canada, 1982
*In the King of Prussia,* Emile de Antonio, U.S.A., 1982
*Jane,* Richard Leacock, U.S.A., 1962
*Journal Inachevé, Un,* Marilu Mallet, U.S.A., 1982
*Joyce at 34,* Joyce Chopra, U.S.A., 1972
*Kid Who Couldn't Miss, The,* Paul Cowan (NFB), Canada, 1982
*Land, The,* Robert Flaherty, U.S.A., 1942
*Life and Times of Rosie the Riveter, The,* Connie Field, 1980
*Lonely Boy,* Wolf Koenig and Roman Kroitor (NFB), Canada, 1961
*Louisiana Story,* Robert Flaherty, U.S.A., 1948
*Man of Aran,* Robert Flaherty, U.K., 1934
*Marjoe,* Howard Smith and Sarah Kernochan, U.S.A., 1972
*Masculine Mystique, The,* Giles Walker and John Smith (NFB), Canada, 1984
*Mental Mechanisms* (series), National Film Board of Canada, 1947–50
*Michael, A Gay Son,* Bruce Glawson, Canada, 1980
*Milhouse, A White Comedy,* Emile de Antonio, U.S.A., 1971
*Middletown* (series), collective, U.S.A., 1982
*Moana,* Robert Flaherty, U.S.A., 1926
*Mourir A Tue-Tête (A Scream From Silence),* Anne-Claire Poirier (NFB), Quebec, 1979
*Nanook of the North,* Robert Flaherty, Canada/U.S.A., 1922
*Native Land,* Leo Hurwitz and Paul Strand (Frontier Films), 1942
*Night Mail,* Basil Wright and Harry Watt (G.P.O. Film Unit, Grierson, producer), 1936

*Ninety Days,* Giles Walker (NFB), Canada, 1985

*Not A Love Story: A Film About Pornography,* Bonnie Sherr Klein (NFB), Canada, 1981

*Not Crazy Like You Think,* Jacqueline Levitin, Quebec, 1984

*Painters Painting,* Emile de Antonio, U.S.A., 1973

*Passiflora,* Fernand Belanger and Dagmar Gueissaz (NFB), Quebec, 1985

*Paul Tomkowicz Street-Railway Switchman,* Roman Kroitor (NFB), Canada, 1954

*Pink Triangles,* Cambridge Documentary Films, U.S.A., 1982

*Portrait of Jason,* Shirley Clarke, U.S.A., 1967

*Portrait of the Artist—As an Old Lady,* Gail Singer (NFB), Canada, 1982

*Power and the Land,* Joris Ivens, U.S.A., 1940

*Primary,* Richard Leacock, U.S.A., 1960

*Prostitute,* Tony Garnett, U.K., 1979

*Pumping Iron,* Robert Fiore and George Butler, U.S.A., 1976

*Pumping Iron II: The Women,* George Butler, U.S.A., 1985

*Quebec-Haiti,* Tahani Rached (NFB), Quebec, 1985

*Queen, The,* Frank Simon, U.S.A., 1968

*Quel Numéro What Number?,* Sophie Bissonnette, Quebec, 1985

*Quiet One, The,* Sidney Meyers, U.S.A., 1949

*Rape,* Jo-Ann Elam, U.S.A., 1977

*Rate It X,* Lucy Winer and Paula de Koenigsberg, U.S.A., 1985

*Right Candidate for Rosedale, The,* Bonnie Sherr Klein (NFB), Canada, 1979

*Salesman,* Albert and David Maysles, U.S.A., 1969

*Seventeen,* J. De Mott and J. Kreines, U.S.A., 1982

*Shoah,* Claude Lanzmann, France, 1985

*Silent Pioneers,* Lucy Winer, U.S.A., 1984

*Soldier Girls,* Nick Broomfield, Joan Churchill, U.S.A., 1981

*Spanish Earth, The,* Joris Ivens, U.S.A., 1937

*Stop Making Sense,* Jonathan Demme, U.S.A., 1985

*Store, The,* Frederick Wiseman, U.S.A., 1983

*Storytelling,* Kay Armatage, Canada, 1984

*Strange Victory,* Leo Hurwitz, U.S.A., 1948

*Streetwise,* Martin Bell, Mary Ellen Mark, and Cheryl McCall, U.S.A., 1984

*Striptease,* Kay Armatage, Canada, 1980

*Three Songs of Lenin,* Dziga Vertov, U.S.S.R., 1934

*Times of Harvey Milk, The,* Richard Schmiechen and Rob Epstein, U.S.A., 1984

*Turlute Des Années Dures, La (The Ballad of Hard Times),* Richard Boutet and Pascal Gélinas, Quebec, 1983

*Two Laws,* Carolyn Strachan, Australia, 1980

*Underground,* Emile de Antonio, U.S.A., 1976

*Union Maids,* Julia Reichert and James Klein, U.S.A., 1976

*Vie Est à Nous, La,* Jean Renoir and collective, France, 1936

*24 (Vingt-Quatre) Heures Ou Plus,* Gilles Groulx (NFB), Quebec, 1972

*Waiting For Fidel,* Michael Rubbo, Canada (NFB), 1974

*War At Home, The,* Barry Brown and Glenn Silber, U.S.A., 1980

*Warrendale,* Allan King, Canada, 1967

*What Sex Am I?,* Lee Grant, U.S.A., 1984

*What You Take For Granted,* Michelle Citron, U.S.A., 1983

*When the Mountains Tremble,* Pamela Yates, Thomas Sigel, U.S.A., 1983

*Woodstock,* Michael Wadleigh, U.S.A, 1970

*Word Is Out,* Mariposa Film Collective, U.S.A., 1978

# 5. *UN CERTAIN REGARD:* Characterization in the First Years of the French New Wave

**Bart Testa**

## I. ANTOINE

IN HIS CAREER PROFILE ON Jean Pierre Léaud, James Monaco would like to argue a difference between the Hollywood star systems and the position of actors within the French *nouvelle vague*. The latter he sees as collaborators in a *cinéma des auteurs* rather than as merely performers in the movies. But once Monaco begins to discuss Léaud's critical importance, he collapses any difference between the actor and a conventional movie star.[1]

Léaud is very closely identified with a single character, Antoine Doinel. François Truffaut introduced Antoine as the protagonist of his debut feature film, *The 400 Blows* (1959), when Léaud was just 14, and reprised his hero three years later, in *Antoine et Colette* (1962), a short in the omnibus film, *Love at Twenty*. After six years, Antoine returned to *Stolen Kisses* (1968), *Bed and Board* (1970), and *Love on the Run* (1978) to complete a nearly twenty-year career on the screen. A few years after his first two Antoine roles—Monaco points out that Léaud was between 15 and 19—the actor played roles in Jerzy Skolimowski's *Le Départ* (1967) and for Jean-Luc Godard's *Masculine-Feminine* (1966), *La Chinoise* (1967), *Week-End* (1967), and *Le Gai Savoir* (1968). Truffaut also featured him in *Two English Girls* (1971) and *Day for Night* (1973). At about the same time, Bernardo Bertolucci cast him as the hapless rival of Marlon Brando in *Last Tango in Paris* (1972), and Jean Eustache made him the center of a stormy love triangle in *The Mother and the Whore* (1973).

Monaco believes these later films somewhat freed Léaud from

Antoine Doinel. In retrospect, however, it seems more likely that Godard, Skolimowski, Eustache, and Bertolucci deployed the actor as an already well-established type, the young French Everyman Léaud had developed in *Antoine et Colette* and who had come of age in *Masculine-Feminine* and *Stolen Kisses*. Monaco goes on to make precisely this point when he praises Léaud in this summary of his career:

> As Antoine, Paul, Guillaume, Emile, Claude, Alphonse, Tom and Alexandre, he has created a subtle and various persona that explains much about his generation.... He represents for many of us the actor surrogate, not portraying a whole gallery of strange, distant and objective characters ... but rather illustrating our own deeper selves, subjectively holding the analytical mirror up to our natures.[2]

This encomium draws on one of the ways in which a movie star can be understood as a repeatable yet variable character who provides a body of films with a revealing and attractive type representative of a moment, class, or generation in the form of an individuality.[3] Indeed, Monaco only draws out such an understanding with his further praise: "Like Bogart, he (Léaud) has provided an ironic model which viewers of his films can use therapeutically within their own lives."[4]

While one might concede that Léaud has not succeeded as a star in some respects—he does not seem to have crossed genres or national boundaries effectively—and that he has distinguished himself from many movie actors in being a *cinéaste* (he worked as Godard's production assistant for a few years in the mid-sixties), it is hard to see how Monaco might maintain a fundamental distinction between this *nouvelle vague* actor and a conventional movie star. Yet, such a distinction can be drawn and maintained. However, to do so, we must shift our focus away from impressions of audience reception—and talk about Léaud as "analytical mirror"—and over to ways that actors are constituted as characters in a *cinéma des auteurs* such as that of the French New Wave. Throughout this essay the often repeated critical generalization that the French cinema of the sixties uses actors mainly as characters developed by directors in single films or across groups of films will be taken to be true. While the French New Wave did produce stars like Jeanne Moreau and Jean-Paul Belmondo, their stardom was conferred on them, as it were, in the aftermath and as a residual benefit of the *nouvelle vague*. The principal film-culture effect of the New Wave was the realization of the *cinéma des auteurs* so insistently trumpeted in *Cahiers du Cinéma* in the years before the debuts of Godard, Truffaut, and Resnais. This realization of film practice of *la politique des auteurs* saw the installation of the film director as the crucial determinant of meaning and style in the New Wave. More specifically, screen acting lost the privileged place it had enjoyed in the two prevailing styles of filmmaking that preceded: the classical style of the Hollywood cinema and the "realist" articulation of "human presence" associated with the work of Rossellini and De Sica.

In one of the paradoxes of the *nouvelle vague*, both these styles of film performance were admired in the criticism that preceded the films of Resnais, Truffaut, and Godard and both were dissolved by their films. The New Wave directors selected and combined, revised and recast the elements of those acting styles they admired in accord with their overall approach to cinematic technique, and little of the "classical" or "realist" emerged from the films of these directors with much of the former significance left intact.

The classical style privileges "star presence" by bending the cinema to support the authority of the actor. A variety of lighting codes, framing, design, and editing position the star in relief against the *mise-en-scène*, and the actors' sight-lines direct the gaze of the viewers through the space and across shots so that the actors effectually organize cinematic space and temporal order around performance. In Neorealist cinema, this system is modified. Here, the actors do not appear in sharp relief against the field of view, though they do remain centered, inside this space. The actor's gaze is only weakly accented, promoting only "objective" identification, and his or her performance seldom mediates cuts. The editing does, however, characterize by organizing the narrative around the actor's presence and by using the durative characteristics of longer takes and reframing camera movements. As a consequence, the actor does not seem to control, and instead screen space assumes a role of its own, that of place. Especially in De Sica's films, the actor is enfolded and often isolated by a *mise-en-scène* no longer responsive to his controlling authority, precisely the control enjoyed by the classically constituted star presence.

The relationship between actor and film style in both the classical style and the Neorealist style can be considered integrated. The early period of the New Wave cinema breaks that unity through a variety of means, four of which will be discussed here. First, the actor behaves as if he were a star in a classically constructed film, but the screen space is not constituted to respond to him, as exemplified by the later Doinel films. The largely comic effect is accomplished by Truffaut through the disjuncture of Antoine fully armed with the elaborate gestures of an actor in charge of the cinematic world around him, while the film he is in persists in behaving rather like a quirky Neorealist movie. Second, the director returns to a style of cinematic construction antedating the classical style or eccentric to it in ways that call attention to film technique, as in Truffaut's *Shoot the Piano Player (Tirez sur le Pianiste),* (1960). Third, the actor persistently quotes a star, or famous classic performance, in order to behave like a star and thus, foregrounds the fact of playacting. The films of Godard, notably *Breathless (A Bout de Souffle)* (1959), deploy acting composed of quotations. Fourth, New Wave films often tend more radically to disrupt the way "human presence" is conventionally constituted in films. Perhaps the most successful and successfully innovative of these disruptions is the breaking of the unity of image and sound, of body and voice, in the films of Godard and Resnais, instanced in this essay by *Hiroshima, Mon Amour* (1959).

The filmmakers of the *nouvelle vague* did not change the codes of cinema that are so important to screen performance because they were mainly interested in film acting *per se*. However, interpretation of acting in the New Wave has lent itself to the critical generalization about the change from star-acting to character articulation. We would question critics who argue that this change manifests the film-historical destiny of the New Wave to take the narrative film further along the path of the novel toward richer characterizations. However, this inquiry does seek to make more specific the general assertion that actors do not function as stars in this cinema but largely as characters.

Antoine Doinel is an interesting place to begin, partly because the cycle of films that reprise him, particularly *Stolen Kisses* and *Bed and Board*, are rather conservative works. Monaco is certainly correct when he claims that Antoine's character recurs as a character-type in a number of movies. We should, then, at least sketch out Antoine but refrain from making Monaco's leap into talk of Léaud being a generational surrogate or mirror. Our preliminary sketch deals with the grown Antoine of the later films in the cycle. Then we turn back to his genesis in *The 400 Blows* for a somewhat closer look.

Antoine is narrowly characterized; he serves specific narrative functions that can be condensed to two elements. He is a gazer, often toward the reverse angles that hold Colette, Christine, and the other women who figure so largely in his romantic life. A good example is the sequence in which Madame Tabard appears before the hero of *Stolen Kisses* as an apotheosis of the feminine. The dreamy tracking shot in which she appears combined with the presence of Delphine Seyrig in the role and the fact that she is worrying her broken shoe constitute a deft homage to Seyrig in *Last Year at Marienbad* (1961), but the immediate effect is to articulate Antoine's gaze as a vision. The moment typifies the exaggerations Truffaut brings to Antoine's look: it is comically heroized, for it has only one goal, the idealized woman, and in her presence Antoine's gaze leaves him speechless, transfixed. Antoine is also a solitary declaimer, the giver of speeches, of declarations of love, the writer of letters and, later, of novels. His declaiming is without narrative consequence for, like the charming awkwardness that accompanies his speech—the rapid hand gestures, shrugs, spins, and strides of his nervous body language—his declaiming is essentially a theatricalization of himself. Truffaut relishes it primarily to set up Antoine to be alternately frozen by his own gaze or silenced, as when Madame Tabard comes to his room and addresses him during their tender morning love scene, or when Christine lectures him in *Bed and Board*. In the interim, whenever

Antoine does perform some bit of narrative business—visiting a brothel in *Stolen Kisses* or dyeing roses in *Bed and Board*—Truffaut handles it elliptically. Principally interested in repetition as the chief means of characterizing Antoine, the Doinel films progress from comically ineffectual episodes of energized self-dramatization (Monaco rightly observes that these underline the character's solitude)[5] to static "privileged moments" (the phrase is Truffaut's) of female authority. Antoine's energies effect nothing. A character of great agitation, he actually performs few actions. Sweetly solipsistic, he certainly is the surrogate of the viewer in the sense of devouring almost all of the screen time. As both gazer and declaimer, he provides access to the world of films. Equipped with an elaborate set of reactions—glances, double takes, sputtering enchantments—Antoine controls point-of-view in an exaggerated fashion. As a declaimer, he seems likewise to be the speaker of the inner voice of the drama. But neither Antoine's look nor his talk possess authority or hold the center of the film. Antoine is a comic voyeur and speaker who mistakes the films for romances and, concomitantly, himself as a romantic lead. Utterly without a clue about the structure of the drama, he is tellingly off in a corner (the bathroom in *Bed and Board*, for example) declaring another manifesto for the theater of his life. In the end, Antoine always proves to be an inept dramaturge. The Doinel films are indeed romances, but not in the way their hero conceives them. The climactic speeches are made by Madame Tabard and Christine, who intervene seldom and authoritatively, silencing Antoine to instruct him about the story he has actually missed, which has gone on around him and prepared a solution for him.

Léaud's mannered acting is well suited for his character. Slight in build, full of nervous energy, and equipped with flailing gestures, he dramatizes Antoine with a paradoxical swiftness and stiffness. The way he smokes a cigarette, clutches his hands behind his back, and strides around bent forward all telegraph caricatures of deep, intense thought. The way he piles books and papers and a flashlight in his arms and the way he fools with his hair show Antoine's self-involvement and express a constant eagerness that lacks a sense of direction. And, just as Léaud's size and mildly frantic semaphores convey unselfconscious solipsism, contributing enormously to the mechanics of Antoine's comic displacement, so do his anxious, intense eyes. Truffaut constantly plays with Léaud's glances, directing him to exaggerate his sidelong looks and frequent double takes, having him swivel his head around to follow his eyes and clumsily stop short in response to what he sees.

These glances should make Antoine the surrogate of the viewer, giving a point of entry into the *découpage*, but their exaggerations really unmask Antoine as a solipsist and as the false center or mediator. The world of the films goes on all around him, rarely through his eye-line cues. Rather, combined with his elaborate interpretations of his situation, his gaze continually returns back to him ironized, back to the solitude that Truffaut delicately builds up around him. Léaud executes his solipsistic displacement with boundless enthusiasm and sincerity, missing everything he should see in flourishes of false discovery. He is a mirror for the viewer, but doubled, because the viewer constantly sees past him; Truffaut's long takes and depth-of-field composition, derived largely from Renoir, allow the viewer to place Antoine in a rich diegesis while Antoine himself acts as if he were the absolute center of his world. The effect is comical throughout.

In contrast, the privileged moments find Antoine speechless and motionless, often off-screen, as in the climactic love scene in *Stolen Kisses* where the camera finds him and Christine in bed.

By the end of *Bed and Board*, Léaud's Antoine was probably developed about as far as he could be. Truffaut parodies him with Léaud's Alphonse in *Day for Night*; Godard uses only parts of the character in various films, especially the declaimer in *Le Gai Savoir* and *Weekend.* It was left for Eustache to draw out Antoine's deeper possibilities in *The Mother and the Whore*, though he accomplishes this mainly through the actresses in that film. Bertolucci simply inserts Léaud, in full frenzied flight, for his brief moments in *Last Tango in Paris*.

The first incarnation of Antoine Doinel, in *The 400 Blows*, long before he became Truffaut's Parisian Everyman, is a character differently drawn and performed. Truffaut suggests his first feature is Hitchcockian. Although the later films in the cycle openly parody some of Hitchcock's devices (particularly the voyeuristic ones), this seems at first to be a rather perverse suggestion to make about *The 400 Blows*, a movie taken to heart by so many as the most humane of the early *nouvelle vague* and given film-historical coordinates along an axis running up from Vigo through Renoir and De Sica. The customary categorization of Truffaut's work provides two main sectors: the "Renoirian" Doinel cycle and literary adaptations (e.g., *Jules and Jim*) and the Hitchcockian "genre cycle" initiated with *Shoot the Piano Player*.[6] These categories depend on critical consideration of narrative material and dramatic design. Truffaut's countering suggestion points to questions of point-of-view construction and the play between Léaud's characterization of the young Antoine and Truffaut's *découpage* of the film.

Recalling the critical generalization mentioned above, that the *nouvelle vague* foregrounds the authorial presence of the director at the expense of certain types of acting, sometimes on behalf of a deepening of cinematic characterization, *The 400 Blows* can be taken as an ideal example of the interplay of screen performance and cinematic style. The film is carefully structured so that the viewer remains with Antoine and both sees him and sees with him. This is not to say that Truffaut's camera is entirely controlled by his central character, as is sometimes said of Hollywood point-of-view structures, but rather that *The 400 Blows* centers its point of view on Antoine and the camera always returns to him and takes up his feelings and perceptions. Dramatically, no one listens to Antoine, no one pays attention to him, except to reprimand, bully, and punish him. His mother's indifference, instanced in the early scene where she removes her stockings in his presence while ordering him about, is typical. For much of the film, Antoine is simply alone—his first night as a runaway with its lyrical evocations of Paris; his private letter writing and devotions to Balzac; his night in jail; his run to the sea that concludes the film. These episodes form the narrative of *The 400 Blows* as a drama of a solitude.

*The 400 Blows* has been seen to continue some cinematic usages of Renoir, De Sica, and Rossellini, such as long takes, free camera movement, location shooting, de-dramatizing mixed tone, and, our main interest here, the moral privileging of the child's point of view that can be specifically traced to Rossellini's *Paisan* (1947) and De Sica's *The Bicycle Thief* (1948). On closer examination, however, *The 400 Blows* reveals that it uses Antoine's gaze not primarily as the moral witness of the child who, through its presence, criticizes the compromised world of adults in which the child figures as a character. Rather, Truffaut creates with Antoine a character whose world is constituted as solitude; the character is its center, not its critic. Antoine's rather limited virtues, already expressed through Léaud's self-dramatization, are crucial: indeed, the film folds back onto Antoine as a whole. With its *mise-en-scène* of mild squalor and drama of loneliness, *The 400 Blows* articulates a will and freedom that lend authority to the pathetic tale quite different from the comic displacements of Antoine later in the Doinel cycle. The hero's being-at-odds is key to the dramatic structure of the story; Truffaut's handling of that drama makes the character's reactions the visual center of the film, so that we neither gain distance from Antoine, nor does he from his world. It follows that the fulcrum of the film is Léaud's performance. And, though his gestures and the use of his eyes are quite consistent through the whole cycle of Doinel films, Léaud's performance has a different effect in *The 400 Blows*. Whereas Antoine grows up to be slight, nervous, and awkward, the young Antoine is sturdy, self-contained, and deliberate. Antoine/Léaud is a "little man" who grew up into an adult little boy.

To take two examples, one brief and the other involving a whole sequence, we turn first to Antoine's discovery of his mother and her lover on the street and then to Antoine's night in jail.

Antoine discovers his mother embracing her lover during a day when he and his friend René have been playing hookey, immediately after his ride on "The Rotor," a sequence that encapsulates Antoine's solitude (he rides alone) and his role as mediator (the viewer sees him, then what he sees—dizzily); it also serves as a sort of metaphor for his life—he is thrown to the wall of the cylinder and pinned there by forces he cannot control. The embrace sequence opens with two long shots that carry Antoine and

René from the amusement arcade to the Place Saint-Augustin, where the boys pass an embracing couple in front of the Metro entrance. A medium close-up and close-up of Madame Doinel and her lover are followed by a close-up of Antoine and René, followed by a close-up of Antoine alone, who looks out of frame. His point-of-view shot is a close-up of the couple, and Madame Doinel glances out of frame. However, the next shot is not Antoine's reaction to his mother's discovery but a medium close-up of the boy's response to the spectacle. The shot does not exclude René; on the contrary, his presence in the shot underlines the privacy of what Antoine sees but René does not. Léaud slightly exaggerates his reaction, as he always does in such dramatic moments. Truffaut holds this shot for a few beats longer than the others, impeding the narrative flow and extending the look beyond what is merely functional for the sequence. It is followed by a close-up of Madame Doinel as she pushes her lover away and then quickly by a medium close-up of Antoine, still staring for a moment before he ducks his head and tugs at René to get going. The sequence then breaks off into two subsequences: three medium close-ups of Madame Doinel and her lover discussing what has just happened, and two medium shots of Antoine and René rushing off. The abruptness of Antoine's walk and his bitter delivery of lines typify a difference between Truffaut's original conception of Antoine as "more delicate and more timid" and Léaud's quickness and aggression. Léaud's handling of the moment, which could have carried a sense of betrayal on the boy's part, is a bit gruff.

The actor's self-containment suggests that he has absorbed a truth of the adult world (his mother has a lover) that he will use (she won't tell his father he was not at school) though the scene also advances Antoine's isolation. The sequence is Hitchcockian precisely in the way Truffaut carves out a dilated moment so that the narrative information settles on a character, Antoine, and on the viewer but is not available to anyone else in the diegesis. The secret, as often in Hitchcock, is thereby shared by the protagonist and viewer; and, just as often, the secret carries a sexual charge and guilt. The secret Madame Doinel and her son share after this sequence comes out when she visits him at the Observation Center and taunts him with her control over her husband and Antoine's imprisonment as a sort of revenge. That much more painful sequence, which follows René's attempt to visit Antoine, occurs after Truffaut has carefully isolated his protagonist dramatically. The earlier sequence in front of the Metro entrance only begins that process.

The night Antoine spends in jail, one of the longest and saddest in *The 400 Blows*, serves several functions in the drama of Antoine's solitude. Dramatically, it separates him from René and from his parents. Kinesthetically, the sequence finishes Antoine's free mobility through the film's space: there will be no more lyrical flights of the camera and character until Antoine's climactic run to the sea.

For this discussion, the sequence can be divided into five segments. The first is the "interrogation," actually a discussion between Antoine's father and the police chief. Having picked his son up at the scene of his "crime," the return of the stolen typewriter, Doinel drags his son to the police station and turns him over to the authorities. The segment opens with an establishing medium shot; the two adults are in the foreground of the frame with Antoine placed toward the rear. The two men discuss the boy as if he is not there. A medium shot of Antoine and his father follows: Antoine looks at the ceiling (it is one of Léaud's little exaggerations) and his father says, "Do you think when we speak to him he is there? Do you think he's listening now?" In fact, Antoine is immediately dispensed with: a series of three shots follow as the Chief arranges for the boy's arrest. Then, in medium close-up, Antoine is led from the room, while the discussion between the two adults continues: Antoine's father turns him over to the police for processing. Then follows the "interview"—taken in a single medium close-up—during which Antoine gives a detective his "statement." Truffaut interrupts for a cutaway showing Antoine's father leaving the police station, then returns to the previous medium close-up just as the detective finishes reading back the statement. A medium close-up from behind Antoine shows his signing the form; then another policeman enters and takes Antoine away, the action followed by a pan. A series of three set-ups using limited depth-of-field follows

Antoine toward a cage-like detention cell. The second of these shots reveals a point of view from behind a small window in a door, but no one is shown having this point of view. The third shot, a dolly right, shows Antoine's hesitant entry into the cell, pauses for a view through the mesh covering the cell, and then moves back to show the surrounding space with the jailers before there is a dissolve.

These two segments, joined at their trunk by the cutaway of Antoine's father leaving, sharply separates Antoine's connection to the world, first by eliminating him from the "interrogation" that will seal his fate (enacted in two stages—Léaud's glance at the ceiling and then the cut to the Chief, who sets the processing of Antoine into motion); second, through a sketchy alternate syntagma that places him in the "statement" shots while his father turns him over to the police and leaves. The succeeding shots in which Antoine is handled by the jailers and is seen through the door window and the cell meshing complete his isolation (figs. 5.1–5.3). The compositions of these shots do not hint at a specific intradiegetic point of view but do position Antoine in a way that visually expresses his situation. Indeed, Truffaut deliberately postpones a point-of-view shot in these segments.

Léaud's performance, consisting simply of a steady, slow walk, despite being shoved and pulled and the way he bends his head, is stoic and empty of reactions such as fear, confusion, or sorrow. His only line, in response to his cellmate's question about his crime, "I ran away from home," is delivered flatly. The irony of the criminal treatment conveyed by the surrounding shots and the childish offense is carried by Léaud's understated reading.

Truffaut's postponement of Antoine's point of view underlines Léaud's underplaying of the scene and the delicately expressionistic images of imprisonment call attention to the act of looking at Antoine (because the camera looks through things), but what is seen remains, at the level of the performance, flatly literal: a boy in a jail cell. Truffaut's postponement, moreover, continues when he fades in on a medium close-up of the room, picking up, after a lapse of time, where the previous shot left off. The camera pans to show Antoine sleeping on the cell floor. Off-screen, a jailer

Fig. 5.1

Fig. 5.2

Fig. 5.3

wakes Antoine with the line, "Ah, sweethearts ...," followed by a cut to a medium shot of a policeman bringing in a trio of prostitutes. They enter the cell holding Antoine, who is roughly removed and shoved into a smaller cage (a pan follows the action) where he sits on a small bench. A close-up follows, from Antoine's point of view, a hand-held pan taking in the whole room; then a close-up of Antoine, who pulls his turtleneck sweater up over his mouth and nose, crosses his arms, and watches sleepily but intently (fig. 5.4).

This segment finally introduces Antoine's point of view in an emphatic manner: the isolation of his small cage to one side of the room positions Antoine as the intradiegetic viewer of the main action. Léaud's bit with the sweater, which isolates his eyes, strongly but quietly accents his role as holder of the camera's pan. The constantly implied point of view of the previous segment, in effect, finally settles on Antoine. Viewed in isolation, he now assumes the proper place prepared for him by the whole sequence, the source-point of the camera's view, the place he usually occupies throughout *The 400 Blows*. This place in the sequence is prepared

**Fig. 5.4**

through the habitual constructions Truffaut uses in the film; but, in this segment, Antoine's point of view has been postponed so long, and its absence felt so strongly because of the compositions of the shots, that this last shot, so emphatically performed by Léaud, organizes the sequence retroactively around Antoine's gaze, his situation, his self-containment. Léaud's stoic underplaying carries a tremendous emotional charge, particularly considering that Truffaut withholds the close-up until the end and holds it static for a fairly long while after a set of activity-filled pans.

Fig. 5.5

Having positioned Antoine at the center of the sequence, Truffaut now opens up that center to reveal the heart of the film: Antoine's solitude. Truffaut has never hidden this anywhere in *The 400 Blows*, but Antoine's solitude has until now been played off against his role as one of the schoolboys, as René's buddy, and, in the night scenes, against his poetic sense of himself as a citizen of Paris. The fourth segment of Antoine's night in jail, the ride in the paddy wagon, is the core of the drama of the film. There are no transitions between the close-up discussed above and the rest of the sequence. Or, rather, the close-up is the point of transition. A medium shot follows, busy with action and camera movement, showing the prisoners being taken out to the police van. A medium shot outside the police station shows them being hauled into the van; Antoine is last and stares out the barred window at the back (fig. 5.5). A shot-reverse-shot series begins with a long shot from Antoine's point of view, followed by a medium close-up from the reverse angle. With the exception of a single long shot of the van driving by, the shot-reverse-shot construction is repeated regularly three times. The last is a medium close-up of Antoine crying, his breath frosted by the cold, concluded with a dissolve.

The simple, stark construction of this segment juxtaposes the relative dynamism of the receding view of the street and the close-up static view of Antoine's shadowed face, the emphasis again placed on his eyes. It is the emotional climax of the film, which has a symmetrical structure and reverses its direction after this sequence, placing Antoine again in the company of other boys like himself, etc. There are exceptions certainly, like the psychiatric interview, which has no reverse angles and so places unusual emphasis on Antoine caught in the frame "explaining himself," and René's failed visit in which Antoine is trapped behind a glass door watching his friend try to get into the Observation Center. And, finally, the solitary run to the sea, which is intended to rhyme with the paddy wagon segment as its opposite. Characteristic of all climaxes in the Doinel films, Antoine is motionless and silent in the police van. Léaud's face, the somber "little man" face of *The 400 Blows*, cracks here with tears and the intensity of his gaze. It is the only moment in the film when Léaud allows his diminutive adult's demeanor to flag.

The sequence continues, resuming the "handling" of Antoine by the police, this time elliptically as a résumé of the rest of the night. Six shots joined by dissolves closely controlled by Antoine's point of view or by close-ups of him show Antoine completely isolated in his cell but with the camera inside with him. The last three shots include a close-up of Antoine's fingerprinting, a medium shot of Antoine being roughly prepared for his "mug shot," and then the mug shot itself as it is being taken.

The sequence as a whole moves from a detached view of Antoine, the grown-ups in the office, to a very close intimacy. Truffaut handles the motion through careful shifts of point of view. The last shots seem to break that progression since the sequence ends with the "mug shots." However, Léaud's intense stare at the police camera—in reality, Truffaut's camera—suggests the last shot of the film when Antoine, having made his run to the sea, stares back at the camera in a freeze frame. More importantly, as the conclusion of the sequence itself, the mug shot thematizes the formal arrangement of the sequence, which alternates between a looking at and a looking with Antoine: here he both looks out at and is caught by the camera. The motion toward Antoine, and toward him fixed, still, and silent, finds him diegetically imprisoned by the institutional structures to which his father has cast him, yet still self-contained, the holder of the gaze.

Léaud carries this very spare construction, the most static development of the Doinel character. His stern gaze is at once open and vulnerable yet surrenders nothing. His containment reduces his whole performance to a simple set of gestures—hunched shoulders, the set of his head; his eyes refuse the sentimentality offered by the sequence and no less refuse a "psychology," any reduction to type. Instead, Léaud's Antoine becomes a character. The characterological "capital" that gathers around this sequence takes twenty years to be exhausted.

## II. CHARLIE

Close attention to the whole of *The 400 Blows* that would continue the preceding examination of a key sequence in Truffaut's characterization of Antoine would also continue to reveal the remarkable interplay of the director's filmic and Léaud's performance tactics. The director constructs the place of the character through point of view, and the actor fills that place, the center of the film. To generalize briefly, we could argue that Truffaut returns to the silent cinema's contemplation of the human face to center *The 400 Blows* in privileged moments of solitude. The deep impression of interiority projected onto Antoine is a function of the ways in which the camera's gaze returns to him and is received and intensified by Léaud's performance, especially in the film's infrequent but critical moments of stasis. A fuller examination of *The 400 Blows* would show from where the camera's gaze returns; it is important to Truffaut's formal structure that the relation of the camera and character is attenuated often during the film. Antoine is frequently part of the loosely fitted *mise-en-scène*, the camera takes off "on its own," and so on. The examples we chose to look at indicate, in the first instance of the "embrace scene," how Truffaut usually returns to Antoine in a few carefully accented close-up/point-of-views within somewhat widely flung sequences; the second shows us the same process of construction settling on a long, dramatically intense passage.

After *The 400 Blows*, Truffaut seldom handles actors or structures his films around them in exactly the same fashion. Some of his best films, in part, do return to the strategies of his first feature, however. *The Wild Child's* performances recall *The 400 Blows*; Truffaut's own acting in *Day for Night*, *The Wild Child*, and *The Green Room* (1979); Léaud's work in *Two English Girls*; and Belmondo in *Mississippi Mermaid* (1969) variously recapitulate the acting and formal tactics so important to *The 400 Blows*. Perhaps these films are to be distinguished by a certain deliberate flatness of the acting and perhaps they should be linked to Charles Aznavour's very slight performance in *Shoot the Piano Player*, significantly the first grown-up acting in a lead role directed by Truffaut. However, the overall direction of this film works on principles different from those Truffaut uses in *The 400 Blows*. Like the later Antoine, Charlie is also a displaced and sometimes comic character. But, whereas *Stolen Kisses* and *Bed and Board* use long takes and deep focus that enable the viewer to look past and around Antoine, *Shoot the Piano Player* privileges the viewer through editing. Although superficially much more Hitchcockian than *The 400 Blows*, Charlie should be seen as a return to a style of performance antedating Hitchcock's partial subversion of "star-acting," to the constructed psychological characterizations associated with Lev Kuleshov and his pupil V.I. Pudovkin. What Aznavour brings to the character of Charlie is minimal: a small, dapper body, immobile features, and very sad eyes. What Truffaut's montage does to Aznavour's performance is to break it down through synecdoche, through rapidly cut close-ups of his hands and face.

In an often frantic film, Charlie is static; in a sometimes melodramatic film, Charlie registers almost no emotion, justifiably giving rise to the impression that Charlie is passive, indeed that he is the first in a series of passive leads in Truffaut's cinema. However, this impression needs a context because, while Aznavour's performance is minimal, it is not the entirety of Charlie's characterization.

The narrative design of *Shoot the Piano Player* is circular. Charlie becomes involved in a tragedy that repeats an old tragedy and, it is hinted at the end when he meets the new barmaid, the whole business will begin again after the film has concluded. This fatalistic circularity derives from the American fictional sources and related film genre (e.g., *film noir*, thriller) on which Truffaut has mapped *Shoot the Piano Player*. Although Truffaut intends "an explosion of genres," this generic structure is kept intact and Charlie is its prisoner. Unlike his American forebears, however, Charlie does not struggle against his destiny. Rather, he is a picture of sad resignation at which the viewer peers in the course of the film. It is easy to mistake Aznavour's frozen-faced passivity, the quiescence of his characterization, and the plot's entrapment as Truffaut's essay into a film equivalent of literary existentialism.

Nevertheless, the method of characterization Truffaut uses in *Shoot the Piano Player* has little in common with such a project as it was extended into French film culture. Rather, Charlie Kohler marks a "film nut" experiment in psychological construction modeled on silent—Hitchcock called it "pure film"—cinema models, particularly the "Kuleshov effect." Its central device is the use of cinematic synecdoche, in extreme close-up, to articulate characters' interior states. Aznavour's rather inert performance is a perfect vehicle for this experiment: what we cannot see on his face is counterpointed with what we are privileged to see expressed in close-ups of his hands. A simple example—and it is characteristic of this type of characterization that it is inevitably simple—is provided by the first night of the film, when Charlie walks with Lena and desperately wants to ask her out for a drink but cannot manage even to take her hand or put his arm around her shoulder.

The sequence is preceded by the elaborate and various exposition of the film. The shifts of tone, from a *film noir* pursuit to a Renoirian long-take dialogue to the nearly slapstick bar scene, do not really settle down until the third sequence, marked by a dissolve. This exposition has introduced Charlie as a somewhat removed figure. He is looked at, addressed, spoken of, but it is not until the bar owner and he have a conversation that the film lights on Charlie as the main character. The conversation is structured in a conventional shot-reverse shot sequence of close-ups. Charlie plays with the line the bar owner feeds him: "I'm scared." Aznavour's several readings of the line, each inflected differently, detach it from any definite inner significance for the character. Meanwhile, Charlie is held in the point of view of the bar owner, or at least apparently, since Truffaut holds Charlie's close-up "too long" and Aznavour does not look in the right direction to return the bar owner's sight-line; instead, the actor looks frame right, as if looking inward, and the effect is to separate the close-up from the sequence.

This short sequence, first of all, openly acknowledges that acting is "playacting." The loose fit of characterization on actors that is frequently taken to be typical of *nouvelle vague* screen performance is here foregrounded by Truffaut. Second, the sequence parodies the classical cinema's convention of the close-up dialogue sequence as the vehicle of characters' interiority. (Whether directly addressing the character held in the reverse angle or, like Charlie, looking inward by not meeting the other's sight-line, such set-ups are frequently used in Hollywood films as a rough equivalent of the stage soliloquy.) By setting up Charlie so early in the film for such a dialogue and then having Aznavour detach the significance of this key line in his characterization, Truffaut neatly severs the expectation that Charlie will possess an adequate interiority in Aznavour's impersonation.*

Leaving the bar, Charlie begins walking down the street but is called back by Lena, the barmaid, and joins her (in a medium

---

*It is beyond the scope of this essay to address the system of direct and indirect allusions Truffaut works into *Shoot the Piano Player*, but this line, voiced so early in the film, is doubtless part of the *Citizen Kane* allusions of the film. "I'm scared" is Charlie's "Rosebud," the critical clue to his whole character. Like "Rosebud" too, knowing the line and knowing it to be true is, paradoxically, the way we do not know the secret of the character, do not have the key to who and what he is and for the film.

shot). She borrows some money and they begin walking. This brief encounter sets up the walking scene which consists of an interrupted "master shot," a backward dolly medium close-up with Lena and Charlie at the center of the frame in rather shallow focus. In addition to the interruptions, which are cutaways, the shot is reframed several times, including three reverse angles. Making the transition from the preface to the walk itself, Charlie looks at Lena in a medium close-up, the master shot, followed by a close-up of his hand going to hers and withdrawing quickly (figs. 5.6–5.8). Truffaut returns to the medium close-up master shot and then repeats the close-up of the hand: the rhythm carries the sense of Charlie's anxiety. A variation of the master shot, another medium close-up, slightly farther away and from behind (i.e., a reverse-angle dolly shot) shows Charlie lifting his hand to put it around her waist (fig. 5.9). A quickly cut in close-up matches the previous shot, as if Charlie will complete the action by showing his hands behind his back counting quickly with his fingers. Truffaut cuts to a medium shot (a dolly) from behind as Charlie continues counting, then back to the "master shot," this time closer so Charlie is seen alone in close-up. He begins a voice-over (interior monologue) with, "She'll think you odd," his eyes slightly to the right, away from Lena and out of frame. As he continues ("Say something. You act scared"), a close-up of his hands from the front is intercut, followed by a close-up of Lena as Charlie's monologue begins to describe her character ("She's the serious type"); the camera pans to include Charlie in the shot. Lena looks at him, his eyes are glancing down, out of frame; he screws up his face, unaware she is watching. Charlie's inner monologue continues, "She seldom laughs. Only when it's really funny." She laughs at this point, interrupting his reverie; he looks at her. "What's so funny?" he asks. "Your face." This break in Charlie's monologue is followed by a bracketed subsequence of several shots that work the "crime story" of the film into this sequence. Lena directs Charlie to look into her hand mirror, followed by a close-up of the mirror image—two pipe-smoking bad guys—and several shots in which Charlie and Lena hide in an alley and shake their pursuers.

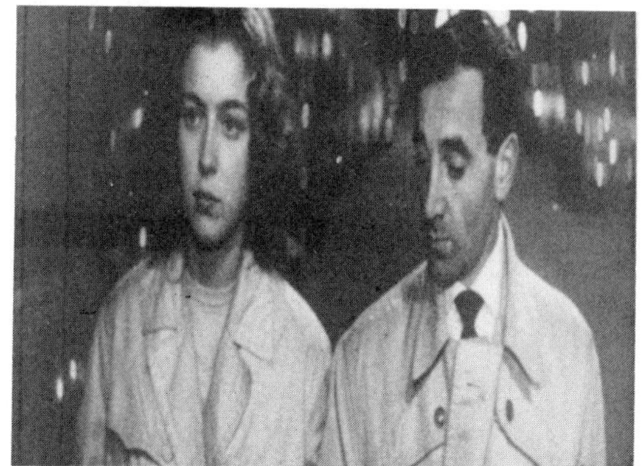

Fig. 5.6

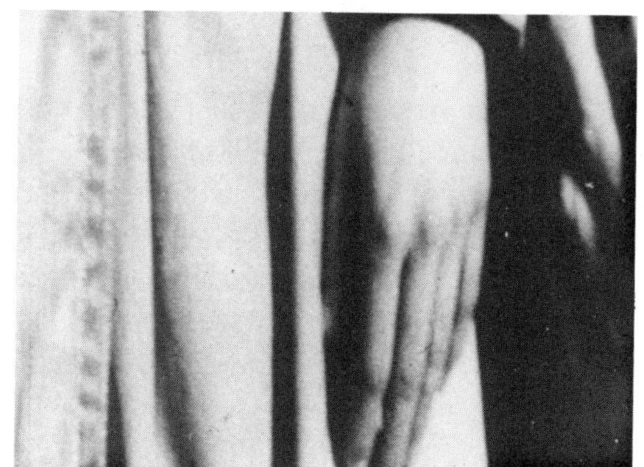

Fig. 5.7

Fig. 5.8

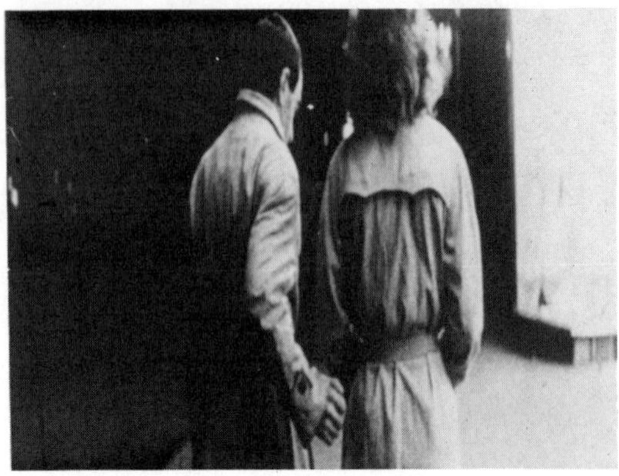

Fig. 5.9

The last shot in the sequence returns to the "master shot" set-up, a close-up of Charlie dollying back as before. A slight pan to the left includes a woman's shoulder, assumed to be Lena's. Charlie has resumed his reverie and the camera moves closer to Charlie, whose inner monologue is working up to an invitation for a drink. At last, he turns and asks out loud, "Want a drink?" The camera continues to track back as Charlie looks around for Lena, who has vanished. He finally stops stumbling around for her and his monologue continues, "Just as well," and his thoughts turn to jazz pianists as he looks down again, and the backward dolly continues until a concluding cut.

The sequence follows up on suggestions laid in the preceding discussion at the bar. Truffaut uses the voice-over apparently to interpret shots from Charlie's perspective, a position soon revealed to be false. The camera never assumes Charlie's point of view or otherwise comes under his authority. On the contrary, the business with the hand mirror shifts visual control of the sequence to Lena for a time, though as a whole it belongs to an anonymous narrating construction. Aznavour's veritable immobility as an actor here serves the director's purpose well by focusing the interiority of the character completely on his hesitant and anxious inner voice, which actually draws further and further from the images until the joke—Lena's unseen departure—is followed through.

Truffaut shows Charlie's psychological state through a rapid series of close-ups of his hands, a montage separated from the actor's integral performance. He repeats this procedure again in the flashback sequence when "Edouard Saroyan" goes for an audition, jump-cutting Charlie's hesitant finger on the doorbell. In this sequence, Truffaut follows an anonymous female violist down a corridor and outside immediately afterward, significantly jerking the camera's gaze away from Charlie. The detachment of the camera from the character could not be more whimsically yet bluntly stated. Truffaut also repeats the voice-over/image disjunction in the flashback when Charlie says to himself that he must embrace his wife just before he runs out into the corridor. The camera does take his point of view on his sudden return to discover his wife has committed suicide, the trauma and the conjunction of point of view punctuating the moment with a very fast tracking movement.

Generally, however, the camera never returns to the protagonist of *Shoot the Piano Player* as it does in *The 400 Blows* and consequently does not provide a place of performance. Instead, Aznavour's minimal acting is shattered into synecdoche. An ensemble of shots, put together by director/viewer, substitutes for the mediation of the central character in the intimate moments of the drama.

Widening our discussion a little, we should circle back to some preliminary generalizations: the New Wave directors foreground their authorial presence and depart from the predominant types of screen acting that preceded them, in part by selecting elements from the history of screen performance, modifying and recasting them. These generalizations seem to be verified by Truffaut, who combines aspects of Neorealist and Hitchcockian styles, but a bit more needs to be said about *Shoot the Piano Player*. In this film, the central character is barely created by Aznavour's performance, which serves as a sort of blank screen on which his psychology is projected either by other characters, like Lena, or by Truffaut's montage. The way the film shatters Charlie, empties him and displaces him as the nominal protagonist of the film, indicates that the main interest of *Shoot the Piano Player* lies in the assertion of cinematic style and the free arrangement of narrative material. Such a displaced, cipher-like central character, who can become a function of filmic articulations made independently of the actor, is the logical outcome of the filmmaking mode that replaced "star-acting" with the stylistic assertions of the director.

It is perhaps a sign of the director's conservatism as an artist that Charlie Kohler is unique in Truffaut's films and that his later work remains within the stylistic performance orbit of *The 400 Blows*, a movie that deepens, varies, and mixes types of acting but does not break entirely with previous conventions of screen performance. The mediating authority of Truffaut's central characters is by and large sustained after *Shoot the Piano Player*, even though there is much of Charlie in the later Antoine, as there is in Adele H., the heroes of *The Soft Skin, Fahrenheit 451*, and especially *Such a Gorgeous Kid Like Me*. Moreover, the acting styles at play in the films of Rohmer, Chabrol, Eustache and others in the New Wave, though distinctively handled by these directors, have much in common with Truffaut's work.

## III. MICHEL

The tendencies we have seen at work in *Shoot the Piano Player* are also present in *Breathless* (1959) but further developed by Godard and inflected quite differently. In looking at the segment of Truffaut's film where Charlie and the bar owner exchange a bit of dialogue, we noted how Aznavour's several readings of the line, "I'm scared" exemplified the play-acting side of the *nouvelle vague* by exposing the fact of acting itself. Jean-Paul Belmondo's notorious mimicry of Humphrey Bogart in *Breathless* is often taken to be the *locus classicus* of this aspect of New Wave screen performance. The film suggests that such acting consists of a concoction of film-historical quotations, just as the stylistic and narrative conventions brought into play make the film an assembly of allusions and readymades. While such a view of Belmondo's (and Jean Seberg's) acting in *Breathless* leaves a considerable surplus untouched, there is a great deal of truth in such a reductive reading, and the film actively solicits it.

As a critic at *Cahiers du Cinéma*, Godard was the most enthusiastic celebrant of *découpage classique* and his 1952 essay, "Defense and Illustration of Classical Construction," written against André Bazin's historicist critique of Hollywood classicism, argues for the classical psychology of screen characterization.[7] Godard contends that the special strength of classical construction is the way it permits the camera, the actors, and the editing to conspire together to signify nuances of behavior, especially through the articulation of the gaze. However, eight years later, when he comes to make *Breathless,* Godard does not deploy the set-ups and editing of the classical style, nor is he directly interested in the style of characterization to which it gives rise. Yet his interest in that style is hardly absent in *Breathless*; while he does not seek to replicate it, he does gloss it, and our consideration of the film should begin by examining how he does so.

Unlike the light, inward actors Truffaut chose for *Shoot the Piano Player*, Godard selected two forceful performers: Seberg, a Hollywood star of the 1950s, and Belmondo, a stage actor whose physical grace and charming arrogance in *Breathless* soon made him a durable international star. Belmondo does look a bit like Bogart, but only as a young Frenchman might—taller, more muscular, and infinitely more narcissistic. Playing on the resemblance, Godard directs Belmondo to decorate his performance with a few carefully chosen gestures associated with Bogart, like running his thumb over his upper lip. These gestures do not make a whole impersonation, nor are they intended to. Rather, they gather on the surface of the actor's performance, signifiers of "Bogart-ness," an idea of Bogart affected by Michel Poiccard, Belmondo's character, detached from Bogart's screen persona. In fact, these gestures merely supplement the characterization of Michel. The moment when Michel contemplates the marquee poster for *The Harder They Fall* (Bogart's last film), enjoying an exchange of glances with "Bogie" across matched close-ups, is a homage on the part of Godard and the film that forms a break in the illusion of self-contained textuality. However the moment also thematizes Michel's self-invention: Michel is playacting his criminality. It is important to realize that Michel is mimicking Bogart and that Belmondo is not putting on a new version of a classic movie persona, as do Albert Finney in *Gumshoe* and Elliott Gould in *The Long Goodbye*. Rather, the use of secondhand start gestures actually impedes identification of Belmondo as a new Bogart as well as blocking association of Michel with the tradition of criminal outsiders of the Bogart (and Jean Gabin) stripe. Michel affects such a character. He is an esthete; he is playacting.

Godard works this playacting into the structure of the film as a narrative system, particularly in the extended passages that depict Michel's first day in Paris. For example, between his arrival in the city and his first conversation with Patricia (Seberg), Michel hurtles through several brief scenes in which he reads a newspaper, makes a phone call, rummages through Patricia's apartment, and so on, until he visits Lilianne (Lilianne Robin), the young woman from whom he steals some money. Godard handles this fragmented series of shots with fast panning camera movements cut together in elliptical chains. Each bit of the narrative progress is a self-contained shot (with a few minor exceptions, like the inserted close-up of Michel counting his change at a coffee bar).

The segment is important in emphasizing some features of Michel's characterization: his impatience and impetuosity. The segment also exemplifies some of the tactics Godard uses to establish the relationship between the camera and the actors, as that between the "container" of action and its performance. Godard's camera simply registers behavior in a series of elliptically arranged takes. The camera placement rarely enters into the space of the performance—the only close-ups are bracketed inserts—and the mismatches of the shots seldom even suggest sight-line matches. The performance is observed, or contained, in the structure of each composition; in contrast to Truffaut's usages, acting in *Breathless* is neither aided nor cued by the ensemble of shots. The elliptical montage chains of shots do not respond to nor do they privilege the actor; for the most part he is "found" by the camera. The style here registers expository narration: Michel moves around Paris. The quick pace of the pans and montage breaks contribute to the abruptness that will envelop Michel during much of the film, but do not operate to reveal his character; they do not center on him, and the camera does not rebound back on his point of view. Instead, the camera outruns him or snaps away from an action only to pick him up elsewhere. This slippage between the actor and the camera effectively reduces all performance to playacting. It reveals how the supports of the classical style are necessary for behavior on screen to become a psychology of character.

Godard interrupts the rapid narrative progression of this long expository segment several times, notably during Michel's stop at Lilianne's, the visit to the travel agency, and the first conversation with Patricia in the scene where she is selling the *Herald Tribune* on the Champs Elysées. Here Godard uses a long take/moving camera which might seem to be the opposite of the rapid and elliptical montage sequences that surround it. However, the Godardian long-take only dilates the function of the shot as a container of action and provides no more support to the actors than his montage segments. To turn briefly to this first conversation with Patricia, it is introduced by several elliptical pans and settles into a long backward traveling shot which bears comparison with the sequence discussed above in *Shoot the Piano Player*. In the Truffaut film, the characters stand revealed to the viewer through two tactics of interiority (the synecdochic close-up and inner monologue voice-over), while Godard keeps his distance and allows the characters to display themselves through performance. Openly carried by her accent and more subtly by her walk, Patricia is quickly established as an American, even a parody of the American woman of the fifties. Her cool flirtatiousness and standoffish sarcasm are transparent codes of the fifties Hollywood feminine masquerade. Michel's pantomime and speech are no less broad, playing on his abruptness, to make him the courtly gangster (he is proposing to take her away to Italy). Both characters are playacting roles, a doubling within the container-shot of the actors' work.

Following this encounter, Godard returns to the quick montage as Michel resumes his travels around Paris. It is within this segment that he encounters the Bogart poster, and for a good reason, because it is within this sequence that Godard essays a critique of character-mediation of the *découpage*. Simply put, what Godard does is to insert medium close-up shots of Michel into the progression of the sequences. The place he holds in the montage should be the place of the star-mediator of space and time, a place similar to the one Bogart-Marlowe holds in the "Acme Bookshop" section of Hawks' *The Big Sleep*,[8] where an elliptical arrangement of subsequences center on the protagonist. In *Breathless*, however, the shots of Michel, usually performing his Bogartian gestures, are not smoothly woven into the cutting and do not function as conventional reaction shots or sight-line cues. Rather, they foreground Michel's playacting, his "Bogie on the street" affectation.

Although sustained through the film and important to its self-reflexive project, these shots and this segment are not the whole story of screen performance in *Breathless*. Godard opens other spaces in the film by shifting his style toward sustained sequence shots and segments that build on them. What occurs in these segments of the film is that the shots are extended as containers of performance, but with the difference that in the more sustained, slower sequences blocks of material are related differently than they are in the faster montage sections of the film. To understand this difference, we should briefly discuss the role of the sequence shot in Godard's early style.

Godard's use of the sequence shot develops out of Rossellini's long-take style rather than Renoir's, which so influenced Truffaut. Whereas Renoir uses depth-of-field and camera movement to construct complex continuity across complicated actions, Rossellini joins segments of rather simply composed blocks of material. In *Breathless*, Godard accelerates Rossellini's shooting methods through faster camera movements and jump cuts that create a false continuity around Michel. The quickened pace and harsh textures of Coutard's cinematography contain Michel without elaboration; the pans and disjunctive cuts refuse the character a center in the *découpage*. His weakened mediation of the shots falls under the velocity of its execution and the refusal of privileging camera angles. Moreover, in each image Michel rushes through the composition or mugs, halting the camera to transmute his presence into a quotation.

This use of the accelerated sequence shot is fundamentally subversive and it greatly diminishes the force of the actor. When Godard slows the pace, the actor seems to return and does more than allow the bare registry of behavior or quotation so that, despite the frequent agitated passages of *Breathless,* a potential space is prepared by this style which achieves a certain purity in the sustained segments of the film.

With *Vivre sa Vie* (1962), Godard perfects the relationship between actor and camera in a meditative mode, but we can see that relationship begin in *Breathless* when we turn to the slower passages. What has been called the "container" can be characterized simply. Camera placement neither enters the space of performance nor supports it. The acting, then, is contained inside the structure of each shot, and Godard rarely carries an actor across shots without shifting the temporal and often tonal aspects of the scene. As a result, dramatic moments are not allowed to develop through a sequence: in the longer encounters between Michel and Patricia, the actors have to recompose their characters around sudden transitions. In this way, *Breathless* is that prototypical *nouvelle vague* film in which the director's style asserts itself against the actors. On the other hand, Godard's style opens a space for performance that moves in an opposite direction: the editing may interrupt the acting, but it never controls its significance; the camera contains, then elides over performance, and this allows performance to rediscover itself across the interruptions. That rediscovery occurs frequently whenever Godard thickens the language with dialogue, speeches, voice-overs, and, finally, titles. By the time of *Alphaville* (1965) and *Pierrot le Fou* (1965), the relationship between accelerated, asynchronous passages and long-take, medium-paced passages of dialogue has become systematic. In *Breathless*, the distinctions are still jagged so that performers have to restate their presence across ruptures of the style. This process can be traced in a comparatively gentle example by examining a part of the long sequence in which Patricia and Michel resume their relationship in her room.

The sequence begins with Patricia looking at herself in the mirror in medium shot; a reverse angle (the expected point of view of the character) does not follow, but rather a jump-cut to a space behind her so that the viewer sees her looking at herself, patting her stomach (we learn later that she may be pregnant). Alone, Patricia is quite taken with herself, like the heroine in a musical; the moment is special, a star's moment, and Godard follows it through with a shot that carries Patricia past the lobby counter. She stands on tiptoe—it is a sort of dance step—and Godard cuts on an off beat to a black space.

A light comes on. There has been an ellipsis while Patricia traveled to her door. When the light comes on, it exposes Michel on Patricia's bed. He quickly goes for his gun under the pillow. This too is a star's moment. The shot is a conventional set-up for a gangster film, but it is not reduced to a quotation. Belmondo's rapid movement is not thrown away but is performed with a panther grace that ends with him falling back onto the bed, then reaching out for a cigarette. The two subsequences, then, set out the two actors in ways that underline their beauty and grace, a moment in the film where Godard's containing style supports the screen performance.

The next shot, a postponed medium establishing shot taken from a slightly high angle, shows the two of them, Michel sitting on the bed looking to the rear of the frame as Patricia enters and then leaves the shot with clipped, dismissive movements as she puts her things away. Their exchange is sarcastic and quickly decays, with Patricia lapsing into English and Michel, no longer the rakish gangster, resorting to Gallic gestures. The charm of the opening segment is dissolved. A straight cut, covering an ellipsis, finds Patricia in the bathroom, a light goes on to reveal her in the mirror with the back of her head to the camera. As she brushes her hair, Seberg restores the Patricia seen downstairs, the star, though the exchange continues with Michel's voice heard off-screen (figs. 5.10–5.12). She is pleased with herself and secure—her secret, her problem, seems a comic matter—Michel is excluded, his voice ignored. A brief set of shot-reverse-shots ensues, with the actors making faces in the mirror, breaking the privileged gaze the camera had set out with Patricia. In a panning medium shot, Patricia walks past Michel but, on a cut, the camera returns to him, now doing his Bogart thumb-over-the-lip gesture. Then he turns, looks out of frame, and the camera pans as he addresses Patricia. Godard cuts to Patricia on the bed in an almost prayerful pose (fig. 5.13).

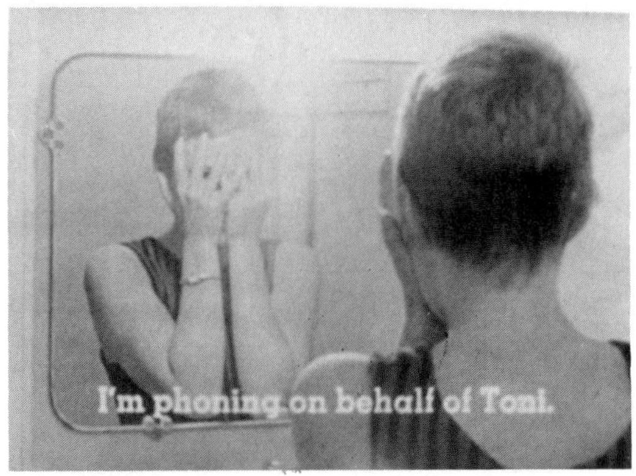


**Fig. 5.10**

The sequence has already fallen into the alternation that will more or less sustain throughout, a three-part alternation between a silent gaze or pause and somewhat acerbic exchanges or "philosophical" speeches. At each transition, the actors abruptly switch moods, display their technique, pose, and improvise a new piece that oscillates between "star" and "character," self-involvement and exchange. In this early section, the shifts come quickly, but as the sequence develops the changes are farther apart and the breaks between them cause the scene—as a unit of drama—to collapse.

When Michel enters the frame, a hand-held camera reframes the space a bit while the actors settle in. This section begins to relax and the dialogue is delivered slowly. They are disputing the terms of their relationship and, when they come to an impasse, Godard cuts to a close-up of Patricia from behind; she sighs and looks out of frame. The shot seems at first to be a conventional medium-to-close-up progression in the development of the scene. However, the next cut does not follow Patricia's sight-line: the shot

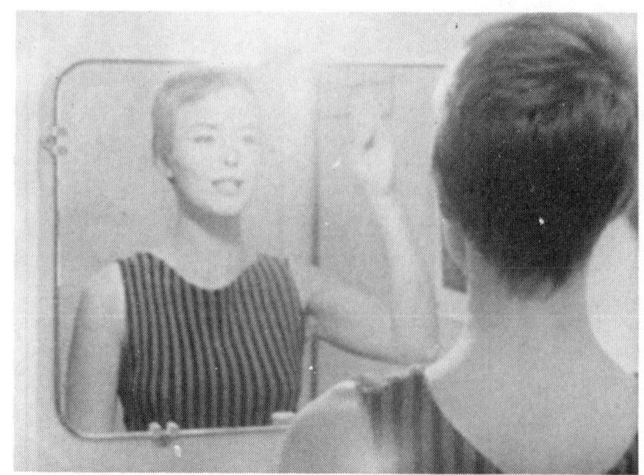

Fig. 5.11

Fig. 5.12

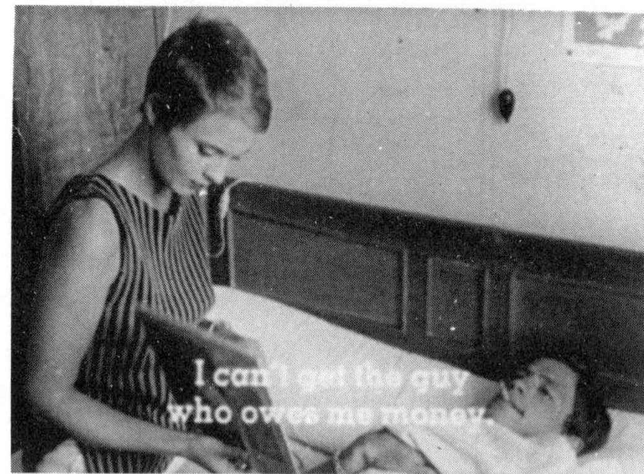


Fig. 5.13

is really a break, a portrait out of the sequence, her gaze an interruption rather than a cue to the next cut. The following shot, which is a very long take, is taken from the foot of the bed. The rhythm of the shot is marked by Michel pulling the bed cover on and off his head as he delivers his dialogue, an inquisition about where she has spent the night, broken off suddenly as Michel declares his love. This long take modulates the more acerbic argument that had developed a few shots before. But instead of continuing, Michel picks up a magazine and Godard inserts a series of close-ups, "art shots" of naked women, and Michel makes a general declaration on them.[9] This subsequence is clearly a rehearsal for the "essays" of *Une Femme Mariée* (1964). Patricia joins in the voice-over to make her declaration of love, and Godard cuts, still in inserted close-up, to an art poster of Romeo and Juliet.

Both actors have vanished, their voices becoming disembodied voice-overs accompanying the pop-vulgar, romantic-sentimental graphic visual material that encapsulates one of the central oppositions of Godard's filmmaking. Without recourse to "acting" at all, Godard situates the characters within the mythologies of culture that precisely determine them as characters. The absent voices—the performers out of character—discuss the history of the personae that the characters exemplify. This variation in the development of the sequence introduces another alternation important to the segment: the end of acting, the disembodiment of the actors into the play of voices/language. While the use of voice-over/graphic material anticipate *Une Femme Mariée*, in terms of screen acting this alternation is also a rehearsal of the way Godard systematically organizes the Belmondo/Karina characters of *Pierrot le Fou* into twin sets of coded playactors (the poet and the femme fatale) and voices (the poetic text/adventure story).

Patricia and Michel return to the screen as abruptly as they left, in medium shot, then a close-up of Patricia who leans forward prettily and laughs when Michel calls her a coward. A medium close-up follows as the sequence shifts suddenly into comedy with some horseplay—he lifts her skirt, she slaps him. The hand-held camera moves in on Michel, who repeats the accusation. A bit of play with cigarettes, likely an allusion to Hawks, who often uses ritual with cigarettes among characters who are "good enough," finds Patricia backlighted against a window trying to light hers. Michel continues his insults off-screen, saying that a woman who can't light a cigarette is frightened. The moment is an interesting "essay" on the way behavior is actually used in classical cinema to show character traits, but it is more importantly an instance of Michel's affectation of those film codes as an ethic, while the viewer sees the backlighted Patricia encoded as a romantic heroine, recalling the Juliet of the poster. Godard then cuts to a medium shot from a slightly high angle, shifting the tone of the scene as Patricia asks, across the cut, if Michel wants a cigarette. He has her get one from his coat and she discovers a passport bearing the name Laszlo Kovacs. As she kneels by the bed, he lights his cigarette and she goes to the window as if resuming the portrait pose of the previous shot as she says that he always thinks of dying. She turns away, demanding that he say something nice.

The dramatic tension in this portion of the sequence arises from Michel's assumption of a B-grade existentialism in the train of the action with the cigarettes while Patricia maintains her pretty romanticism; the brief essay on cultural types, then, sets the text for this ensuing exchange. Patricia is defeated; the scene shifts again, when she comes near, Michel grabs for her and she runs across the room to touch a Renoir poster. The scene collapses. When it resumes, after a cut, Michel is looking through a newspaper and she is rolling up a poster. In several shot-reverse-shots, the two of them resume their characters, he with his thumb gesture and she with very American movements. The two of them have pulled apart, as had occurred in the bathroom, and their dialogue takes up differences between Frenchmen and Americans. When they resume friendly communication—Michel delivering a speech declaring that he wants to sleep with her—Godard repositions the camera so that the viewer watches Patricia move around the room from Michel's point of view, then breaks into another elliptical shot-counter-shot series that concludes with a "double portrait." Silently, Michel performs his Bogart lip gestures while Patricia wipes her eyes as if she had been crying, then regains her composure with a very American fifties shrug of her shoulders and announces, "I'm going to outstare you." From her point of view through the rolled up poster, Patricia sees Michel as a cute, even sweet boy in a movie star pose as the camera zooms in for an extreme close-up. Following a cut, a zoom out of them kissing begins a short ellipsis that breaks the scene down into a series of brief, disjunctive takes.

This section of the overall segment in Patricia's room, approximately half of it, suffices to indicate the characteristic way Godard handles screen performance in his slower, more sustained sequences. First, as we have seen, he seldom really sustains a scene for long, allowing it to "collapse" into ellipses even when the time and space of the overall action remains stable. He has the actors slide, often quickly, from performing one aspect of their personae to others. Here, from fifties movie star/B-film tough guy to girl and boy, the shifts form an alternation; then Godard breaks down these personae into disembodied voices/fixed graphic images. What is perhaps most remarkable about all this is that Godard dispenses with the interval between the moments, refusing the possibility of a synthesis of them for the characters. Indeed, the final resolution in the section of the sequence we have examined is the collapse of Michel into a sort of still portrait of a boyish Belmondo, a process that reverses a whole series of shots of Seberg/Patricia that connects her to the Juliet of the poster. By eliminating the interval between moments, Godard foregrounds acting precisely as performance, playing off distinct screen "identities" and finally fragmenting the actor into voice and image that extinguishes the psychology of screen acting which Godard had discerned in the classical cinema. More than merely subordinating the "star actor" to the style of the director, presumably a task already accomplished fully by the construction of the montage earlier in *Breathless* and often assumed to serve the enrichment of "character" in contradistinction to "star," Godard successively subordinates acting itself to the play of its codes and components. The "textual" ones of film-historical screen characterizations (Michel and Patricia "play" at being stars) are de-authorized. Patricia melts into traditional portraiture; Michel only parodies the position of the mediator within the *découpage*. Then Godard dissolves the material conjunction of voice and image that subtends conventional film acting. Of course, none of the states in this progression is permanent, for the film is but an alternation within and across sequences, which is why the actors were said above to recompose their performances across interruptions.

In his subsequent films, particularly after *Vivre sa Vie* where Godard systematizes his use of the sequence shot to create tableaux,[10] the playacting aspects recede in importance, though of course without ever disappearing (See *Bande à Part, Alphaville, Made In USA*, for example). Concomitantly, there is a noticeable shift toward voice/image separations, a declamatory performance style (see *Le Mépris, Pierrot le Fou, La Chinoise*), though this too is already apparent in this bedroom sequence of *Breathless.*

## IV. NEVERS

While introducing her script of *Hiroshima, Mon Amour*, Marguerite Duras explains that the first sequence of the film should be understood to be "an operatic exchange."[11] It begins with dark shots of intertwined bodies cross-cut with a tour of Hiroshima and its war museum accompanied by a voice-over dialogue between a man and a woman. Whether this sequence resembles what Duras intended with her expression "operatic exchange," assuming that she meant a direct allusion to operatic conventions, Duras still points us in the right direction. The beginning is a duet for two performers in which language rises above the naturalist conventions of screen dialogue. The script possesses a density and rhythmic eccentricity that does suggest the operatic, and the performance powerfully exploits these aspects of Duras' writing. In opera, stylization in the duet is achieved through the musical transformation of language. In Duras' films, like *India Song* (1974), its equivalent is accomplished in a two-fold fashion. First, by severing actors' voices from the *mise-en-scène*, Duras places extraordinary emphasis on the highly literary texture of her dialogue. Second, she freezes their images in static tableaux with the result that the actors' voices accompany the action in a manner suggestive of operatic recitatives rather than conventional dramatic interaction of characters.

The performative stylization of Duras' cinema, which she initiated only some years after her single collaboration with Resnais, suggests, retroactively, that the separation of voice and image that marks the film's style so deeply has a significance not at all like Godard's at first apparently similar disassociation of these fundamental components of film acting. In *Breathless*, Godard breaks down acting into its material elements in order to put a distance between the characters of his fiction and the performers. He uses this fracture to open a space in which to inscribe an essay about the cultural sources of the characters: Patricia-as-Juliet, Michel-as-Bogart. And then he turns back. The actors recompose their performances (their presence and personae) across the alternations of his style. We generalized above that Godard seeks to foreground the idea of acting as playacting. Aside from the salient fact that Resnais' style is slower, more stately, than Godard's, the significance of Resnais' handling of acting in *Hiroshima, Mon Amour* is different from Godard's in *Breathless*. Resnais severs voice and image in order to construct complex, "literary" characters rather than to deconstruct conventional star-acting. If *Breathless* is the classic example of New Wave playacting, *Hiroshima, Mon Amour* is the key instance of a director revising conventions of screen acting in order to articulate characters in film that bear comparison to the literature of interiority, doubt, memory, and displacement in which Duras, as well as other of Resnais' scriptwriter collaborators, figure prominently and in which characterization is central to narrational systems.

In Resnais' earlier nonfiction films, like *Nuit et Brouillard* (1955), before his feature debut with *Hiroshima, Mon Amour*, he problematized the documentary mode by making voice-over an issue. Conventionally, the off-screen narrator has complete authority in nonfiction film to interpret the meaning of the images. Resnais called this into question by allowing the narrator to poeticize, ironize, even to doubt the status of his own discourse. The first sequence of *Hiroshima, Mon Amour* resumes these concerns in fiction form. What Duras calls "an operatic exchange" is a debate between two characters on questions of memory, knowledge, representation, and perception. It accompanies an image track composed in the register of documentary witness. A woman's voice insists that because she has seen these images, she has grasped the reality of the nuclear devastation that befell Hiroshima; a man's voice denies her claims. This debate and the images occupy two different spaces and times: the night in a hotel room, the bodies intertwined, and the poetic and insistent murmurings of the lovers; a complicated and varied construct—a pseudo-documentary—that tours Hiroshima past and present in the days (weeks, perhaps) prior to this night of lovemaking. As the segment develops, extending to the next morning, Resnais identifies the characters, the French actress (Emmanuelle Riva) who has come to Hiroshima to make an anti-nuclear war film, and the Japanese architect (Eiji Okada) who has become her lover. Although the first sequence is redolent of a serious parody of documentary filmmaking, the initial disassociation of voice and image is not something from which they must recover their characters' personae, as is the case with Seberg and Belmondo in *Breathless.* On the contrary, when Resnais' couple awake to the light of the next morning and they appear and talk on the screen just like any characters might in a classically made movie; the night's "operatic exchange" has enriched them as characters, given them a wealth of interiority that the rest of the film will plumb and explore.

In *Hiroshima, Mon Amour*, the disassociation of voice and image is crucial to the development of the film's drama. It occurs often, although never again so ambiguously as in this first segment of the film. It never signals the dispersion of the characters as such a gesture does in Godard. On the contrary, it expands their psychologies, opens new depths to the characters. Resnais complicates screen performance; his stylizations are not reductive or auto-critical or deconstructive at the level of film conventions. The starting point for Godard's semioclasmic handling of film acting and Resnais' subversion of the authority of the voice-over bear comparing, for both open toward a critique of film realism. However, each director develops the gesture differently and to a different end. In Resnais' films, the disjunctures of performative elements raise issues of a psychological (at times, ethical) kind, particularly in his collaborations with Jean Cayrol (*Nuit et Brouillard* and *Muriel*, 1963), Alain Robbe-Grillet (*L'Année Dernière à Marienbad*, 1961) and David Mercer (*Providence*, 1978). *Marienbad*, with its deployment of Resnais' meta-cinematic strategies—the film's hieratic tableaux recast aspects of silent film performance—shows that the director is no less interested in experiments with film acting than Godard. Nonetheless, with *Hiroshima, Mon Amour,* Resnais uses an authoritative naturalist actress, Riva, and builds a film around her intense performance that places the director squarely within the strong art-film tradition of the European cinema. In the late fifties and early sixties, Resnais' formal rigor surpasses the extent, daring, and control of others in the *nouvelle vague*. Yet, as a director of actors, Resnais circumvents the playacting aspects of the New Wave. Of all the French directors of this period, he is most the contemporary of Antonioni and Bergman; Riva's performance in *Hiroshima, Mon Amour* suggests comparisons with Ingrid Thulin (Bergman), Delphine Seyrig (*Marienbad* and *Muriel*), and Monica Vitti (Antonioni) in ways that Seberg's and Moreau's performances for Godard and Truffaut do not. Such comparisons suggest themselves within the understanding that in this group of otherwise diverse directors, the break from conventional star-acting subtends the construction of characters possessed of psychological complexity and density; in the case of Resnais, these characters arise from the director's preference for ambitious literary collaborators.

Acting in *Hiroshima, Mon Amour* can be broken down into four modes corresponding to four of the five types of sequence that make up the film. The first of these reproduces the classical style in its essentials. The second is the recitative, (named after Duras' suggestion of "operatic exchange"): Resnais uses the actors' voices as voice-overs, as in the opening passages and the many flashbacks of the film's second half, and the *découpage* is a complex of images from the past—the Riva's character's memories—and the present—her conversations with her Japanese lover. The third style is a subjectivizing long-take extreme close-up mode similar to that found in the films of Bergman and Antonioni. Appearing between the flashback segments and of varying lengths, these long-takes contain some of the most intense acting in the film. Resnais' fourth style of acting/shot construction is a silent pantomime that appears within the flashbacks, usually in very brief and elliptically arranged takes. In addition, *Hiroshima* has a fifth style, a sort of pseudo-documentary mode that, after the long opening sequence, is used for brief expository transitions such as the shift in locale from the Japanese man's home to the Tea House. In some passages, such as the demonstration sequence, Resnais mixes the classical mode and these "documentary" passages.

By way of illustration, two sections of the film will be examined. The first is the scene when the couple go to the architect's house during the afternoon following the demonstration. The second is the Tea Room flashback segment.

When the actress and her lover go to his home, Resnais reverses the progression of styles in *Hiroshima* that precede the sequences. As we noted above, the film begins with the lovers entwined. It moves then toward a classically constructed segment, the next morning, and then toward a loose pseudo-documentary style to register the anti-nuclear demonstration. On arriving at the architect's house, the film returns to the classical style. A medium master shot introduces the couple and then breaks down into a shot-counter-shot succession with eye-line matches and careful delineation of off-screen spaces. The dialogue, significantly, concerns the lovers' ordinary lives outside the events of the film. When they embrace, Resnais cuts to a close-up. The phone is ringing off-screen, the last ambient sound until the end of the scene, which now slips into a recitative.

This classical sequence is almost merely functional: it conveys the characters into position for what follows, removing them from a public sphere—the demonstration—into the sort of intimacy they had at the beginning of the film. However, these few shots have another significance, for it is important to see Riva's character here as a poised and beautiful French woman of a certain class, age, and intelligence. It is this nameless, public persona that Resnais and Duras will soon draw aside like a curtain when she descends into painful memory. (This contrast is a favored device in Duras' fiction, which often juxtaposes a somewhat stiff social milieu with the inner storms or melancholies of her characters.) Riva's poise is constituted by dress, lighting, her voice and posture, all sustained by camera movement and cutting which pulls the sequence toward the embrace with a series of exchanged looks that, in the manner of innumerable classic films, tactfully but inexorably overpowers the characters' dialogue. The embrace dissolves to a close-up of the two of them in bed as they begin a dialogue about the past. The language here is different—imagistic, slightly incantatory—from the previous sequence and gradually becomes more so as Resnais begins to cut in flashbacks, isolated shots at first, then, as Riva's voice becomes more musical and ruminative, longer passages. This recitative does not operate precisely like a documentary voice-over here; the actress hovers over the flashbacks, the texts do not exactly correspond to the images. Rather than demanding interpretation (as is the conventional position of such images), they are redundant, as if fragments of memory were being summoned by the words. The sequence is centered in the present; the woman has not yet begun her descent into her memories though they are starting to come to her. Her monologue gives a brief précis of her wartime romance with a German soldier in Nevers, the town where she was raised. Resnais does not parallel her words with a succession of narrative images. Rather, he depicts their trysts in a frequentative tense, a selection of shots showing the encounters in various locales and times. When the woman stops speaking, the architect delivers a speech in the same style as her soliloquy, saying that to know her past is to know her. Toward the end of this exchange, the camera is positioned behind her as she looks at him and demands he tell her why he wants her to speak of Nevers. When he answers, she replies sharply, "No, that's not the reason." Resnais zip-pans to her in extreme close-up and holds the shot in silence. The man tries two more explanations, which Resnais covers in two jump-cut close-ups, then returns to her in extreme close-up when he finishes speaking. She is silent, very serious, haloed by side-lighting.

Taken as a whole, the segment exemplifies the long-take extreme close-up style used between flashbacks: the shots are tightly framed "portraits" of the woman; the performance becomes very tense, as if the character were drawing material up from some emotional depth. It stands in harsh contrast to both the poised manner of the earlier dialogue section and to the ruminative, quite musical monologue of the flashbacks immediately preceding.

A dissolve follows and when it is complete, she is dressed, lying on the bed, relaxed, seen from a somewhat high angle. Ambient sound returns. She sits up, the camera pulls back to reveal that the shot is from his point of view. It is a deft and somewhat deceptive return to the classical style—with the camera and the space cued by the character—that ends the scene. She says she wants to leave.

This section of the film encapsulates the three crucial acting/film styles Resnais uses in the second half of *Hiroshima, Mon Amour*. The transitions from one to another are signalled by shifts in Duras' script, shifts that progress toward the subjectivity of the characters, finally to the disassociation of voice and image. There is a change in the viewer's reception of the Riva character here, from assured French woman to a pained soul of great seriousness. This change is doubled by a parallel treatment of the architect, who is gradually assuming the position as "witness" to the drama of her interiority.

Although Duras' script marks it off as Part IV, the Tea House sequence expands on the previous scene in the architect's house and is, in turn, extended by the several sequences moving to the end of the film, in which the couple grapple with the intimate knowledge they have shared. The segment is constructed almost entirely of sustained recitative accompanying the flashbacks.

The two of them are sitting at a table in a two-shot. The camera pans right and cuts to the first flashback of Nevers, a tracking shot (left) of the River Loire, as he says, "I can't picture Nevers." The brief tracking shot is interrupted by a close-up of her, left of screen, as she begins to speak at length. At first the words of her narration seem to be a bald recital of facts—about the river, the cellar where she was imprisoned after the liberation, and so on. Riva reads the lines very softly and musically, and the cutting and camera movements of the flashbacks are matched to her reading. She plays with a glass; he touches her face to encourage her to go on. In the flashbacks, which become a bit more frequent, the acting is extremely bare, as if she were not a subject inside her memories, as if this set of flashbacks are to be as enigmatic as those seen before. The camera is positioned, in the past, as if she were not a subject of her own story—it stands outside the spectacle. Then, on the sharply spoken lines, "You are dead … and … how is it possible to bear such pain?" the body of her German lover appears in a very brief flashback. In the present, she draws back from the table and relaxes, again speaking in a soft, ruminative tone, "The cellar is small." In a moment, however, she blocks her ears and the sounds of the Tea House vanish.

The real descent into memory begins. She starts the long narration of her imprisonment in the cellar; now, in the flashbacks, the camera is intimate with the spaces of her memories and Riva's performance, as both her younger self and grown woman in the present, takes on a grueling intensity. Shots of her bleeding hands in Nevers and other elliptically edited images of her ordeal make her narration almost tactile. In the present her eyes do not seem to see her Japanese lover, but he clutches her hands in close-up inserts.

At the end of this portion of Riva's recitation, Resnais cuts from Nevers to a pan that follows her hands and her manicured nails clicking on her glass, which she lifts and drinks from, the camera following with a tilt. The subsequence here establishes the basic alternation from past to present, from the intensity of memory to the comparative calm of the immediate moment. But it is more than a formal alternation, for it is accompanied by an ironic juxtaposition: the bleeding hands in the cellar and the manicured fingers of the woman in the present. The shot prefaces the theme of memory's loss, to which the scene soon turns.

Resnais introduces a close-up of the architect and he asks, "Do you scream?" In her reply, a long incantatory speech, she addresses him as if he were her lost wartime lover. Now he can be heard over the flashbacks (rather like the first sequence of the film), which resume their penetration of the past. Riva's reading now becomes steadily, though quietly, furious. There is no trace of pillow-talk murmuring in her voice. She bites into Duras' lines, which become so abrupt that they could almost be a shot list; the character has been fused to the images of the past. The flashback performances are extended into a cryptic pantomime repeating what she narrates, a matching of voice-over and images. A fresh source of tension is introduced into the sequence: the shots of action in the past are brief, while shots of stasis—the girl lying on her bed—are held quite long. The silence that separates the present and past is unbearable: her remembered past-self is adamantly inarticulate. The woman breaks off.

The architect moves back from her and offers her the glass, pressing her to continue, describing the cellar himself. She continues, and the flashback shows her in a tight close-up biting on the cellar walls and she says, "Sometimes a cat comes and looks . . ."; there are three extreme close-ups, her eyes and the cat's. He asks how long she was there. "Eternity," she replies, as the third extreme close-up of her eyes ends (figs. 5.14–5.15).

Resnais then cuts suddenly to a long shot from another corner of the Tea House. It is a deep-focus composition, the couple is visible in one corner of the frame. A close-up shows a record coming down in a jukebox; ambient sound resumes (figs. 5.16–5.17). Resnais then returns to the couple, medium close-up. She is screen-left, just finishing her drink; he is to the right, with his back partly turned to the camera. The moment is intentionally a *caesura*. He pours another drink, the jukebox playing a ridiculous French "bistro tune." Then, suddenly, she explodes with fury, "Oh, how young I was once." She pounds her fists on the table—once—and throws herself back from the table in anguish (fig. 5.18). The camera pans and tracks to reframe, pushing him almost completely out of view. Then, calmly, she continues.

The recitative quickly achieves a new plateau of intensity, centered now by a single sound—a scream, from the past—as a flashback shows her coming down some stairs in an exterior. It is the eidetic image of herself—in the reverse angle of her shattering gaze toward her lover—shot and dying, around which the whole of her memory revolves. But Resnais and Duras take some time in identifying the significance of this shot and of the scream. Resnais cuts to the aftermath—the public shaving of the girl's head by the liberated townspeople, the last weeks of her imprisonment (fig. 5.19). She tells, in close-up detail, her memories of the passage of time and her struggle to remember, and her failure. Riva recites the words in a rhythmic incantation that is immensely sad. As she continues, the flashbacks grow longer and clearer, becoming an intelligible narrative of their own for the first time, as she tells about her return from the madness of her grief. Finally cutting back to the present, the camera shows the couple leaning closely toward each other.

Then, she breaks off with, "It's horrible. I'm beginning to remember you less clearly." She is shaking, extremely distraught, reliving now not the memory of her pain and suffering but the memory of how she emerged from the "eternity" by forgetting her great love. He makes her drink. She gulps fiercely and says, "I'm beginning to forget you.... [then to the Japanese] More." He holds the glass for her to drink again (fig. 5.20). When she finishes, she moves back into the shadow and her face becomes invisible. Resnais has taken this exchange in a single long take and Riva performs the passage with a terrible mixture of authority, carried by her extraordinary voice and face, and awkwardness, the way she drinks almost convulsively from the glass he holds for her. It is a terrible moment in which the actor has to be in the past and the present at the same time, addressing her dead lover while nearly being nursed by the man across the table. Her voice and her image, her actual presence and her inner feeling, even inner speech, are being pulled to the breaking point. Once she retreats into the shadows, Riva almost vanishes—her voice alone carries the next subsequence. A few shots fit together the tale of the lovers' last embrace as he dies in her arms; these are the shots the flashbacks have avoided and around which her speech and the images have circulated. They are the woman's darkest and most precious memories, the ones she is terrified of losing, perhaps of having lost already. In this passage, Riva uses a higher, thinner voice to read Duras' almost viciously objective rendering of the incident, until the last lines, which rise up in what is almost a wail: "All I could find between his body and mine were obvious similarities, do you understand?" Then screaming, "He was my first love...." She

Fig. 5.14

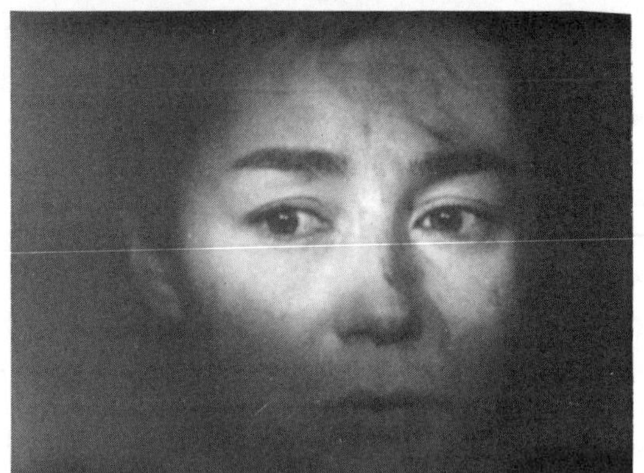

Fig. 5.15

Fig. 5.16

Fig. 5.17

Fig. 5.18

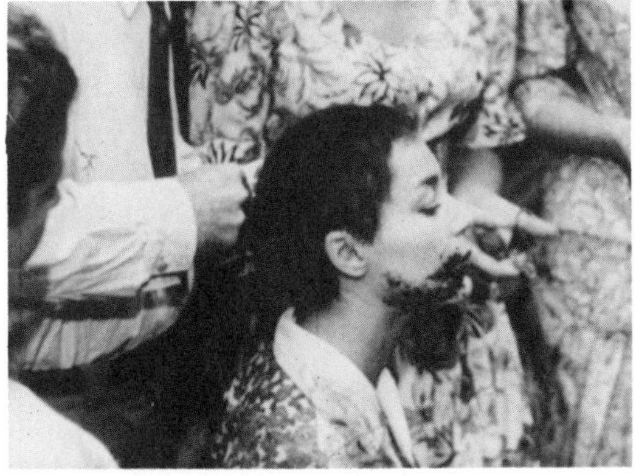

Fig. 5.19

emerges from the shadow. Her Japanese lover slaps her sharply (fig. 5.21), which is followed by a rapid montage of shocked faces around the Tea Room. Ambient sound returns again and Resnais cuts to a high-angle medium shot as she continues, her voice returning to normal; the flashbacks are an anticlimax dealing with how she finally left the cellar, took her parents' money, and went to Paris. The camera returns to its rather distanced rendering of these events. Another jukebox record comes on and she concludes. She takes a drink and grows very calm and puts her head on the table, resting it on his arm (fig. 5.22).

The conversation continues, but already prepares us for the next long sequence at the hotel as Resnais slowly draws the scene back toward the classical style.

This sequence is one of the most extraordinary in the cinema of the *nouvelle vague*, certainly in regard to its performance, which contains within its textures the realization of the characterological project attributed to the New Wave by many of its sympathetic critics. What is so fascinating about the passage is that it is almost entirely a recitation by Riva, sitting on a chair at a table. Yet, in intense collaboration with Resnais' montage, which brings her voice in and out of relation with her image, the passage brings us into astonishing emotional contact with the character. Nonetheless, there is nothing about this sequence that smacks of the melodramatic devices of conventional star-acting—the presence and authority of the actor has been diminished by the simplicity of the *mise-en-scène* and, indeed, Resnais inverts the customary relationship between voice and flashback. The woman is pulled toward her memories; she does not conjure them from her words. And she becomes precisely a Durasian "character" through the decorum that Resnais and Riva have achieved, in a way that not even Resnais would ever again accomplish.

## NOTES

1. James Monaco, "Coming of Age: Jean-Pierre Léaud," *Take One*, vol. 5. no. 4, (October 1976), pp. 16–20. Reprinted in James Monaco, *Celebrity, The*

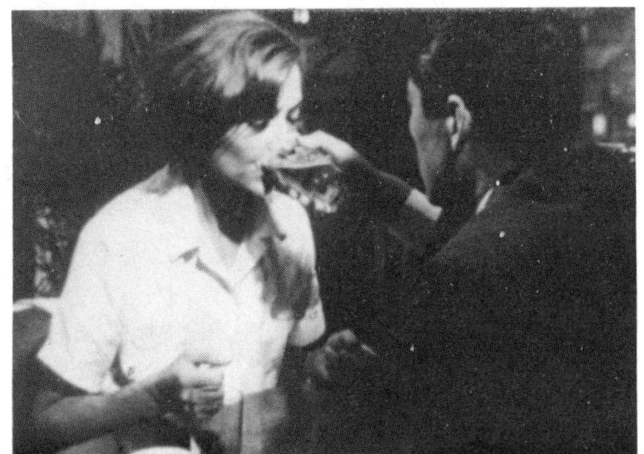

Fig. 5.20

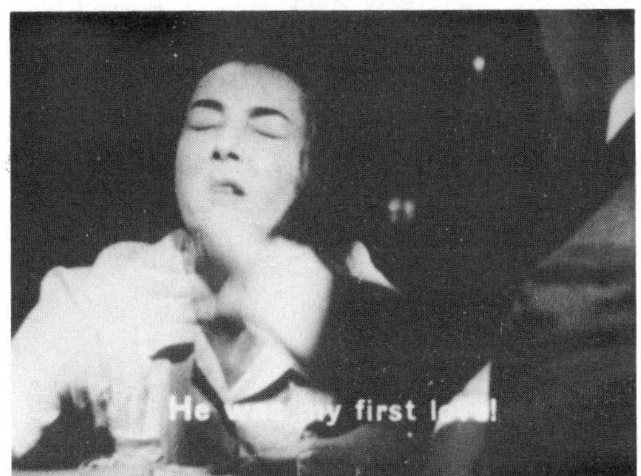


Fig. 5.21

Fig. 5.22

*Media as Image Makers* (NY: Dell, 1978), pp. 134–143. Citations here from *Celebrity*.

2. Monaco, p. 143.
3. See Stanley Cavell, *The World Viewed: Reflections on the Ontology of Film*, enlarged edition (Cambridge: Harvard University Press, 1979), pp. 41–55, for a discussion of screen personae that develops this widely held notion.
4. Monaco, p. 143.
5. James Monaco, *The New Wave: Truffaut, Godard, Chabrol, Rohmer* (NY:Oxford University Press, 1976), pp. 29 ff.
6. See Monaco, *The New Wave, passim* and Annette Insdorf, *Francois Truffaut* (NY:William Morrow, 1979), *passim*. Insdorf entitles two successive chapters, "The Hitchcockian Strain" and "The Renoirian Vision."
7. Jean-Luc Godard, *Godard on Godard*, edited by Jean Narboni and Tom Milne (London:Secker and Warburg, 1972), pp. 27–30.
8. See David Thomson, "At the Acme Book Shop," *Sight and Sound*, vol. 50, no. 2, (Spring 1981), pp. 112–125 for an analysis of such "star mediation."
9. See Marie-Claire Ropars-Wuilleumier, "The Graphic in Filmic Writing: *A Bout De Souffle* or, the Erratic Alphabet," *Enclitic*, vol. 5, no. 2 and vol. 6, no. 1, (Spring 1982), pp. 147–161, for a full discussion of this imagery in the film.
10. See Brian Henderson, *A Critique of Film Theory* (NY:E.P. Dutton, 1980), pp. 62–81, for a discussion of Godard's later long-take style.
11. Marguerite Duras, *Hiroshima, Mon Amour* (NY:Grove Press, 1961), p. 9.

# 6. THE LIVES OF PERFORMERS: The Actress As Signifier in the Cinema

Lucy Fischer

> Of all the arts that mankind has invented to clothe its concept of reality and to ornament its leisure moments, none is more suited to the genius of the female of the species than that of theater.—Rosamond Gilder, *Enter the Actress.*[1]

## I. INTRODUCTION

OVER THE PAST DECADE OF FEMINIST film criticism, studies have been written that analyze the *persona* of notable actresses: critics have discussed the screen character of Mae West, arguing for or against her liberating aspects; writers have examined the image of Bette Davis, noting her incarnation of a strong woman model; scholars have also investigated the figure of Marlene Dietrich, citing her highly ambiguous sexuality. During that same period, articles have appeared that study the fictional roles assigned to women in film: be they positive or negative, be they prostitute, lawyer, or mother.

What we have not seen, however, is these two concerns come *together*: the question of the actress in film and the role she embodies. Where these issues quite naturally collide is in films that depict the life of a fictional actress, raising the question of woman and performance, simultaneously, on two levels. In *Stage Fright*, for example, the entertainer character, Charlotte Inwood, is played by the real actress Marlene Dietrich; while in *Sunset Boulevard*, the movie-queen figure, Norma Desmond, is played by the real star, Gloria Swanson. Perhaps the only critic to underscore the import of this genre has been Molly Haskell, although she notes it only in passing. In *From Reverence to Rape*, she writes:

> The actress—whether as literal thespian…or as a symbol for the role-playing woman—is a key female figure throughout film history… In one sense the actress merely extends the role-playing dimension of women, emphasizing what she already is.[2]

Haskell's observation that the actress role has been a "key female figure throughout film history" is certainly confirmed by a brief listing of the films in question, all of which portray fictional performers. In the American cinema alone one thinks of *Dangerous* (1935), *The Velvet Touch* (1948), *All About Eve* (1950), *Torch Song* (1953), *The Barefoot Contessa* (1954), *Indiscreet* (1958), *Inside Daisy Clover* (1965), to name but a few. Interestingly, one cannot come up with a comparable list of films about the actor. In a chapter of *Cinema and Sentiment* concerning the performer character in film, Charles Affron mentions only George Cukor's *A Double Life*, starring Ronald Colman.[3] While other films on the topic do exist (*The Entertainer*, 1960/1975, *The Dresser*, 1983), they fail to represent as impressive a subgenre as that of the actress.

This relative imbalance may signify something important. If the actress has appeared as fictional film role more frequently than the actor, what does that mean? Why has she proven a "key figure"? What might her privileged position tell us about woman and performance, or about the positioning of woman in traditional culture? How does the actress emphasize what woman "already is"?

To pursue these questions, we will first examine the issue of female "theatricality" and then trace its manifestation in two relevant works: Ingmar Bergman's *Persona* (1966) and Mai Zetterling's *The Girls* (1968).

## II. TWO-FACED WOMAN

On the topic of female "theatricality," Molly Haskell's reference to woman's role-playing dimension is clearly central. Critics like Jean Duvignaud in *Spectacle et société* have indicated how the lives of all human beings participate in the dramatic. As he writes:

> Notre existence à nous, disons celle de la culture, est une représentation jouée, des instincts et des pulsions. La sexualité, la mort, l'échange économique ou esthétique, le travail, tout est manifeste, tout est joué. L'homme est la seule espèce dramatique....[4]

But feminist criticism has argued that women, more selectively than men, have been forced to role-play in society. Cast as the "Other" to the male norm, they have been urged to embody a wide range of *dramatis personae*: from earth mother to temptress, from madonna to whore. As Simone de Beauvoir has pointed out, these roles are frequently incompatible, placing the woman who seeks to fulfill them in a hopeless double bind.[5] In particular, women have been encouraged to dissemble for their man—to appear submissive (though they may be strong), to seem dumb (though they may be intelligent)—all to create a safe and appealing image. Magazines like *Cosmopolitan* offer women scenarios for catching or keeping a lover; books like *How to Find Another Husband by Someone Who Did* provide game plans for landing a man; and movies like *How to Marry a Millionaire* (1953) picture woman's role in romance as a mode of theatrical deception.

*Two-Faced Woman* (1941)—though not a film about an actress—highlights the pressure placed on women to role-play for their man. Starring Greta Garbo, it tells the story of a ski instructor, Karin, who meets a vacationing magazine publisher, Blake (Melvyn Douglas), when he hires her for ski lessons. Blake is attracted to her wholesome appearance and way of life, and when they are stranded together in a snowbank overnight, they fall in love and elope. We learn that Blake has promised to reform his mad, workaholic way of life. When he does not appear in his New York office, two assistants come to find him and convince him to return to the magazine world. When he orders Karin to go to the city with him, she refuses, being a highly independent woman. He leaves, and through a montage of telegrams, we learn that he keeps postponing his return to the ski lodge and has taken up with an old flame who works in the theater. Karin decides to fight for her man and, abandoning her earthy looks, gets dolled up for a trip to New York. When she arrives at a theater (where Blake's secretary has said he will be), she sees him with his old lover and slinks off, depressed and unnoticed, determined to return home. On her way from the theater, she encounters one of Blake's assistants whom she had met at the lodge. He addresses her as Karin, but to cover herself, she pretends to be Katrin, Karin's imaginary twin sister. She behaves in a highly sophisticated, vampish manner to convince him that she is someone else, but this only attracts him, and he asks her out for dinner. At the restaurant, she encounters Blake and continues the deception. Though he suspects some ruse and seems aware of her "trick," it is clear that he falls in love with this second Karin—the one who is consonant with the traditional male ideal. The film ends with Blake confronting his new wife with her duplicity, but her "split personality" is never resolved. He calls her, lovingly: "Karin/Katrin."

What this film reveals is the need for all women to be "two-faced," to cover their true selves with a theatrical mask. The real Karin is never as appealing to Blake as the role of Katrin that she plays, a persona embodying male desire. If this notion of female "theatricality" surfaces in films that have nothing to do with the drama, it will be even more intriguing to trace its appearance in those that do. In *The Velvet Touch,* Rosalind Russell plays a musical comedy star who has worked throughout her career with a domineering male impressario who is also her lover. In the opening scene she tells him that she will terminate their association in order to appear in a serious drama, *Hedda Gabler*. She also reveals that she is involved with another man. The producer is enraged and threatens to sully her reputation. In the heat of the moment, she strikes him with a statuette and kills him. Rather than report the crime, she flees. During the rest of the film we see her "act" the role of an innocent bystander to both her suitor and a policeman. When it becomes apparent that blame for the crime will be placed on another woman, she is tortured with guilt. In the film's final sequence, she is playing the last scene of *Hedda Gabler* and we fear that she, like the drama's heroine, will commit suicide. When the curtain rises for the actor's call, she is still alive, but she sends a confessional note to the police investigator.

What is most interesting about *The Velvet Touch* is its emphasis on the actress' need to role-play off the stage. As a woman, her career has been at the mercy of a powerful man who has exacted a sexual, as well as professional price for his support. When she vows to end that relationship, he threatens to ruin her with some unstated innuendo. Though she has killed him by accident, she feels unable to reveal her situation. Here her role as Hedda Gabler seems significant, since both women are independent and unable to play the prescribed societal role.

Other films about actresses display a similar fascination with extra-theatrical role-playing. In *Stage Fright*, Marlene Dietrich plays a performer who has feigned romantic interest in a man to tempt him to murder her husband. When he does, he tries to pin the blame on her, then calls upon another actress, Eve Gill (Jane Wyman), for help. Since Eve is in love with the man, she assists him and, in order to discern the truth, enacts many roles off-stage, including a reporter and a maid. Similarly, *Indiscreet* finds Ingrid Bergman as an actress who has fallen in love with a businessman (Cary Grant) who claims that he is married. Being an unconventional woman, she completely accepts the situation and is content with their affair. When she learns, however, that the man is a bachelor (who has lied to her to avoid marital pressure), she is furious. In retaliation, she plans and enacts a dramatic scenario for making him jealous. *Indiscreet*, once more, portrays the actress role-playing off-stage, and her need to dissemble is tied to her relationship with a man. Ironically, in *Indiscreet* the actress' impulse to deceive is caused by her lover's mistaken assumption that she will demand to play the role of wife.

Although this need for woman to role-play in society may, in part, explain the popularity of the actress figure in the cinema, it does not address the entire issue. There would seem to be deeper reasons for her favored position, and these lead back to the history of western theater. In *Enter the Actress*, Rosamond Gilder discusses the common belief that the first performers were religious leaders enacting sacred rituals. And, as she points out, in most cultures such figures were originally women. She writes:

> In Phrigia she was called Cybele, Great Mother of the Gods; in Babylonia and Phoenicia, Ishtar and Ashtoreth; in Egypt, they hailed her as Isis, Queen of Heaven; but wherever she appeared, she was the prototype of that first actress-priest of the primitive grove, and her attributes remained the same—the symbols of fertility—the child who dies to be reborn and the band of attendant women dancing the drama of birth and death and resurrection.[6]

As Gilder notes, however, eventually the cult of the mother was replaced by that of the son, and with it came the banishment of women from primary roles in religious ritual. Gilder sees the same process at work in the exclusion of women from ancient drama, an exile that lasted some two thousand years. As she observes, during this period some of the greatest theatrical roles depicted women, but they were enacted by men. As she writes:

> From the technical point of view, the fact that women were not allowed to act on the Athenian stage would present little difficulty to the poet or choregua superintending the production of a play. All the actors wore masks and flowing robes which entirely covered them.... The voice alone could betray the fact that Antigone, Electra or Clytemnestra was being portrayed by a man, and this particular difficulty was overcome by the great care given to the training of the actors, for in the Greek theatre, flexibility, power and beauty of a voice was the actor's greatest glory.[7]

When women eventually returned to performance, their position was far below that of sacred priestess. As Gilder notes, "When ... the nobler aspects of the theater were closed to her, [the actress] came in ... by the Devil's way."[8] Thus, during the Roman era, female mimes performed during the interludes of the drama or in the street or marketplace. According to Gilder, such actresses were officially classed as prostitutes and were legally prohibited from marrying Roman citizens. Beyond that, the audience had "the right on certain days, to force the actress to strip themselves naked on the stage."[9]

What this review of theater history reveals is that (1) woman's original sacred position in the drama was deposed through exclusion or association with prostitution, and that (2) the absence of women in the theater (from the Classical period until the Restoration) was compensated for by acts of female impersonation. At the center of this issue would seem to be female sexuality: woman's original role of actress/priestess was dependent on her powers of fertility; her fallen position of actress/harlot was tied to her promiscuity. Thus, within the history of the drama, female sexuality would be entirely banished or else degraded.

The modern fascination with woman as actress may reveal ancient attitudes and ambivalences toward that role. Consider the fact, for example, that many female stars of the Hollywood classical cinema have been noted for their androgyny: Marlene Dietrich, Katharine Hepburn, Greta Garbo, Joan Crawford, to name a few. According to certain feminist critics, their masculinity represents a fetishization of the female body, making it less awesome to the male spectator.[10] But no critic, to my knowledge, has linked the aura of masculinity to the ancient practice of male cross-dressing in the theater, yet another technique for dispelling the threat of the female. Thus, the male discomfort with the actress figure may live on in a more subtle fashion. In this regard, I am reminded of Kenneth Tynan's remarks on Greta Garbo. He writes:

> I half-believed, until I met her, the old hilarious slander which whispered that she was a brilliant Swedish female impersonator who kept up the pretence too long; behind the dark glasses, it was hinted, beneath the wild brown hair, there lurked the features of a proud Scandinavian diplomat, now proclaiming their masculinity so stridently that exposure to cameras was out of the question.

Tynan eventually assures us that, upon meeting Garbo, "this idle fabrication was demolished" and that "this was a girl, all right." He closes by explaining that it was "an indication of the mystery which surrounds [Garbo] that [he] felt pleased even to have ascertained her sex."

On another note, Leo Braudy, in *The World in a Frame*, sees the contemporary obsession with the lurid sex lives of Hollywood stars as linked to the ancient association between drama and prostitution. But he does not seem to realize that this connection has obtained only for women. He writes:

> Gossip about the fact that film actors and actresses may have been prostitutes or may have performed some kind of sexual acts to get their jobs has often been used as a way of minimizing them.... But such charges show an ignorance of stage history. Many great stage actresses in the Restoration, when women were first allowed onto the English stage, often kept up their practice as prostitutes.... There is an aesthetic continuity between all the professions that display the body. Prostitution like acting emphasizes individual pleasure through a kind of benevolent deception, a "trick."[12]

Why, however, if all acting foregrounds the body, was it only the female who was traditionally associated with prostitution?

But perhaps there are even more deep-seated connections between women and acting that explain the blending of the actress with her sexuality. Rosamond Gilder points to one when she traces the actress' appearance back to Genesis. She writes:

> Ever since Eve invented costume, and coached by the serpent, enacted that little comedy by which she persuaded Adam that the bitter apple of knowledge was sweet and comforting, there has been something satanic in the very nature of the theater.[13]

In her characterization of Eve as actress and her linkage of Eve's "performance" to the original sin, Gilder reiterates ancient notions of woman as dangerous dissembler. As we well know, Eve's punishment will be a biological one—the menstrual cycle and the pangs of childbirth—thus demonstrating once more the connection between acting and female sexuality.

But beyond this biblical association of women and theatricality, there may be other, more psychological reasons for this characterization of the female sex—and here I am offering pure speculation. As many literary and film critics have shown, the root of classical narrative is in the male Oedipal situation, and countless analyses of fictional works have revealed an Oedipal trajectory.[14] At the heart of this psychological conflict is both the infant boy's desire to cast the mother as his sexual partner, and his *méprise* that she will accept that role. After all, doesn't she shower him with love and affection? Doesn't she tend to all his bodily needs? Doesn't she create for him a world of sensual pleasure linked to her very own body? When this fantasy is denied (at the entrance to the Symbolic stage), is it not possible that the son misconstrues his mother's prior behavior as a deceptive "act"? Perhaps this explains some of the male hostility to women that has been part of men's development in traditional society. Perhaps, too, this explains the tendency of men to see woman as archetypal actress.

## III. *PERSONA*: MOMMIE DEAREST

There is no film that so confirms this speculation on the formulation of woman as actress as Ingmar Bergman's *Persona*. On a narrative level, it is the story of an encounter between Elizabeth Vogler (Liv Ullmann), an actress experiencing a nervous breakdown, and Sister Alma (Bibi Andersson), a nurse who has been assigned to care for her at a seaside home. Since Elizabeth's primary "symptom" is her refusal to speak, Alma passes time by talking to her in lengthy monologues, confessing private details of her life. Elizabeth responds with mute but supportive silence, and Alma imagines that they are friends. One day, while taking Elizabeth's mail to the post office, Alma notices an unsealed letter and succumbs to the temptation to read it. She finds to her dismay that Elizabeth has been corresponding with her husband about Alma's secrets, boasting that it has been fun to "study" her. Alma returns home, enraged, and without telling Elizabeth why, becomes extremely hostile to her. At this point, the narrative (as realistic story) breaks down. What transpires is a series of confrontations between the women that seem to exist at a purely psychic level, that may or may not have "happened."

But to analyze *Persona* one must begin before the emergence of the narrative, for it is a work that opens with an abstract prologue. After a group of images depicting an arc lamp illuminated and a film projector set in motion, we see a montage of shots of such things as: a spider, a bloody sheep's head, a crucified hand, a winter forest, and silent movie footage. Eventually, our attention is directed to the figure of a young boy, who seems to be lying on a morgue slab or hospital bed. He sits up, puts on glasses, reads a bit, and then, facing us, touches what seems to be the surface of the screen. The shot then changes to a reverse angle (from behind him), and we see that he is caressing huge photographs of women's faces that dissolve into one another. It is here that we first see the title of the film: *Persona*.

In an interview about the work, Bergman has stated that he "made believe [he] was a little boy who'd died, yet who wasn't allowed to be really dead...." One would have to look far and wide in the history of cinema to find a better symbol of the Oedipal perspective on the art than this one of a little boy (identified with the male director) who quizzically caresses the image of women on the film screen/mindscreen. But the Oedipal thrust of *Persona* goes far beyond the prologue and works its way into the narrative itself. On one level, the story told in *Persona* can be viewed as a universal human drama, and it has been seen this way by many critics. Susan Sontag, for instance, reads it as enacting a primal struggle of human existence. She writes:

> If the maintenance of personality requires the safeguarding of the integrity of masks, and the truth about a person is always the cracking of the mask, then the truth about life as a whole is the shattering of the total facade behind which lies an absolute cruelty.[15]

Although this theme of the duplicity of all human life is certainly existent in *Persona*, it must be remembered that Bergman has chosen to dramatize it in a film exclusively about women. So the question arises: are there themes in *Persona* that selectively stress the inauthenticity of the female? A close look at the narrative will conclude the affirmative: the mental breakdowns of both women seem tied to their sexuality and to their romantic relations with men.

Let us first examine the character of Elizabeth Vogler, since she is the professional actress and the one, ostensibly, who is disturbed. Because *Persona* is not a conventional film, we are denied the usual exposition of Elizabeth's problems, but over the course of the film a pattern nonetheless emerges. We are told that she first fell silent during a performance of the Greek tragedy *Electra*. And, while still in the hospital, we see her upset by a letter from her husband and watch her tear up a photograph of her son. Already the matricidal theme of *Electra*—the torn image of her child, her anxiety about her husband—makes us suspect that she is uncomfortable with her maternal and marital roles.

But the primary revelation about Elizabeth comes later in the film, after her relationship with Nurse Alma has entirely deteriorated. Alma finds (or imagines that she finds) Elizabeth hiding the snapshot of her son in her hand. She asks Elizabeth what she is concealing and then says that they must talk about it. What follows is a speech by Alma about Elizabeth. It is rendered in a voice-over monologue as the camera focuses on images of the actress.[16]

Alma begins by describing how Elizabeth made the decision to have a child, making clear that it was tied to her profession as an actress:

> One evening at a party. It was late and pretty noisy. Sometime in the early morning someone said, "Elizabeth Vogler has practically everything she needs as a woman and an artist." "And what's missing?" [you] asked. "You're not motherly." [You] laughed because [you] thought the whole idea was ridiculous. But after a while [you] found yourself thinking about it every now and again. [You] got more and more worried and then [you] let [your] husband give you a child. You wanted to be a mother. So Elizabeth Vogler, the actress, got pregnant.

Alma then goes on to recount how Elizabeth soon grew severely apprehensive about her pregnancy, though she continued to play the role of the radiant madonna:

> When [you] realized [you] couldn't change your mind, [you] got frightened. Didn't you?—frightened of the responsibility, frightened of drifting away from the theater, frightened of dying, fright-

> ened of your body swelling up. But the whole time [you] played the part of a happy young expectant mother. And everyone said: "Isn't she beautiful now she's pregnant. She's never been so beautiful."

Finally, Alma relates how Elizabeth's doubts about pregnancy grew into loathing and violence, and how she succumbed to murderous impulses:

> In the meantime you tried several times by yourself to abort. And you failed. In the end you went to a doctor. He realized it was no longer possible. When [you] saw there was no way out, [you] became ill and began to hate the baby and wished for it to be stillborn. It was a long and difficult delivery, [you] were in agony for days. In the end, the baby was pulled out by forceps. Elizabeth Vogler looked with disgust and terror at her crippled, piping baby. Left alone with her first born she kept hoping and muttering: "Can't you die now, can't you die." And [you] thought what it would be like to kill the baby, smother it under the pillow, as if by accident, or crack its head against the radiator. But he survived.

Alma concludes her monologue by describing Elizabeth's hostile feelings toward her son after his unwanted birth:

> The child survived as if to spite [you] and [you] were forced to hold this repulsive shaking creature to your breasts, which ached and pained from the milk which refused to come.... Finally the boy was taken care of by a nurse ... and Elizabeth Vogler was allowed to get up from her sick-bed and return to the theater. But the suffering was not over. The little boy had an incredible, violent love for his mother. [You] protect [yourself] ... because [you] know [you] cannot repay it ... [you're] cold and indifferent, and he looks at [you] and loves [you] and is so soft [you] want to hit him, because he won't leave you alone. [You] find him disgusting with his thick mouth and ugly body and wet appealing eyes.

What this text makes clear is an association between Elizabeth's breakdown and her failure to fulfill the maternal role. Beyond that, it seems to mark as the site of authenticity in woman the reproductive function. Surely, if the crisis had occurred to a man, it would have been about something different: we think of Dr.

Borg's career concerns in Bergman's *Wild Strawberries* (1957) or of the Knight's religious doubts in *The Seventh Seal* (1956).

But the text of this confrontation also makes clear the association of woman/actress with the maternal role. Alma accuses Elizabeth of playing the part of the glowing pregnant woman, even though she hates her unborn child. The monologue also voices the Oedipal complaint of the unloved son, who continues to adore his mother despite her rejection of him. What this emphasis on the son accomplishes is to urge us to see retroactively the boy of the film's prologue as a surrogate for Elizabeth's child. It would seem to be he that caresses the images of his mother, trying to possess or fathom them. It is interesting that as Alma intones her monologue, we see ever-larger close-ups of Elizabeth's face—until they reach the proportion they assume in the prologue, when the boy tried to grasp them.

Not only must Elizabeth fake her maternal role, she must also feign the sexual duties of a wife—further evidence of her need to perform off-stage. Later in the sequence, Alma is surprised by a visit from Mr. Vogler, who is apparently blind and approaches the nurse as though she were his wife. Alma enacts the role of Elizabeth for him, with the actress looking on. When the couple goes into the bedroom to make love, Mr. Vogler asks: "Do you like being with me? Is it good with me?" At first, Alma responds that he is a "wonderful lover," but then she shouts: "Give me something to stupefy my senses, or beat me to death, kill me, it's a shame, a dishonour, it's all counterfeit, a lie."[17] Thus, she reveals that her sex life has been a sham, similar to a prostitute's "trick."

Clearly, we cannot regard *Persona* as a realistic drama that creates fully rounded characters. Nonetheless, it is significant that the sketchy "motivations" Bergman provides for his abstract personae so completely conforms to the stereotype of woman as archetypal actress. Again, in *Persona*, the actress/woman must role-play in life. Again, her status as performer is tied to her fertility and to her sexual relations with men.

That Bergman intends this picture of woman/actress to hold for all women is clear from his portrayal of the other character in the film: Nurse Alma. Though, on a diegetic level, she is not an actress like Elizabeth Vogler, she is shown nonetheless to dissemble. Once more her theatricality will center on her maternal function and on her sexual encounters with men.

In the beginning of the film Alma views herself as a well-adjusted woman who knows what she wants, personally and professionally. As she goes to sleep one night in the hospital, she tells herself:

> I'll marry Karl-Henrik and we'll have a couple of kids that I'll bring up. That's all decided, it's in me somewhere. I don't have to work things out at all, how they're going to be. That makes you feel very safe. And I'm doing a job I like. That's a good thing too—only in a different way. I wonder what's really wrong with Mrs. Vogler.[18]

Thus, she sees herself in opposition to the actress—and, for the time being, so do we.

As the narrative progresses, however, and Alma begins to confess more about herself, her life begins to seem less ordered and coherent. She reveals that for years she was involved with a married man, and that, although she will marry Karl-Henrik, "You only love once." She also tells Elizabeth about an orgy that she experienced with a girlfriend and some young boys. Though she never told Karl-Henrik abut it, sex with him has never again been as good as on the night of the debauch. Finally, she tells Elizabeth that she became pregnant from the orgy and had an abortion. She is clearly tortured with guilt, and in recounting the incident she breaks down in sobs.

Evidently, she has been as much an actress as Elizabeth. Though she imagines her life in order, she clearly has severe doubts. Significantly, her concerns are identical to those of Elizabeth: she questions her maternal impulse and her ability to love a man. This sense of the two women as co-equal, as doubles, is made most explicit in the sequence of the film in which Alma describes Elizabeth's experience of maternity. In the original screenplay, Alma keeps interchanging the pronouns "you" and "I" in addressing Elizabeth, making it clear that she confuses herself with the actress. In the film that verbal slippage is eliminated, but Alma's monologue about Elizabeth is repeated, the second time presenting images of Alma on the screen. Clearly, Bergman sees this taint of inauthenticity as applicable to both figures. But this charge seems to go beyond them, to envision all women as actresses in their maternal and sexual roles. The film ends with an abstract epilogue that mirrors the opening sequence. Just before the arc lamp dies out, a boy is seen, once more, to caress the facial images of Alma/Elizabeth projected on a screen. Beyond simply representing the Oedipal perspective on narrative, which *Persona* so clearly articulates, this final trope is suggestive of something else more relevant and more profound. In his essay, "The Apparatus," Jean-Louis Baudry examines the inherent ideological implications of the cinema machine. Through a discussion of Freud and his use of optical metaphors for the unconscious, Baudry concludes that, for the spectator, film viewing is analogous to dreaming. Baudry then reminds us that Freud saw the oneiric state as harkening back to an earlier experience.

> Sleep, he tells us, from a somatic viewpoint, is a revivescence of one's stay in the body of the mother, certain conditions which it recreates: the rest position, warmth and isolation which protects him from excitement. This makes possible a first kind of regression in the development of the self back to a primitive narcissism....[19]

Thus, if the cinema is like a dream—and dreaming is reminiscent of the womb state—then the film-viewing experience may give us pleasure through its association with the mother. Baudry goes even further in this comparison by discussing Betram Lewin's notion of the dream-screen:

> According to Lewin's hypothesis, the dreamscreen is the dream's hallucinatory representation of the mother's breast on which the child use to fall asleep after nursing.[20]

Thus, the cinema apparatus may be likened to the mother not only by its replication of a dream state, but by its presentation of a screen for imagery, one like the maternal breast on which the dozing infant projects its fantasies.

With this in mind, *Persona's* figure of the boy at the screen becomes even more resonant and symbolic. For in this film—which on a dramatic level sees woman as mother, and mother as quintessential actress—Bergman presents us with an image that not only literalizes the Oedipal perspective of the narrative, but also associates woman's maternal body with the cinematic apparatus itself.

## IV. *THE GIRLS*: THE ACTRESS AS ACTIVIST

Having analyzed *Persona* for its patriarchal view of woman as actress, it is useful to compare it to another film on the same subject: *The Girls*, directed by Mai Zetterling. By placing the works in such a diptych frame, it is possible to foreground their opposing assumptions about women. There are additional reasons why the films can be easily paired. Both were made in Sweden in the late 1960s and are, essentially, modernist works that dispense with realistic narrative to present an interior world where fantasy and reality blend. And both films cast the actress Bibi Andersson in leading roles, which creates an even greater symmetry.

On a dramatic level, *The Girls* concerns a troupe of touring actors appearing in a production of Aristophanes' *Lysistrata*. Though the film presents the group as a whole, it concentrates on three actresses; thus, the male director and performers are decidedly minor characters. Rather than follow the external action (the company's trip across Sweden), the narrative focuses on the consciousness of the women and constantly shifts from exterior to interior views. Real events continually merge with the womens' thoughts, memories, and fantasies, and the status of screen events is highly ambiguous. Unlike *Persona*, however, this move into woman's consciousness is not read as a descent into madness; rather, it is seen as a sane perspective on a sexist world.

While *Persona* takes a patriarchal and mythic approach to the figure of the actress—identifying her with woman as "duplicitous" mother or lover—*The Girls* presents a far more realistic picture of the female performer despite the films' fantastic aura. Motherhood, for example, is a central issue in the film, but it is treated without the Oedipal overlay of *Persona*. Instead, it is seen within the context of the working woman and the problems associated with her stressful, divided life. In the opening sequence of the film, Marianne (Harriet Andersson) runs onto the stage, late for a rehearsal. The director curtly asks her where she has been, then criticizes her for the delivery of certain lines. "An actress who wasn't late," he says, "could make it sound urgent." The narrative then enters her mind and depicts, in flashback, a scene of her wresting her son from a man whom she threatens to leave. The child's scream heard in the flashback merges with the sound of her son now crying from the theater wings. The director snaps: "I hope you're not taking *him* on tour!" Clearly, the point of the sequence is to show us the tensions that the actress faces as working mother and the insensitivity displayed by her male employer.

Several other sequences in *The Girls* concentrate on the question of motherhood and again approach it from this concrete perspective. Early in the film, Marianne leaves a store and hears a child screaming on the street. As she runs home, the noise continues on the soundtrack. When she opens her apartment door, we find that her own son is perfectly content. Clearly, the child's cry has made her anxious about the son she has had to leave at home. We later learn that Marianne is a single parent and that the father of her child has refused to marry her.

Here, and throughout the film, the free-associational logic of Zetterling's audio/visual editing gives us access to the actress' minds and allows us to empathize with their psychological plight. Beyond that, it gives voice to their true selves—a perspective we are denied with the mute Elizabeth Vogler, whom we see only from the outside. Unlike the women in *Persona* or in other films about female performers, the actresses in *The Girls* do not dissemble or wear masks off-stage: they boldly and aggressively speak their minds.

A second actress in the film (played by Gunnel Lindblom) is also seen as a mother. In one sequence, she stands in a travel agency recalling or fantasizing a scene of her children draping toilet paper around the house as the father looks on hopelessly. At other points in the film we see her signing a postcard "Mama" and notice a child's drawing tacked up in her hotel room. Much to Zetterling's credit (as co-scenarist of the film), she's careful to script the role of one actress, Liz (Bibi Andersson) who is apparently not a parent, so there is no attempt to impose motherhood as a universal or favored role. Unlike the case of Elizabeth Vogler, Liz's lack of maternity is not portrayed as a problem; rather it seems to liberate her for feminist/political action.

But aside form the question of motherhood, many women's issues are raised in this film through its focus on the figure of the actress, seen as archetypal female living in a paternalistic world. The women are clearly devalued by their male director and co-performers. As the men watch the actresses being interviewed on television, they chuckle together and ask, "Have you ever met women who could take things seriously?" What makes the men's position all the more outrageous is the fact that they are appearing in *Lysistrata*, a play that details women's crucial role in stopping war. Like the men in *Lysistrata*, it is really the actors and directors who fail to see what is serious in life.

The actresses are also shown to face sexism from their male audience, who are trained to see them as "showgirls." When Liz has dinner with a local couple in a tour town, we enter the mind of the man who thinks that the actress is "beginning to look old" and wonders whether she "could be fun." Clearly, these would not be his thoughts concerning an actor, whose age, beauty, or sexual availability are not traditionally associated with his role. This issue reappears later in the film, during a fantasy sequence in which Liz imagines herself stripping for a group of male reporters. We are again reminded of the historic root of the actress profession in prostitution and of the Roman crowd's right to demand that the actress undress. During the course of the film, these women face sexual innuendo in other areas of their lives. When the actress played by Gunnel Lindblom goes to a market to buy some cheese, the salesman comments lasciviously that she can have "anything [she] wants." When the actresses go to a restaurant one evening on tour, some men try to pick them up and are insulted when the women do not respond. "Don't you know how to be polite?" one man shouts, and then rudely informs them that they should be "grateful" for not being left alone. Zetterling follows this encounter with a whimsical scene of the women back in their hotel room, dancing together and having fun.

During the course of the film, the actresses face other problems that riddle women's lives. Some have to do with question of career, especially as it affects male mates. In a flashback, one actress' husband inquires sarcastically how long the tour will last, indicating that he resents being left alone. The husband of another actress lets on that he is uncomfortable earning less money than his wife. One actress complains to a friend that her husband does not take her work seriously.

Still other questions are raised about the double standard that applies to men's and women's sexual lives. Liz's husband, Carl, is having affairs with at least two women. Ironically, his wife's career as a touring performer enables him to conduct these liaisons quite effortlessly. Though Carl thinks he is being discreet, Liz knows about these trysts and seems to find them rather ridiculous. In one of her fantasies she imagines Carl arriving to visit her and unpacking his mistresses from his suitcase. He then proceeds to use them as hangers on which to drape his clothes. He implores his wife to be gay and understanding and to welcome his friends. In the final scene of the film, Liz fantasizes that she publicly announces their ensuing divorce.

Thus, throughout the film, Zetterling rejects Bergman's formulation of the actress as mythic screen on which to project male fears and desires, and instead envisions her as incarnating socialized woman, confronting myriad untenable roles. But Zetterling's interests go beyond the question of sexism to the broader issues of phallocentric culture. While Bergman's actress performs in *Electra*, a drama of matricide and a daughter's revenge, Zetterling's actresses appear in *Lysistrata*—a comedy in which women take an active role in opposing war. Though within the play women are mocked for their attempt to confront affairs of state, it is clear that they (and not the men) have the humane and rational perspective on politics. If male expertise is associated with death, then female power will be aligned with life. As she performs the role of *Lysistrata*, Liz becomes convinced that in order to prevent massive global destruction women must take action. Thus *The Girls* not only traces Liz's attempts to position herself as an actress, but to forge a political role for herself in society. As she performs the play in various cities, she perceives the audience's inattention and becomes angry and upset. During one performance, she finally breaks character and directly addresses the spectators. She asks them if it is possible to change the world, or to change themselves. She tells them these are the issues which Aristophanes wishes to raise in writing the play. The director shouts, "What? Another revolt among women?" and takes her off the stage. Thus, the events of *Lysistrata* are doubled in the story of Liz, who becomes progressively more interested in a political role. The fact that she has dared to take seriously the drama she enacts solicits a hostile response from the press. One reporter asks: "What do you want the audience to do when they're here for a good time?" It is at this point that Liz fantasizes her striptease—behaving in a manner more consonant with what is expected of actress.

Thus, the male world portrayed in *The Girls* is not only one of sexism, but one of phallocentric violence. At one point on their tour, the women sit in a train comparing photographs of their men. One actress asks, "How could we manage without them?" while another declares that she finds them "a load of shit." This scene is followed by a fantasy in which the women sit in a movie theater jeering at filmed images of Lyndon Johnson, Benito Mussolini, and Adolf Hitler. They throw pies at the screen as their own men appear on stage in front of the images of goosestepping armies. In the next scene, the actresses tour a bomb shelter as a guide proudly shows them the youth club, bar, and theater. This is followed by a fantasy depicting one actress' husband complacently sitting in an armchair in a war-ravaged forest, ignoring the detonating bombs around him. On the soundtrack we hear lines from *Lysistrata* in which a man tells the women: "You haven't the least idea what war means."

Throughout *The Girls*, Zetterling utilizes this play-within-a-play motif to demonstrate parallels between the world of Aristophanes' ancient drama and that of three contemporary women. Early in the film, Marianne recalls a sexual romp with her lover which ends with her in tears. Intercut with this flashback are scenes from the play in which women discuss the strategy of withholding sex from men in order to force them to cease warfare. One woman shouts: "I won't lift my legs to the sky" or "crouch on all fours"; another promises that she will "stiffen and reject" her lover. We have the sense that Marianne, too, should adopt this posture as a way of terminating her unhappy affair. This parallel between the actress and the world of *Lysistrata* is underscored at a later point in the film, when, in a performance of the play, Marianne's lover suddenly and fantastically appears on stage. In another scene which interweaves the theater and real life, Liz, costumed as *Lysistrata*, magically appears in the stock exchange where her husband works. Thus, throughout *The Girls*, Zetterling harks back to Aristophanes' drama, demonstrating that the problems and solutions facing women in ancient times are still relevant today.

It is clear that, as in *Lysistrata*, Zetterling sees hope for the world in women's political action, action aimed simultaneously at countering male sexism and militarism. Within the play, the character of Lysistrata calls women "a helpless lot" and sighs: "No wonder tragedies are written about us." Later, as she calls the women to action, she cries: "Now it's up to the women folk to do something about the world." Liz shares the ideology of her stage persona. After noticing the men asleep in the audience, she suggests a performance for women alone. Moreover, she dares to break out of her dramatic role and admonish the audience to attend to the message of the play. "I know," she says, "I shouldn't say something apart from the play," but she proceeds to speak in her own woman's voice, discarding the lines of Aristophanes' text. Though Zetterling can be applauded for having her female protagonist call for political action, she can be criticized for leaving the solutions vague. If men have failed to lead the world, how will women succeed? What kind of positions must they take? Aside from leaving these questions unanswered, Zetterling seems even to undercut her call for a women's movement, since in one fantasy sequence a group of demonstrating women begin to fight with one another.

Bergman's *Persona* in its representation of the actress, and

Zetterling brings to her film a concrete sense of the parameters of that way of life. Unlike Bergman, Zetterling does not mythify the actress figure or overlay it with male ideals or stereotypes. Rather, the actress stands as a woman in the world—destined to play a role not only in the household or theater, but on the political stage.

## V. CURTAIN CALL: ALL ABOUT EVE

Through our discussion of various films, we have seen that the actress role has, indeed, been a "key female figure throughout film history." And we have found that there are reasons for her privileged position in fictional screen narrative. Taking a cue from Molly Haskell, we have noted woman's societal "role-playing dimension," finding that many films about the actress (*The Velvet Touch, Stage Fright, Indiscreet*) focus on her need for deception both on and off the stage. Furthermore, these films have stressed the actress' need to perform for men—to enact the feminine Other.

But in addition to this sociological notion of woman as quintessential role-player, there are deeper, more concealed reasons for her association with theatricality. In reviewing the early history of the western drama, we have traced the trajectory of the actress' fate: from her original sacred position to her exile from the stage to her degradation to prostitute. What strikes one is the association of the female performer with her sexuality, be it the fertility of the actress/priestess or the taint of the actress/harlot.

Going beyond theater history, we have speculated on the psychological causes for the male formulation of woman as actress, finding the Oedipal perspective of son confronting mother central in this regard. Also important is the male fear of woman performing disingenuously in sex—feigning pleasure, enacting the prostitute's "trick."

We have also unearthed the biblical characterization of woman as actress and theatricality as original sin. This notion finds its way into a contemporary film like Hitchcock's *Stage Fright*, where one actress is literally named Eve. Moreover, the second actress, Charlotte Inwood, is linked to a murder by a bloodstained skirt. One evening, while she is performing, Eve's father tries to force a confession from her by bringing a doll into the theater which wears a similarly besmirched costume. What better symbols could there be of Eve's biblical punishment than the bloodstained dress and the childlike doll—icons of the "curse" of maternity.

Having unpacked the notion of woman as actress, we have witnessed its expression in two modernist films, united by their focus on the lives of fictional performers. In Ingmar Bergman's *Persona*, we have found a confirmation of the male stereotype of woman as dissembler—especially in her primal roles of mother and lover. In Mai Zetterling's *The Girls*, we have found a rebuttal of this view. Zetterling does not mythify the actress but treats her as a working woman, juggling maternal and career goals in a hostile, male-oriented world. Rather than see the actress' role as inherently perverse, Zetterling sees it as potentially redemptive, giving woman a platform to articulate her voice. Instead of envisioning the actress as passive (like the mute, withdrawn Elizabeth Vogler), Zetterling sees her as a vital figure. Zetterling's actress does not simply perform, she acts—she makes an impact on the world.

Perhaps, in the aggressive stance of Zetterling's heroine, we can imagine that Eve gets her revenge for being "miscast" in the long-running, patriarchal drama.

## NOTES

1. Rosamond Gilder, *Enter The Actress* (Boston/New York: Houghton Mifflin, 1931), p. xv.
2. Molly Haskell, *From Reverence to Rape, the Treatment of Women in the Movies* (New York: Holt, Rinehart and Winston, 1974), p. 242.
3. Charles Affron, *Cinema and Sentiment* (Chicago/London: University of Chicago Press, 1982), pp. 132–157.
4. Jean Duvignaud, *Spectacle et societe* (Paris: Editions Denoel, 1970), p. 17.
5. Simone de Beauvoir, *The Second Sex*, trans. H.M. Parshley (New York: Random House, 1974).
6. Gilder, p. 2.
7. Ibid., p. 6.
8. Ibid., p. 9.
9. Ibid., p. 16.

10. See Laura Mulvey, "Visual Pleasure and Narrative Cinema," in Gerald Mast and Marshall Cohen, *Film Theory and Criticism* (New York: Oxford, 1985), pp. 803–816.
11. Kenneth Tynan, "Garbo," in Mast and Cohen, p. 772–3.
12. Leo Braudy, *The World in a Frame* (Garden City, NY: Doubleday, 1976), p. 214.
13. Gilder, p. 8.
14. see Teresa deLaurentis, *Alice Doesn't* (Bloomington: Indiana University Press, 1984); E. Ann Kaplan, *Women and Film* (New York: Methuen, 1983).
15. Susan Sontag, "*Persona*", in *Styles of Radical Will* (New York: Delta, 1969), p. 141.
16. The text below is taken from the published script for *Persona.* The pronouns in brackets were originally "I" in the script, but in the film Alma speaks them as "you." See Ingmar Bergman, *Persona and Shame*, trans. by Keith Bradfield (New York: Grossman, 1972), p. 94.
17. Ibid.
18. Ibid., p. 32.
19. Jean-Louis Baudry, "The Apparatus," in *Camera Obscura*, no 1 (Fall 1976), p. 114.
20. Ibid., p. 117. Baudry is referring to Bertram Lewin, "Sleep, the Mouth and the Dream Screen," in *Psychoanalytic Quarterly*, vol. 15 (1946), pp. 419–43, and "Inferences from the Dream Screen," in *International Journal of Psychoanalysis*, vol. 29 (1948), pp. 224–431.

# 7. THE GREAT PROFILE: How Do We Know the Actor from the Acting?

Marian Keane

> Admiration directed at reflection must be expressed in the language of reflection, not that of immediacy. Reflection is this: Why?—because.... Why is the whole thing constructed in this way?—because.... Why is this little stroke here?—because....[1]

## I.

TWO VIEWS PREDOMINATE ABOUT John Barrymore. He is considered one of the twentieth century's greatest tragedians, and he is thought of as one of the world's biggest—or as he says in *Twentieth Century,* "cheapest"—hams and most pathetic public figures. Film critics, when they have thought about Barrymore, have not been alone in feeling on the horns of a dilemma with regard to the value of his acting. Theater critics also have been divided on his work, sometimes proclaiming his genius and at other times bemoaning his histrionics.

There were high points for both views during Barrymore's lifetime. In 1920, after months of studying Shakespeare and elocution, Barrymore performed Richard III on Broadway. Critics who had dismissed Barrymore's acting—finding it hyperbolic and overly praised by Broadway's inner circle—and critics who had only hinted that he was a great actor when they saw him play Falder in Galsworthy's *Justice* (1916) and Peter Ibbetson in the play of that title (1917), found themselves awed. With his performance in *Hamlet* in 1922, a consensus was reached: Barrymore was the greatest actor of his time and the worthy successor of Edwin Booth's mantle. In 1924, Barrymore produced and starred in

Plate I
(Courtesy of Harvard Theatre Collection)

**Plate II**
**(Courtesy of Harvard Theatre Collection)**

The Aspect that Peter Ibbetson (Mr. Barrymore) Turns Oftenest to the Illuded Public Looking Upon Him

*Hamlet* again in London and accomplished the impossible: an American actor stunned British audiences with his performance of Shakespeare.

In the thirties and forties, Barrymore continued to be in the public eye, but for different reasons. In movies, plays, and on radio shows, alcoholism seemed to engulf his superior abilities and deteriorate his beauty, in particular the beauty of his profile (plates I and II). The idea that his acting was empty theatricality resurfaced. Incomprehensibly, Barrymore participated in this idea of himself and his work, devastatingly mocking his famous Shakespearean roles and his identity as a Shakespearean actor in films such as *The Great Profile* and on the Rudy Vallee radio shows. The press had a field day with his private life, which grew increasingly tortured and pathetic. Although he parried reporter's barbs with his characteristically ironic and literate wit, his retorts were more biting and bitter than they had ever been before. In 1942, when he died at the age of sixty, Barrymore's reputation was at an all-time low.

The disturbing and pathetic qualities of Barrymore's later years make him, and consequently his place in the histories of theater and film, subjects complicated by emotion. The emotions Barrymore aroused have faded as the world has come to regard him as a supreme artist whose promise was not fulfilled, a genius whose darker angel conquered him. But those views are partly the result of time's passage. In 1939, when Barrymore appeared in his last play on Broadway, *My Dear Children, Life* magazine was prepared to give equal coverage to the "episodes of pathos and domestic discord" that marred the evening. Of his performance, *Life* reported: "For New York sophisticates he toned down his ad-lib buffoonery. He did tricks with his eyes and larynx, winced at thunderous belly-laughs; but the impression left with critics was that of a fine virtuoso burlesquing his own imcomparable art."[2] We should compare this to F.P.A's (Franklin Pierce Adams) review of Barrymore's Hamlet in 1924 : "... in the evening [I went] to see *Hamlet* and J. Barrymore's acting of it the finest I ever saw, and all about it as close to perfection as ever I hope to see, and when my grandchildren say to me, This or that is a great Hamlet, I shall say,

Ay, but not so fine as Barrymore's. And I will disinherit those babes."[3]

Partly because Barrymore has called forth confused emotions of awe, disappointment, anger and even betrayal, he has been the subject of biographies almost since the moment of his death. With varying degrees of sentimentality, these biographies, such as Gene Fowler's unabashedly loyal *Good Night, Sweet Prince* (1944) and Hollis Alpert's thorough *The Barrymores* (1964), set out intimate and sympathetic accounts of his glamorous, glorious, and finally tragic life. Identifying him with the Shakespearean roles for which he is best known and for which he received the greatest praise, *Richard III* and *Hamlet,* and setting his life, in particular his later years, within a context of Shakespearean tragedy, those authors pay homage to one of the century's most complex and gifted artists.

These books portray Barrymore as a tragic figure and their tones at the end are melancholy. Speaking for themselves and for their readers, Barrymore's audience, the authors mourn his self-destructiveness. Wanting his greatest achievements, understood as *Richard III* and *Hamlet,* to represent him in history and to displace the bad memories of his later years, his biographers suggest that had he stayed with the classics, had he disciplined and restrained himself, Barrymore would have achieved a place in the history of theater that he, alone in his generation, could have attained.

The understanding that his performances of Shakespeare contained and revealed his genius more consummately than any others underwrites the view that Barrymore participated in his downfall by choosing work unworthy of him. His biographers record this as the prevailing view in the loyal circle of Broadway figures who had pinned their hopes for a renaissance of American theater on the three Barrymores, and especially on John. Barrymore was thought to have betrayed Broadway, and betrayed himself, when he went to work in Hollywood. His biographers' tendency to skim over Barrymore's work on film constitutes an endorsement of theater's view. Chronicling behind-the-scenes intrigue in Hollywood and often only cataloging the titles of his films, Barrymore's biographers do not argue for the idea that film acting is a lesser endeavor than stage acting: instead, they take it for granted, as does most of the world.

Barrymore's decision to act on stage and in movies—in fifty-four of them between 1914 and 1941—is a fact that causes both theater and film critics some trouble. Neither theater criticism, which neglects Barrymore's film acting, nor film criticism, which neglects Barrymore's work more or less entirely, has come to terms with the complex relation between theater and film. Nevertheless, the prevailing critical views are not without interest. They reveal the circumstances for Barrymore's unrecognized importance in the history of film acting and for the partiality of his acceptance by the world of theater criticism.

Barrymore's biographers emerge more from the world of the theater than they do from film. They put forth a conservative view of Barrymore's importance when they prize his Shakespearean performances above all the others. Doing so, they invoke a standard of classical theater compared to which nothing is as good or as important. Since Barrymore was famously a man of excesses, buffoonery, and scandal, defining him as a classical actor is a way of downplaying everything about him that is hard to accept. His performances of Shakespeare are seen as testaments to his seriousness and thus as antidotes to the ways in which his life undermined, challenged, or avoided "seriousness" altogether.

There are film critics who claim that Barrymore's best performance on film was in William Wyler's *Counsellor at Law* (1933). I understand this judgment to endorse, or to emerge from, theater's view of Barrymore. I also see it as a declaration that film criticism can make no independent claim about the meaning and the value of Barrymore's work. Both are positions I will contest in this essay. Barrymore's performance in *Counsellor at Law* is praised for being more restrained, serious, and sober than any of his other work on film. He appears "toned down." If one has the idea that his stage acting was toned down, then one has the feeling that Wyler's film comes closest to presenting an unadulterated Barrymore, the Barrymore of theatrical greatness.

In my view, Wyler avoids issues about Barrymore and his acting, issues that are directly confronted in a number of other films. In particular, the film presents no interpretation of his absorption in his thinking, which in George Cukor's *A Bill of Divorcement* (1932) is interpreted as madness and in Howard Hawks' *Twentieth Century* (1934) as genius. For example, in *Counsellor at Law,* when Barrymore leaves his office en route to a meeting with the figures who are bringing about the end of his career, he is in a highly agitated state, absorbed in his thoughts. His gestures are charged with confusion as he struggles against unleashing his enormous capacity for physical violence. Yet the camera makes no declaration about the depth or meaning of Barrymore's agitation. Rather, it identifies with Barrymore's secretary, who is in love with him and interprets his actions as rejections of her. Barrymore is thoroughly preoccupied; his mind is elsewhere. His exclusion of this woman, or unwillingness to reveal himself to her, is a real consequence of his self-absorption, but it is not his primary reason for being preoccupied. What thoughts are in his mind and what emotions fill him at this moment are not the subject of the camera in the same way that his secretary's thoughts and emotions are. A real question is raised here: does Barrymore's absorption in his own thoughts bar him from a satisfying romantic union? But it is a question about the implications of Barrymore's mood, not about its origin and meaning.

When the camera presents the secretary's comprehensible emotions rather than attempt to interpret Barrymore's complex emotional state, the film effectively denies the obvious—that Barrymore's inner agitation, potential for violence, and absorption in his thinking make the camera's access to him problematic. The consequences of Wyler's failure to interpret Barrymore's mood or nature at this moment are clear in the film's ending, which unites Barrymore and his secretary. We do not believe that this woman possesses a deep understanding of who this man is, largely because the film itself presents no such understanding. Because of this, we feel his romantic attachment to her is partial. Wyler's film is unsatisfying because it limits, not our sense of Barrymore as a romantic figure, but our understanding of what is required for a romantic partner, or for the camera, to acknowledge him.

Like Barrymore's biographers, the critics who praise Barrymore in *Counsellor at Law* assume that Barrymore's stage acting and his acting on film are separate: one was serious, the other not. This distinction is less argued for than it is founded on, or fueled by, an assumption about film acting which seems to account for Barrymore's work. The assumption is that he was not (it is all but said, how could anyone be?) serious about film acting.

Partly as a consequence of this view, the world is unprepared to accept Barrymore as a serious film actor. His theatricality and his clowning seem to contradict his reputation as a "classical" actor. But Barrymore's ambition, and his understanding of his acting, are to my mind unacknowledged when his classical roles are understood as the only fulfillments of his art. This view denies the ambition behind, and the meaning in, Barrymore's decision to act in films.

Why did Barrymore leave the stage at the moment of his greatest success and the height of his powers as a stage actor? Did he squander his genius? What did acting in movies mean to him? This question cannot be satisfyingly answered except in light of, and on the basis of, Barrymore's film acting itself. For me the question, what did acting in movies mean to Barrymore? becomes, what is the meaning of Barrymore's acting in specific films?

Let me say a word about two common responses to the first of these questions. Barrymore's biographers and friends maintain that he left the stage primarily because he couldn't tolerate playing the same role six times a week for weeks on end. He says as much in his autobiography.

> People ... often ask me why I stop a play in what seems to them the middle of the run and while there is still a demand for seats.... It is not easy to explain, but it is because I lack something that is a very valuable quality for an actor to possess.... I am not a trouper. To have that quality that makes for a good trouper is, as I say, of great value, but there are many valuable qualities that bring no particular pleasure to the possessor.[4]

I accept this explanation, but I don't think it explains everything. After all, Barrymore could have written his own ticket on Broadway, done the plays he wanted and ended runs when he wished, as he had done already. This explanation tells us something Barrymore didn't like about the theater but leaves unanswered other questions: Why movies? Why radically change mediums? And what does Barrymore's film acting mean? Surely Barrymore would not have dedicated himself to acting in films if he thought nothing of them or thought he could not work in the film medium. What was Barrymore's understanding of film and of acting on film?

Another frequently heard explanation for an actor's switch from stage to film is that an actor like Barrymore went to Hollywood solely to make a lot of money and thereby compromised his work. This view goes hand in hand with the view that Hollywood studios made stage actors of stature offers they couldn't refuse solely in order to upgrade the status of film to an art. In this regard, there's no denying that Barrymore signed a lucrative contract with Warner's or that some executives at Warner's probably harbored the thought that Barrymore's name would add prestige to their products.

When one thinks that Barrymore acted in movies simply to make money, and thinks that this is enough to say about Barrymore's film acting, however, not only is Barrymore underestimated as an artist and his ambitions and thoughts about his work unacknowledged, but a serious discussion about film acting is avoided. Theoretically speaking, Barrymore's—or anyone's—acting on film cannot be called compromised in the abstract, in the absence of close examination of the work itself. I find the term "compromised" strangely empty in the context of discussing Barrymore's film acting, specifically because it does not describe or give an account of my experience of Barrymore on film. There are no moments in Barrymore's work on film that I would call compromised, no moments that I understand as calling for being understood as compromised.

In Barrymore's work, rather than compromises, there are moments, and even whole films, that call for being understood as failures. *The Great Profile* (1940), for example, contains hardly a moment of Barrymore's acting that I find as interesting or worth studying as many of his other film performances. On the other hand, both *Dr. Jekyll and Mr. Hyde* (1920) and *Counsellor at Law* (1933), two films that are clearly superior to *The Great Profile,* contain failed moments, moments in which it is apparent that a failure of understanding between director and actor has occurred. Failures of understanding like those that occur in these films are expressed, or exposed, in the fact of the camera being placed badly, that is, in a position out of synch with—and thus in no position to reveal or to acknowledge—Barrymore's thinking, identity, and acting. Though both of these films are good, they are also, at moments, failures, not because Barrymore "compromised" his acting, but because—as has been pointed out—the films' directors shied away from, or were unaware of, the meaning of Barrymore's acting and identity on film.

*Beau Brummel* (1924), directed by Harry Beaumont, starred Barrymore and, at his request, the then little-known actress, Mary Astor. As one of the first films Barrymore made in Hollywood,[5] *Beau Brummel* stands to reveal aspects of Barrymore's work at a crucial, not to say momentous, juncture of his life. The object of my reading of *Beau Brummel* is to investigate Barrymore's acting and the film's understanding of him. The first argument of my reading of the film is based on reading a number of Barrymore's recurrent or signature gestures. Reading these gestures allows us to address the meaning of Barrymore's acting. My reading of Barrymore's performance in *Beau Brummel* undertakes to reveal Barrymore's thoughts about acting and to reflect upon who he is as seriously as he does in his performance.

The second argument of my reading is composed of reflections on who Barrymore is within the world of *Beau Brummel,* specifically on how his presence on film, and chiefly his beauty, are interpreted by the film. (This is a subject of pre-eminent importance to my study of film acting, because central to the work of filming Barrymore, as it is in filming any star, is the work of identifying and interpreting his romantic identity.) Barrymore is a unique figure in the history of film in this regard, because his romantic identity is declared to the camera and to the viewer by a signal framing, or a signature pose: his profile. Barrymore's profile is the emblem of his romantic identity; thus, the meaning of his romantic identity must be understood in terms of the meaning of his profile.

The third subject of my reading of *Beau Brummel* is the romance in the film, or the conditions of Barrymore/Beau's romance with the Mary Astor figure. In my view, the conditions of their romance are inseparable from Barrymore's beauty on film and his theatricality. *Beau Brummel* does not set out an original interpretation of Barrymore as a romantic figure (as Hawks and Cukor do, in different ways). Instead, the film appears to derive its interpretation of Barrymore as a romantic figure from *Peter Ibbetson* or at least to share, to an uncanny degree, the concept of romance and the understanding of Barrymore that lie at the heart of that important romantic work.

The 1917 play *Peter Ibbetson* was adapted quite faithfully from the popular novel of that title written by George du Maurier (who also wrote *Trilby*) in 1891. It tells the story of Peter and the Duchess of Towers, childhood friends who are separated when their families, for different and tragic reasons, move. Peter and Mimsy, as he calls the Duchess, meet again after many years, recognize one another, and recognize too that they are in love. But they cannot marry. The Duchess is married already to an older man she does not love. Shortly after their reunion, Peter, enraged at his uncle's slanderous remarks about his mother, kills him and receives a sentence of lifetime imprisonment.

Peter and Mimsy's attachment is unbreakable. They continue, for the rest of their lives, to meet by the extraordinary process of "dreaming true." Dreaming true is accomplished by gathering all of one's inner being and thinking very hard about where one wants most to be, and with whom, just before one goes to sleep. While one's outer shell remains in place, one's inner being is transported to that special place and experiences life, and a platonic love, with great intensity.

By dreaming true every night, Peter and Mimsy live the lives they wish to live: they travel together, stay home together, dine together. Dreaming true "was a life within a life—an intenser life," announces Peter, whose memoirs make up the book. "No waking joys the world can give can equal in intensity these complex joys I had when I was asleep; waking joys seem so slight in comparison."[6] The characters inhabit the world of their childhood, or any other place either of them has ever been in real life, as ghosts, invisible to others who dwell in real time, visible only to one another. Both characters die in the novel, but death is not the end of their life together: it is the beginning of uninterrupted "dreaming true."

In a moving introduction to a collection of du Maurier's novels, John Masefield describes the book as "a complete statement of destiny."

> It begins with suggestions from a far past, and ends with suggestions of a lasting future. In between these eternities are the lives on earth of hero and heroine, both in some measure thwarted as earthly lives, both amended and completed by inner lives of an intensity and interest not before known. [du Maurier] put his two spirits in exceptional situations in which passion might have no play, and the separation of the two mortals [was] almost complete. He imagined two spirits of exceptional quality ... [and showed in their love] something which made life more wonderful, more full of meaning, more glad with powers of sympathy.

"*Peter Ibbetson's* effect ... upon [its] generation was profound," Masefield writes.

> We who were young then could have dispensed with many of the great writers, but without du Maurier life would have been bleak. He, and a few others, heightened the sense of life in us, and gave us something of beauty and wonder, which the mind must ever hunger for.
>
> Even now, after fifty years, I can think of no book which so startled and delighted the questioning mind.... [It] leaves the reader sure that what [they] achieved by "dreaming true" may be done by people with the right kind of will.[7]

Du Maurier's novel was the basis for several movies as well as an opera. One of the movies, *Forever,* made in 1921, seems to have been an outgrowth of the popular Broadway play starring Barrymore and Constance Collier and was a major success in its own right. I mention *Forever* because *Beau Brummel*'s debt to

*Peter Ibbetson* is sufficient for us to assume that Harry Beaumont saw some version of *Ibbetson* before he directed Barrymore in *Brummel.* Though Beaumont may not have seen *Ibbetson* on Broadway, it is quite possible that he saw *Forever* and derived much of his direction of *Beau Brummel* from it.[8]

Barrymore, however, could not have been in the dark as to the origins or the meaning of the romance at the heart of *Beau Brummel.* It might even be that Barrymore was drawn to act in *Beau Brummel* because of the opportunity it gave him to deepen his understanding of his centrality to the romantic genre epitomized by *Peter Ibbetson.* What, then, do Barrymore's theatricality and beauty mean within the terms of *Ibbetson*'s or *Beau Brummel*'s concept of romance and romantic happiness? How do the romantic conditions of these works interpret Barrymore, and how does Barrymore interpret the romantic conditions of these works?

## II.

John Barrymore is introduced ironically in *Beau Brummel* as "A young man of no importance—a captain of the 10th Hussars—George Byram Brummel." The film starts its story of Beau's life at the moment of his doomed love affair with Lady Margery (Mary Astor). It chronicles Beau's subsequent rise to prominence in court society, his introduction of trend-setting fashions, and his numerous heartless dalliances with women of high status. Beau's conniving, sarcasm, and treatment of others finally leads to his downfall. He is exiled from England and lives the rest of his life in France. In the end, Beau is a broken man whose astounding youthful beauty is completely gone. He is also mad and hallucinates that King George, who had been an unwitting object of Beau's dersion and mockery, and Margery, still his true love, visit him in prison, where he is confined.

In Beau's fantasy, the King and Margery appear in superimposition on the screen. Beau humiliates the King by forcing him, a fat man, to display his clothing, a duplicate of one of the fashions that Beau had introduced long ago. Shortly after the King disappears, Margery appears in her wedding dress and Beau, once again, is taken by her. But the effort of hallucinating seems to overwhelm him; suddenly he collapses and dies. Seconds later, he rises as a ghostly presence in superimposition on the screen and, like the figures in his fantasy, he is restored as the younger version of himself. All of his dashing and elegance returned, he and Margery embrace. Their marriage, never a possibility on earth, takes place in heaven.

The opening sequence of the film is set in the garden of Margery's parents' estate. A bit like Juliet, Margery stands on the balcony of her room, clad in her wedding dress, lost in thought. Tonight, at her parents' bidding, she will marry a man she does not love. Beau, dressed in his officer's uniform and a flowing cape, steals into the garden. Calling her, he wakens her from her reverie and begs her to join him in the garden, where they have a desperate exchange. Her parents will not allow their marriage both because Beau is from a lower class and because they think him a fortune hunter; Beau cannot elope with Margery because he's been called to battle. In the midst of their despairing declaration of love, Margery's parents enter the garden and force her into the house. The wedding march begins and Beau, despondent, leaves the garden.

The second sequence opens with a medium shot of Beau, deeply depressed, in his apartment. He picks up a cameo of Margery and gazes at it. Turning it over, he writes, "This beautiful creature is *dead*," and places it in a box. He thinks for a moment, his posture inflected with sadness. His shoulders sag and his eyes stare out dully, without focus.

He turns and walks to frame right where something catches his eye. He pauses, looks, and then shakes his head, dismissing a thought. He continues to walk to frame right. We cut to a perpendicular framing of Barrymore that also contains the doorway of the room and a mirror with an ornately carved frame. It is clear that his reflection in this mirror had caught his eye a few seconds before. We cut to a new medium framing of Barrymore with the mirror prominently placed in the foreground. Slowly, he walks forward toward the camera and the mirror. His gaze cast down, he is deep in thought (fig. 7.1).

He arrives in the foreground of the frame and stands next to the mirror. His head still bent, he remains absorbed in his thoughts. Absentmindedly, as though he were a sleepwalker, he places his left hand on the mirror frame at a height level with his shoulder (fig. 7.2).

A moment later, he looks up, gazes at his reflection, and blinks rapidly several times as he beholds himself (fig. 7.3). Leaning forward, inspecting his reflection, he gives himself a cool and dispassionate look. Then, still facing himself in the mirror, he steps back, smooths his cummerbund, and gives his reflection an up and down look (fig. 7.4). He takes a few more steps back and is behind the camera. All we view is his reflection, framed within the mirror's frame.

Not taking his eyes from his reflection, Barrymore makes alterations in his appearance and performs gestures of decorous behavior with the clear goal of perfecting his performance of them. He holds in his abdomen, pressing it with his fingers (fig. 7.5), adopts a Napoleonic pose and adjusts it a couple of times, and rehearses a courtly bow. As he rehearses the bow, he motions quickly toward himself with his right arm, as though beckoning an imaginary person to come forward and play opposite him.

Barrymore bows several times to his imaginary partner. At just the moment in the last bow when his face would be out of sight from the person to whom he is bowing, Barrymore sneaks a look at himself in the mirror (fig. 7.6). This is a gesture filled with subtle meaning. It acknowledges his awareness of being viewed and therefore acknowledges us, our attention and our view. It tells us that at this moment we do not have more access to Barrymore than he has.

While he has this privileged view of himself, Barrymore takes the opportunity to adjust his pose. He flexes one knee a few times to get his leg to bend at a certain angle, for example. But this knee-flexing is, we should note, unnecessary: his leg is as perfectly bent the first time as it is the last. Barrymore understands this

Fig. 7.1

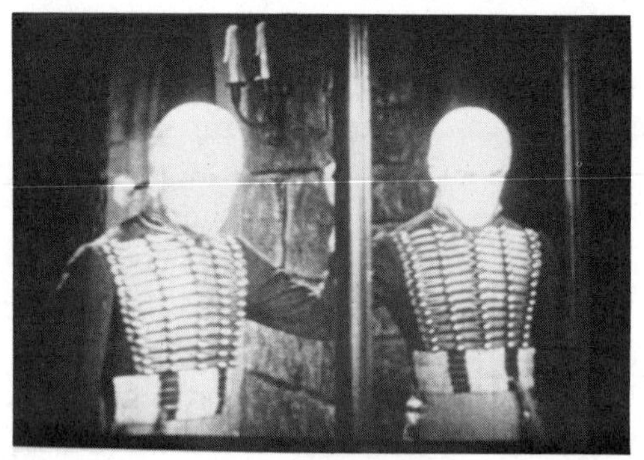

Fig. 7.2

Fig. 7.3

Fig. 7.4

Fig. 7.5

Fig. 7.6

moment as one in which he can declare his theatricality. Thus, though the adjustments Barrymore makes at this moment are on one level comical, they are also serious, partly because they are explicitly offered or performed for us. As declarations of his knowledge of our presence as his audience and of himself as theatrical being, these are self-conscious gestures. Partly, what this means is that Barrymore's gestures declare his identity as the pre-eminent actor, John Barrymore.

Abruptly, we cut to an unmatched shot of Barrymore gazing off, to frame left (fig. 7.7). The mirror is not in the frame, and Barrymore is in a significantly different mood. His lips are tightly drawn; his brows are low over his eyes. No longer absorbed in a contemplation of himself, his thoughts are filled with anger, his eyes direct and full of vengeance. An intertitle declares: "Revenge was all he thought of now. He would use all his charm, wit, and personal appearance in a game against the society which had robbed him of his love." We cut back to the shot of Barrymore that preceded the title, and his expression is unchanged.

Fig. 7.7

The sequence ends with the next shot. We return to the framing of Barrymore in the mirror (fig. 7.8). As in the previous shots from this angle, he is framed within the frame by the mirror and unviewed in the original. There is, however, a striking difference between this shot and the shot that made up most of the sequence. In the final framing, Barrymore no longer studies his reflection or occupies himself with his appearance and postures. He is motionless and framed in profile. His jaw is set squarely and his right hand is clenched in a tight fist. If the early part of the sequence showed him engaged in the creation of "Beau Brummel," this shot declares that his creation is complete. We behold the product of Beau's rehearsing and self-absorption.

Fig. 7.8

Why does Beau incarnate himself as "Beau?" The intertitle offers one explanation which, I take it, Barrymore at least partially endorses. It tells us that his revenge will take the form of using "all of his charm, wit and personal appearance" in "a game against his society." Beau, the beautiful, heartless seducer, is created in order to declare Beau's denial of love.

Beau's incarnation as "Beau" begins when he declares that the love of his life "is dead." What this means is realized only at the end of the film, when the lovers are reunited, first in Beau's fantasy and then in the next world. *Beau Brummel* posits that these lovers can know romantic happiness only if they know freedom from the world. When Beau declares Margery dead, he is engaged in a fantasy not only about her death, but about his own as well. Or we might say his fantasy is about the death of the world, since that would also make possible his and Margery's happiness. Beau's vengeance, then, is partly directed at himself and partly directed at the world. Feeling himself condemned by the world to live without his love, Beau wants to put his anger and bitterness into action.

After Beau places the cameo of Margery in a box, he turns to frame right. When he sees his reflection in the mirror, an idea enters his mind which, with a shake of his head, he dismisses. Is this the idea of "Beau," the crystallized facade he will present henceforth to the world, and is its origin his view of himself in the mirror? Does he dismiss the idea because it is too vengeful, too bitter? Does he dismiss it at first because he is not certain he can play "Beau"?

He does not completely dismiss the idea that enters his mind, but rather remains absorbed in it as he crosses the room. He walks up to the mirror without hesitation, in a state of preoccupation, and it is in this state that he places his arm on the mirror. What does this gesture, which appears to be an embrace of himself, mean?

The gesture of embracing someone around the shoulders is a gesture that recurs in Barrymore's acting, not just in *Beau Brummel* but in all of his films. In fact, it is one of a number of gestures which, because they recur with great precision in Barrymore's acting, call for being understood as a repertoire: a system of thoroughly thought-out movements that express meanings of crucial importance to Barrymore's identity and thinking. These gestures declare Barrymore's thoughts at particular moments in given films and, as importantly, they declare that what he is doing at certain moments is thinking. These gestures are motivated by events that occur in the worlds of his films, events that challenge him and call upon him to declare who he is.

In "What Photography Calls Thinking," Stanley Cavell discusses at length the ways in which motion picture photography presents human thoughtfulness, or the fact that what human beings do naturally is think, in the "fidgetiness" of individuals gazed upon by the camera. The subject of Cavell's essay in this regard is Frank Capra's *Mr. Deeds Goes to Town,* where Cavell finds Deeds' (Gary Cooper) summoning of himself to speak for himself in the courtroom scene when he "[defends] his sanity" to be "the climax ... expected in a melodramatic structure": "[It is] a version of Descartes' *cogito,* taking on the proof of his own existence, as if against it's denial by the world."[9]

I mention Cavell's essay because of its relevance to the fact and the meaning of Barrymore's gestures. Barrymore's gestures, announcing his thoughts and the fact of his thinking, can be understood to be melodramatic in the way Cavell interprets Deed's declaration of sanity in *Mr. Deeds*. Barrymore's gestures do differ from Deeds' in certain respects. They are, for one thing, continuous, not found at climactic moments in a film and not called attention to by the narrative. They are also not gestures singled out by the camera in most cases. They are instead gestures that Barrymore simply performs, gestures that constitute his ordinary actions within the worlds of his films.

These differences, however, do not undermine or contradict the central arguments of Cavell's essay. It remains as true for Barrymore as Cavell argues it is true for Deeds that declarations of this order, declarations of the proof of one's existence as a human being—as a thinking being—are the substance of film melodrama. Barrymore's acting can be understood as further and important evidence for the central claim Cavell makes in his essay, a claim about the metaphysical importance of film itself: "... While thinking is no longer secured by the mind's declaration of its presence to itself, it is now to be secured by the presence of the live human body to the camera, in particular by the presence of the body's least intelligent property, its fidgetiness, its metaphysical restlessness."[10]

Some of the gestures in Barrymore's repertoire are: double takes; repeated staccato jerks of his head when, told a certain piece of news, he is filled with disbelief; the gesture of raising his hand to his head, which can take the form of running his fingers through his hair or brushing his forehead lightly with his forefinger, also registers a sense of disbelief or perplexity; turning his profile to the camera; arching his hands at the palm, palm face down, with his fingers fiercely taut, which I take to originate in his understanding of Richard III and in particular to invoke Richard's spider-like villainy; a look of innocence or discovery that I call his "slate-wiped-clean-look," which expresses a mental dawning, an illumination, either of a better world or of a second chance in this one; his direct look into the camera; his slumped and immobile posture, which is a registration of depression, hopelessness, and declares his knowledge of, and at this moment his dwelling in, a deep metaphysical abyss; and specific eye movements, such as widening them, closing them to near-slits, or blinking rapidly many times in quick succession.

In *Beau Brummel,* Barrymore employs the gesture of embracing someone around the shoulders several times. He embraces the King this way at the end of the scene in which they become fast friends as a result of Beau's quick-wittedness (he saves the King from a scandal involving his seduction of an innkeeper's wife). And he embraces a foppish courtier of the King's when he asks the courtier for some money (fig. 7.9). At both moments, Barrymore's embrace is ironic: he never means the loyalty implied by the gesture. On both occasions, Barrymore's gesture of embracing another around the shoulders expresses two facts: he is certain of his superiority to both men, and he is dedicated to betraying them.

**Fig. 7.9**

The gesture of the shoulder embrace also occurs in *Twentieth Century*. In the scene of the morning after his outburst at the prospect of Lily's stepping out to attend a gala benefit in her honor, Jaffe (Barrymore) places his arm around Lily's shoulders as he walks her to the door. Soberly, he announces he's had "a change of heart." Happily surprised, Lily asks him what brought it about. "That moment at the window," he replies, raising his eyebrows and tipping his head toward the French window he had thrown open the night before in a suicidal fit. he promises her that he will never be a jealous maniac again. "I trust you implicitly," he says in an even and subdued tone. But he's lying. The very instant Lily leaves the apartment, he is at the telephone, dialing the McGonigle Detective Agency, arranging to have Lily's every move watched and reported to him. Except for the fact that he's become utterly surreptitious (the price of which will be Lily's departure from his theater, from the stage, and from him), there has been no change in his nature at all.

When Barrymore puts his arm around his own shoulder by placing his hand on the mirror frame in *Beau Brummel,* the gesture's meaning is complicated by the fact that it is directed at himself. As in its other instances, his gesture here implies loyalty, honesty, and intimacy, three qualities that have enormous importance in Barrymore's relationships in each of his films, perhaps most explicity in *Twentieth Century,* where his two cohorts and Lily are essential to his well being, but also in *Dinner at Eight,* where his agent's repeated betrayals cause him palpably deep pain.

In *Beau Brummel,* Beau's only real friend is his valet, whom Beau frequently embraces about the shoulders and who remains loyal to Beau all his life. But the valet is clearly not Barrymore's equal. Loyal and often uncomprehending of Beau, he is like Oliver and Owen in *Twentieth Century,* and the two oddly-shaped mates Barrymore has in *The Beloved Rogue*. These figures' relationships of loyalty with clear inferiority to Barrymore resemble most, to my mind, the relationships secondary characters have with heroes in Shakespeare's plays.[11] Barrymore will, upon occasion, put his arm around the shoulders of such figures and, clearly, loyalty and a certain kind of intimacy is expressed in the gesture. But it is not deep intimacy: because these figures cannot comprehend Barrymore, what's in his mind, his passions, and his art, they are always distanced from him. He needs them and surely values their loyalty, but he also knows it is a blind loyalty. Such loyalty is never a component of the relationships Barrymore strives to attain with women in his films; indeed, such loyalty poses a threat to romantic happiness.

When Barrymore embraces his reflection in the mirror, his gesture has several layers of meaning. On one level, he indicates that he believes his reflection is an inferior being to himself; indeed, his scene of rehearsing in front of the mirror has the quality of a puppet show. His reflection in fact has no mind of his own; it is at his beck and call, subject to his will. On another level, Barrymore's embrace of his reflection in the mirror announces that, this time, the figure whom he betrays is himself. His gesture posits that theatrical incarnation—the incarnation of "Beau"—is an act of self-betrayal.

What is Barrymore's relation to his reflection in the mirror? When he raises his eyes to look at himself in the mirror, lifting from his state of self-absorption for the first time, he blinks rapidly a number of times. Once again, this is an ordinary gesture, over so quickly that we might not be inclined to pay it any mind. But it is charged with meaning that, as with the gesture of the shoulder embrace, becomes clear when we apply ourselves to thinking about it.

Barrymore blinks rapidly many times in succession when, for example, he hallucinates that the King and Lady Margery visit his cell in the closing sequence of *Beau Brummel*; during the first rehearsal scene in *Twentieth Century*; and during the centerpiece romantic scene of *The Beloved Rogue*. When he blinks this way in that early scene of *Twentieth Century*, the object of his gaze is his theater manager, Oliver. Oliver confides in Jaffe (Barrymore) that he's spoken with Francine Anderson (whom Jaffe will call "that piece of human tripe!"), told her that Lily is not working out, and induced Anderson to take the play's leading role. Jaffe, blinking throughout Oliver's story, erupts in anger when Oliver is through. Clearly, Oliver has usurped Jaffe's authority: he's told stories out of school (that Garland is not any good) and hired another actress without Jaffe's knowledge or approval.

But this isn't all that Oliver has done. Jaffe might well be incensed by a usurpation of his authority, but where does Jaffe's greatest authority lie? His power in *Twentieth Century* is identified as the power to create a *star,* to, as he puts it, "find the gold that's inside" of Lily and "to mine it." What Oliver's actions, which Jaffe rightly identifies as "treachery," betray are his doubts about Jaffe's creative and directorial powers. No one, in his view, can make Lily a star, not even "The Master." But this is not what Jaffe thinks; indeed, he is certain he can make Lily a great star because he is certain of his powers.

In the same way that Oliver's doubts dumbfound Jaffe, the doubts expressed by the woman he loves in *The Beloved Rogue* shock him. He blinks in that film at the moment Charlotte wakens from a state of romantic entrancement and rebukes all of his grand plans, his vision of the perfect world they will inhabit as lovers, a world without class distinctions and a world of bliss. To be sure, Charlotte had been captivated by Villon's dream. Clasped in his arms, they had both gazed off, absorbed in the fantasy of what will be that Villon ardently sketched.

Once again, as *Twentieth Century,* Barrymore bursts into a furious tirade after he blinks. He informs Charlotte that his art will keep her alive long after her class has disappeared. This time he explicity declares something that had been implicit in his creation of the star Lily Garland in *Twentieth Century*: his powers as an artist are so great that they assure immortality.

Barrymore's blinks declare that he is, at first, struck dumb by what is said to him at these moments. He simply cannot believe what he hears: he cannot believe that Oliver and Charlotte can't see what he can see so clearly, in one case, the star within Lily, and in the other case, a world made perfect by perfect love. Why can't he believe Oliver and Charlotte? Both seem to be telling Barrymore things that are true: Plotka (Garland) doesn't show much talent, and the world is not going to be transformed before their, or our, very eyes. Is Barrymore insensible of such facts?

If we assume that these are just dreams that Barrymore has, that they are unattainable and exist in his mind like wishes, then Barrymore emerges as a madman. And, in fact, this is precisely the interpretation of this deep feature of his identity that *A Bill of Divorcement* and the closing of *Beau Brummel* explore. (*A Bill of Divorcement* only covers the fact that it is a study of this feature of Barrymore's mind or imagination or identity with the story about familial "bad blood.")

Barrymore's ability to conceive a reality beyond what anyone's, including his own, ordinary senses deliver, or beyond what others in the worlds of his films can know, means he is considered mad by others in many of his films. A central question in this regard is: does Barrymore take himself to be mad? *A Bill of Divorcement* provides one answer. In that film Barrymore summons his capacity for extreme and violent behavior *as an actor* when he exploits his daughter's sympathy and terror of him and convinces her to send her mother from the house. The revelation that Barrymore's madness can be an act, and thus can be under his control, is *A Bill of Divorcement's* deepest declaration about the nature of its leading man. Cukor's film's meditation of Barrymore complicates whatever we might go on to say about Barrymore's acting, about his powers, his genius, and about his theatricality, by revealing in a way no other film does that he is always acting.

In *Twentieth Century* and in *The Beloved Rogue,* the possibility that Barrymore is clinically mad does not arise. The fact that he possesses a private vision of things others cannot see is interpreted within his identity as an artist—in Hawks' film, he is a supreme figure of the theater, and in Crosland's film he plays the poet François Villon. These films identify the power of Barrymore's imagination as genius.

Barrymore's blinks at Oliver and Charlotte are expressions of disbelief. He cannot believe that they don't see what he sees, and he cannot believe they doubt him. Barrymore's blinks reveal him as a figure whose artistry, genius, or madness separates him from others, even from those who love him. His blinks declare, then, not only that he is convinced of his genius—and outraged when others underestimate it—but that to be an artist, to be Barrymore, is to be alone.

Barrymore's blinks made an important feature of his condition as a figure of tragedy knowable. It seems appropriate here to add that I take the fact that they are common in his acting as proof that Barrymore read scripts with an insightful and educated eye and that he recognized, throughout his career, the occasions that called upon him to declare not only his understanding of himself as a supreme artist, but his knowledge of himself as a tragic figure.

Barrymore's blinks at his reflection in the mirror are, as always, partly comical. They suggest that he's surprised at what he sees, quite as though he had never looked at himself before, and they suggest he had never gazed at himself with the particular idea he has in mind at this moment. They also show that he feels mocked by his reflection, which he sees as an appearance without a mind of its own, a shell that simply mimicks him. At this moment, neither an Oliver nor a Charlotte mocks, underestimates, or challenges Barrymore, but his own reflection. Thus the rehearsal that follows feels like a puppet show with the puppeteer, Barrymore, behind the camera, out of sight in the original, and Barrymore or "Beau" the puppet on stage.

Gazing at his reflection, Barrymore realizes he can make anything of his appearance. Part of him is always on display, while part of him, his inner self, remains concealed. He gazes here upon his reflection with eyes of an author or a creator, or an actor, who examines the unmolded stuff of a character. If the issue in *Twentieth Century* is how will he make Lily Garland a star?, here the issue is, how will Barrymore bring his powers to bear upon himself? What will he become?

Before and after he blinks, Barrymore's gaze at himself is cold and dispassionate. Why? Why not, for example, a look of frustration or disappointment? A knowing look? A smile? Barrymore regards his body in the mirror impersonally, as a vessel into which he must breath life. His body does not become a mask when he creates "Beau." It was already a mask. As "Beau," his body merely becomes a better mask, a fully conceived covering of his inner being.

By denying that his reflection is himself, Barrymore denies the humanness of "Beau" and makes of the reflection a monster. (Richard III and Mr. Hyde are monsters of this sort too.) But "Beau" is also Barrymore. "Beau" thus reveals Barrymore as a figure at once human and monstrous. In other roles Barrymore played, the possibility or fact of his monstrousness is somewhat easier to see. In *Dr. Jekyll and Mr. Hyde,* for example, Barrymore becomes a hideous creature when he transforms himself into Hyde; as Svengali in *Svengali,* Barrymore distorts his evenly proportioned body by elongating his features with makeup and heeled boots and masks his face with a beard and unkempt, long hair; even as Ahab in *The Sea Beast,* a romanticized version of *Moby Dick,* we find Barrymore's naturally graceful body disfigured by the loss of his leg to the whale.

"Beau" is another of these masks. To be sure, it is their opposite on one score: "Beau" is not hideous, like Mr. Hyde or Svengali, and neither is he comical, like (what I'll call) Barrymore's Colonel Sanders disguise in *Twentieth Century.* "Beau" is a mask of beauty. In *Beau Brummel,* Barrymore's beauty is the emblem of his monstrousness; his beauty is the feature of his presence that declares his hideousness.

Barrymore's masks meditate theatricality itself by taking up a condition of human existence and reflecting upon it. His masks deform him, camouflage his inner being, clothe him and keep him from our view. The deformities of his masks stand as proof of what I'll call, taking a cue from *Richard III,* the "accident" that places each of us, our inner beings, within a particular body. This metaphysical condition meditated in Barrymore's theatricality received perhaps its fullest examination in *Richard III,* in which deformity is understood as the sign that Richard was "sent before [his] time," and was pushed into the world "unfinished." His inner being is not one with his outer being. Cast—imprisoned, locked up—into the body he inhabits, he is a stranger in that house just as Barrymore is a stranger inside of his own body, inside of "Beau," of Mr. Hyde, of Richard III.

All of Barrymore's acting meditates the metaphysical disjointedness of his body and his inner being. The closing sequence of *Beau Brummel* literalizes this subject of Barrymore's acting by presenting him as an inmate in a prison. It is here that *Beau Brummel's* indebtedness to *Peter Ibbetson* is most apparent. *Ibbetson* employed a complicated system of transparent screens to achieve the illusion of the other world Peter and Mimsy occupy when they "dream true" and after their deaths; *Beau Brummel* uses the device of superimposition to a similar end (figs. 7.10-7.11).

The freedom longed for by both Ibbetson and Beau is freedom from the body, from the mortal world itself. In both, romantic happiness exists as only a dream until the body is finally disposed of and the inner being liberated. Only then is theatricality no longer a necessity; only then can a marriage of true minds occur.

Barrymore's performance in *Beau Brummel* reveals his acting on film to be deeply consistent with his work on stage. The idea that Barrymore was required to "make a transition" from stage to film may have its superficial claims, but close examination of Barrymore's career overall shows up that argument's irrelevance. The fact is that Barrymore established himself as the pre-eminent

**Fig. 7.10**

actor on stage in a genre of romance that was fundamentally based on, and no doubt inspired by, his presence, beauty, and understanding of theatricality. Barrymore continued to work in that genre in Hollywood and to meditate on the conditions of his theatricality in his performances on film. Barrymore's film acting, like his stage acting, is nothing less than a meditation on and an acknowledgement of his mortality.

Fig. 7.11

## NOTES

1. Søren Kierkegaard, "Herr Phister As Captain Scipio," *Crisis in the Life of an Actress and Other Essays on Drama,* trans. and intro. by Stephen Crites (London: Collins, 1967), p. 112.
2. *Life,* vol. 6, no 5, January 30, 1939.
3. F.P.A., "The Conning Tower," *The World,* November 18, 1922.
4. John Barrymore, *Confessions of an Actor* (New York: B.Blom, 1971, 1926), vs. unpaged.
5. *The Sea Beast*, an adaptation of *Moby Dick*, followed in 1926; then *Don Juan* (1926), Warner's first Vitaphone film; then *When A Man Loves* and *The Beloved Rogue* (1927), both directed by Alan Crosland, one of the best directors Barrymore worked with in Hollywood.
6. George du Maurier, *Peter Ibbetson,* Intro. by John Masefield (London: Peter Davies, 1947), p. 45.
7. John Masefield, "Introduction to *Peter Ibbetson* and *Trilby*," *Novels of George du Maurier: A Pilot Omnibus* (London: Peter Davies, 1947), pp.ix–x.
8. For information about *Forever*, its importance, its condition (It is, I understand, a film so deteriorated that it cannot be seen), and the insight that Beaumont (who was not the most erudite director Barrymore worked with in Hollywood) in all likelihood saw it rather than the play, I am grateful to William K. Everson.

9. Stanley Cavell, "What Photography Calls Thinking", *Raritan: A Quarterly Review.* (New Brunswick, N.J.: Rutgers University Press), 4.3 (Spring 1985), pp. 15–16.
10. Cavell, p. 19.
11. See Northrop Frye's valuable discussions on the nature of loyalty and its meaning in Shakespeare in *Fools of Time: Studies in Shakespearean Tragedy* (Toronto: University of Toronto Press, 1967).

# 8. KEATON: Film Acting As Action

Noël Carroll

## I. INTRODUCTION

CERTAIN IMAGES UNAVOIDABLY CONJURE up the idea of silent film: Chaplin in his derby; Lillian Gish swathed in mountains of curls; and of course, Buster Keaton with his deadpan intensity and his porkpie hat. In one sense, Keaton played a number of different roles; but, in another sense, these were merely surface variations of one underlying character, one underlying set of preoccupations which Keaton explored in different fictional guises. The purpose of this paper is to isolate the core structure of the Keaton character as found in his mature silent films.

When we think of "film acting" what comes first to mind, generally, are the pretenses, mannerisms, and implied motives that a performer employs to give substance to a certain fictional being. However, when applying the notion to Keaton, we must also bear in mind a much more basic sense of "acting," viz., the sense of acting as being involved in a process of doing. Keaton's character, it could be said, is a product of a series of doings; his film acting, in a manner of speaking, is rooted in action. That is, in important respects, Keaton's character emerges not through declaiming, posturing, or emoting, but in the process of action, or better, in interactions, specifically with things. If such a rough distinction may be drawn, Keaton emphasizes the behavioral—the engagement with objects—rather than the psychological, where that category signals interest in the affective and in motivation. Moreover, the terrain of Keaton's activity is less significantly the social or the interpersonal and, more importantly, the realm of objects and the physical world. But though Keaton's traffic is most arrestingly with mute objects—or with people treated as objects, like so many weights in precarious balance—Keaton nevertheless is able to create a structurally rich and compelling character, one that calls attention to a dimension of human existence—what I call concrete intelligence—that is rarely explored in art, and even more rarely with the finesse found in Keaton's works.

Keaton's film acting is concerned, first and foremost, with the manipulation of objects and, by extension, with the manipulation of people as physical objects. This is not to say that Keaton's films lack dramatic or social dimensions, but rather that what is distinctive about the films and the character they are designed to showcase is a concern with the interaction between human life and things. Specifically, I shall claim, Keaton's preoccupation is with exemplifying what intelligence, and the lack thereof, amounts to in our interaction with things. The dramatic conflicts in the films and their subtending social relations are, for Keaton, pretexts for a series of feats and failures in the realm of micro-engineering.

Of course, other silent comics, such as Chaplin, build their characters through interactions with things. However, there is something special about the way in which the Keaton character approaches physical objects. One way to get a sense of this is to recall that many of the most memorable moments in Chaplin films involve the metaphoric transformation of objects into other kinds of objects; the alarm clock becomes a sardine can; the shoe laces become spaghetti; the buttons on a lady's dress become bolts. In Chaplin this transformative vision is the mark of the Tramp's imagination, of his ability to see the world differently. But Keaton's commerce with objects is generally much more mundane, and yet gloriously so. In his films, the physical world is not treated poetically and metaphorically, but manifests itself, as it were, through the sensibility of an engineer. It is a matter of weights and volumes, angles and balances, causes and effects, and of the special kind of human intelligence the physical world calls forth. Keaton's character, as he grapples with objects, shows us how things work and how things fail to work, and in the process the Keaton character shows us what it is to have and to lack a concrete intelligence of things—an ability to accommodate our actions to physical objects and forces, and to assimilate those objects and forces into our activities. Keaton's great theme, embodied in his "acting" (his "doings") is the mechanics of work and of ordinary life, and of the bodily intelligence they require.

I have asserted that Keaton's film acting is profitably approached as a series of doings, as a series of interactions with things in their physical dimensions. A convenient way to explore this issue is to focus on Keaton's gags; they are the crux of his films and the crux of his doings, and it is through his gags that we primarily derive a sense of his character. In what follows, I will examine the recurrent gag structures in Keaton's 1926 film *The General*, suggesting, as well, the extent to which similar structures can be found throughout Keaton's silent work. I shall argue that two significantly interrelated structures—what I call automatism gags and insight gags—dominate Keaton's work, and that the contrast between the characters presupposed by these gags sets forth the terms of the Keaton character's meditation on concrete intelligence.

## II. OUTLINE OF *THE GENERAL*

The story told in *The General* is based, ever so loosely, on an event that occurred during the American Civil War—the hijacking of a Southern locomotive, The General, by Union spies. In Keaton's uproariously fictional retelling, the engineer of The General, played by Buster himself, is Johnny Gray. Johnny's abiding preoccupations are his locomotive and his beloved Annabelle Lee. The opening of the film involves comic observations upon Johnny's courtship of Annabelle.

In the midst of their romance, however, the Civil War breaks out. Annabelle's father and brother rush off to enlist. Johnny follows suit and deftly reaches the head of the enlistment line. But the South needs engineers to win the war, and Johnny's application for military service is rejected. Johnny tries several ruses to enlist, but each is unmasked by the conscription board, and Johnny is unceremoniously ejected with a swift kick to the rear.

Annabelle's family sees Johnny and offers him a place with them on the enlistment line. Recalling his aching bottom, Johnny declines, an action Annabelle's family interprets to Johnny's discredit. Annabelle seeks Johnny out and demands to know why he didn't enlist. When he explains that they wouldn't take him, she accuses him of lying and says, "I don't want you to speak to me again until you are in uniform." This sets up two dominant questions whose answers we await until the end of the story: Will Johnny re-win Annabelle's affections, and how, in order to do that, will he ever be in a position to enlist?

After a short interlude—in which we are privy to the Union plan to seize The General as part of a larger offensive—the hijacking scene commences. The General is about to depart from Marietta, and Annabelle, who is still not speaking to Johnny, is a passenger. When the train stops for a layover, the hijackers make their move while Johnny is washing up. But Annabelle is on board, checking her luggage. As the train pulls away, Johnny pursues it on foot. Two more key narrative questions arise: Will Johnny recapture The General, and, in the process, will he rescue Annabelle?

The seizure of The General and Johnny's subsequent pursuit make up much of the first half of the film. This section is very eventful, challenging Johnny with a wealth of physical tasks whose performance or, rather often, whose misperformance, enable Keaton to define one antipode of his character. The spies pull up rails and litter the tracks with debris in order to impede pursuit, and Johnny must mediate these obstacles in order to continue. The sequence is virtually pure action, providing a comic forum of mishaps through which Keaton projects one side of his characterization of Johnny.

At one point, Johnny reaches a Southern encampment. Troops load onto another train pulled by a locomotive called The Texas. But Johnny, characteristically, forgets to attach the troop car to his engine, and he chugs out of the depot without his army. Nevertheless, the hijackers believe they are being pursued by estimable forces, and so they flee their lonely Fury, Johnny. By the time the Northerners realize that there is only one man chasing them and they counterattack, both trains are in Union territory. Johnny abandons The Texas and makes his way through a dark and rainy forest to a house which turns out to be the Union headquarters. There he learns of the impending Northern attack and of Annabelle's captivity. He must save Annabelle, retrieve The General, and speed South to warn the Confederates of the Union offensive. Which he then does.

Once Johnny has secured both Annabelle and The General, the chase resumes, only this time it is, so to say, in reverse: the Union soldiers are the pursuers, and Johnny is the pursued. Many of the gags from the earlier chase are recycled; however, this time around, most frequently, the Northerners serve as the butt of the humor. Johnny—heaping the tracks with barriers and boobytraps—does unto the Union what it had done to him. Whereas in the first half of the film Johnny had generally shown himself to be inept at or unaware of the tasks set before him, in the second chase, he becomes progressively more adept; his assured, stunningly co-ordinated and insightful manipulations of the physical world reveal the second side of the Keaton character. For in this second chase, not only has the literal direction of the race reversed, but that reversal itself marks the overall reversal of Johnny's relation to the world around him.

Johnny reaches Southern forces, delivers Annabelle to safety, and is able to warn the confederates of the Union advance in time for the boys in gray to ambush the boys in blue. A battle ensues in which Johnny distinguishes himself; he is made a lieutenant. And now that he is in a Confederate uniform, his courtship with Annabelle proceeds toward an implied blissful future.

Before turning to Keaton's acting here, it pays to remark upon the extreme elegance and economy of the plot of *The General*. For not only was Keaton the star of the film, but, as was the case with most of his major works, he was effectively a writer and director as well. Thus, many of the qualities that mark the exposition of *The General*—precision, sharp structure, studied reversibility—are applicable, in a different register, to Keaton's performance style. That is, Keaton's character and the fictional world he creates for it are of a qualitative piece.

The first thing that strikes one about the plot of *The General* is its smoothly coordinated narrative logic. The film presents four prevailing narrative questions which it answers with sequentially dovetailing events: will Johnny win Annabelle, which depends upon the question, will he be enlisted? And will he rescue The General and thereby be able to reach Southern lines in time to warn the Confederates? In interlocking order, he recaptures The General and warns the South, for which he is rewarded with a commission which paves the way for a happily-ever-after reunion with Annabelle. Very neat, no loose ends, and tight connections revealing a taste for a clean, logical line of action in Keaton the storyteller, which matches a similar penchant for clear, uncluttered lines of cause and effect in Keaton the performer.

Also, the plot of *The General* is, like that of certain other Keaton films, possessed of a doubling structure.[1] The two chases make for a pattern of theme and variation: first, Johnny derails; then, later, the Union soldiers derail. This gives the film a strong architectonic flavor. Indeed, there is an early scene in which the Union command peruses a map of their attack. It might as well be a diagram of the plot, very linear, but of course reversible. Here one has the sense of a narrative imagination characterizable in scientific and mechanical metaphors. It is a very "geometrical" and "rational" imagination, very linear and likely to be fascinated with erector sets, while the concerns with reversibility and variation suggest an experimentalist mentality. It should come as no surprise that Keaton believed that had he not been a comedian, he would have become an engineer. Moreover, the "mechanical" sensibility expressed by Keaton's narrative preferences are echoed again and again in his gags, which are obsessed with concrete manipulations.

But the doubling structure in *The General* is not only expressive, it is also functional. For it enables Keaton to divide his character into roughly two phases which reflect the two sides of concrete intelligence. Through the first chase, the Johnny Gray character is predominantly, though not always, inept, while from his rescue of Annabelle onwards, Johnny perfects his ability to manipulate the physical world. *The General*, like many other Keaton films, offers us a Keaton character split into two strongly contrasting parts, what we might call the inept and the adept, which, in turn, shows us two antipodes of concrete intelligence. The inept character emerges through the physical action of Keaton's "automatism" gags, while the adept character figures in Keaton's "insight" gags.

## III. AUTOMATISM

To begin to get a feeling for the theme of automatism in Keaton's character, one can look at the first gag proper in *The General*. Johnny is going to visit Annabelle. The gag is composed of a string of six shots. First there is a medium close shot of Annabelle, apparently borrowing a book. She turns to walk toward a gate, her back to the camera. Then there is a medium long shot of Johnny, followed by local town boys, walking past a hedge. The boys imitate Johnny's every move. The third shot is a medium shot which places Annabelle, book in hand, at the end of a pathway that cuts through a hedge. Shot four establishes that the hedge in the previous shot is the one that Johnny is passing. This shot puts Annabelle in the background and Johnny and his entourage in the middle ground. Since Annabelle is just back from the hedge, Johnny doesn't see her. He walks right by and Annabelle, seeing him, falls into step behind the boys. Shot five is a long shot that shows the whole parade turning into Annabelle's front yard, and the last shot establishes the group at Annabelle's door. Johnny adjusts his coat, cleans his shoes, and slicks down his hair. Of course, Annabelle is watching the entire procedure. Thus, if Johnny's last minute touch-ups are meant to suggest to Annabelle that he is always so precisely presentable, his vanities are exposed, since Annabelle, unbeknownst to him, witnesses his entire ritual. Finally, Johnny knocks; he stands back and sideways, adopting a dignified *contrapposto* stance. At that moment, he is virtually face to face with Annabelle. He looks momentarily ruffled—she's on the wrong side of the door—and his jaw drops in a flustered sort of way. (Parenthetically, it pays to note that this gag is significantly enhanced by Keaton's facial gestures. He is not a great stone face except in respect of not smiling. Otherwise, his face is quite expressive.)

He is not a great stone face except in respect of not smiling. Otherwise, his face is quite expressive.)

The preceding gag is certainly at the expense of Johnny Gray. What is humorous is what is revealed about his character. As he walks along the street, Keaton portrays Johnny as though he had no peripheral vision. Likewise, when he turns into Annabelle's yard, he is oblivious to lateral presences. What is being represented is a character with an awesome fixity of attention, with acute tunnel vision. His orientation is relentlessly frontal. The character has the idea that Annabelle is at home and that he will visit her. His determination leads him to travel in a manner that suppresses normal perceptual habits, namely he ceases to respond to glimpses on the periphery of his visual field, an impression that Keaton-the-actor reinforces by the rigid way in which he holds his head. The character overvalues the way he thinks things are, and he simultaneously undervalues new input. He's stuck on automatic pilot, so to speak. The result is that he functions almost completely in terms of his idea of the situation without bothering to modify that idea by means of new data. It is the kind of fixity of attention, or rather spectacular inattention, that provokes our laughter.

The courtship section of *The General* concludes with a particularly famous inattention gag. Annabelle has just spurned Johnny unless he joins the army. Dejectedly, Johnny slumps back onto the drive-rod of his engine, completely absorbed in his misfortune. The camera pulls back for a long shot. We see an engineer enter the cab and stoke up the engine. Johnny continues to sit forlornly on his drive-rod. We see that he is out of the engineer's field of vision and that he, Johnny, is ignorant of what is going on in the cab, since his glance is directed at the ground. Suddenly the engine starts. The wheels turn several times, then, just as the train enters a tunnel, Johnny finally realizes that he is lethally balanced on the drive-rod of a moving engine.

Our reaction to this scene is undoubtedly complex. Obviously, the stunt is dangerous—what if the wheels lost traction? But aside from the danger, we can also see that the basis of this gag is two simultaneous acts of inattention. The engineer carries on unaware of what is in front of him on the wheels of his locomotive. He relies on his conception of things, not on the actual situation. Johnny, of course, raises the level of inattention by virtually a quantum leap. For he is initially inattentive to the fact that the train is moving. He is so preoccupied that presumably he not only fails to respond to the sound of the train, but even to his own bodily sensations, which ought to provoke a feeling of rising and falling. This gag is an example of Keaton's "slow burn," i.e., the character's coming to awareness of a (usually untoward) state of affairs over an inordinately long time interval. Here, the "slow burn" is used to bring the theme of the scene to a crescendo by compounding the engineer's initial act of inattention with an almost inconceivable act of inattention on Johnny's part.

So far we have seen that important gags in the first section of *The General* underscore the character's inattentiveness, his inability to register that the world around him has changed in ways that diverge radically from his settled idea of how things stand. How does this connect with the notion of automatism? Well, Johnny is not only inattentive to changes in the environment, but he continues behaving in the way that his preconceptions dictate, often on the way to a pratfall. That is, Johnny behaves automatically or like a preprogrammed automaton, blind to new information. Johnny's path, most often to his chagrin, seems set in stone. Many of the gags of the first half of *The General* rely on this connection between inattention and automatism.

For example, Johnny and four volunteers charge on foot after the hijacked General. We see that Johnny's cohorts give up the chase almost immediately. But until the Union spies subdue Annabelle and sever Confederate telegraph wires, Johnny does not realize that he is alone. Indeed, one feels Johnny would never have turned around, had he not reached a handcar siding. Again, the character's tendency is to adopt a rigid and fixed viewpoint, attending only to what is directly in front of him, assured that the rest of the world is as he supposes it to be. And this, in turn, sends him hurtling forward more like a car without a driver—or a train without an engineer—than a sentient being.

Undoubtedly the most elaborate example of Johnny's tendency to maintain a single track of behavior despite changes in the environment is his entry into Northern territory. The scene begins with the title, "The Southern Army facing Chattanooga is ordered to retreat." There is a shot of Confederate cavalry troops withdrawing. Then a shot of the Union spies shows them crouching in the cab of The General. Finally, we see Johnny, from overhead, cutting wood in the timber-car of the recently acquired locomotive, The Texas. The film then cuts to a shot of the retreating Southerners. Initially it is a long shot. Next, all of a sudden, The Texas pulls into the foreground from screen left. The Texas drives past the camera, revealing that Johnny is still chopping wood with his back to the battle. As the battle continues, the South turns heel and the Northerners take the field. Johnny continues to chop. At one point he breaks his axe handle. But even with this rupture in his work pattern, he remains unaware that he is completely surrounded by Union troops. In all, it takes twelve shots before Johnny realizes his predicament, so absolutely engrossed is he in his work that he never once glances outside the narrow ambit of his wood pile.

In many ways, it seems that the railroad is an appropriate central image in *The General*, for there is a way in which imagery of railroads supplies a source in ordinary language for our metaphors of the type of automatism that is so characteristic of Johnny. We speak of people as having "one-track minds" in order to underscore the fixity of their ideas. The notion of a track in this metaphor emphasizes the rigidity with which the single-minded person maintains his preconceived idea. In this light, Johnny's conceptions of things are analogous to a track. The imagery of the film virtually demands this analogy. And Johnny himself is rather like a locomotive. He travels along his track, oblivious to what the changing environment has placed in his way. Within this context, the recurring derailments and track switchings in *The General* become a kind of objective correlative to the way in which Johnny's "one-track mind" constantly—both figuratively and sometimes literally—derails his schemes and sends him barreling in the wrong direction.

The action of these gags incarnates the automaton aspect of the Keaton character. The acting, i.e., the pretense they require from Keaton, is an impression of utter absorption, a rigidly narrow scope of attention, and a kind of perpetual momentum, often in the service of a repetitive, even mechanical task, such as chopping wood.

The preceding discussion of automatism gags, it is hoped, establishes that there is, in *The General*, a character-based theme of rigidity or inflexibility of behavior patterns, premised on Johnny's inattention to changes in the environment. Of course, inattention, in and of itself, is hardly a theme specific to the Keaton character, but can be found in other comic types. However, within the class of Keaton's automatism gags, we can distinguish a core group which define the special emphasis Keaton exerts in regard to automatism. Those gags are ones that involve physical tasks requiring the manipulation of the natural and industrial environment.

A perfect example of this kind of gag occurs in the first short that Keaton released for distribution. In *One Week*, the Keaton character marries. The newlyweds are given a house that Keaton must assemble. A disgruntled former suitor of Keaton's wife vengefully changes the numbers on the crates that contain the prefabricated house. The instructions for assembling the house are based on the numbers on the crates. Keaton persists in erecting the house according to the instructions, despite the fact that the numbers on the crates match up with the numbers in the instructions with outlandish results: second floor doors open onto thin air, and the roof has a valley in it. Obviously, the Keaton character has willfully followed the instructions despite these incongruities. An abstract, preconceived idea, represented by the instructions, completely governs the character's mediation with the environment. The madcap house that emerges is a literal monument to the character's single-track mind.

Turning back to *The General*, we see that a large number of central automatism/inattention gags are also involved with the manipulation of the physical environment, for instance, the derailment of the hand-car and the attempt to shunt the box car onto a siding.[2] Of course, most of the gags involving the train chases are obviously concerned with physical manipulations. A particularly emblematic gag in this respect occurs when The Texas, sidetracked by Union spies, nearly runs off an abruptly ending spur. Johnny manages to stop the train at the last minute. He then attempts to reverse the engine. However, the wheels of the engine spin impotently on the track. There is no traction. Johnny leaps from the engine and begins to shovel sand onto the track in an effort to give the wheels something with which to engage. At one point, Johnny turns his back to the engine. He tries to kick loose a clump of grass so that more dirt can be freed to shovel onto the track. While his back is turned, however, the wheels of the locomotive catch on the sand that Johnny previously put on the track, and the train pulls away. But Johnny is too preoccupied to realize his train is gone.

Similarly, when Johnny recovers The General, he and Annabelle stop it to refuel at a corral fence composed of long beams piled carefully on top of each other. Johnny rushes from the locomotive, grabbing the long unwieldy fencing and hurtling it over the tender. Johnny is so utterly immersed in his work that he fails to notice that he has pitched these railings clear over the timber car. All his effort succeeds in achieving is to pile the lumber on the opposite side of the train. At points in the gag, Johnny's behavior is almost robotlike; he works in a preprogrammed manner that takes no account of the actual results of his own actions. It is as though he were devoid of feedback.

All the gags discussed so far involve a duality[3] of viewpoint. There is the situation seen as it actually is—e.g., the train pulling away while Johnny's back is turned—and the situation as the character misconceives it. The audience is privy to both these viewpoints; the gag emerges in the discrepancy between the actual situation and the way the character misapprehends it. To work, such a gag requires a character with a certain type of mentality, and Keaton's acting or action fulfills this requirement by proposing a character who, against the reality principle, fixates on an inflexible mental map of a situation and behaves, with often disastrous effect, in accordance with that mental map.

Though most of Keaton's film acting is a matter of doing, nevertheless, the character that he evolves through his automatism gags is essentially a portrait of a state of mind, of a way of thinking. Rigidity of thought, the incapacity to reevaluate the situation and to modify behavior accordingly, represent a form of dimwittedness or slowness of thought. That Keaton restages these automatism gags very often with reference to manual work, suggests his acknowledgment that such "merely physical" activity requires an intelligence and has a cognitive dimension, cultural prejudices to the contrary notwithstanding.

Through automatism gags, the Keaton character explores the relation of intelligence to physical activity, such as manual work, through a kind of process of negation, viz., Johnny's errors in carrying out physical tasks. By means of this *via negativa*, Keaton outlines his understanding of concrete intelligence through the enactment of gags that exemplify a paradigmatic lack of responsiveness to the environment. To confirm the centrality of the theme of intelligence for the Keaton character, one need only consult one's experience of Keaton's automatism/inattention gags. These gags presuppose alertness on the part of the viewer versus the character's rigidity—a perceptive response versus a virtually blind response. What the audience must do to appreciate the automatism gags is to make up the difference between the rote behavior of characters and an alert, intelligent comprehension of the situation.

The notions of fixation, rigidity, inflexibility, inattention and automatism deployed in our discussion of the Keaton character so far, of course, are derived from the comic theory of Henri Bergson. Moreover, we have also followed Bergson in holding that the appeal made by such themes is concerned at root with the issue of intelligence. However, Bergson's theoretical machinery is not embraced here in the belief that it is a perfectly adequate theory for all comedy, of which *The General* and the rest of Keaton's oeuvre are but particular examples. Indeed, in the next section it will be shown that as a general theory of comedy, Bergson's approach cannot work, in part because it can't handle certain key aspects of Keaton's comic character. Nevertheless, Bergson's framework is useful for discussing at least that aspect of the Keaton character that is embodied in the automatism gags. For in both Keaton's comic practice and Bergson's theory, there is a high premium placed on responsiveness to the environment. That is, independently of each other, both Keaton and Bergson construe intelligence in terms of adjustability and adaptability.

For Bergson, comedy performs a social function. Laughter is a corrective. It taunts people away from undesirable modes of behavior. Bergson identifies the most undesirable form of behavior as that which is rote, habituated, or routinized, i.e. "mechanical" in the most negative sense of the term. The absentminded, the inflexible, the unobservant, all these are to be chastized by comedy, thereby driving us to a "wideawake adaptability and the living pliability of a human being."[4] Truly human life, Bergson believes, adjusts itself to the novelty of each situation. In this approach, intelligence, which is very much influenced by Bergson's conception of evolution, is the ability to adapt and adjust to each new circumstance.

Though Keaton appears to lack a view of laughter's role in society, through his characters he seems to share Bergson's conception of intelligence as adaptability, and at least part of his comic practice rests on something very like the Bergsonian connection between adaptability and intelligence. In *The General*, the bulk of the gags involving inattention and automatism all project a picture of mental operations on the part of Johnny Gray that are fixated on a notion of a situation and that are heedless of the need to constantly replenish that idea with fresh details from the environment. Johnny's stupidities, moreover, illuminate what would be a contrary state of affairs, one where the character is intelligent, one where the character behaves as the audience perceives he should, in short, where the character is adaptable.

The importance of the theme of automatism for the Keaton character, and the related opposition of adaptation versus failure to adapt, can be easily identified in Keaton films other than *The General.* Consider the famous projection sequence in *Sherlock Jr.* Sherlock Jr. walks into a scene that is being projected on a motion picture screen. As he goes up to the door of the house in this film-within-a-film, the scene shifts. What is odd about this cut, however, is that the character remains in the same exact screen position that he previously occupied. From the shot of the character before the door, we cut to a garden, and Sherlock begins to sit on a bench in the garden. There is another cut, this time to a city street. Since Sherlock's position and movement remain continuous over the cut, he falls backward into the busy thoroughfare. Sherlock straightens up and starts to walk down the street. All of a sudden, there is yet another cut, and Sherlock nearly walks off a cliff. He looks over the cliff, sticking his neck out. There's a cut, of course; he's in a cage; his neck is invitingly poised in a lion's maw. He backs away from the lion. Cut—he's in a desert. A train just misses him. He sits down and the location changes to a rock surrounded by water. He dives off the rock but a devilishly placed edit lands him headfirst in a snow bank. Standing upright, he reaches out to lean on a tree. A final cut—he is back in the original garden, falling on his head because the tree is no longer there.

This sequence is perhaps Keaton's most delirious exploration of the themes of automatism and maladaptation. Undoubtedly the most frequently invoked example of poor adaptability in the whole evolutionary bestiary is the dinosaur. That dimwitted beast, though suited to tropical climates, supposedly could not survive the rigors of the ice age. The environment changed on him when he wasn't looking. Environmental change is also key to the automatism/inattention gag. And there is hardly a more radical series of environmental changes in all of Keaton than one finds in the preceding sequence of *Sherlock Jr.* Via incredibly precise editing, Keaton is able to draw an image of a character sustaining without modification a set of behaviors appropriate to one environment into another environment where it is inappropriate. This sequence from *Sherlock Jr.* seems to be one of the most symbolic and abstract in all of Keaton, summarizing in almost schematic fashion the Keaton character's underlying tendency toward inadaptability by setting out environmental variations in the most hyperbolic manner imaginable.

Another outstanding automatism gag is the sparring sequence in *Battling Butler*. Here, Keaton, as Alfred Butler, tries his hand at fisticuffs. A professional trainer instructs Butler to watch him. He will make the appropriate countermoves to the thrusts of Butler's sparring partner. Butler need only imitate the trainer, supposedly, in order to protect himself and to win. The hitch in this plan, however, is the time lag between Butler's opponent's punch, the trainer's reaction, and then Butler's reaction. By the time Butler reacts, his opponent's jabs have already landed. The result is a kind of bizarre dance—Butler's opponent throws a punch, the trainer raises his arm in a blocking motion, the punch lands, and Butler, reeling, raises his arm to meet a phantom blow that has already come and gone. The rhythm is repeated again and again until Butler is staggering. As we have seen in *The General*, this is based on Butler's failure to attend to the situation he is actually in. His glance, directed to the trainer, is really a species of deferred attention. Butler is out of synchronization with his environment. Moreover, this notion of being out of synchronization underpins all Keaton's inattention/automatism gags. For synchronization between plan and action, on the one hand, and the environment, on the other, is the very essence of adaptability.

## IV. INSIGHT

Keaton's film acting is primarily a matter of the way in which he acts, in the sense of doing things, most often in the context of gags. It is through these doings that his character emerges. So far it has been stressed that automatism and inadaptability comprise a key aspect of the Keaton character, one developed through Keaton's performance of certain types of gags. But this is not the whole story. For the same character who is inattentive, unheeding, and maladapted to some situations can suddenly manifest an awareness, sensitivity, and control over the environment that is nothing short of breathtaking (as well as laughter provoking).

A famous example of this, one concerned with a physical task, occurs during the first chase in *The General*. The Union spies have thrown railroad ties on the tracks in order to derail Johnny. Johnny slows The Texas down and runs alongside the engine. Carefully he slides down the cow-catcher on the front of the engine and runs to dislodge the first tie from the tracks. With great difficulty, he lifts it off the track. Unfortunately, he has not worked fast enough. The Texas has inched up behind him as he struggled with the first tie, and, by the time he picks it up, the front of the engine sweeps him off his feet and lands him on the cow-catcher. The beam that he removed from the track is so heavy that it pins him to the cow-catcher. Suddenly, he sees that there is another tie on the tracks less than ten feet ahead of him. Thus, the locomotive is about to derail with him on the front of it. Yet Johnny sees an avenue of escape. He realizes that the tie on the track is straddling the rails. So if he can hit the overhanging end of the tie on the track, he can knock it out of the way of the oncoming train. He lifts the tie on his chest over his head and hurls it at the one on the track, banging the latter out of the way of the oncoming train, and thus casting two worries aside with a single blow while "inventing" the catapult in the process (figs. 8.1–8.4).

The presuppositions of this gag are quite different from those of the automatism gags. Whereas the automatism gags seem to presuppose a character whose concept of a state of affairs is rigid, this type of successful adaptation involves a character who can rethink a situation and arrive at insights and inventions. Johnny, pinned to the cow-catcher, is able to break out of a single picture of the situation and is able to think of those threatening railroad ties not as mere beams, but as a lever and a weight. He is able to mentally reorganize the elements of the visual field in a new way—significantly, a new way that will save his life. A monkey, given two separate sticks, has an insight when he realizes that he can combine those two sticks into one in order to reach outside his cage and hook onto a bunch of bananas. Similarly, Johnny has an insight when he thinks of the ties not as ties but as elements of a catapult. His state of mind is one that recognizes this picture of the state of affairs. This stands in striking contrast with Johnny's state of mind during the automatism gags, where his mental map of the situation is irremediably frozen.

The sequence of the railroad ties in *The General* is structurally reminiscent of the scene in *Our Hospitality* where the Keaton character, John McKay, struggles to free himself from a rope that binds him to a log which overhangs a waterfall. This rope originally attached McKay to one of the Canfields. For a long section of the film, it has been a bane to McKay's existence. Finally, it binds him to a log which may at any moment loosen and go shooting over the falls, dragging McKay with it. As McKay tugs on the rope, hoping to free himself, he sees his girlfriend being borne to the edge of the waterfall by a swift current. Suddenly, he rethinks his situation. Instead of conceiving of the log and the rope on the model of a ball and chain, he thinks of it as a crossbeam with an attached rope. Seen this way, he can use the former detriment as a device to save his girlfriend. As she crosses the edge of the falls, he swings over and catches her just before she is about to plummet to the bottom of the falls. Again, the character's behavior is predicated on an ability to reorganize his way of seeing and comprehending the situation. In contrast to automatism gags, inflexibility of thought gives way to flexibility.

Another successful adaptation gag in *The General* occurs when Johnny is chopping wood. As The Texas is passing into Union territory, Johnny breaks his ax handle. He desperately needs wood for his engine. He looks at the broken handle forlornly, but only for a second, because, all of a sudden, he realizes that the handle is wood, the very thing he needs to stoke his engine. He dutifully carries this "newly discovered" piece of kindling to the furnace. Here, as before, the character must shed a characteristic way of thinking. He must switch from thinking of the handle as a handle to thinking of it as wood. A process of discovery, a new way of seeing, is called for. Johnny must decenter his concentration on the functional properties of the object *qua* ax handle and shift his way of thinking about the object in terms of its material properties. This involves both cognition and perception. Refocusing the center of attention from functional properties to materials involves a mental reorganization of Johnny's visual field. The moment of recognition of such a shift is the moment of insight.

The gag that concludes *The General* is also an insight gag, actually one that transforms lovemaking into a problem of concrete intelligence. Like so many comedies, such as Chaplin's *The Gold Rush*, *The General* ends with a hero and the heroine united. Johnny has his uniform, so they can run off and romance. Predictably—since that's where all the trouble began—they nestle on the drive-rod of The General. But since Johnny is an officer now, he must

Fig. 8.1

Fig. 8.2

Fig. 8.3

Fig. 8.4

salute every passing soldier. And given the way he is positioned vis-à-vis Annabelle, this military ritual means that his every attempted kiss is interrupted. Suddenly, it looks as though the whole army is about to march by. In a flash, Johnny realizes that if he switches positions with Annabelle he will be able to kiss and salute simultaneously. Unlike Chaplin, who would play a final love scene like this for feeling (vide *The Gold Rush*), Keaton treats the kiss as an engineering problem, returning once again to the theme of concrete intelligence. Like so many of the gags in *The General*, this parting joke concerns the manipulation of the right/left operations. Mastery of this basic physical category is the foundation for the comic surprise which accompanies the reversal of Johnny's predicament. Johnny must envision himself as opposite his actual position. He must be able to recognize that in such a position his right arm will be able to freely negotiate his salutes while his left arm caresses Annabelle. That is, what is required of Johnny is an insight which is based on a mental reorganizing of the constituents of his visual and kinetic fields.

The preceding gags all presuppose insight on the part of the Keaton character, especially in terms of concrete operations. As such they stand in sharp, systematic contrast with the automatism gags examined in the previous section. It is for this reason that I noted earlier that Bergson's theory of comedy was not perfectly general for all comedy nor even specifically for all Keaton's comic invention. Bergson is aligned to a tradition of comic theorizing that associates comedy with stupidity, the nonrational, the irrational, or the absurd. Freud, though quite different from Bergson, also stands in this tradition. However, such approaches to comedy cannot comprehend all the data. In particular, they cannot accommodate Keaton's successful adaptation gags. For these gags involve insight on the part of the character, rather than stupidity. In terms of the audience, such gags involve a shift in our mode of organizing the situation as well. This shift, often abrupt, is surprising. For example, our expectations are brought up short when Johnny comprehends a new way of employing his broken ax handle. Here the Bergsonian idea, that laughter serves to humiliate the character as a behavioral corrective, is completely untenable, because in fact the character's thinking is far ahead of the audience's.

Rather, the audience laughs at these adaptation gags with a variety of laughter that one indulges when a particularly brilliant checkmate is executed or when a tricky mathematical problem is ingeniously solved. Similarly, we sometimes laugh at the intricate movements of a precision machine, or at the solution of a puzzle. That is, there is a category of laughter that is evoked when, so to speak, "things fall into place." This is a kind of laughter prompted by the apparition of pure intelligibility. This is the kind of reaction that greets Keaton's successful adaptation gags. The basis of these gags cannot be given a Bergsonian formulation. For a theoretical framework, one must turn to the kind of configurational theory of comedy proposed by Quintillian and Hegel and by psychologists of the Gestalt tradition in the thirties. From that tradition of psychology, the following characterization is offered of the relevant mental processes of the humorous experience. Note how aptly it describes the Keaton gags of the successful adaptation variety.

> Wertheimer has shown that the meaning of elements depends on the configuration of which they are a part. When the configuration suddenly changes, the meaning of the elements suddenly changes as a consequence.... Direction is a determining factor underlying the formation of configuration. A problem is always looked at from a certain point of view and this point of view determines what one will do about it (i.e. what direction one's mind will take). A particular direction facilitates certain configurations and inhibits others. Thus, when we are presented with any facts we tend to organize them in a certain way. Usually past experience gives us the point of view; we organize the facts accordingly and consequently miss a new organization or interpretation. A humorous incident is told so as to encourage a certain point of view. Then in the end we are given a conclusion (an organization of the facts presented) which is very different from the one we anticipated. It is like the experience of insight except for certain differences.... [5]

Keaton mixes gags that have apparently very different explanations. There are inattention/automatism gags that are based in the presupposition of the character's fixation on a certain idea of a situation, and there are configurational gags that are based on the character's reorganization of his mental map of the situation. Neither the Bergsonian theory nor the Gestalt configurational theory offers an account of all Keaton's gags. Here, we must turn elsewhere for an understanding of Keaton's themes. The obvious place to look, however, is not far off. The intersection of Gestalt theory with Bergsonian theory may provide the location of Keaton's particular subject. Both theories are concerned with thinking and intelligence, but each places different emphasis on the subject. The automatism gags involve failures of thinking, while the configurational gags involve successful thinking. But both are concerned with thought.

Structurally, Keaton seems to counterpoint the ineptness of Johnny's performance of some physical tasks with moments of resourcefulness and quickly calculated judgment that seem to establish new levels of precision in human activity. Thus, through the action of the character, humor of the inflexibility variety is balanced by humor of the configurational sort. Two contrary modes play against each other. Insofar as a task is an amalgam of thought and action, the formal opposition of successfully executed tasks with failures presupposes an opposition of two different aspects of intellectual activity—fixation versus insight. Analysis of major Keaton gags in *The General* constantly leads one to postulate either fixation or insight of characters (Johnny and others) as the predominant focal points of laughter. From this emerges recognition of the locus or subject of Keaton's character, viz. intelligence, especially concrete intelligence, of which insight and fixation represent two poles, positive and negative.

Similar contrastive structures can be found throughout Keaton's work. That automatism gags abound is undoubtedly obvious. But insight gags are also recurrent, especially in terms of physical manipulations. In *Cops*, the Keaton character "invents" a signal arm from a boxing glove and a scissors lamp. Also in *Cops*, the Keaton character evinces insight when he turns the teeter-tottering ladder on which the police have him cornered into a virtual catapult. In *One Week*, Keaton uses the front porch balustrade as a ladder. In

*The Blacksmith*, an engine hoist becomes the means to offset variations where the Keaton character was thwarted, through his nonadaptability, in his attempt to manipulate the same kind of objects previously encountered. In The Navigator, he is first daunted by the ship's awesome kitchen that was designed to feed hundreds. Disastrously, the Keaton character, called Rollo, tries with a splashing effect to open an outsized can of food, and he fails to boil eggs in a large pot. But the second time around, Rollo has insightfully and humorously adapted to the environment. He uses a crab trap to boil eggs in the enormous cauldron, and he attaches a saw to the wheel of a grindstone to serve as a makeshift can opener. In the scene in *Steamboat Bill Jr.*, where Keaton, as Bill Jr., rescues his father, he has harnessed the objects that earlier bedeviled him—the ropes, throttle and levers—into a mechanism that enables one person to run the entire ship. One can also group the skillful finale of *College* with these "adaptability" performances. Here, Keaton, as Ronald, must run across town to save Mary Haines. There are many obstacles, human and inanimate. Ronald must be especially acute to navigate across parks and landscapes covered with hedges. Nevertheless, he bolts across town at top speed, running around pedestrians like a football player, and leaping over shrubs without missing a stride, like an obstacle course runner. These feats reverse his earlier mishaps with the selfsame academic sports. As he heads towards Mary's second-floor window, he has an insight. Without breaking pace, he grabs a pole that is holding up a clothesline and uses the pole to vault through Mary's window, thereby again reversing his earlier sporting failure. Ronald, in this case, shifts from thinking of the pole's function to simply thinking of it in terms of its length, shape, and weight. Seeing the pole apart from its function enables him to see it as an aid to his jump. Here insight combines with action in a feat of adaptability as the character assimilates the environment to his needs.

The notion of assimilating the environment, of course, applies to key aspects of Keaton's screen action apart from what might be narrowly construed as gags. It extends to feats of superadaptability of the sort that David Robinson has called Keaton's trajectories,[6] i.e., runs such as those at the end of the Roman sequence in *Three*

*Ages*, in *Seven Chances*, and of course in *College*. In these sequences, match cutting facilitates the production of a cinematic image of astounding speed, judgment, and dexterity. Because shot segments of movement are being elided, the composite picture is of sustained continuous movement. It is as if Keaton runs for miles without breaking stride, whereas, of course, he is only actually running for several hundred feet at a time. The appearance is of virtually superhuman alertness and adaptability capable of assimilating every obstacle of the environment into awe-inspiring yet giddy, flabbergasting, unbroken vectors of movement across impossible steeplechases. These feats bespeak and celebrate a bodily intelligence in respect to inanimate things which subsumes them as articles for human use.

In cases such as *Steamboat Bill Jr.* and *College*, the Keaton character becomes possessed of insight and superadaptability at those crucial narrative turning points where he is called to the rescue. In *The General*, insight and adaptability gags are distributed throughout, though with a greater preponderance in the second chase. Obviously, these shifts from inept to adept correspond most often to changes in the direction of the story. However, as to the question of whether these gags are meant to serve the story, or vice-versa, I believe that it is the story which functions as the armature for the gags. Keaton's profound theme is not "Love shall overcome," as a purely narratological exegesis might suggest, but rather is an examination of the parameters of human intelligence, specifically bodily intelligence, conceived in terms of adaptability, whose conditions Keaton reveals rather than analyzes through the contrast of automatism and insight which is developed through his actions.

## CONCLUSION

It has been the thesis of this paper that Keaton's film acting—i.e., the screen performance elements that shape what is key to our perception of the Keaton character—are his actions, often task-like performances, which occur in the context of gags and his famous "trajectories." Through the contrast of automatism and insight, the Keaton character and his "doings" are preoccupied with the theme of intelligence, particularly bodily intelligence, which is ultimately celebrated in terms of adaptability. In this way, the Keaton character presents us with a reflection upon a dimension of human existence infrequently explored and acknowledged, let alone celebrated, in art: our relation with objects *qua* objects and the special intelligence that that relation requires. Perhaps this can be employed in an explanation of Keaton's ever-rising fortunes in respect to critical and popular response. For Keaton celebrates bodily intelligence with things, a dimension of human skill progressively in diminishing demand in societies where the division of labor and service occupations prevail. Keaton recalls for the salesperson, the clerk, the teacher, the computer programmer, and the journalist a time when the intelligent interaction with things was the fulcrum of a daily life, a time past but not lost.

## NOTES

1. For sustained analyses of the doubling structure throughout Keaton's narratives, see Daniel Moews, *Keaton: The Silent Features Close-up* (Berkeley: University of California Press, 1977).
2. For analyses of these gags from *The General*, as well as others not discussed in this paper, see Noel Carroll, *An In-depth Analysis of Buster Keaton's The General* (Ph.D. dissertation, New York University, 1976). The director of that thesis was Annette Michelson, whose influence on my approach to Keaton and to film in general has been profound.
3. The gags that I describe in terms of a duality of viewpoint can also be seen as a subset of what Bergson calls the reciprocal interference of (event) series: see Henri Bergson, *Laughter in Comedy*, ed: Wylie Sypher (Garden City: Doubleday Anchor Books, 1956), p. 123.
4. Bergson, p. 67.
5. Norman Maier, "A Gestalt Theory of Humor," *The British Journal of Psychology,* vol. XXIII, part I. (July 1932), pp. 69–70.
6. David Robinson, *Buster Keaton* (Bloomington: University of Indiana Press, 1969), p. 79.

# 9. ACTOR AND TEXT: LA GRANDE ILLUSION

**Sylvie Gendron**
**translated from French by Anne Golden with Carole Zucker**

## INTRODUCTION

THE ESSENCE OF FRENCH CINEMA during the thirties and forties is inexorably bound to what has been called poetic realism. Clair, Feyder, Duvivier, Becker, Carné, and Renoir are the famous *école française*, who would change and influence the history and evolution of French cinema. Some of the key actors were Jean Gabin, Michel Simon, Louis Jouvet, Pierre Fresnay, as well as Michèle Morgan, Simone Simon, and Françoise Rosay.

The development of poetic realism coincides, by a few years, with the advent of sound in films. In the French cinema, we can identify the desire to develop a literary quality, borrowed from playwrights, novelists, and poets, and its infusion into the stories, characters, and dialogue of the films. This development did not occur simply because of sound, but because of the nature and identity of the language in its incomparable diversity of expression.

In French cinema, the changes were the catalyst for the appearance of a new type of artist: the screen-dialogue writer, who was most often from the world of theater, literature or radio. This phenomenon is often ignored or neglected in discussions of French poetic realism, but in fact the importance of story and dialogue (or text) cannot be overstated. The *dialoguiste*'s* position was ex-

**Ed. note*. There is no precise English equivalent to the French *dialoguiste*. The word *screenwriter* does not have the same connotations as *dialoguiste*, although the work of a screenwriter and *dialoguiste* would overlap. Gendron points out that the *dialoguiste* is more intensely involved with character and language.

tremely important. His tasks were to verbalize a director's ideas, to make the characters appealing to the public, and to give the actor the basis for the creation of a character.

Names linked with the development of screen-dialogue writing include Pierre Bost, Jean Aurenche, Henri Jeanson, Jacques Prévert, and Charles Spaak. Today, when certain films of this period are mentioned, the name of the writer comes up as often as that of the director (for example, Carné-Prévert, Feyder-Spaak).

Film historians cite the films not only for the quality of their technical achievement, but for their unique dialogue and sensitive character development. Throughout these films, we can clearly identify a desire to go beyond simple storytelling using words and images. There is a seductive power in the themes, characters, and dialogue. It can be found in the humor, poetry, and imagery of the script and in the character development. The need to surpass the banality of words and their primary function as a tool of communication corresponds to an aesthetic end. The public recognized and welcomed the final product (called *l'esprit français*) as something unique and distinct. It became a culmination, as well as an index, of cultural and social traditions.

The spirit is manifest, first and foremost, in language since the latter is the most accessible and pervasive means of communication. But it goes beyond the written word and its various modes of expression (theater, novels, etc.), although it is inspired by all of these. Quite simply, words are of prime importance for the French. Language is more than a means of communication. For example, the appearance and development of *argot* is more than a characteristic of a social class and milieu. Slang as a "language" is the earmark of a love for colorful sounds and images.

When one studies this period of French cinema, certain tendencies become apparent. The form of the novel can be found at the level of narrative structure, while themes and characters attain "literariness" through the precision and piquancy of their expression. On the other hand, there are striking examples of film used in a theatrical manner, as in the case of Pagnol and Guitry. Pagnol's trilogy (*Marius–Fanny–César*) fueled the public appreciation for characters and dialogue. These examples of "canned theater" (as

Pagnol himself put it) are successful for the strength, quality, and color of their scripts and the intense rendering of the characters; they serve as proof that words and dialogue were essential to this period of French cinema.

Once aware of the importance of words, scenario, and the *dialoguiste*, we can study the work of the actor from within the same era. The dialogue in French films (perhaps more so than in other national cinemas) is an integral part of the whole and is at least as important as actions and gestures. Renoir understood this fact. With speech, the character attained a level of authenticity that went beyond filmic representation. Speech became the primary element in the definition and incarnation of a character.

The relationship between an actor and his text is privileged. It is the result of contact between inert material and a diverse and complex individual. If scripts are a favored aspect of thirties and forties French cinema, they are also extremely important as a tool for actors. The work of an actor might be cursorily summarized as actor-text-character.

In the beginning, the essence of a character is provided by the *dialoguiste* through verbal construction. The nature and thrust of a script destined for a particular character allows the actor to realize an imaginary being. A character's identity, inspired by the script, takes shape with vocal intonation, pronunciation, physical aspect and attitude (gesture, appearance), and state of mind.

One film that best lends itself to a study of actors—the characters they embody and their impact—is Renoir's *La Grande Illusion*. The film boasts performances that stem from different acting techniques. From every point of view, the film asserts the power of the text. Because the action of the film takes place in a prison camp during World War I, the characters' lives unfold in specific, limited locations. Details that point to ideas about their normal ways of life and their personality traits come primarily from the text and from those props associated with each character. We will now turn to a detailed analysis of three central performances in the film.*

---

**Ed. note:* Gendron originally included an analysis of Dalio's performance in *La Grande Illusion.* She believes a consideration of Dalio's work is both crucial and instructive. We have excluded this section of her article due to its lengthiness.

## JEAN GABIN

Jean Gabin is probably the best known French prewar (and postwar) actor on an international scale. During this period, he was never referred to as a star (in the purest sense of the term); the American star system was alien to prewar French cinema. The French adaptation of the star system evolved gradually and was set in place only after World War II. But it is unlikely that the prewar public associated Gabin, the actor and the man, with today's concept of a star, French or American.

Gabin's image is that of man-of-the-people. For the public, seeing a film featuring Gabin must have been a bit like a reunion with an old pal. Gabin's presence in prewar French films had an incredible impact and influence on French cinema.

Gabin had no formal education. He learned his trade by following his parents into the great tradition of music-hall and cabaret performance. He played in light comedies and even sang operetta in his 1930 film debut. It took seventeen films in five years for the public to unanimously adopt Gabin. In 1935, Gabin was finally given a springboard role in Duvivier's *La Belle Equipe*. It was a "popular" role in which Gabin played a worker searching for simple happiness. From this point on, Gabin's roles would have more or less the same flavor. In 1936, he played a philosopher-thief in *Les Bas-Fonds*. He was the legendary *Pépé Le Moko*, gangster and victim of fate in Duvivier's film. In 1937, Renoir cast him as Maréchal in *La Grande Illusion*, in which Gabin plays a soldier who comes from the people.

Until World War II, Gabin would affirm his talent and forge his image with the same type of character: a man both strong and vulnerable, an exceptional man of humble origin whose fundamental simplicity and honesty is at odds with the universe embraced by poetic realism. In this character, we can recognize the deserter of *Quai Des Brumes* (Carné, 1938), the train engineer of *La Bête Humaine* (Renoir, 1938) and the hunted worker of *Le Jour Se Lève* (Carné, 1939).

The representative image projected by Gabin and the characters he portrayed rapidly won favor because he symbolized the dreams of the average French citizen. Gabin personified the ordinary man who pursued the simplest and, inevitably, the most wrenchingly inaccessible of dreams; Gabin became a popular hero who remained faithful to his deepest personal convictions. In this sense, Gabin symbolized the honor of the public. The actions of the characters he played gave the public a dignity that reality did not.

When analyzing the characters Gabin incarnated, it is obvious that Gabin the actor does not exist in the traditional sense of the word. This is hardly an original observation. It is a common fact when dealing with actors who have strong personalities or who are "stars." What must be noted are essential points that define the nature of a talent, that erase the abstraction of a character and replace it with a concrete personality.

Generally, the most striking element of Gabin's talent was his capacity to project an emotional quality that resounded in his character's human dimension. This emotional quality probably stems from the fact that Gabin seemed to act instinctively, that is, with a naturalness that banishes rehearsed effects, calculated gestures, and premeditated reactions. He always gave the impression of spontaneity. From one role to another, Gabin cultivated this style. Familiar traits of a Gabin performance are a unique set of vocal modulations and intonations, silences, and facial expressions all with an emphasis on economy. There are other elements that illustrate and explain the power of his appeal. These elements are the most striking, but are difficult to explain in a rational manner because they deny objectivity.

Gabin possessed an incredibly powerful and intense gaze. During periods of silence, the eloquence of this look could betray more emotion than the most beautiful of speeches. The honesty and frankness of thoughts laid bare were revealed in the fixed stare of his eyes. Gabin also possessed a distinctive voice, deep and a bit raspy. He was able to make it sound soft and tender, but it could easily sound desperate and furious. The public never forgot Gabin's gaze and his voice; they became the actor's trademarks.

It is necessary to consider Gabin's very strong personality, which permeates his particular acting technique. The essence of this strength is the total of his inherent contradictions. There is, at once, strength and vulnerability, the disarming charm of his imperfect face and the intense beauty of his gaze, the grace and heaviness of his features and body and the softness and overwhelming power of his voice. There is a profound conflict between his general appearance—bulky and imposing—which is at odds with the poetry of his movements and gestures. There is an undercurrent of violence and menace, never wholly developed but ever present. He is a rare example, for the period, of an actor playing against type. He was not a leading man; Gabin obliterated this classical notion. The amalgamation of Gabin's contradictions produces a fascinating appeal that eventually led to the creation of the Gabin legend.

Gabin rapidly became an irreproachable *monstre sacré*. But if Gabin was a great actor, it was only within certain limits. Can we honestly imagine him playing anything other than a man of the people, a laborer, or an essentially good man at odds with the law? He was an instinctive actor who did not possess the ability to transform himself. In any case, Gabin was never an imposter, even as he became a legend. He never tried to become what he was not or give a performance of which he was not capable.

The power of his legend was such that it is easy to suggest that the French public went to see Gabin and not the films he appeared in. This complicity between public and actor was the guarantee of his success; Gabin was predictable. But it was this predictability—as is the case with most stars—on which his career was built. Fundamentally honest in his performances, the actor never tried to break free of those limitations that established his image.

### Gabin As Maréchal

Gabin as Maréchal in *La Grande Illusion* has a physique that vaguely recalls rural origins. Gabin is stocky, and solid, but moves with the grace and suppleness of one who is comfortable with who and what he is. Gabin makes Maréchal a figure of stability, equilibrium, calmness, and wisdom. Maréchal, as created by Gabin, behaves with the instincts of someone who understands people and life. He has simple needs and his happiness lies in everyday things.

Gabin as Maréchal inspires comfort and tranquility. This

notion is conveyed entirely through physical means. By simply noting his garments, one has the impression that his clothes are comfortable or that he wears clothes in order to be comfortable. His cap is askew and pushed slightly back to accommodate his unruly hair. The cap might recall the one he typically wears in civilian life.

As always, Gabin infuses Maréchal with the familiar air of someone who is not afraid to reveal his identity. His walk is heavy, slow, and assured. At the same time, his movements never suggest languor, laziness, or fatigue. This physical impression, the rhythmic movement, contributes to and reinforces the idea of peace and all-encompassing tranquility that are suggested by other elements of his image.

His moral sense and general outlook tend to convince us that this man does not deal with the superfluous. He possesses a frankness and honesty in his gaze that translates the integrity and candor of his thoughts, words, and feelings. This direct gaze (the famous Gabin look, figs. 9.1–9.2) automatically denies apathy and boorishness. The gaze reveals a no-nonsense dignity, that of an honest working man.

**Mise-en-scène**

Maréchal (Gabin) is the first character introduced in the film. From the very beginning, it is clear his character will be associated with particular objects in his environment. We discover him in a *café-canteen*, bent over a *phonograph* listening to and half singing along with a popular song, "*Frou-Frou.*" Maréchal is very much at home in the canteen. He loves the warm atmosphere. The phonograph supplies him with material for a sentimental reverie about a simple love affair. Soon after, we learn that the woman is named Josephine, "la fille à tout le monde," everybody's girl. Maréchal smokes a *cigarette*, fully appreciating the small pleasure. When he is put in isolation in Hallbach prison camp (later in the film, after the French have recaptured Douaumont), he fights boredom and despair by playing his favorite tune, "Frou Frou," on the *harmonica.* In Wintersborn prison camp, he easily makes the *rope* that will help him escape. On Elsa's farm, he takes care of the *cow* and helps with the housework (especially the making of the coffee).

Fig. 9.1

Fig. 9.2

All of the objects and actions are associated with the character Gabin portrays. The objects are essential to the story line, but more importantly, they permit Gabin to forge Maréchal's image. They tend to accentuate the image of a simple man who adapts and copes easily with different situations (freedom, imprisonment, group life, family life). The objects and actions of the character reveal his tastes. He loves nature, popular culture, and everyday things.

**Text/Dialogue**

There is a more striking means of discovering the essence of Maréchal. Certain lines can lead us to imagine the actions and settings of his life beyond the story told by the film. During the dinner sequence after he and Boeldieu (Pierre Fresnay) have been captured by the Germans, Maréchal has a conversation with his neighbor. We learn that he is a mechanic. In another sequence, in the cell/chamber of Hallbach during the first meal with his new companions, he indicates his preference for a nice cheap bistro where he can drink good cheap wine. Later still, while at Elsa's farm, he says to her cow that he was born in the twentieth *arrondissement* in Paris (a region populated mainly by workers).

We know that he is a mechanic, enjoys the habits and pleasures of a worker, and is a genuine Parisian. The script, therefore, is important as a source of practical information. We are given a dimension of Maréchal thanks to little touches that indicate a character's past. Quite simply, we can imagine the character in different settings and circumstances other than those of the film.

The script contains lines that transcribe Maréchal's fundamental personality traits. Gabin's distinctively calm, deep voice and careful pronunciation are important in the reading of the lines. The voice corresponds to and completes the image we have of Maréchal; Gabin's elocution is marked by a smooth delivery. Maréchal does not use a great deal of slang, but he does skim over certain syllables and accentuate others, characteristic of a popular mode of expression. His manner of speaking creates a modulated rhythm, one that resembles the rhythmic quality of his movements. His speech is agreeable to listen to, like a familiar song. His voice has an ease and flow that suits his physique and his motion. The charm of the Gabin voice produces a warmth that suffuses each line. It is necessary to pay full attention to the lines because we often discover the depth, emotions, and thought processes that determine a given character's individuality. In Maréchal's case, his remarks parallel his image: direct, but not without a certain poetry.

When there is a search at Hallbach, he tells the soldier, in a tone both mocking and calm: "Ah! moi, j'ai rien, mon vieux...Si j'avais su que je venais ici, j'aurais pris un peu d'argent sur moi. Je regrette!" ("I've got nothing on me! If I'd known I was coming here, I'd have brought some cash. Sorry.")

While conversing with the Actor (Julien Carrette), he explains with an enthusiasm that stops short of being an outburst that he prefers cycling over theater. During the same welcoming meal offered by Rosenthal (Marcel Dalio), Maréchal responds to spirited comments from the Actor; with a slight appreciative smile, he tells him: "Dis donc, t'es un drôle de petit comique toi?" ("Say, you're quite a joker, aren't you!")

Later, when the engineer asks him whether Boeldieu can be trusted, he says, with conviction: "Bien! Il a un drôle d'air, mais, malgré ça, c'est un brave type! Oh! oui, tu peux avoir confiance...." ("Well, he looks bizarre, but he's O.K. You can trust him.")

During a military exercise, the prisoners, leaning out a window, observe the maneuver. Maréchal, apparently touched and gazing fixedly, says softly: "Ce qui purce, mon vieux, c'est pas la musique, c'est pas les instruments, c'est le bruit des pas." ("What hits you isn't the music, or the instruments, it's the sound of marching feet.")

We can observe Gabin's work in the way he delivers the words of the text designated for Maréchal. Integral to his technique is the importance of the spoken word that helps define the character and thus permits Gabin to perfect Maréchal. For example, Gabin omits the use of the French negative qualifier, *ne* or *n'* (the contraction). He says, "je *vais jamais* au théâtre" instead of "je *ne* vais jamais au théâtre" ("I never go to the theater"), and "c'*est pas* les instruments, c'*est pas* la musique" rather than "ce *ne* sont *pas*, ce *n'* est *pas*." This is typical of popular usage. These involuntary grammatical errors are natural in people of Maréchal's background; they also have a particular charm. The flow of words is more supple and the word *pas* provides a harder sound, thus giving the phrase a certain rhythm, like the beat of a musical note that falls heavily on the ears. It is important to remember this trait, which is particular to Maréchal, because it plays an important role in the nature of the character and his social identity. Therefore, we have to pay attention not only to what is said but how it is said.

Another example indicates Maréchal's social identity through the nature of terms he uses to express himself. At the Wintersborn fortress, the French prisoners watch as Russian prisoners open a package from home. Amid the confusion, slightly apart from the others, Maréchal says, admiringly: "C'est une bien brave femme l'impératrice." ("The Empress is a good woman.") The sentiment is perhaps naive, but the accent is on good or *brave*. *Brave* in French also means "honest" and, by extension, someone who is essentially good. When someone shows kindness or generosity, s/he can be called *brave*. This expression is of a popular nature and rural in origin. It is a qualifying adjective that is meant as a compliment.

Maréchal, for the most part, expresses himself by using a minimum of simple words that translate his deepest thoughts. He voices his opinions in a precise manner, regardless of whom he is speaking to and the topic of conversation.

While discussing music with Boeldieu, Maréchal states without embarrassment: "Oh! comme ci comme ça. Une bonne valse, oui!" ("Me, sure! I like music. A good waltz, yes.") From his lines, we become conscious of the essentially simple, honest nature of the character. When he has an emotional outburst, it is time rather than physical suffering to which he reacts. Maréchal lets loose with an anguished torrent of words (another Gabin trademark) that allows a brutal outlet for his despair. He then calms down very quickly, purged of the unbearable pain that provoked the outbreak. In these intense moments, we discover that Maréchal is a profoundly social being who finds it difficult to be alone. When he argues with Rosenthal (Dalio) during their escape, cruelly shouting insults that mask his own sorrow and despair, the outburst is as violent as it is brief. It is in these instances that Maréchal is most touching. Gabin is stunning in these sudden and total transformations, while remaining believable and true to the character.

If we consider the purely visual elements of the character as well as his manner of speaking, there is harmony between these two aspects that generates the construction of a character. There is, therefore, a unity in the actor's creative work. Maréchal's lines are indicative of his vision of the world and his sense of values. Gabin speaks the expressions and characteristic words with the ease of one who uses them regularly.

### Gestures/Movements

Generally, Gabin as Maréchal displays an economy of gesture. His stocky body relegates the importance of expression to his eyes and face. He keeps his hands in his pockets. In this film, he has been wounded in the arm. The imposed immobility does nothing to rob him of his hands when he talks. The contained physical energy is in his voice, eyes, and face. Everything is imparted to the viewer by Gabin's face.

The absence of superfluous gestures and movement correspond to Maréchal's personality. He does not become animated unless absolutely necessary (this may be what Gabin wants us to think). Along the same lines, he probably sees no use in motion for its own sake. For example, during the entire sequence in the room/cell at Hallbach in which his companions sift through costumes destined for their performance, Maréchal is the only one (with Boeldieu, but for different reasons), who touches nothing. He prefers wordlessly to observe the hurly-burly.

Another sequence reveals the economy of gestures particular to Maréchal. During a reading of the regulations upon their arrival at Hallbach, Maréchal and Boeldieu (Fresnay) seem imperturbable. Maréchal yawns unabashedly. His indifferent expression then returns, as if undisturbed. This non-gesture, that of not covering the mouth as he yawns, indicates certain things. We can interpret it as an involuntary neglect, an unconscious manifestation of his refusal or disgust concerning proper social gestures. He probably considers them useless and so ignores them without remorse or shame. And when the rules have been read, Maréchal makes a face (another Gabin trademark) that seems to say what he thinks of the edifying nature of the document. In essence, it might be interpreted as something like this: "I could not care less, they are exaggerating and they are boring me to no end."

To conclude, Gabin does not use his body in a traditional way. He emphasizes this non-movement, in order to invent facial expressions that add directly to the creation and expression of a character. It must be noted that these elaborate gestures are not always in evidence. Gabin's gestures are concentrated principally in the expression of his eyes; it is his way of moving. Maréchal/Gabin is more nuance than substance.

## PIERRE FRESNAY

Pierre Fresnay was never a star. Even so, he left his mark on prewar French films, without making a big splash. Fresnay stood for a certain image of French "quality" associated with good taste. Fresnay had his moments of glory. He did not possess an image that inspired sympathy and endeared him to the public. In any case, Fresnay never sought to play sympathetic characters. In this sense, he was not worried about a positive screen image. His criteria in choosing a role apparently did not include the congeniality of a character. Fresnay's relative popularity was probably stirred by respect and admiration.

Fresnay did everything the "right" way. He studied with George Berr at the Conservatoire, then entered the Comédie Française in 1915 at the age of seventeen. He remained with the Théâtre Français until 1928. Fresnay was, above all, a theater actor trained by classical rules and the repertory of traditional roles. The stamp "theater actor" would influence the public's appreciation of Pierre Fresnay, film actor.

Fresnay began his film career in 1915, but it took ten more films for the public to discover him. In 1931, he played Marius, the eponymous character in Alexander Korda's film. The screenplay was by Pagnol, adapted from the play in which Fresnay also had the title role. It is surprising to see Fresnay—with a coarse appearance—hanging around cafés. He dreams of the sea and escape. The principal physical elements of the characterization are a lock of rebellious hair falling on his forehead, sleeves rolled up to reveal muscular arms, and a cigarette dangling from the corner of his mouth. It is also surprising to hear Fresnay speaking with an accent characteristic of Marseille. Fresnay as Marius is, therefore, a popular hero.

As his career progresses, he plays more or less interesting roles. He is Marius again in *Fanny* (1932) and *César* (1936), which complete Pagnol's trilogy. In 1937, Fresnay plays Boeldieu in *La Grande Illusion*. Marius and Boeldieu are at opposite poles. Fresnay is able to "construct" credible characters. In 1942, Fresnay's image undergoes a change when he plays Inspector Swen in *L'Assassin Habite au 21* by Clouzot. He would then play a stubborn doctor in *Le Corbeau* (Clouzot, 1943). Another important role in his career is that of Vincent de Paul in *Monsieur Vincent* (Maurice Cloche, 1942), a historic figure of rare intensity.

It is difficult to pinpoint Fresnay's acting technique. He approached the notion of realism or naturalism in acting. The creation of a character was strongly bound up in his physical appearance; his biggest handicap was his slight build. But within this limitation, Fresnay exploited his attributes: a voice that possessed a cutting tone, sharp facial features, and an intelligent gaze. In each of his roles, he used these characteristics to full advantage.

## Pierre Fresnay as Boeldieu

Pierre Fresnay has the difficult task of making Boeldieu—a slightly stuffy aristocrat—a sympathetic figure, while never betraying the character's essential image. The script certainly contributes to the spectator's idea of the character, but Fresnay's work was cut out for him. From the first, Fresnay is a perfect Boeldieu, with his refined tastes, chiseled features, and immaculate appearance. His carriage and his impeccable demeanor peg him as a man of the world who represents tradition and personifies, by right, a certain social class. From this perfection is born a coldness, an insurmountable barrier that sets him apart from others. In addition, his aloofness can engender the feeling that he is a bothersome prig, not worthy of the viewer's sympathy.

If Boëldieu must remain true to what he is, Fresnay found a way of playing him so that the viewer can recognize his essential goodness and accord him a certain amount of sympathy, respect, and, perhaps, admiration. The only way of making Boeldieu someone who is not simply detestable because of his peculiarities is to play him straight. Fresnay does not make Boeldieu a caricature. There are traits worthy of caricature, but Fresnay makes these traits into qualities that are a part of Boeldieu's life and social standing. For example, everything he does or says is done without animosity or disgust, with a tone of voice that merely indicates observation, criticism, and commentary. This is central to the creation of Boeldieu.

It is striking to find no trace of affectation in the character's manners. The first impression is that everything about him is innate. His entire physical makeup and attitude is due to the simple fact of his birth; Boeldieu does not proclaim his aristocratic upbringing and lifestyle. Fresnay confers on Boeldieu an image that corresponds to his character definition, without using exaggeration or mannerisms.

Boeldieu always walks with his head held high and his body arrow-straight, in a posture that manifests his commanding attitude. It comes to him naturally and, so, is irreproachable. Fresnay is not tall, but he seems tall. His disposition expresses the idea that he is a man who knows his duties and responsibilities and is aware of the burden that falls to those of his class. Boeldieu does not play an active role in society; he assumes a function and believes in it even as he understands the derision associated with this state of affairs. Unconsciously, he knows he must set an example; therefore, he is that example. On the other hand, he understands that he has no rights over anyone, except those who are conscious of his status and treat him accordingly. His appearance suggests rigidity and constancy of thought, leading us to see him as a just man in the sense that his most profound motivations are order and fairness. Because of this, Boeldieu is not a figure of fear but one of respect.

It is for this reason that, despite the first impression of Boeldieu, as a whole he inspires sympathy.

The wearing of a uniform has special significance in relation to Boeldieu. Regardless of the type of uniform he wears, whether it is the complete military issue or a pullover, he is at ease. He projects a sober and refined elegance at all times. The way he wears his clothes indicates that he is a man of taste who possesses an ever-present practicality. He sits and crosses his legs with an ease entirely devoid of rigidity. His image encourages the label "perfect," yet he never looks constrained. Boeldieu's image, his physical presentation, corresponds to his interior makeup on every count: ease, discipline, dignity, finesse, intelligence, rigor, and authenticity.

### Mise-en-scène

Boeldieu is contemplating a document when we are introduced to him. Dressed from head to toe in military uniform, he is imposing because of his apparel and attitude. Instead of tilting his head, he lowers his eyes, adjusting his *monocle* with a *gloved* right hand, with the precise and natural gesture of one who has the habit of doing so. His *riding crop* is firmly held under his folded arm.

At Hallbach prison camp, Boeldieu learns from the engineer (Gaston Modot) that all sorts of goods can be acquired. He intends to buy a "comfortable" *arm chair*, *playing cards*, *books* and *English cigarettes.* At Wintersborn fortress, as he prepares to play his diversionary role in the escape, he quietly occupies himself by washing his *white gloves.* During the first meal provided by Rosenthal (Dalio), Boeldieu and he are talking about *Paris* and *Maxim's.* As Rauffenstein (Stroheim) gives them a tour of the fortress, we hear this commentary as Rauffenstein recalls Maxim's and a pretty girl named Fifi. Boeldieu responds, in the most natural of tones: "Je l'ai connue aussi." ("I knew her too.")

The white gloves, monocle, and riding crop are characteristic accessories of Boeldieu; during the film, they are irrevocably associated with him (fig. 9.3). He has a practical spirit. War does not keep him from indulging his habits. Boeldieu wants a comfortable armchair, *at least*; playing cards that calm; a distinguished pastime—books—a sign of a cultivated spirit; and English cigarettes, indicating a refined taste. He is a man of the world. Paris, for

Fig. 9.3

him, is summarized by Maxim's, the sophisticated place to go. Yet, he is not totally without passion; he too has had a brief love affair.

Boeldieu amuses himself while adhering to the rules of his class. He surrounds himself with objects and people who correspond to his social rank and consequent tastes.

### Text/Dialogue

As usual, it is through Boeldieu's lines that we discover exactly what kind of man he is. His voice and elocution correspond to the visual information particular to Boeldieu.

Tone of voice, elocution, and rhythm of speech make up the most interesting facets of this character. Boeldieu speaks with a certain dryness that does not indicate a disagreeable personality so much as a form of discipline. His pronunciation is perfect. Every syllable is clear. He utters every word and makes each pause with the same methodical nature that makes up his entire being. Boeldieu never raises his voice. He is in control.

Words also permit us to understand Boeldieu's thought process more clearly. The three principal traits of his personality are revealed through his dialogue. Perhaps the most remarkable of these traits is his ever-present sense of humor, which is both refined and subtle. Boeldieu expresses the simplest of things with words and turns of phrase that are surprising for their ingenuousness and bite. More often than not, his observations are stated seriously, but with a trace of irony. At the beginning of the film, Maréchal and the soldier cannot agree on what elements make up the aerial photograph he has been studying. Boeldieu says, in a manner both serious and mocking: "Touchante unanimité! Cette précision donne une riche idée de la perfection de notre matériel photographique." ("What touching unanimity! It gives one a good idea of the perfection of our photographic techniques.") Once they have decided to verify the actual contents of the photograph, the soldier asks Boeldieu what type of flying suit he would prefer. Without missing a beat, he responds dryly: "Aucune préférence: les combinaisons sentent mauvaises et les peaux de bique perdent leurs poils." ("No preference: flying suits smell and goatskins shed their hair.") This line contains two interesting elements. The grim humor touches on details of daily military life. The second part of the line is said with astonishing rapidity. It resembles a tongue twister like "she sells seashells...." The recurrence of *p*, *d*, and *b* makes it a perilous sentence to say quickly. Fresnay makes it comical thanks to his dry, distinct pronunciation.

At Hallbach prison camp, during their first meal, he responds to a "bon mot" from the Actor with a raised eyebrow, a thin smile, and a soft voice: "Le jeu demande-t-il que l'on fasse semblant de trouver ça drôle?" ("Do the rules of the game require that we pretend to find that funny?") Still at Hallbach, when he is designated by the engineer to dig part of the escape tunnel, he says, very seriously: "Avec plaisir! Je me suis laissé dire que la reptation était un exercice des plus salutaires." ("With pleasure. I have been told that crawling is a salutary form of exercise.")

Another of his personality traits indicates that this man, thanks to his social conditioning, understands that there is a code of honor and that, regardless of circumstances and no matter how exceptional, the code must be upheld. During the search upon their arrival at Hallbach, Boeldieu's attitude reveals itself:

BOELDIEU (protesting vigorously): "Mais, dites donc, qu'est- ce que c'est que cette façon de procéder?" ("Say, what sort of procedure is this!")
KRANTZ (a bit surprised): "Mais ... c'est la guerre!" ("This is war!")
BOELDIEU (with dignity): "Nous sommes parfaitement d'accord, mais on peut la faire poliment (...)" ("I could not agree with you more, but there are polite ways of doing it.")

At night, when the role is being called:

KRANTZ (dryly): "Boeldieu!"
BOELDIEU (just as dryly): "Vous pourriez dire: Capitaine de Boeldieu!" ("You ought to say: Captain de Boeldieu.")

His sense of humor and sense of values are complimented by a practical spirit that is based on observation and logical reasoning. Boeldieu exercises his discipline constantly. As they discuss their various reasons for wanting to escape Hallbach, Boeldieu explains his motives. He proceeds methodically, demonstrating his theory point by point in the tone of one who believes his logic is irrefutable: "Pour moi, la question ne se pose pas. A quoi sert un terrain de golf? A jouer au golf. Un court de tennis? A jouer au tennis. Eh bien! Un camp de prisonniers, ça sert à s'évader (...)." ("In my opinion, the question need not arise. What is the purpose of a golf course? To play golf. Of a tennis court? To play tennis. A prison camp exists to effect an escape.") Boeldieu's discipline is also present in his expression of feelings. As the tunnel is reaching completion, Maréchal is still held in isolation. Rosenthal speaks of the sadness he feels at having to leave without Maréchal. Boeldieu, bothered by this fact, says, with a harder tone than necessary: "Ça m 'est très pénible. Moi aussi ça me gêne, mais c'est la guerre, les sentiments sont hors de question." ("I feel badly about it, too. It's bothersome. Well, this is war, feelings are out of the question.")

Boeldieu's feelings and sense of justice are revealed at the same time as his calm and realistic personality. A surprise awaits the characters after Boeldieu's line. The door to the room is opened. Maréchal has returned. Boeldieu advances towards him and says, in a dry tone that masks his emotion: "Je suis rudement content de vous voir, mon vieux." ("I am really delighted to see you again, old chap.") The words that betray emotion are "old chap" (*mon vieux*). It is the only time Boeldieu will use an expression of familiarity, when addressing Maréchal (or anyone else). The use of "*mon vieux*," usually associated with Maréchal, expresses Boeldieu's fondness for his comrade.

Boeldieu's lines, rendered by Fresnay, are a means of discovering everything about the personality of this complex character—physically, spiritually, and intellectually. What we learn is gleaned through the information the dialogue provides and the way the lines are spoken. The dialogue realizes the hidden facets of Boeldieu and confirms the first impression evoked by his visual representation.

## Gestures/Movement

Boeldieu is inconceivable without certain gestures and movements. Fresnay moves in a manner that is the visual counterpart of his manner of speaking. We can see his movements as an extension of Boeldieu's sharp features, elegant personality, and precise thought patterns. For example, it is impossible to miss the accurate, supple movement with which he adjusts his monocle. When he puts on his gloves, the gesture is both methodical and nonchalant, mechanical and reverential. In movement or speech, the essence of Boeldieu is calculated with precise economy.

During the sequence in which the rules are read, Maréchal yawns without restraint. Boeldieu yawns, too. However, he elegantly covers his mouth with the back of his hand. It is a natural gesture. It is amusing to note the subtle looks the two characters give each other during the sequence. Boeldieu's raised eyebrow and pinched expression offer a light reproach to Maréchal and his no-holds-barred yawn (figs. 9.4–9.5).

When the prisoners go out to the garden to dispose of the dirt from the tunnel, most of them chatter. In the foreground, slightly apart from the others, Boeldieu silently empties his sack, shakes it gently and neatly folds it. Even while doing the most mundane things, Boeldieu exhibits the same methodical control.

This character, in his entirety, represents the quintessential

Fig. 9.4

Fig. 9.5

French spirit in the sense that he is everything that France showcases with pride. He is the image of culture with refinement and a glorious, mythical nobility. Boeldieu is a luxury item. In the eyes of the world, he is the *crème de la crème*, the living end and the *ne plus ultra* with the right amount of intelligence, taste, and sobriety. Boeldieu is part of an endangered species that inspires admiration and reverence. He is not the popular France of folklore, like Gabin. Boeldieu is the official and immortal France.

## ERICH VON STROHEIM

Erich von Stroheim is an example of a tenacious legend made up equally of myth and reality, gossip and scandal. This man of multiple talents, "the man you love to hate," carried an impressive reputation with him all his life.

Stroheim was born in 1885 in Vienna, the son of merchant parents. In 1906, he headed for America and went to California to launch an assault on the Hollywood studios. By 1914, he was featured in films. In 1915, as military advisor, he had an active role in the shooting of *The Birth of a Nation* under the direction of D. W. Griffith. Stroheim had a passion for uniforms, an interest that would mark his career. In 1916, he was an assistant and actor for *Intolerance* (Griffith). From this apprenticeship, Stroheim went on to direct his own films. He made, among others, *Blind Husbands* (1919), *Foolish Wives* (1926), and the unfinished *Queen Kelly* (1928). For most of his films, Stroheim was the director, screenwriter, art director, editor, and costume designer. And if there was a suitable role, actor. To the filmgoing public of the time, Stroheim was the archetypal perverse German officer, sadistic and cruel, delighting in the debauchery and corruption of innocent young women.

Stroheim's incredible demands and obsessive procedures would win him a reputation as an impossible director. After 1929, he abandoned directing to pursue a career as an actor. In the eyes of the world, Stroheim the director no longer counted. He made his mark as an actor and became associated with an ensemble of tailor-made roles that, more or less, followed the same pattern. It took Renoir's meeting with Stroheim and the character of Rauffenstein to reveal an actor who had become a victim of his own myth. The role was written by Renoir with Stroheim in mind. Rauffenstein is, once again, the familiar German officer. But the officer in *La Grande Illusion* has nothing in common with his predecessors. Stroheim participated in the creation of Rauffenstein; designing his costume, choosing every element with extreme care.

Stroheim's biggest handicap was, without a doubt, his physical appearance. It is hard to envisage any type of exterior transformation because his appearance would be so difficult to alter. Stroheim's body is heavy and massive. His face is lined. His eyes betray a melancholy beneath the oblique angles of his eyebrows. His neck is shaved in a severe army cut and his chin juts out. All these characteristics make for an almost obsessive presence. His voice bears an undeniably Teutonic accent. Its timbre has a certain lassitude and its tone is admonitory, making it unforgettable and unique. Stroheim's voice and the expression of his eyes (like Gabin's) are the most striking traits upon which his talent is built. But Stroheim transcends the handicap inherent in his physical appearance because he knows how to create a fictional character.

Stroheim displays astonishing sobriety and an understanding of the link between action and emotion. For example, we can cite his performance in *Les Disparus de Saint-Agil* (Christian-Jaque, 1938). Stroheim makes an important figure out of the character he plays, an English professor in a small provincial school. He is surprising in the role because the sympathetic tone is so unexpected for Stroheim. His image is essentially the same, but it is at the service of a different type of role. Stroheim is equally remarkable in *Sunset Boulevard* (Wilder, 1949) as the devoted, tenderhearted majordomo who loves Gloria Swanson from afar.

Stroheim was unique. If the public forgot the legendary filmmaker, it is harder to neglect the acting talent that certain films allow us to discover.

**Erich von Stroheim as Rauffenstein**

Visually, Stroheim's body is as imposing as Gabin's. The difference is that Stroheim possesses none of the suppleness evident in Gabin's movements. Gabin has an understated grace that is agreeable to watch. However, Stroheim's appearance is perfect for the character of Rauffenstein.

His rigid posture becomes an important quality. Because he plays an officer, the impression is that his stiff movements were produced by the discipline and austere temperament of the German military. Behind the image of the quintessential officer, we discover the aristocrat, who has a certain elegance and severe dignity; the uniform he wears reinforces the rigidity of his inflexible posture. Stroheim takes full advantage of the military accessories. He is impeccable in the uniform that is a symbolic tie to the obligations that correspond to his social standing and military rank. It is the carefully constructed image that expresses his inflexible honor and sense of duty in their most noble and sacred traditions.

The impression of rigidity is confirmed in the sobriety of Rauffenstein's walk and appearance. The features of his face are immobile. His occasional, slight smile indicates a thorough control of his emotions. Rauffenstein's close-shaven skull reflects his adherence to military discipline and his obsessive need for perfection, making the character more impressive and austere. He is an aristocrat; he is of an elite class of men who believe that they are the guardians of order and tradition.

Stroheim has acquired the attitude of a military man. Even if all the visual elements that compose the character seem to be pushed to the limits of possible expression, what remains is the notion that it is not Stroheim who encourages this, but Rauffenstein, the character evolving within the story.

### Mise-en-scène

Rauffenstein's first appearance occurs as he returns from an expedition crowned by his capture of a French plane. He enters the barracks with a conquering stride, a *cigarette* in his mouth. He removes his flying suit with the help of an aide-de-camp and knocks back a shot of *alcohol*. A little while later, when the group is seated, Rauffenstein turns to Boeldieu, adjusting his *monocle* with mechanical precision. At Wintersborn, the important objects in his apartment are a small table with a *photograph of General von*

*Hindenburg*, a carefully made regulation *army cot*, a *potted flower*, a *bottle of champagne in a bucket*, a *portrait of a woman*, an assortment of *sabers* and *riding crops*, *white gloves*, and a *monocle*. From a conversation with Boeldieu, we learn that he knew *Fifi* from *Maxim's*. Another conversation with Boeldieu informs us that he rode the race horse Blue Minnie in the 1905 Prince of Wales Cup at the "Military" in Liverpool.

Rauffenstein smokes cigarettes, drinks alcohol, and is a sportsman. He cultivates respect for the hierarchy, venerates his superiors, and guards the memory of his wife. The last three points indicate that he is a staunch defender of traditional values and intends to perpetuate them.

Within all this rigid discipline, one detail is extraordinary because it is so at odds with the pervasive sense of order: it is the flower. Rauffenstein possesses a romantic spirit that gives birth to his subtle melancholia. Thanks to a single flower, we discover another Rauffenstein beneath the quest for discipline and order. This Rauffenstein hides behind discipline to mask his "imperfect" existence as an emotional being. It is this fact that gives him a slight quality of sadness. Through the flower, we understand that Rauffenstein is an unhappy man fighting for survival in a world that is no longer up to his standards.

**Text/Dialogue**

In his tone of voice, elocution, and use of French verbs, Stroheim has given Rauffenstein a style of verbal expression that corresponds to his physical appearance. What he says, and the way he says his lines, are in perfect accord with his physical aspect and costume. Rauffenstein is almost always unfailingly polite, but it is not an effortless quality. His gentlemanly manners have none of the sympathy and spontaneity to be found in Boeldieu's politely ironic remarks. This corresponds to the notion that Rauffenstein (or Stroheim) is not fluent enough in French to make clever remarks or to know what is and is not acceptable. What surfaces from his reading of the lines is that Rauffenstein is using language as a form of protocol that is sympathetic to his rank and class.

Rauffenstein's tone is dry. The rhythm of his speech is staccato, like a military march. There is a slight hesitation between each word that adds a delicacy not apparent in his elocution. He also possesses the studied tone of one who is not entirely comfortable speaking a language. This explains the impression of softness in Rauffenstein's voice. If his French is perfect, it is because he is extremely careful about what he says. Careful listening reveals that the order, discipline, and control that dominate his personality are also found in his speech.

Through the script, we learn that his attitudes correspond to those of Boeldieu. Rauffenstein believes war can be waged politely and one must respect the enemy, even as prisoners. Rauffenstein admires the legendary France of powerful lords and ancestral traditions. France is, for him, the aristocracy and everything it represents.

The first time we see Rauffenstein, he is returning victorious from an expedition. Speaking to his aide-de-camp, he informs him (in German) that he shot down an enemy plane and he adds: ("If they are officers, invite them to lunch.") When Maréchal and Boeldieu are brought in, Rauffenstein bows stiffly and says, weighing each word: "Très honoré d'avoir des hôtes français." ("Very honored to receive French guests.") As he receives new prisoners (Maréchal and Boeldieu, again) at Wintersborn, he advances towards them, bows slightly, and addresses them in a respectful tone. Then addressing only Boeldieu, he adds: "Enchanté de vous revoir Boeldieu. Je suis désolé de vous revoir ici." ("Delighted to see you again, Boeldieu. I deeply regret seeing you here.") Nothing in Rauffenstein's face or voice indicates that he is delighted to see Boeldieu again or sorry to see him in the prison camp. His voice and features remain expressionless. He cannot permit himself to express his feelings more openly. He is, however, a frank and honest man. Therefore, when he says he is at once delighted and sorry, it is because he means it. Through his manner and speech, we realize his preferences (toward Boeldieu, and so the aristocracy) and his respect for convention and established standards. All these elements become clear in Rauffenstein's conversations with Boeldieu. For example, during a surprise search of the prisoners' quarters at Wintersborn, the two men have a conversation that demonstrates their privileged rapport. Rauffenstein advances towards Boeldieu and says:

RAUFFENSTEIN (with dignity): "Donnez-moi votre parole d'honneur qu'il n'y a rien dans la chambre qui soit interdit par les règlements." ("Give me your word of honor that there is nothing in the room which is against regulations.")
BOELDIEU (serious): "Je vous donne ma parole d'honneur. Mais pourquoi ma parole et pas celle de ces messieurs?" ("I give you my word of honor. But why my word and not that of these gentlemen?")
RAUFFENSTEIN (disgusted and skeptical): "Hum...! la parole d'honneur d'un Rosenthal?...ou celle d'un Maréchal?" ("Hum...! The word of honor of a Rosenthal ... or that of a Maréchal?")
BOELDIEU (dropping his ironic tone; with a dry persuasive tone): "Elle vaut la nôtre." ("It is as good as ours!")
RAUFFENSTEIN (sarcastically): "Peut-être." (Perhaps.)

Rauffenstein is inflexible, even when faced by facts which undermine his way of seeing things. But slowly he begins to recognize the signs of change and to rationalize them in his own way. A second conversation with Boeldieu indicates this change. Rauffenstein invites Boeldieu for a tête-à-tête in his private quarters. Boeldieu wonders out loud why an exception to the rules has been made. Rauffenstein replies with somber conviction and dignity, but is almost astonished by the question: "Pourquoi? Parce que vous vous appelez Boeldieu, officier de carrière dans l'armée française, et moi, Rauffenstein, officier de carrière dans l'armée Impériale d'Allemagne." ("Why? Because your name is Boeldieu, career officer in the French Army, and my name is Rauffenstein, career officer in the Imperial German Army.")

Boeldieu replies, a bit incredulous: "Mais...mes camarades sont aussi des officiers." ("But...my comrades are officers, too.")

Rauffenstein retorts, maliciously: "Un Maréchal et un Rosenthal...officiers?" ("A Maréchal and a Rosenthal, officers?")

Boeldieu, insisting, serious: "Ils sont de très bons soldats." ("They are good soldiers.")

Rauffenstein reveals his thoughts on the subject: "Oui!...Joli cadeau de la Révolution Française." ("Yes, a charming legacy of the French revolution.")

Boeldieu, (insistent, with a "what-can-one-do?" attitude): "Je crains que ni vous ni moi ne puissions rien faire pour empêcher la marche du temps." ("I fear that neither you nor I can stop the march of time.")

Rauffenstein ends by confiding the source of his agony: "Boeldieu, je ne sais pas qui va gagner cette guerre mais je sais une chose: la fin, quelle qu'elle soit, sera la fin des Rauffenstein et des Boeldieu." ("Boeldieu, I do not know who is going to win this war; the outcome, whatever it may be, will be the end of the Rauffensteins and the Boeldieus.")

Rauffenstein is trying to safeguard his way of life and reason for living. His inability to renounce his standards makes for a wrenching dilemma that tinges his loss with poignancy. Stroheim successfully illustrates this loss in the way he delivers his lines in an obstinate and insistent tone, and by underscoring all the elements that characterize Rauffenstein. To make it perfectly clear that he will not conform, he goes to the extreme in his ideas and conduct.

### Gestures/Movement

Rauffenstein does not indulge in extraneous movement. Obviously, this corresponds to his personality, his character, and his physical aspect. Every gesture is ordered, precise, and methodical. Economy of movement completes the picture of austerity. The sequence that serves as introduction to Rauffenstein, the one in which he returns from his expedition, marks this spareness. During the meal that honors the French prisoners, we cannot help but notice the dry, precise manner with which he adjusts his monocle or the stiffness of his body as he leans towards Boeldieu.

Each gesture Stroheim makes is truncated, robot-like, and exact. There is not an ounce of grace. An accident has forced him to wear an orthopedic corset that reaches up to his chin. Before the accident, he has the same impossibly straight posture. Rauffenstein already seems to be enclosed in a steel casing; his tight constraint is forged by his thorough discipline.

As Boeldieu lies dying of his wounds, it is through

Rauffenstein's solicitous, almost tender movements and gestures that we can discern the depth of his pain and sadness. It is the only time that Rauffenstein departs from his usually plain, strict gestures. We can sense the depth of his emotions. During the entire film, his physical aspect and his manner of speaking transmit Rauffenstein's *public* image. Nothing betrays this appearance. Thanks to these little gestures, we discover his secret, or what Rauffenstein is really like. Rauffenstein may be a man of iron, but the solid casing encloses a tormented individual.

## CONCLUSION

Several specific points emerge from a study of performance in *La Grande Illusion*. The film is representative of a type of cinema from a certain period. The lessons we take from *La Grande Illusion* may be easily applied to other French films of the era.

One is immediately struck by the classicism that colors the actors' performances. The term "classicism" is not employed to impose a narrow definition on the acting styles. It must be understood in the context of the period of French film now referred to as classical. Classicism in the performances is suggested by the use of well-developed characters, characters who invoke the possibility of real lives beyond the fictional. The credibility of the character is valorized, and a quest for a harmonious integration of the actor and his role is implicit in the performance of this type of text.

Despite the different types of training experienced by each of the three actors who have been profiled, all three try to protect the basic idea of the character they portray. Their work leads to well-rounded, unambiguous characters who function in accord with elements of the mise-en-scène, script, and gestures/movements. In this context, a character will not suddenly do or say something that is at odds with his entire conception. Consider Gabin as Maréchal: every aspect of his character's makeup is complementary—a thought corresponds to a look, a reaction to a silence, a spoken line to a physical expression. The same phenomenon is present in the case of Fresnay and Stroheim.

We can also make other claims that relate to all three actors. We can say that a particular actor's training, whether academic or based on experience, does not alter the tendency toward classical harmony and logic. Each character corresponds to an ideal notion of how a character should be portrayed in a film. If we discover differences or variations among the performance styles, these are not found at the level of the general, abstract idea of a character or in the character's final representation. Differences are, rather, to be found in the actor's training and in the impact of this formation on his method of rendering a character. Put simply, the point of departure and the route taken by an actor may differ, but the goal itself is the same.

There is another crucial factor at the base of any portrayal—the actor. In the case of actors dealing in the creation of a unique persona, we must be aware of the different nature of observations relating to their work. It is clear that Gabin and Stroheim cannot be seen in the same light as Fresnay. In Gabin's case, it is necessary to consider how he adapts his roles to fit his physical aspects, personality, and acting trademarks (his voice, gaze, and sparse movements). If this process permits Gabin to render an intense, individualistic character, it also forces him to play a specific type. His work differs compared to that of actors whose images are less well-defined. The same phenomenon occurs in Stroheim's case. It is inconceivable to disregard Stroheim's physical presence on screen; observations must be directed at another level. In the case of Stroheim and Gabin, we must first observe the impact of unchangeable elements on their styles and then consider how they exploited these elements to correspond to their characters.

The inverse of this methodology is one we traditionally reserve for actors whose physical aspect does not impose an a priori type, as is the case with Fresnay. The approach to his performance is different because his physical appearance can be used as an instrument of transformation, through which he explores different character types. In the case of Gabin and Stroheim, our attention and interest gathers around the actor as a total entity; our understanding of these immutable figures allows us to better comprehend their work. With Fresnay, we are more likely to study what the actor is like each time he is on screen in order to discern what constitutes his work.

No evaluative statements should be made about whether a "real" actor is the one who distinguishes himself on screen through the character he plays or the one who offers a performance that depends heavily on his personal appearance and qualities. One would be reluctant to say that Gabin is a better actor than Fresnay because he had a bigger impact on the filmgoing public. Who can say that Fresnay is a "real" or better actor because he could play all sorts of characters and his classical training gave him the stamp of a "serious" and "official" actor?

Finally, it is clear that we must consider the actor's work while looking to the work of the *dialoguiste.* If this aspect is particularly relevant to French films of this period, it remains a somewhat forgotten element, privileged in the theater and neglected in the very visual medium of film. Film makes use of text both aurally and visually (in the sense that the words affect a character's image and portrayal). The script becomes a tool that an actor uses to forge his character. We can gauge the work done with the text by noting the way in which the printed word is transformed into a performance. The word is brought to life; to ignore the script is to return to the silent era.

The script is not just a creative tool, but an aesthetic object. It possesses a seductive power in its poetry, intelligence, and vivacity. It also permits the actor to create with the sound of language, using the unique capacity of the voice to add breadth and dimension to the character he incarnates.

**Author's notes**

I wish to cite Alexander Sesonske's *Jean Renoir, The French Films 1924–1939* (Harvard Film Studies: Harvard University Press, 1980, 463 pages) as a source of inspiration in the writing of this critical essay.

**Editor's note**

I wish to thank Mario Falsetto for editorial assistance in the preparation of this article.

# 10. "I AM DIETRICH AND DIETRICH IS ME": An Investigation of Performance Style In *Morocco* and *Shanghai Express*

**Carole Zucker**

THE DIETRICH OF THE 1930s is usually taken to be a paradigm of Hollywood glamour and/or an example of the tough-minded, independent, and subversive "new woman."[1] Thus, it is natural to regard Dietrich as a "persona" actor (of whom Bogart is the archetype) and worry the issue no further. When she performs she is merely fulfilling the variety of constitutive elements which taken together compose her image.

When the angle of attack is shifted from her image to her acting, from a generalized view of her career in the '30s to her work with one director—Sternberg—a substantially different and far more complex version of Dietrich emerges. Her acting becomes an integral part of the director's design in which each aspect of the film (the frame, *mise-en-scène*, performance, etc.) is mutually interdependent in the realization of the film's meaning. One becomes cognizant of the way Dietrich's acting in these films is unlike the acting of any other actress in that decade—in its extraordinary rhythm, deployment of artifice, and confrontation of acting as acting. The mode in which Dietrich performs her roles denies the production of character in a traditional sense; i.e., one who thinks, believes, and feels in specific ways; one who has a past and a future; one who is, above all, a collection of traits that work in a cause and effect relationship with other characters to drive the narrative.

Dietrich's centrality to Sternberg's work engenders several questions. Considering their almost exclusive collaboration (with the exception of Dietrich's role in *Song of Songs*, 1933, Mamoulian) for six years and seven films, is there a trajectory in the performance style? Is it viable to claim that the authorship of this style is the province of the director or the actress? Or, in work that represents for both artists a period of intense collaboration, is this a false issue?

To entertain these speculations, one must return to their source; a close analysis of several films illuminates the conundrum that is the work of the director and performer. Further, highly descriptive criticism is one of the ways film acting may be approached meaningfully. It is through the fine details of performance—eye movements, gestures, body positions, line readings, pauses, etc.—that the film actor articulates his or her role.

I have chosen to concentrate on two films because it is my sense that these films represent a clear stylistic progression. In *Morocco*, the primary performance strategies are laid out; in *Shanghai Express* they are developed and refined. In the preceding film, *The Blue Angel*, we witness a level of psychological verism and artlessness (on Dietrich's part) never to be witnessed again in Sternberg's films, while the later films—*The Scarlet Empress* and *The Devil Is a Woman*—present a radicalized version of performance that goes beyond the scope of this essay.[2]

In the initial encounter onboard ship between Adolphe Menjou and Dietrich in *Morocco*, one becomes aware of the remarkable nuance and rigor of the performance style. The process of pursuit and rejection is enacted in this sequence from *Morocco* through the subtle use of eye movement, the direction of the glance, gesture, facial expression, and vocal intonation. When Menjou retrieves the contents of her suitcase, Dietrich thanks him, turning her face toward his direction, saying, "Merci, monsieur, you are very kind"(fig. 10.1). He performs a civility, she is grateful; that is the termination of their contact. When Dietrich turns nearly left profile, it is a formal rather than a friendly gesture. She does not encourage further intimacy; she does not extend her hand, a matter of conventional decorum among many European women. Her use of "monsieur" indicates both a wish to keep her distance and an acknowledgment of Menjou's superior social status. (She never addresses Gary Cooper in the same film as "monsieur.") After duly expressing her gratitude, Dietrich returns to a frontal position, concluding their exchange (fig. 10.2). Yet Menjou remains in his previous position, facing Dietrich's space. Either he does not

Fig. 10.1

Fig. 10.2

Fig. 10.3

recognize or (as his later behavior would indicate) does not concede the completion of their dialogue and continues it by uttering a line to Dietrich. His line: "Your first voyage to Morocco?" claims a desire to persist in developing their acquaintance. When Dietrich returns to the "court," as it were, it is with the realization that Menjou is proceeding against her unspoken injunction to desist (fig. 10.3). She looks at him, moving her eyes up and down, assessing her opponent. When she replies to his question, her one word answer, "Yeees," is unlike anything we have heard Dietrich say before, but its protracted vowel sound will become familiar in her repertoire of intonations. It is the expansion of a word which enables it to become a repository for a great number of meanings. It gives Dietrich more time to appraise the potential of engaging the interest of Menjou. At the same instant it declares her suspicion of him, of his insistence in speaking to a woman who obviously wants to be left alone, of his desire to help her in the first place. Finally, and most vividly, her phrasing and intonation invoke weariness, a sense that it is tiring to speak (thus her agony in extracting the word), and tiresome to reply to Menjou's demand for an answer. The "Yes" becomes a prolonged sigh which raises the specters of all the men who have hounded her, who have made her a "suicide passenger" with a "one-way ticket" to a "country like this." When Menjou extends his offer, Dietrich turns her eyes toward the foreground. Her look into space completes her previous reply. Her wariness, her fatigued answer, become more and more clearly the correct response to this man. The other side to his overture of assistance is her reciprocal role, the part that must correspond to his "service." Her look outward is one of recognition, an acknowledgment of this eternal drama (fig. 10.4). Dietrich's head returns to Menjou's area again, momentarily perpetuating the business of courtesy, as if to try to recoup their meeting at a level of vague affability (fig. 10.5). He declares that he would be "happy to help" her. At this she retreats to the frontal position, except that in this case her position favors the right (away from Menjou) and her eyes look in the same direction as she says, "I won't need any help." Her body position signifies a rejection of their continued exchange with a literal and figurative turning away that oversteps the limits of good

Fig. 10.4

Fig. 10.5

Fig. 10.6

Fig. 10.7

Fig. 10.8

Fig. 10.9

conduct. The direction of the glance affirms her disentanglement from the playing ground of the dialogue (fig. 10.6). The movement away becomes a representation of Dietrich's resolution to liberate herself from all the "reciprocal arrangements" of which Menjou is but a reminder. In the next shot Menjou still pursues the matter, handing her his card even while she clasps her suitcase against her body, as if arming herself against his advances (fig. 10.7). She takes the card, looking in his direction, although the axis of her glance does not appear to cross his; she looks beyond him. (This observation takes into account the "cheating" of sight-lines that is common in films; it seems clear that their sight-lines were not meant to appear to converge.) In the next shot Dietrich turns her head in a close shot; the corners of her mouth rise very slightly (fig. 10.8). This look was present to some degree in *The Blue Angel*, but the facial expression in *Morocco* is far more subtle and resonant. The look is cryptic and clandestine; it is capable of suggesting at once the foolishness and the pain of desire and the endless cycle of romance and loss. It is a glance meant only for the camera; it marks the beginning of Dietrich's communion with the camera which will become one of the privileged tropes in the performance style of Sternberg's films. Because her look is not meant for the observation of the other characters, it is a way in which Dietrich becomes detached from others in the film. Dietrich thanks Menjou and walks out of the frame. He tips his hat to her, knowing she cannot see him (fig. 10.9). This is Menjou's acknowledgment of his high regard for her and the first indication of civilized suffering and mute admiration that will characterize him throughout the film. In the next shot of Dietrich she is leaning on the railing, chin cupped in her hand, perusing Menjou's card (fig. 10.10). From the way she turns it back and forth it becomes evident that she is not reading the card (because business or personal cards are not imprinted on both sides), but determining the significance of it. When she disposes of the card, it is a gesture of great deliberateness. It would be a very different act if Dietrich had merely ripped up the card and tossed it into the water. But she tears it slowly and rhythmically, then collects the small pieces in the palm of her hand before blasting them with the released coil of her index finger (fig. 10.11). This is not a direct physical and emotional attack, as it is when Lola blows face powder at Rath in *The Blue Angel.* Yet by virtue of its indirectness, the assault accrues a greater measure of intensity and cruelty. When Dietrich thanks Menjou and removes herself from the conversational position to the ship's railing, she is presumably at a distance from her would-be suitor. Yet when she performs her action she is certain that she is retaining his glance. And in fact there is a cut to a reaction shot of Menjou faintly smiling as Dietrich finishes her "performance" (fig. 10.12). He is looking at her illicitly because their communication has "officially" terminated; her action needs his glance to affirm its effectiveness. Menjou is cast in the role of a Peeping Tom beholding his own humiliation. Dietrich's gesture is conceived as an "act" that will demonstrate her indifference, rudeness, and insolence to Menjou. Dietrich has told Menjou repeatedly in more subtle ways that she is rejecting him. Without confronting him directly—direct emotional confrontation is rare in the Sternberg/Dietrich films—Dietrich tells Menjou, in a detached and methodical way, that she doesn't want to be bothered. The confluence of gesture, glance, and body position succinctly inscribe an intricate psychological configuration of voyeurism, impotence (in Menjou's inability to respond to Dietrich's abuse), and sadomasochism. The elaborate, premeditated gesture offers the sting of mortification rather than the provocation of immediate aggression. Ironically, this corresponds precisely to Menjou's desires.

The performance in this sequence consists of a series of movements interspersed and/or coupled with lines of dialogue. I claim that each position of the body, each gesture, each facial expression and vocal intonation is rigorously selected and controlled by the director. The degree of Sternberg's manipulation from *Morocco* through *The Devil Is a Woman* is evident, not only from his and Dietrich's accounts and that of the " ... long list of actors ... outraged by [his] tuition,"[3] but from the testimony of the performances themselves.[4]

The performances in Sternberg's films resist any claims of "naturalism" or "realism," if we take those much-abused terms, for the sake of the argument, to be meaningful. We are not likely to mistake the performers in any film for "real" people. But in

Fig. 10.10

Fig. 10.11

Fig. 10.12

Sternberg's films any resemblance between "real-life" behavior and the behavior of his performers is strictly disavowed. The regulation and co-ordination of the smallest detail of the performance and the resulting artificiality assist the removal of the actors from the arena of verisimilitude. They are located by the special nature of their actions and speech only within their own fiction.

A special endowment of the performance style in Sternberg's films (which is effected partly by the exertion of the director's control) is their theatrical quality. It is this theatricality that creates a further withdrawal of the films from both a reality which parallels our own and, in most cases, from the fictive worlds portrayed in other films.

The acting is theatrical in two senses. First, because it transgresses the type of expressive behavior that is considered "lifelike" in films. "Theatricality in ordinary life consists in the resort to this special grammar of composed behavior; it is when we suspect that behavior is being composed according to this grammar of ... conventions that we regard it as theatrical. We feel that we are in the presence of some action which has been devised to transmit beliefs, attitudes, and feelings of a kind that the 'composer' wishes us to have."[5] An example of this type of behavior in *Morocco* occurs when Dietrich is brought into Ulrich Hauptmann's (Captain Caesar's) office, where Gary Cooper is being held for his assault on two Arabs the previous night. There is a shot of Hauptmann in which he says, "Nice of you to have come, Mademoiselle." She has been brought in to bear witness to her part in the action or her knowledge of Cooper's part. There is a cut to Dietrich, her back to the camera. She raises her arms with her finger extended, sweeps it along the window sill, and holds it up, as if checking for dust. Her "reply" to the officer's greeting is a gesture that is invented to tell those present what her sentiments are toward the Captain and the trial. It is an "acting out" of her contempt for the proceedings. She is manipulating certain behavioral conventions in order to make her point clear. She does not respond to her interrogator either verbally or by visual salutation. She turns her back on the audience. When she mimes her examination for dust it signifies a careful concealment of her anxiety for her lover (and she wishes to prevent the

Captain from knowing he is her lover), an assertion of her contempt, and/or utter lack of interest in her surroundings. It is a gesture designed for the purpose of communicating these attitudes to the watcher.

The second way the performances in Sternberg's films are theatrical is in their utilization of behavior and conditions peculiar to the stage. The dressing room shot between Paul Porcasi and Dietrich provides examples of the various ways in which the performances are invested with theatricality. The shot begins with Dietrich standing in mid-frame in a medium shot. Her head turns to look as Porcasi enters from the right, then she returns to her original position, looking left and down. Porcasi fumbles into the room, waving a handkerchief as he speaks in a Turkish-accented voice. He is short and heavy and wears a gold hoop earring in one ear. When he reaches a position level to Dietrich, he says, "This is a great night for you. If you make a hit you can stay here as long as you like." As he speaks, Dietrich takes a cigarette and a candle in a holder from her dressing table in the lower foreground, brings the candle up to the cigarette in her mouth, and lights it (fig. 10.13). She puts the cigarette down on the candle holder. Porcasi crosses to Dietrich's right and gazes at her. He speaks: "You may have heard of me in Europe or not. My house is patronized by the finest society in Morocco." He waves his left hand toward the background. During this speech Dietrich picks up a flattened top hat and precisely at the moment Porcasi ends his line, she pushes the crown of the hat out with a pop (fig. 10.14). She places the top hat, cocked to the left side, on her head. Porcasi wipes his forehead with a handkerchief (fig. 10.15). Porcasi: "Now, what is it I was going to say, oh yeah. ..." Dietrich picks up a mirror, fixing her bowtie (she is attired in a male dress suit, without a jacket), smoothing her hair near the hat. Porcasi continues, "Pick yourself a protector," he places a monocle in his left eye, "it will give you some prestige ... an officer." Dietrich turns to face the camera, still looking left and down, holding her suit jacket with her right hand. Porcasi is waving his hands as he speaks, looking at Dietrich. "They will tell you that the officers in the Legion are unimportant, that the common legionnaire is the thing." As he speaks they walk in unison toward the camera. Dietrich stretches out her right arm slightly with the jacket on it; Porcasi takes the jacket and helps her on with it as she continues looking away from his direction (figs. 10.16–10.17). He cites reports " … that Private So-and-So is a Russian Prince or an ex-General, that he joined the Legion to forget his past." Dietrich looks toward him momentarily on this line. She takes a handkerchief from her pants pocket and puts it in her outside breast pocket. Porcasi: "Don't believe it. The private in the Legion is no bargain." Dietrich hands the fan right without moving her eyes or head in that direction (fig. 10.18). Porcasi takes the object, rapidly fans himself and continues, " … For 75 centimes a day. Thank you." He puts the fan down right. "Pick the officers, they have the money." He turns his back to the camera and rushes to the door. Dietrich picks up a mirror from the lower left quadrant, looks at herself, puts the mirror down, looks forward and down, and adjusts the bowtie at her neck.

This long take demonstrates the three main ways in which Sternberg's films engage in conventions of the theater:

*(A) Stylization and Exaggeration*: Sternberg utilizes a series of gestures, movements and positionings that counterpoint Porcasi and Dietrich in this shot, contributing to its highly stylized quality. The conflict of their styles, coupled with the hyperbolizing of their individual mannerisms, produce "stylization" and "exaggeration." Dietrich is cool both in temperament and in response to the tropical heat. (In the scenes taking place in the nightclub there is a continuous fluttering caused by a multitude of patrons' fans; the bandleader has removed his jacket and undone his collar; La Bessière and Caesar, when they first meet, both remark on the heat; Brown refuses a cognac because it's "too hot." Yet throughout the film Dietrich never perspires and never uses a fan except to flip it back and forth decorously.) Porcasi enters the room, sweating profusely, continuously wiping his brow with his handkerchief. Dietrich displays an unwillingness to expend energy, perhaps thus accounting for her apparent immunity to heat. Her only reaction when her employer enters the room is to turn her head to see who has entered, then turn away. In this perfunctory action she establishes her disdain for Porcasi; she does not bother to greet him and

Fig. 10.13

Fig. 10.14

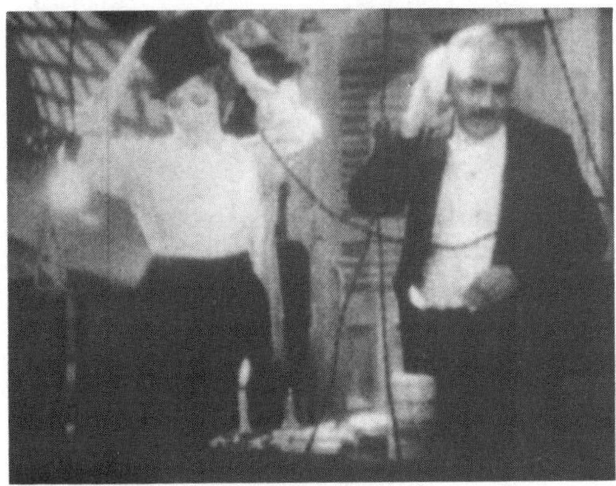

Fig. 10.15

Fig. 10.16

Fig. 10.17

Fig. 10.18

averts her face as he speaks to her. In fact, during the entire take she never glances in his direction, except when he says, "... he joined the Legion to forget his past." This phrase momentarily causes her to turn her head in the speaker's direction. Dietrich's actions are economical, as when she lifts the candle while picking up her cigarette, bringing the candle to the cigarette in her mouth in one movement. Porcasi on the other hand moves uninterruptedly throughout the shot. He gesticulates with his arms as he speaks, waves his handkerchief, and, in contrast to Dietrich's languid walk, virtually seems to hop around. He is squat to Dietrich's tall and slender. He speaks quickly and constantly with a comical Turkish accent, while Dietrich never utters a word throughout the shot. Dietrich affects "masculine" mannerisms: she dangles her cigarette between her lips on the side of her mouth when she smokes; she places her top hat jauntily to the side of her head like a "swell" (pushing it down from the crown as a man would, rather than arranging the brim to suit her hairstyle); takes a handkerchief out of her pants pocket and places it in her breast pocket; plucks her bowtie to straighten it and pulls the tie away from her neck as though it were constricting an adam's apple. When she holds out her arm with her jacket on it, it is not to remind her employer of his "duty" as a gentleman, but to assert the natural prerogative of the master. Porcasi just as naturally assumes the "inferior/female" role. Even though he is the proprietor, he behaves as though he is Dietrich's valet. He plays the femme to her butch; he is fluttery; his voice gallops at an emotional pace; he wears a gold hoop in one ear and gives Dietrich matronly advice on how to do well with the men in the audience. Her reaction to his nagging is to turn her back contemptuously on him as he says, "Pick yourself a protector, it will give you some prestige...."

The counterpoint of this duet is interspersed with gestures performed in unison. One of these is the business with the jacket; Porcasi responds to Dietrich's outstretched arm with an alacrity and unquestioning obedience that might suggest a familiar routine, although this is her first night in his club. When he announces that his clientele is "the finest society in Morocco," at the exact moment he completes the line she pops open her compressed top hat. It is a consummate jest on the "cream" of Morocco's society, and represents Dietrich's response to her employer's pretensions. The precise timing endows the shot with a sense of contrivance that situates it unmistakably in the sphere of stylization. Similarly, when Porcasi's exhortations and accompanying movements reach a fever pitch, as if telling him to "cool down," Dietrich hands a fan to him without moving her eyes or head. He agitates the fan while continuing to counsel her, then adds, "Thank you," to the end of his sentence. It is a number that bears the mark of repeated rehearsal; it resembles the performance of straightman and comic in a vaudeville team, not the interaction of people who have just met. Sternberg is acknowledging and underscoring the artifice in acting.

*(B) Frontality*. For the greater part of the dressing room shot, Dietrich is positioned frontally, or nearly so, with respect to the camera. She does not glance directly at the camera, but her body is frontal while her head is generally turned to the left or right, or looking downward. Because Porcasi is the only one who speaks, it is clearly not a question of having to maintain Dietrich in a position close to a microphone or a moving sound blimp. (In any case, post-dubbing was available at this time.) Partly, the frontality is an attempt to distance the audience's emotions. The frontal position of the performer coupled with the placement of the camera at a medium distance creates both a real and an affective distance. It is as if the camera is recording a stage performance rather than a dialogue scene in a film; the actors play to the stationary camera as they would to an audience in a theater. Dietrich is in fact "performing" in this shot; it is more an "act" than an interaction with the other character, although he is necessary to fulfill the conditions of her performance. Sternberg always prohibits identifying with or "knowing" the Dietrich character, while equally essential is the provision that we must watch her. Both of these conditions are preserved by the frontality. Dietrich's position is frequently posed, rigid and unnatural; her attitudes are not "normal"; Dietrich is unrecognizable as belonging to any natural order of things, and thus she is not susceptible to the penetration of our knowledge or understanding. Yet these very same qualities make her interesting

to view. Frontality is a way of placing Dietrich on display, at a distance.

*(C) Theatrical Space and Time*: The distinction between theater as a " ... materially enclosed ..." place and film as " ... the moving world before us ..."[6] has surely in large measure broken down since the thirties. (In some measure, this is due to cross-fertilization between two mediums; the use of long takes with a stationary camera—Straub, Snow, Fassbinder, etc., in film—and the development of mobile space in the theater—Schechner, Serban, Monk, etc.) But the demarcation of space Sternberg chose to use can be seen as an invocation of theater. He deliberately does not cut or alter the position of the camera, thus asserting the contiguity of characters and the duration associated with theater.

The theater-like continuity-in-space-and-time directs the viewer's attention to what is in the space and to what the space is. A three-minute take without camera movement impels us to attend to the only motion within the frame: the action of the characters. We observe the careful positioning, gestures, and movements of the actors, which are so crucial to the shot. Because our field of vision is unchanging, the actor's performance is privileged; it becomes more substantial in a "plastic" and in an expressive sense. The long take/stationary camera transforms the frame into a theatrical space. Dietrich is about to perform on stage in the next scene, and yet her "act" in the theatricalized space of the dressing room is no less choreographed, prepared, and accomplished. The two major differences are that Dietrich sings on stage, and that her audience in the dressing room is only Porcasi, the film crew, and the film's viewers. These two sequences are juxtaposed to underscore that there is an "act" Dietrich performs that is not relegated to the stage. Her behavior in front of the cabaret audience in many ways mirrors her conduct with Porcasi. She strides out from behind a curtain to the center of the stage and, in the next shot, sits on the arm of a chair. She reclines her body rightward and looks, without interest, in a leftward direction as the off-screen audience boos loudly. Her masculine walk, her studied lack of concern, and her nonchalant pose recall her attitude in the Porcasi scene. She smokes a cigarette, dangling it between her lips as she walks to an area where the patrons are seated in the background of the iron railing. She swings one leg over the railing and straddles it. When she sings she keeps one hand in her pocket; the cigarette is in the other hand. When a man seated at a table reaches out to touch her arm, the instant before he grasps her sleeve she rises and moves away. Dietrich pushes her top hat back on her head as she is about to end the song, then pushes the brim down on her forehead in perfect synchronization with the closing chord. The timing and stylization of her gesture and her composure in the midst of disturbance are echoes of the dressing room scene. The question becomes whether there is any time in the film when Dietrich/Amy is *not* supposed to be performing.

The space of the dressing room is like a stage in the sense that it encloses action within its borders; it does not open "out"; the action does not continue in the "wings." If we look at a shot in which stage-like space is rejected, the consequences of Sternberg's particular use of space becomes more clear by comparison. In the famous sequence from Jean Renoir's *Le Crime de Monsieur Lange* (1935), a camera positioned outside a building follows Lange's trajectory from room to room as he goes outside to shoot Batala. Lange exits through a door on the ground floor and the camera moves forward (toward Lange) and then in the opposite direction, making a circular leftward pan sweeping the court as Lange walks rightward out of the camera's range. The camera movement evokes the courtyard community—those who have inhabited this space—and summons up its collective role in the killing. The dressing room shot in *Morocco*, by contrast, excludes both the continuity of space and the suggestion that anything exists beyond the borders of the frame. André Bazin draws a lesson from the camera movement in Renoir's film:

> Since what we are shown is only significant in terms of what is hidden from us … the mise-en-scène cannot limit itself to what is presented on the screen. The rest of the scene, while effectively hidden, should not cease to exist. The action is not bounded by the screen, but merely passes through it. And a person who enters the camera's field of vision is coming from other areas of the action and not from some limbo, some imaginary "backstage." Likewise, the

> camera should be able to spin suddenly without picking up holes or dead spots in the action.[7]

Sternberg's work precisely counters Bazin's understanding of the screen when he promotes the sense that the action is completely bounded by the frame, that there are no other areas of action occurring beyond the frame. Even when Sternberg moves the camera, his *mise-en-scène* creates a closed-off quality. The sense of confinement, in concert with the frontality and stylization of the acting, creates an emotional arena that is at a remove from the viewer. For Sternberg the screen is circumscribed by his ideas and intentions. It is not a "place" that has any other existence. Bazin writes: "We are prepared to admit that the screen opens upon an artificial world provided there exists a common denominator between the cinematographic image and the world we live in."[8] In Sternberg's films, however, any such "common denominator" is disavowed.

Another constituent of performance style that is introduced in *Morocco*, and which further contributes to the stylization of the acting, is the choreography of movement. An example of distinctly dance-like motion occurs after Dietrich ruins her engagement party by running into the street to meet the returning Legion troops. She learns that Cooper has been wounded and returns to Menjou's house. She walks forward looking to right, left, and background, clutching the skirt of her long black dress. She turns 360 degrees, then walks into the dimly lit foreground. Her head is bent down and leftward. She no longer holds her skirt, and her hands clutch her hair, pulling it back. Because of the backlighting she is nearly in silhouette. She turns clockwise to right profile, making her second complete circular motion, lets go of her hair, and walks right to the background as the camera follows her. A palm tree obscures the foreground as she exits in the right background. The movements are stylized; Dietrich is not aimlessly pacing, but dancing steps that have been worked out for her. She has just broken her relationship with her fiancé. Upon learning of Cooper's condition, she must act. She returns to Menjou and tells him—in front of the assembled guests—that she must go to Cooper. When Dietrich enters the hall, she is trying to decide whether she can impose further on the man she has recently humiliated. Her circular movements in space externalize, literalize her mental gyrations. The exaggeration of the movements is underscored because they are performed in silence and placed between two dialogue sequences. Because of their execution in near-silhouette (figs. 10.19–10.22), the viewer can concentrate on the choreographed movement of the body as a form.

Choreography, on a smaller scale, can be found throughout *Morocco* in conjunction with other elements of the performance. In the sequence in which Menjou finds Dietrich drunk in her dressing room, there is a long take that begins with a medium shot of Dietrich in the left foreground with her back to the camera. Behind her is a table with a vase of flowers sent by Menjou. She pushes the vase to the side of the table as we hear the off-screen sound of crashing glass. She turns toward the camera, looking down, smiling drunkenly, then—as if challenging Menjou—looks up. In the mirror at the center of the background, Gary Cooper's farewell message ("I changed my mind. Good luck.") remains inscribed. She pushes aside the flowers so that Menjou can witness her humiliation by Cooper, the message of rejection. She looks up at him, as if to repeat her question when he first entered the room, "How do you like me now?" Menjou's face is reflected in long shot in the left side of the mirror, superimposed over Cooper's communication. Dietrich places the flowers down

**Fig. 10.19**

Fig. 10.20

Fig. 10.21

Fig. 10.22

in the right foreground and, feigning indifference, turns her back to the camera, fixing her hair in the mirror. But the alcohol makes her primping gestures visibly over-deliberate. In the face of the triangular configuration—Menjou, Cooper, and herself—her cool nonchalance is undermined; she is unable to carry on the "act." She pulls a weed out of the bouquet on the right and holds it upright left, grinning. She looks at the mirror, then turns again to face the camera and says, "Not badly written for a soldier." Menjou enters the frame and says, "Perhaps it was for the best." She looks down right, then her head moves to left profile: "Give me a drink." Menjou pours the champagne; Dietrich extends her arm to take the glass, still smiling. She looks again to the background, at the mirror, then turns right to look at her drink, holding it up to her face. She repeats this movement from mirror to drink once more. Then Dietrich turns her back to the camera, throwing the contents of her glass at the mirror (fig. 10.23). After this she quickly turns left profile, throwing her glass downward; an off-screen crash is heard. She turns back to the camera fully, then ¾ left, then frontal again with her head bowed down ¾ right, arms crossed in front of her body (fig. 10. 24). Menjou regards this scene, hesitates for a moment, then walks out of frame. A click of a door is heard.

**Fig. 10.23**

When Dietrich throws her drink, she turns more than 180 degrees to do so, then makes the same turn to end up in a frontal

Fig. 10.24

position. It is a startling moment in the film because it seems at first glance to be a spontaneous reaction, an instance in which the character loses the ability to govern herself. But the tension in the shot lies in the completely regulated enactment of impulse. When one breaks down the components of this "spontaneous" demonstration of passion, they are fully as proportioned and designed as any other display of feeling in *Morocco*. The reiterated looks at the mirror foreshadow the climactic hurling of the champagne. They are like repeated motifs in music that receive expanded treatment in the final movement. The repositioning of her body in the striking left profile of body and head, as she smashes the glass, is a dramatically emphatic pose. When she switches back to the frontal position, she does not merely turn around, but places her body in several situations first, as if enacting the final convulsions of her grief and anger. These movements have a highly predetermined quality because she moves herself fully into one position, stops momentarily, and changes to the next pose. Impulsive movement, especially in rage, does not have this elaborate posturing, with the individual parts of the action having the clear "beginning" and "ending" Dietrich observes in this scene. Sternberg stylizes even this evocation of sudden anger. When Dietrich crosses her arms and bows her head it signifies a desire to conceal herself after her indecorous behavior; it is an expression of shame. She was betrayed and reacted, in public, with passion. She has ripped off the mask of apathy which was so carefully constructed. Her posture is also one of exhaustion after the violence of her display. And finally, it is a tragic pose, an expression of grief at suffering an insupportable loss.

In *Shanghai Express*, the acting style becomes more refined, its elements remarkably concise. Paradigmatic is the early scene between Dietrich (Shanghai Lily/Madelaine), Louise Closser Hale (Mrs. Rafferty), and Anna May Wong (Hui Fei). Hale drops in to chat with the two women and produces a card advertising her boarding house in Shanghai. She insists that she "... only takes the most respectable people." Dietrich receives the card, flips it back and forth, and remarks, "Don't you find respectable people terribly ... [long pause; she seems to search for the correct word as she waves the card, placed between two fingers like a cigarette] ... dull?" There is a cut to Hale; she speaks rapidly, flustered, "You're joking aren't you! I've only known the most respectable people. You see I keep a boarding house." She looks left and then right at Dietrich and Wong. The light dawns; she narrows her eyes and purses her lips. There is a cut to a close-up of Dietrich looking down at the card and squinting, as if she could not have read the card properly (fig. 10.25). She looks up, her eyes wide with expectancy and wonder (fig. 10.26), "What kind of house did you say?" Dietrich phrases the question with a rising inflection that suggests both astonishment and ingenuous curiosity. There is a cut to Hale as she manages to eject, through clenched lips, "A boarding house." Cut to Dietrich as she looks at the card, moves her eyes up and down, pauses, makes her lips into a small circle and says, "Oh" (fig. 10.27). She lowers her eyes. She has set up the joke by feigning an avid interest in the proposition; her lips are parted in attentive consideration, she seems to peruse the card repeatedly while turning it in her hands. The rapid up and down movement of her eyes displays at once simulated contemplation of the situation and equally false dismay at her profound error. The extended pause and final lowering of her eyes is a parody of embarrassment and shame at the base of which is an infinite contempt for bourgeois respectability. Dietrich's performance has the precise timing of a great comedienne. Indeed, Dietrich's acting in *Shanghai Express* differs

Fig. 10.25

Fig. 10.26

Fig. 10.27

from that in *Morocco* partly because she is permitted to indulge her humor; she is no longer the "straight man." Her gestures, eye movements, and facial expressions are crisper and more definite. There appears to be a physical accompaniment for every line, and every phrase has a distinct nuance that evokes numerous interpretations. In *Shanghai Express*, Dietrich exhibits a new assurance and poise.

With this new confidence, Dietrich's ability to sustain and juggle "acts" becomes more virtuosic. The scene described above is emblematic of her "profane" act, a self-representation to which she retreats after being attacked or wounded; Clive Brook (Captain Harvey) performs such an aggression prior to the boarding house sequence. In *Morocco*, Dietrich's tough, cold, "masculine" aspect is set in opposition to the warmer, more vulnerable, "feminine" role she assumes at other times. In *Shanghai Express* these distinctions obtain, but Dietrich's relationship to these roles is not nearly as discrete; she slips from role to role with astonishing dexterity. Dietrich performs her "acts" so skillfully that it becomes impossible to define her real character. In the boarding house sequence she plays Shanghai Lily, a role she presumably created in response to Clive Brook's defection five years earlier. She plays Lily for Louise Hale because she wants to shock her and because Hale, with her rigid morality, is a stand-in for Brook. Shanghai Lily is a role she is capable of acting or not acting at any particular time. She can even play Shanghai Lily playing someone else, as in her mock-innocent question ("What kind of house ...?") to Louise Hale.

In her enactment of different roles within a single character—roles which are, moreover, in a continual state of flux—the performance of Dietrich (and the direction of Sternberg) acquires a new dimension. Not only is there an increased complexity in the execution of the performance, but in its conception as well. The stylization of the performance is heightened, withdrawing the character more explicitly from the conventions of "life-like" behavior. And there is also in the film the declaration and development of a labyrinthine relationship between director, actress, and role that creates a kind of puzzle for the spectator to solve.

Sternberg enlists numerous modalities of performance in the

sequence that takes place on the observation car of the train. Clive Brook is seated frontally when Dietrich walks on to the platform. He looks in her direction. When she asks if he wants to be alone, he returns to a frontal position, giving her a curt, formal response. Brook's frontality here, whatever else it may be, is a way of characterizing his rigidity. He is, as it were, locked in an unbending confrontation with the camera. This is in character for a man distinguished throughout the film by his stiff military bearing. Consider when he refuses to extend his hand to Anna May Wong and instead places his hands behind his back and bows from the waist, his legs clamped together. When Dietrich joins Brook, they are in two-shots, he on the right, frontal, she above him in the left background. Dietrich says, "Do you expect to stay in Shanghai for awhile?" She looks up and right and then down with her eyes (fig. 10.29); Brook answers, "I think so," as he takes a drag from his ever-present cigarette. She replies: "Then we ought to see a lot of each other." Her eyes move back and forth as she says this line, then she looks down, smirking (fig. 10.30). Brook looks straight ahead, smoking, and says, "Perhaps." Dietrich's eye movements have become more exaggerated in *Shanghai Express*. The move-

**Fig. 10.29**

ments of her eyes after she asks Brook the first question admit of many interpretations—anxiety, hopefulness, skepticism, whimsicality—as she waits for his response. They theatricalize the shot, providing movements that are comparable to the gestures of actors on stage, larger than life. They make Dietrich's consciousness visible without divulging what it is, precisely that she thinks. She is endowed at the same time with transparency and opacity, public-

**Fig. 10.30**

ness and privateness. Brook, in contradistinction to the ambiguity of Dietrich's openness, refuses even to glance at her. He delivers an enigmatic answer, but his disposition is rendered clearly by his inflexible posture. By giving an equivocal response, Brook leaves Dietrich room to complete the joke she has set up. Of course they will not see a lot of each other; she is being, in a facetious way, as polite and ceremonious as he. Her smirk at the end of her line resembles her look to Menjou on board ship in *Morocco*, when Dietrich's knowing glance seems primarily centered on bitter and unhappy reflections. Dietrich's look here is sparked by comparable meditations, but it has gained a measure of piquancy. With a greater degree of control, she has drawn Brook into a jest by mimicking his remote civility.

The pattern of the sequence is relatively stable, alternating medium close-ups of each actor and two-shots of both. Brook remains immovable, while Dietrich provides the animation. They discuss Brook's activities since their "smash-up"; he speaks in a voice that is uninflected and swiftly paced. While he attempts to maintain a distant and conversational tone, she interjects comments that are meant to draw him into a more intimate discourse. A change in the order occurs when Dietrich says, "I wanted to be certain you loved me (fig. 10.31), instead I lost you (fig. 10.32). I suffered quite a bit (fig. 10.33), and I probably deserved it." Brook in the next shot rises, smoking his cigarette, his back dramatically to the camera. Brook: "I was a fool to let you go out of my life." She reaches (with her back to the camera) to Brook and pulls him down to her; there is a cut to a closer two-shot of them (fig. 10.34). She removes Brook's hat and brings his face to hers. There is a reverse angle shot favoring her face in close-up (fig. 10.35). The back of Brook's head reaches the level of hers, then there is a cut to a medium shot of the kiss, with both their faces partially obscured (fig. 10.36); a kiss is an act to which Sternberg always forbids the viewer access.

Dietrich performs her four-sentence statement in a way that manages to break the impasse of their dialogue. It appears to be a confessional moment, but I take it that the character is merely discarding one role and adopting another. She discontinues the sophisticated and detached facade, seizing on a character who is insecure, vulnerable, and contrite; she gets the desired result—capitulation—from Brook. Dietrich's lines are broken into four sections divided by a pause during which she moves her eyes. The pauses lend an air of gravity to each phrase, weighting it with significance. The penitent and angst-filled poses—eyes downcast or forward, staring into the abyss—consolidate the credibility of the words. Yet the speech is highly stylized; it is a strictly metered quatrain. Because the tempo is so regular, it gives the speech a rehearsed effect; it seems as if the character has repeated these lines often to herself. (In their practiced quality, these lines are comparable to the routine performed by Dietrich and Porcasi in *Morocco*. In neither case is an effort made to conceal the unspontaneous nature of the actions or the words.) Dietrich's speech causes Brook to abandon his remote and businesslike conduct toward her. He surrenders his "military man" role and appropriates its opposite—the irrational, the impulsive, the emotional—the "feminine." (It is a fundamental Sternberg principle that, for two people to success-

Fig. 10.31

Fig. 10.32

Fig. 10.33

Fig. 10.34

Fig. 10.35

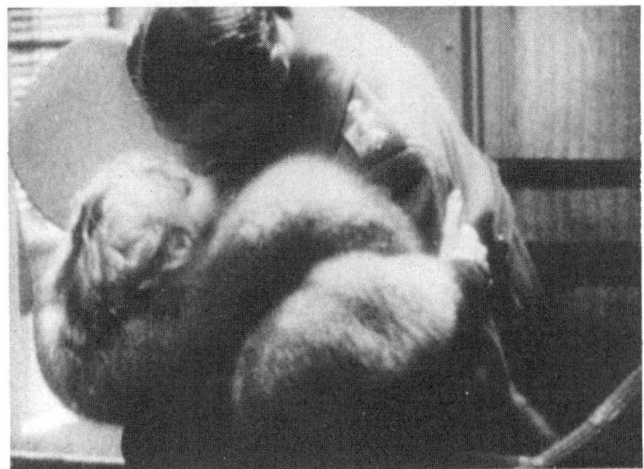

Fig. 10.36

fully conjoin, each must embrace the male-female duality within the self.) When Brook throws down his cigarette and speaks, the modulation of the performance is such that this mundane action acquires, within the Sternbergian scheme, an exalted significance. (Brook's "I was a fool to let you go out of my life." is also in character for Brook's conventional British Romantic Hero; he retains, within a work that transcends such conventions, his status as a recognizable type.)

When Dietrich pulls Brook down to her, the rhythm of the sequence changes again. The shots become longer. Dietrich becomes the aggressor, removing Brook's badge of manliness, his army cap. Yet Dietrich is also in a submissive position: Brook hovers above her, while she is nearly prone in the frame. In the reverse angle medium close-up, for the duration of the fifteen-frame shot where only the back of Brook's head is visible, the face of Dietrich becomes disengaged from all specific roles (fig. 10.35). The status of these shots as interruption is reinforced by the slowness with which the actions are performed, the paucity of motion.

After the "clinch," the actors again change their roles. Dietrich is situated in the lower left quadrant; only the back of her head is visible, and her lavish fox fur can be seen beneath her head and in the lower right of the frame. Brook is above Dietrich, but also in the lower part of the frame, only the top of his head is visible (fig. 10.37). It is as if he has collapsed on her, or is about to rise with blood dripping from his mouth. (In Sternberg's films Dietrich's sexuality has a self-destructive and a murderous side as well.) Brook's torso is in the frame, he remains seated. He looks left, saying: "I wish you could tell me there'd been no other men." Dietrich remains in the same horizontal position, then rises in the frame. We see her brush her hair back with her hand, as her other hand places the army cap on her head. Her head is facing the background. Once again, Sternberg is using forceful and exaggerated compositions to underscore the tensions between the characters. There is a cut to Dietrich as she turns in the frame toward Brook's position. She cocks the hat to the side, pulling on the brim as she does so, saying, "I wish I could Doc ...," narrowing her eyes slightly, "... but five years in China ...." She moves her eyes up and down during this phrase, then pauses and stops the eye movements and looks leftward without any movement, concluding,

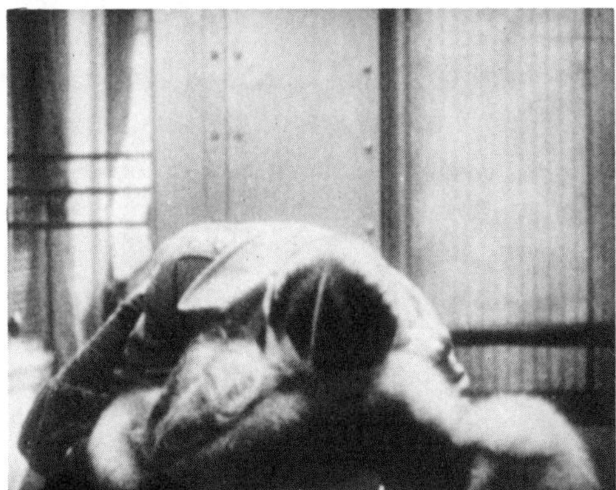

Fig. 10.37

"... is a long time." This final part of the sentence is said in a slower rhythm. In the next shot, Brook is seated frontally, looking straight ahead. Dietrich is in the right background, higher in the frame than Brook; her hand is on her hip. Brook says, petulantly, "I wish I had 'em back"; then Dietrich walks forward, swaggering, hand still on hip, a smirk on her lips. She stands to the right of Brook, putting her left arm over his shoulder. She says, "What would you have done with them? That's the scheme ... ," she looks down and left as she completes the sentence, "... of things. Sooner or later we would have parted anyway. Then [she looks up, her eyes moving] we might never have met again" (fig. 10.38). Brook then speaks insistently, turning his head ¾ to the right, "We wouldn't have parted, Madeleine [her eyes look rightward, her mouth compressed in a cynical smile (fig. 10.39)], we'd have gone back to England [Dietrich raises her eyes upward, then lowers them], we'd have been married ...." She raises her eyes and looks frontally and slightly right, her smile barely contained. Brook looks leftward and says, "There are a lot of things I would have done if I had those five years to live again." During this sentence Dietrich has moved left, taking her hand from around his shoulder, the camera moving with her. There is a cut to a medium close-up of Dietrich, her hat cocked on her head. She looks rightward and speaks, "There's only one thing I wouldn't have done, Doc." She says this quickly, unlike her other lines. There is a close-up of Brook, bemused, "What, for instance?" Cut to Dietrich, smiling openly rather than smirking (fig. 10.40), "I wouldn't have [flicks the visor of the hat] bobbed my hair"; she continues smiling (fig. 10.41). She walks forward and right, and in the next shot replaces Brook's cap and wishes him goodnight.

This dialogue adds new dimensions to both characters. Once Brook inquires about the "other men," Dietrich reinstates the distance previously asserted by Brook but apparently bridged by the kiss. By bringing up the past Brook reveals an unwillingness to accept Dietrich without doubt and reservations; it is the same absence of trust that presumably destroyed their relationship earlier. Brook exhibits a pride and possessiveness that Dietrich immediately attacks by repeating his locution, "I wish I could ...," her toughly narrowed eyes declare her refusal to acquiesce in Brook's conditions. Her eye movements invite the viewer to imagine the multitude of "corruptions" she may have experienced in her "five years in China." When she levels her eyes at Brook as she completes the sentence, it is a firm accusation. She is indicting him for the faithlessness that led her to become "Shanghai Lily" and for his foolishness now in demanding the death of this character born of

**Fig. 10.38**

Fig. 10.39

Fig. 10.40

Fig. 10.41

his own mistrust. The drawn out tempo of this last phrase emphasizes its importance and enhances its suggestiveness. Brook returns to his frontal position after his brief hiatus, telling the viewer that, regardless of the apparent change in his attitude after the kiss, he remains inflexible. He uses the same word—"wish"—when speaking of their lost years; his "wish," his determination, is to idealize their relationship. He affirms this in the longer speech in which he fantasizes about the possible course the five years could have taken. Dietrich's response to his false naiveté is one of almost big-sisterly condescension. She assumes her "tough" pose, her hand on her hip, her aggressive stride, and then, rather than draping her arm affectionately around him as a lover might, she leans on him in "buddy" fashion as she mockingly questions his interpretation of events. During Brook's long speech, Dietrich performs a silent litany with her eyes and mouth. Each ingenuous remark, each invocation of eternal love, marriage, and England, each nostalgic (mis)remembrance of their history elicits silent skepticism from Dietrich. In this sequence Brook betrays himself; when the cool, manly exterior is removed, his romantic dreams and inability to confront reality are revealed. Previously Dietrich was the expectant one, waiting for Brook's exposure. Now she has uncovered his disguise, and she is the one to retreat behind a mask that is at once cynical and mercilessly realistic: Brook finds himself in the presence of Shanghai Lily. Brook's desire for normalcy must of necessity exclude Lily. Yet Brook is, at least partly, responsible for the creation of this figure who is fixed forever within Dietrich. It is only when Brook accepts the totality of Dietrich's character that their relationship can resume. This is Dietrich's condition. When Dietrich makes her flippant remark about her hair and hits the brim of her visor and smiles, it is an act of rebellion against his hypocritical "morality." Her words and her gestures mock Brook's wish for a romance that is "pure."

As Dietrich exits, a porter enters the observation platform with a telegram. Brook is seated and has recovered the grim hard facial expression he had at the beginning of the sequence. As Dietrich reads the telegram, he looks frontally; when she puts the telegram down, he looks left in profile, not at her, saying, "From one of your lovers?" Dietrich responds negatively, and Brook says, "I wish I could believe you." Dietrich asks, "Don't you?" Brook says, forcefully, "No." Dietrich looks left: "Will you never learn to believe without proof?" Brook looks toward Dietrich, "I believe you, Madeleine." She hands the letter to him and looks away, smirking. There is an insert of the letter; it is, in fact, from a lover. There is a cut to a medium close-up of Dietrich. She is positioned frontally, looking straight ahead, and says, "When I needed your faith you withheld it, and now when I don't need it and don't deserve it you give it to me." She leans right. There is a cut to a two-shot as she grabs the letter from him, crumples it, throws it down, and exits through the background door, Brook looking toward her.

This final section of the sequence represents yet another major alteration in tone. Brook returns to his original stance, his body position—frontal and severe profile—once again stiff. After two lines which establish his lack of faith in her, Brook yields. His reason for doing so arises from their interaction in the previous parts of the scene. Dietrich has maintained a measure of authority throughout; either by initiating an act or by responding to Brook, it is she who changes the tenor of their conversation. His grudging claim of belief recalls a scene between a student and his teacher. The teacher poses a question, and the student, wishing to be a "good" pupil, responds in the way he thinks will please the teacher. In fact, a part of Dietrich's stature in many of her Sternberg films is as an instructor in ethics. Brook gives the "correct" answer, but he is wrong because it reflects not belief but the "wish" to be "correct." Just as he "wishes" they had married, that she were not Shanghai Lily, he "wishes" to span by words the unbridgeable gap that separates his fantasy, his desire, from reality. For the first time in the sequence Dietrich assumes a completely frontal position, and her glance no longer seeks his. He has failed to learn the lesson, and she chastises him. Where once she exited saying, "Goodnight Donald," now her action is marked by a palpable hostility.

This sequence has been described at some length because it presents a prototype of performance in the Sternberg-Dietrich films. It contains all of the stylistic traits of Sternbergian performance and, further, is a deep case for thinking about film acting.

There is an elaborate counterpoint created by eye movement, glance, posture, gesture, and movement around the set; they function in rhythmical relation to one another. Further rhythm is produced when these elements of the performance occur in concert with and between lines of dialogue and pauses. Presumably we are never naive enough to believe actors are the characters they play. But in a Sternberg film, the acting is so stylized, exaggerated, and controlled, we may wonder if what is created bears any relationship to what we know as a character. Or is it a new category of film acting which denies the existence of characters and is, instead, a performance?

In *Shanghai Express*, the actors continually appropriate and desert their roles; Sternberg is subverting a more conventional type of acting in which consistency and truthfulness are valorized. By deliberately stressing the artifice in their performance, the director asserts the actors' status as performers. Because the actors are so withdrawn from anything resembling "real-life" behavior, they inhabit roles that are not merely fictive, but which partake of fantasy. There is no call for the spectator's belief, involvement, or identification.

In the observation car sequence, we witness Dietrich and Brook (particularly the former) moving from role to role. The quality of the acting—the rapid oscillation among roles, the extraordinary degree of premeditation and regulation—invokes the author of the performances. The character of Shanghai Lily, also known as Madeleine, might be viewed as a stand-in for the figure of the author; it is she who seems to determine and effect the transitions in the scene. However, throughout the film there is a point of hesitation: when are we in the presence of Lily or in the presence of Madeleine? Who was the Madeleine Captain Harvey knew and who has "changed"? Whom does Harvey embrace at the film's end? Is there any part of Lily or Madeleine untouched by the other? The uncertainty about Madeleine/Lily undermines the character's authority as a representative of the author. While she maintains the on-screen authority for shifting the tone of the sequences, her strong ambiguity, of necessity, causes us to look beyond the filmed image for the source of authorship.

The dual role of Madeleine/Lily replicates the twofold nature of the actress, Dietrich. There are two Dietrichs that are always present in Sternberg's films: the "Dietrich-on-film" and the "real" Dietrich. Shanghai Lily and "Dietrich-on-film" are inventions, public personae, while Madeleine and the "real" Dietrich are, as it were, the media out of which the fictional personae emerge. Both Dietrichs reside in every role in each film by Sternberg; her presence is an ongoing force that dominates any individual role. Her existence overtakes the characters she plays; she is the character in the films. Dietrich may be taken as the author of the performances in the sense that each role is engendered and defined by her persona and could not achieve fulfillment without her.

There is a privileged moment in the observation car sequence. It occurs prior to the kiss, when Dietrich's "act" of contrition causes Brook's surrender. Dietrich is framed in a medium close-up for fifteen frames before embarking on her next "act." For the duration of this shot, she is between roles. It is crucial within the context of the scene, because it is an interruption in the performance; for this instant, Dietrich performs no role. The absence of an act evokes the presence of the acts that enfold this shot. At the center of the sequence there is a moment of recognition, an acknowledgment by the director of the figure who is at the center of his work. The disjunctive pause emphasizes the primacy of Dietrich, her ability to transcend all roles.

Sternberg pinpoints an aspect of stardom in this shot. He compels us to recognize that stardom is (partly) the creation of an image that is esteemed for itself, regardless of the performance. Dietrich relinquishes her roles; she does not need to act. She is revealed as a "pure" image, independent of the fiction that envelops her.

The performances in the Sternberg-Dietrich films raise questions—who creates Madeleine/Lily and "Dietrich-on-film"?—to which there can be no definitive responses. It is by no means clear that Dietrich would not be Dietrich without the assistance of Sternberg, nor can one assert that the director is responsible for "Dietrich-on-film." However, the performance style represents only one significant aspect of Sternberg's films; it is one part of a whole.

When the director writes about *The Scarlet Empress*, "... every single scene [bears] my imprint,"[9] it can be taken as a statement about all of his work. We are bound to accept Sternberg's accountability for the performance in works so strongly marked by the stamp of their creator. "I am Dietrich and Dietrich is me"; Sternberg and Dietrich are indissolubly united in the world of his films.

## NOTES

1. Molly Haskell, *From Reverence to Rape: The Treatment of Women in Movies* (New York: Penguin, 1973), pp. 109–13.
2. See Carole Zucker, *The Idea of the Image: Sternberg's Dietrich Films* (Fairleigh Dickinson University Press, 1988) for an analysis of performance in *The Blue Angel, The Scarlet Empress,* and *The Devil is a Woman.*
3. Josef von Sternberg, *Fun in a Chinese Laundry* (New York: Collier, 1965), p. 127.
4. According to Sternberg's autobiography (pp. 245–51) Dietrich barely spoke English when she made *Morocco*; he recounts his persistent efforts to coach her and correct her pronunciation. This factor may also be seen to contribute to the "control" the director possessed over Dietrich's performance.
5. Elizabeth Burns, *Theatricality* (London: Longman, 1972), p. 33.
6. André Bazin, *What is Cinema?* trans. by Hugh Gray, (Berkeley: University of California Press, 1971), p. 104.
7. André Bazin, *Jean Renoir*, trans. by W.W. Halsey II and William G. Simon, (New York: Simon and Schuster, 1973), p. 89.
8. Bazin, *Cinema*, p. 108.
9. Sternberg, p. 265.

# 11. JAMES DEAN: The Pose of Reality? *East of Eden* and the Method Performance

Johanne Larue
and Carole Zucker

## INTRODUCTION

"METHOD ACTING" HAS BECOME, over the years, a concept as mystical as the persona of James Dean. If one believes that the Method exists in process only when an ensemble of actors, working with a director, is improvising and rehearsing—united in their efforts by common artistic and social ideals—the analysis of the Method actor's screen-work becomes difficult, because the recorded performance alone remains as a testament.

When critical discourse about the Method exists, it's not often that we get statements that move beyond the cliché: "Method acting equals realist performance." The commonly accepted notion is that the Method deals exclusively with real emotion, lived experience, visceral truth, psychological honesty, "reality," as opposed to calculated behavior, empty mannerisms, skillful imitation of life, in short, the artificial world of a more traditional "theater."

At any rate, the Method performance is very rarely analyzed, it is experienced. And if it is experienced by the spectator and the critic as "viscerally real and exciting,"[1] to quote Lee Strasberg, then one can say that it is a good Method performance. Of course, "viscerally real and exciting" are highly subjective terms and will not obtain as valuable criteria nor act as a substitute for formal analysis for many writers and viewers of film. In fact, critical points of view on the evaluation of Method performances have greatly lacked sophistication. The reasoning often seems to go as follows:

We shouldn't sense your acting (You don't need to act); make us believe you're real (you just have to be yourself). One can feel the confusion at work. Either way, such an approach can only lead to unsubstantial analysis, judgement, and understanding of film acting in general while being offensive to Method actors and directors. Are we repudiating their art?

That is exactly what the increasing number of James Dean books on the market do.[2] At their best they may offer a study of the cultural influence of the actor's persona, but if they try to deal with James Dean, the actor, we invariably get a cross between a mythological portrait and a psychoanalytical autopsy. In a sense, James Dean is a threatening performer. Contemporary audiences sometimes laugh nervously when confronted with the more emotional scenes in *East of Eden*; it is embarrassing and shocking to feel that an actor is transgressing the *politesse* of playacting. One way to circumvent this threat is to fetishize the actor. Again, the written "studies" on Dean accomplish precisely this. Supported by references to fellow actors who have argued that the young actor only needed to be himself on screen, they end up negating him as an actor by thrusting his performances into the realm of idealization.

If this is true, there is no purpose in writing a critical essay on Method performance. We claim that one can study Method acting because the enactment of Method tenets is discernible on screen. And, because the range and complexity of the Method piece of work (piece of art) far exceeds the pursuit of the "realist performance," it demands critical investigation. *East of Eden* (Kazan, 1955) is paradigmatic of this claim. What the film reflects is the history and practice of Method acting, from the "affective memory" to the "physical action" and "subtext" of the players to the unorthodox style of Kazan's Method directing and *mise-en-scène*. As for James Dean, though the actor may be one of the last elements of the filmic vocabulary to resist the filmmaker's control (the human actor can be influenced and coached, but he cannot be programmed, nor can his work be physically manipulated by the director while he is performing in front of the camera; thus, the human actor, compared to the lighting or the art design, is still an intelligent and sometimes unpredictable "element" set free on the soundstage by the willing director), once printed on film, the actor also becomes an integral part of that form: a human mask composed of projected light. This enables us to study the actor's work: we won't be looking at "James Dean, cultural icon," but at "James Dean, actor."

## FROM STANISLAVSKY TO JAMES DEAN

In *East of Eden* there is a scene that can be frightening to most viewers unaccustomed to Method performances. Following a racial dispute that leaves Cal Trask (James Dean) defending an old German friend against angry townspeople (the film is set before and during World War I in the Monterey peninsula of California), the movie sets up a brutal confrontation between Cal and Aron (Richard Davalos), two brothers divided over their love for their father, Adam (Raymond Massey), and the same young woman, Abra (Julie Harris).

After the brawl, the two young men are left in front of their German friend's house. The summer night is hot and humid; only the singing of locusts disturbs the newly settled stillness. After refusing Cal's affectionate embrace, Aron angrily reproaches his brother for the violent bravado he displayed against the townspeople. The camera frames the pair in a medium shot; Aron, in the left foreground, menacingly walks towards his brother, standing in the right background. Aron has his back to the camera, but we can clearly see Cal's confused reaction to Aron's unexpected about-face. (Aron, up to now, has been the docile and pacifist half of the pair—the "innocent" and "good" brother, while Cal is "through and through bad.") Aron soon shouts: "... don't lie to me about ..."—the vocal assault is abruptly interrupted by Cal, who slaps his brother in the face, his own features registering shock, his imploring eyes searching Aron's. Cal has become the physical aggressor, but his face tells us he hurts as if he were the victim. To save his brother, to show him his love and the force of his emotion, Cal then strikes Aron twice with his fists, shouting like a wounded beast, while the impact of the blows is reinforced by the sudden transition to a profile half-shot of the pair that shows Cal's punches traversing the full width of the frame. Cal's voice is a roar, and his diction thick as he comes down on his brother: "I was just trying to help [here, Cal's fist reaches his brother's jaw] you!" Again his fist strikes Aron's face as he stretches the word "you" into a cry of pain. Cal has struck his brother to the ground; an inserted close-up of Aron's face gives us a startling insight about his nature: as he starts to rise, he looks in Cal's direction (off-screen) and lets a strange smile pass across his bruised face—a petrified mask of pleasure and hatred. His reaction is then juxtaposed to that of Abra, a witness to the scene, who is isolated in a half-shot; she winces as if registering physical pain. We then see Aron getting up in front of Cal (framed as in the first set-up described). The young man is waiting for Aron, his torso a bit hunched forward, his arms dropping heavily and his eyes bulging in disbelief. Cal looks like a crazed puppet suspended in space. He murmurs: "It can't be, Aron." But Aron doesn't let go and spits back, half crying, "Are you finished?" Again, Cal just stares at him, but now his face relaxes. A silent beat. A second goes by, an enacted still-frame, and then the release, the eruption; Cal screams: "Nooo!!" He grabs Aron, ready to kill.

In all its intensity, violence, and frightening passion, this scene from *East of Eden* was more than thirty years in the making. Said in a different way, our understanding of the different elements and levels of meaning in this scene can be greatly facilitated by our knowledge of the thirty years of System/Method acting that preceded the shooting of *East of Eden*.

James Dean once said that "an actor's course is set even before he's out of the cradle."[3] Consider the graph opposite; it charts the heritage that helped mold Dean's personal style of Method acting. Lest we forget, all Method actors are different, just as there are no two Method teachers or teachings strictly alike. As early as 1933, Stanislavsky, the "grandfather" of the Method, would say:

> People may say that what united my comrades in art, my pupils, and those who share my ideas ... is the "Stanislavsky System." What System? By now in every theater that has sprung from the Moscow

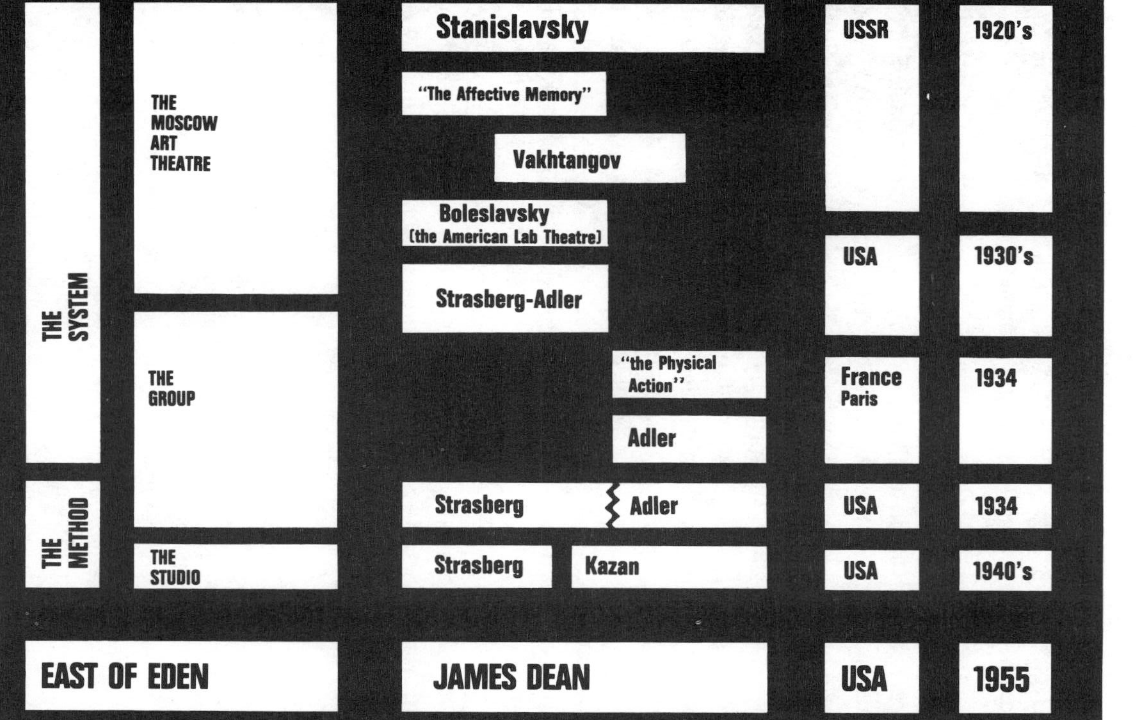
THE SYSTEM
THE MOSCOW ART THEATRE
Stanislavsky
"The Affective Memory"
Vakhtangov
Boleslavsky (the American Lab Theatre)
Strasberg-Adler
USSR
1920's
USA
1930's
THE GROUP
"the Physical Action"
Adler
France Paris
1934
THE METHOD
Strasberg
Adler
USA
1934
THE STUDIO
Strasberg
Kazan
USA
1940's
EAST OF EDEN
JAMES DEAN
USA
1955

> Art Theater, this System has been transformed into something different, new, even contrasting.[4]

The chart on page 299 is the historical trajectory of the System/Method, from Stanislavsky to James Dean.

Constantin Stanislavsky, the famous Soviet actor, director, teacher, and theorist, first introduced his "revolutionary" techniques in the 1920s at the Moscow Art Theater (the MAT). Along with his most important pupil, Eugene Vakhtangov, he developed a new approach to acting. To break free from the codes of artificial behavior on stage, supported by preconceived forms of the representation of emotions, he tried to work with actors from the inside out, striving for the "poetic reflection of life's experience"[5]—acting as a quest for Truth. Of the many theories developed by Stanislavsky to help the actor become a creative rather than an interpretative artist, the "Affective Memory" most impressed the Americans through the teachings of Richard Boleslavsky at the American Lab Theater (the ALT). Boleslavsky himself, it should be noted, probably did not teach the exercises exactly as "prescribed" by Stanislavsky for the simple reason that the theories of the Master were always evolving, and his theoretical writings were never definite. The "Affective Memory" was nonetheless reportedly taught as follows:

> After the performer analyzes his part to see what feeling or emotion is necessary at a particular point in a scene, he searches his own life for a remembered feeling or emotion that parallels the former. He then uses appropriate sensory exercises to retrieve the parallel emotion from his affective memory. He is not to be concerned with how the emotion will manifest itself, but only with finding it, creating the sensory realities that will unlock it, and trusting to his "instrument's" natural and unique response to what is released.[6]

When Stanislavsky spoke these words, Lee Strasberg and Stella Adler were in the audience. They were soon to become part of The Group Theater where a new interpretation of the System would emerge. When Adler came back from a Paris meeting with Stanislavsky in 1934, the news she brought created a conflict that shook The Group's foundations. It seems that after some more work with his pupil Vakhtangov, Stanislavsky now stated that the tapping of the actor's affective memory should be replaced by the development of The Physical Action approach. In Stanislavsky's words:

> ... learn to carry out correctly and organically the simplest physical actions. The logic and consecutiveness of these actions will evoke in you the entire complicated, subtle scale of inner experiences. Carrying out the logic of a physical action will bring you to the logic of emotions, and this is everything for an actor.[7]

This new technique raised interesting questions and dilemmas: with the method of Physical Actions, weren't actors reverting to the use of outer stimuli (preconceived actions) that would lead to dishonesty of emotion on stage? Or, on the contrary, wasn't the method of Physical Actions just another way to tap the affective memory; a safer, "healthier" exercise than the one used by Strasberg?

Strasberg, once he began teaching at the Actors Studio, taught "substitution," where "... a personal reality was substituted for a stage reality to help the actor believe in what he was doing and, therefore, create 'truthful' and 'organic' behavior."[8] In the few classes attended by James Dean in the fifties, it was Lee Strasberg's Method that was explored. If Dean thought that all he had to do was to be himself on screen, he did not learn it from Strasberg. The American teacher may have been far from Stanislavsky's ideal of the System's spokesperson, but he never taught the "heretical" notion that one "shouldn't act" in order to be a good Method performer. "The emotions," Strasberg would say, "must be remembered emotions and not 'real' ones. Real emotion, that is emotion actually provoked on the spot, has no place on the stage.... The art of acting is that the actor has full control of his sensory and emotional apparatus and can bring it into operation at his will, creating the experience over and over solely through the creative manipulation of his imagination."[9]

Before stepping in front of the cameras for *East of Eden*, James Dean would have to go through Elia Kazan's own interpretation of the System/Method. Also a teacher at the Actors Studio, Kazan firmly believed in the existence of the Affective Memory, but following Stella Adler's position, he never taught the exercise of "substitution" but concentrated on "action exercises." What is the intention (the motivation) of the character? To achieve the fixed goal, the imagination lets different physical impulses create the required behavior, with a little help from the director. It is not surprising that a film director would be so attracted to a Method which would depend so much on physical movements. In cinema, one could perhaps create a choreography, a ballet between film form and actor, both concerned with motion/emotion of the body, mind, and soul and the "poetic reflection of life's experience" for which Stanislavsky so hungered.

So James Dean started his film acting career in a starring role within the framework of contrasting, perhaps even contradictory, practical and philosophical notions of what constitutes acting. But his performance still partakes of the Method. It is more than slouching shoulders and slurred speech. An investigation of the oldest and most commonly known Method practice, the tapping of the Affective Memory in James Dean's performance, will be the starting point in the search to locate the Method in the actor's performance of Cal Trask in *East of Eden*.

## THE SOLITARY WORK OF THE METHOD ACTOR

> An actor who can stand in an imaginary snow-drift and actually make an audience shiver has mastered the reality of his art.—Boleslavsky.[10]

The workings of Method performances are often shrouded in mystery. We have been told stories of how actors would hide in their trailers for long stretches of time, ask to be left alone, finally return to the set where the crew waited—to give a transcendent performance as soon as the camera rolled. Such anecdotes, reported by scornful and admiring witnesses alike, do not facilitate our understanding of Method actors. By suggesting that the location of the actual process of creation is **outside** of the frame and takes place **before** the shooting of the scene, makes the resulting performance look like a highly skillful imitation of a preconceived form of behavior; the exact antithesis of the Stanislavskian approach to acting.

If one looks closely at James Dean's performance in *East of Eden*, it becomes apparent that the actor is in fact working constantly. He isn't bringing a completed "sculpture" or "canvas" to the screen, he is creating as the film unfolds before us.

Method actors, we are told, work with emotions that are stored inside their psyche, their "affective memory." To achieve this recall, the actor needs to relax and to concentrate on past sensory experiences. "Relaxation and concentration exercises" were a familiar routine during all classes at the Actors Studio—one might speculate that it is also what goes on in the trailers mentioned earlier—but in *East of Eden* they seem to be part of the Method actor's delivery.

The opening sequence of the film shows Cal desperately trying to communicate to his mother his thoughts and feelings about her. After his somewhat oneiric tailing of Kate (Jo van Fleet), the mother who left him and his family a long time ago, through sunny streets filled with dust and scattered sexual "invitations" (the sailors's boot thrust suggestively at Kate, the faraway laughter of a couple, and the closing of a window shade which momentarily distract Cal, and finally, the provocative and mocking laughter of a dubious-looking black woman), the Trask boy is left in front of Kate's house. In a still and frontal long shot, Dean is seen walking back and forth, from right to left, hiding in the shade of a tree. In the background, the black prostitute sits on her porch, reclining on a chair that bars the way to her front door, her legs suggestively lifted and resting on the banister. Cal is nervously observing Kate's house; he **hesitates.** The prostitute's laughter (she is shown in an isolated full shot) soon drives the boy away to the sunny street. Another long shot, excluding the black woman this time, shows Cal taking a few steps forward while the camera follows him with a rightward pan. The camera tilts up to meet him in half-shot, framing his body in the right foreground. Cal stops, looks at the black woman, looks left (as if wanting to escape the frame), but then turns right and takes a few steps, hands in his pockets, glancing once more towards the prostitute but keeping his head down. After an insert of Kate inside her house, asking her bodyguard, Joe (Timothy Carey), to look into this new problem—she knows she has been followed—we cut to another long shot of Cal standing in the dust-filled street. The young man leans forward **to pick up a rock**. The actor looks at it, **doesn't speak**, and gracefully swivels around to look at the black prostitute while the attentive camera almost imperceptibly follows his movement with a slight pan right, as if nervously anticipating some improvised and abrupt gesture from him. Cal takes a few steps forward but turns his head towards Kate's house. His feet are dragging a bit, he looks unsure; he **holds on** to the rock. Again, an insert of the black prostitute shows her laughing at Cal, a shrill sound that keeps recurring rhythmically on the soundtrack where hypnotic music is heard, underlining Cal's contemplative mood. We come back to a closer shot of him that puts the emphasis on the upper part of his body and not its full febrile length, as had been previously the case. The young man walks towards the camera (it tilts up slightly); we can see his features very clearly: he is squinting a bit, **concentrating** on the house off-screen, the house that shelters the cause of his agony. He opens his mouth a bit, as if to murmur something, **but instead** holds back a sigh. His face is like a screen where multiple emotions appear and dissolve like waves on troubled waters. It seems he is about to cry, **but instead** he suddenly goes through an elaborate pitching motion and throws his rock off-screen, towards Kate's house, while his body, in a blur, almost collides with the camera lens.

There follows an aggressive encounter between Cal and Joe. In a half-shot framing the pair in ¾ profile, we see Joe on the right (his back almost to the camera) holding Cal (frame-left) by the elbows. He interrogates the young boy, but Cal's mind is elsewhere. An insert of Kate's house underlines his obsession: **"Would she talk to me?"** Cal has finally met Joe's inquisitive glance. The mental and emotional currents of both Cal and James Dean are converging.

We cut to a full shot of Cal disengaging Joe's grip and walking towards the house. Again, the camera reframes every shift of Cal's body. Throughout Joe's continuing interrogation, Cal wards off the big man's questions while again intently watching Kate's house, as if brooding over an unreachable but seductive adversary. Soon, in a low-angle, torso-shot (the closest the camera has come to a close-up of him in this scene), Cal will utter what any confused and love-hungry teenager might say to an ungiving parent: "Well you tell her," the comma feels like a period—for the first time since he began talking in the film, his tone of voice is firm and rather assured, "I hate her."

Thus, in the first sequence of the film, Dean's search for Cal and Cal's search for eloquence are united. And if the viewer feels he understands Cal (if the viewer is shivering in Dean's imaginary snowdrift), it is because he has been a witness to James Dean's search for the interiority of his character. The frame is the trailer. The off-screen glances, the hesitations, the sighs, the silences, the aborted gestures, the use of an object as tool of communication, the juxtapositions of contradictory "emotional events" (he wants to cry and is about to, but he resorts to a violent act: the throwing of the rock, etc.), are the basis for the construction of the performance; the text itself isn't nearly as revealing.

Furthermore, it is not surprising that Dean appears to be isolating himself. Joe's questions only seem to be there to help him go deeper into himself: "Why are you hanging around here for, anyway?" "What do you want?" "Why were you following her?" Put those questions in the mouth of a rehearsal director (in Elia Kazan's mouth) and the scene takes on a whole new dimension. Joe is directing Dean, and Dean is alone with his feelings.

Further evidence of Dean's particular work is offered in the bean field scene. Cal has come to witness the "birth" of the green sprouts, an exhilarating event for him: the crop he is cultivating will be sold at a huge profit. He intends to give the money to his father, who lost almost all his savings in a refrigeration venture that failed. He hopes to gain his father's respect and love with this unexpected present. The main part of the sequence is composed of eleven shots: the first, third, fifth, ninth, and eleventh isolate James Dean in the field; number two, four, six, eight, and ten show the reactions of the Mexican onlookers (a friendly farmer who tends to a car, and his children); while the seventh shot establishes the spatial relationship of all the participants. The scene opens on a close view of a green sprout waving in the wind; the camera then tilts up to reveal Cal lying down on his stomach between rows of beans which extend into infinity in the far background of the frame. He smiles and tilts his head to judge the height of the small sprouts. Though he next engages in a short but joyful conversation with the Mexican farmer (they shout back and forth, isolated in their respective shot-countershots), the full extent of Cal's pride and happiness is only revealed in the subsequent shots that show him running up and down the field. Kazan's attentive camera follows, with pans and tilts, the movements of the young man exploring the depth of the frame in his dancing trajectory. Kazan's stand is one of respect for the actor's performance. He juxtaposes the somewhat flat and static shots of the laughing onlookers with the dynamic and deep views of James Dean's crazy dance, and he makes sure that the young actor has the full range of the frame to express himself. Dean can relax and express Cal's euphoric emotions through graceful and seemingly improvised acrobatics. He runs hunched forward; he jumps in the air, arms fully extended, head back; he spins and runs again, with hands near the sprouts, waving an invitation to grow faster and faster (figs. 11.1–11.4). The last shot shows him running at an angle, towards the camera, crossing its axis and exiting the frame, leaving a small cloud of dust behind him.

Whether through concentration to tap the affective memory or with relaxation to express the emotions through "free style" physical action, *East of Eden* abounds in moments where the work of James Dean can be studied.

The ledge scene between James Dean and Julie Harris is yet another such moment. This time, though, it reveals a more troubling aspect of Dean's solitary performance, his being "private in public."

Following his brutal exchange with Aron, Cal seeks Abra's approval and help when, after having had too much to drink, he decides to wake her up to explain the plan he now has for a birthday party that would enable him to offer his father the money he made in his bean venture. The sequence begins with a shot of Cal climbing up a trellis to the second story of Abra's house and knocking on her bedroom window while standing on a thin ledge. After exposing his plan in a soft tone, Cal will next perform a dangerous and seductive "ballet," a combination of imploring, sensuous, hurt glances, vocal variations on taunting questions, and dangerous physical actions carried out in a somewhat erotic fashion.

Cal, still standing on the thin ledge near Abra's bedroom, is framed in a head and shoulder shot; he occupies the left side of the frame, while portions of Abra's long red hair are seen at the right of the frame as she leans out her window. He looks at her, his own face offered to her gaze. He blinks slowly, frowns, and says in a sweet and pleading tone: "Will you do it?" thrusting his face slightly forward. Cut to Abra, also framed in a head and shoulder shot, while Cal's back profile can be seen at frame-right; she responds softly: "I'd like to." Back to the previous set-up, we see Cal smile in response, a bit drunkenly; then he moves his lips (he lets his smile fade away), swallows, and cocks his head in a feline nod while closing his eyes as he nestles his face in profile on the wood clapboards of the house, snuggling his cheek and nose near the window frame. As soon as his skin softly touches the frame, his eyes flash open, and he rests his gaze on Abra's face. He smiles but again slowly closes his eyes and, with a sigh, revolves his shoulders

**Fig. 11.1**

Fig. 11.2

Fig. 11.3

Fig. 11.4

while keeping his head on the wall until his back is flat against the house and he faces a wooden ornament attached to the roof—the camera has followed his movement away from Abra. Cal slowly lifts his right arm and looks at his hand enter the hole of the ornament where it softly comes to rest. We cut to Abra; she has followed his motion with a worried look on her face. Her eyes repeat their up and down glance.

Back to a head and shoulder shot of Cal that excludes Abra, we see the young man say, eyes half-closed, features troubled: "I'm sort of … sort of…." He lets his head fall back squarely in front of the ornament and then, quite suddenly, knocks it sharply on the protruding piece of wood, hurting his forehead. He doesn't respond, but Abra winces in a reaction shot. His head bent on the ornament, he continues: "Why did I hit Aron? Why did I hit him **so** hard?" He lets Abra contemplate his inner turmoil as he rubs his forehead and brushes his hair on the ornament, eyes closed, letting his head follow the curve of the wood until his body seemingly plunges into the empty space below. But as soon as we cut to a high-angle, half-shot of his motion, we see his right arm still holding on to the gingerbread curlicue as Abra, leaning over with her back to the camera, looks on. Hanging on above the ground, his feet reclining on the ledge, he swings his head back to look at the young woman and pleads: "Will you help me? Will ya? Will you really help me?"

We cut to her; the lighting is soft on her face, a subtle iris blurs the contour of the frame; she murmurs: "I'll help you, Cal." As we return to him, we see he is no longer on the ledge: Cal, silently facing Abra, is standing erect on a porch roof below, his graceful figure receding back in the darkness. We cut to a reverse angle, taken from the ground, and witness Cal's near drop from the porch's roof, as he waves his arms to retain his balance while Abra, framed in the upper-right corner of this long shot, gestures to protect him: "Be careful." Cal swivels back and happily exclaims to her: "How'd I get up here? …" The scene ends with a half-shot of Abra sighing and hugging the window frame as she sees Cal depart (off-screen).

Not much dialogue is exchanged in this scene; Dean uses his character's drunkenness to once again isolate himself in his research and intimate rapport with the camera. The emphasis is on the translation of his emotional state into physically intricate actions acted out in an actually dangerous shooting situation that creates an exciting tension. Try to imagine the same scene (the same text) enacted inside Abra's room with the two protagonists comfortably sitting in armchairs. A whole dimension of James Dean's character evaporates: his "dare-devil" stature is absolutely necessary to both his eroticization and his emotional suffering. The camera lingers on his face; every detail of his performance is acted slowly, sensuously, from the caresses of his body to his self-inflicted blow.

We could make a judgment upon looking at this scene; that James Dean is a narcissistic actor. There *is* a strong element of seduction and self-absorption in the sequence. During the moments of intense meditation and brooding contemplation, when he lays bare his painful emotions in front of the camera, using his fellow actors as mere spectators—as Julie Harris surely is in this scene—is James Dean being a true Method actor? Lest we forget, Stanislavsky said: "Collective creativeness, on which our art is based, necessarily demands ensemble.... Those who violate it commit a crime ... against the art which they serve."[11]

Was James Dean's performance heretical to this notion?

## THE ENSEMBLE WORK OF THE METHOD ACTOR

Studies of Method performances that are solely based on statements about the work of individual actors can lead to imbalanced and inadequate criticism. Certainly we are deprived of an understanding of the intricate world of the Method *mise-en-scène*.

We must acknowledge that there is a mediator between the performance of James Dean in *East of Eden* and the spectator: Elia Kazan. An analysis of the Method phenomenon in the film must take Kazan's strategies into account.

When a play or a screenplay is being rehearsed by a Method ensemble of cast and director, preliminary work is done with the text to get to its essence. This is crucial to the Method performance of the written word. The ensemble (or the director alone) has to find a subtextual line that runs through the work and gives logical order and perspective to the various roles, while organically uniting them. Though the screenplay of *East of Eden* would have been adequate in its exploration of the conflict between good and evil (by using the metaphors found in the novel: Cain/Cal, Abel/Aron, exile from Eden, the woman as temptress, etc.), the **subtext** developed by Kazan and his ensemble tells of pain and unshared feelings, and the quest for fatherly love by a boy in search of his own identity. In *East of Eden*, this "through-line of actions"[12] clearly translates into strategies that isolate Cal from the other characters, to further stress the teenage boy's incapacity to adequately communicate his need for love.

Thus if the Cal and Abra scene leaves us with the impression of James Dean as narcissist—which is to say, a poor heir to Stanislavsky's teaching—it is largely the product of Kazan's editing. During the exchange between Cal and Abra, instead of favoring a camera angle and focal length that would frame the two actors together, thereby permitting the necessary communication/communion of Method actors, Kazan chooses to fragment the scene in **shot-counter-shots** that cast James Dean as the "performer" and Julie Harris as the "spectator." In view of this formal plan, the legitimate judgment that one might make is that James Dean's **character** is the one being isolated by the director, the tight frame cradling his pain ("Why did I hit Aron **so** hard?"). This isolation has nothing to do with the "methodness" or "non-methodness" of the actor's work.

One need only look at the scene which follows the ledge sequence above to understand how James Dean can work **with** another actor while his character remains egocentric. Cal and Abra meet the next day in Adam's house, where the couple prepares his surprise birthday party. The scene opens on a shot of Dean swinging the kitchen door open and running past the dining table to the living room, where paper decorations are hanging from the ceiling. The camera pans right to follow his trajectory. Julie Harris enters from the left but remains standing in the midground, at the very edge of the frame. This time, Kazan is setting up a **long take**. In the background, we see Dean running around like an excited child (fig. 11.5). He turns towards Harris and exclaims: "Ooh, I think it looks beautiful, don't you? I love the way it looks." Julie Harris, patient and receptive, just says: "Hmm, hmm," and waits for Dean's reaction.

He promptly continues (his hook accepted by the actress):

Fig. 11.5

DEAN: "It looks festive, don't it?"
HARRIS: "Yes, it does."
DEAN: "You think it looks festive?"
HARRIS: "Oh yes, oh Cal...."
DEAN: "You think this is childish?"
HARRIS: "No, not a bit...."

Dean resumes his dance around the living room (figs. 11.6-11.7). During the exchange, both actors "feed" on each other and work together in what is basically an improvisation on one simple sentence, the "I think it's beautiful" line spoken by Dean. But Kazan manages to divide the two characters spatially, because Abra is never permitted to enter Cal's "playground" (the living room). He also keeps them apart dramatically because the two actors do not deliver the same subtext. Though James Dean asks questions that

Fig. 11.6

Fig. 11.7

Fig. 11.8

hint at his insecurity, his body movements (reminiscent of his "dance" in the bean field) tell us that his character is excited by the party. The character is oblivious to Abra's reserve and her growing concern about his well-being. While she never takes her eyes off him, Dean's eyes are restless, his glance always nervous. Though her words are reassuring, her behavior asks him to be calm, to be careful: something could go wrong; his father might not understand his gift of love. It becomes apparent that Cal does not share Abra's knowledge when the camera moves in to frame them closely near the buffet. Cal performs his actions and continues his own train of thought; he talks to Abra without looking at her. Abra, on the contrary, follows his every move, searches for eye contact, and again pleads for his understanding, for true communication (fig. 11.8). The characters are having a one-way relationship, but the actors are nonetheless **creating together** through careful listening, rhythmical delivery of syncopated lines, and respectful understanding of each other's body language.

Because of their vulnerability and transparent sensitivity, James Dean and Julie Harris have come to form the most recognizable Method-like couple in *East of Eden*. But James Dean's performance, when observed in light of the acting ensemble (particularly in his scenes with Raymond Massey), is even more illuminating in the quest for a deeper understanding of the Method.

For the role of Cal's father, Adam Trask, Elia Kazan chose Massey, a non-Method actor with a more orthodox theater background. While the performance of the veteran actor may seem "wooden"—to paraphrase the director[13]—his resolutely non-Method attitude allows the confrontation scenes between Adam and Cal to become extraordinary examples of dramatic collision.

In the reading of the Bible scene, Kazan stages a confrontation between rebellion and authority, pride and mortification, contemporary teenage angst and Victorian standards; in short, a duel between a son and his father. But it is also a duel between a Method actor communicating through subtext and a non-Method actor hanging on to the written word. Consider the following exchange: Adam Trask has reprimanded Cal for throwing big blocks of ice down an ice-chute, causing them to melt in the sun. He tries to be calm as he questions his son; he is trying to find the real reason for Cal's behavior. For an answer, he can only get the impertinent reply: "I wanted to see them slide down the chute." He is insulted and asks his son to read a passage from the Bible.

Cal is shot from the waist up, in a canted frame, sitting at the far end of the dining table (fig. 11.9). He slides the Bible in front of him. After a sigh and a glance towards his father and Aron (off-screen), he hunches over the book and begins to read, mumbling a bit: "I acknowledge my sin unto thee and my iniquity. . . ." Cal's delivery becomes faster, the syllables indistinguishable one from the other. He ends by delivering the formal notice, "Selah." He then starts to close the book, but his father's voice, from off-screen, interrupts his gesture. He is asked to "go on." Cal slides the Bible back in front of him, sighs, and hunches again over the written words; but instead of reading the text, he announces the verse number. There is a cut to Adam, sitting at the other end of the table, framed alone in an extreme canted shot.

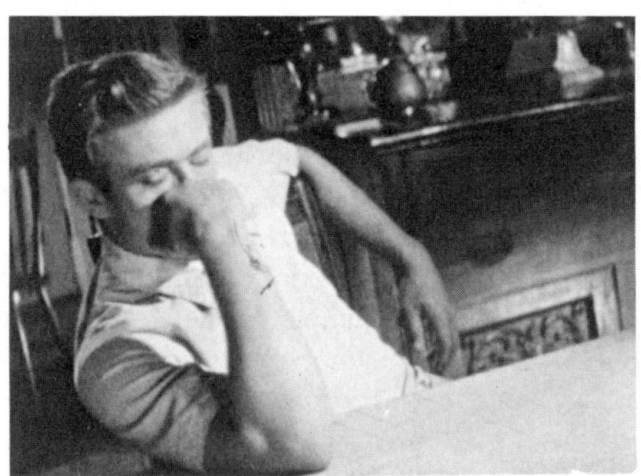

**Fig. 11.9**

He says: "And I suggest a little slower Cal, and you don't have to read the verse numbers." Cutting back to Cal, we see him reading at a fast pace, against his father's recommendation. He ends it defiantly: "Selah." **A beat**. "Seven." He raises his eyes towards his father. We cut to the latter: "Not the numbers, Cal." Adam is still calm. Back to his son; Cal's head is already down. He resumes the reading, more slowly this time, but he adopts a declamatory tone and again ends the sentence with the formal word: "Selah." **Three silent beats**. On the fourth, he looks upward, squints, and almost spits out: "Eight."

We promptly cut back to Adam and Aron, the camera framing them from the side of the table, at a normal angle. The father shouts: "You have no repentance. You're bad. Through and through, bad."

What is important to the father, in this scene, are the words and their meaning; just as they are important to Massey as an actor. In contradistinction, James Dean plays with the rhythm, pauses, and intonations to communicate his frustration and disgust to his "father." The words could have spelled out mathematical rules or been part of a grocery list; the important thing is the structure of the delivery, the projection of the inner feelings associated with the experience of the event. Kazan's masterstroke has been to simply incorporate this Method training exercise into the narrative and let the two opponents battle it out in a series of shot-counter-shots, while retaining James Dean's victory: his masterful control of those three silent beats before the utterance of his defiant cry: "Eight."

The other two members of the main cast ensemble were also used by Kazan in an unorthodox manner. Jo van Fleet, playing the role of Cal's mother, and Richard Davalos, as Cal's brother, were both Studio-trained contemporaries of James Dean (as was Julie Harris), but Kazan rarely let them develop what has been called "naturalistic playacting." Again, to isolate Dean's character more thoroughly, Kazan favors symbolism, caricature in physical appearances, and extreme modes of behavior for the other two actors. In short, a type of performance rarely associated with the Method.

When we first see Jo van Fleet (Kate), she is a darkly clad figure walking in the sunny streets of Monterey. Her face and hands are also hidden behind a black veil and gloves. The only word she utters is a cold and curt, "Deposit," an order she gives to a bank teller while Cal waits outside, spying on her. Her features are never explored by a close-up; her human qualities are hidden. When

Kazan allows her character to fully evolve in dramatic scenes with Cal, he opposes Dean's withdrawal to van Fleet's alternate implacability and near-hysterical gestures.

The scene when Cal comes to ask Kate for money is revealing of Kazan's strategy. While the boy stammers, makes himself small in Kate's armchair, or leans on the wall near her door, talking, face turned away from her (all emblematic of a Method-emphasis on physicalized emotion), Kate energetically walks to and fro in her small office, throws her arms in the air, draws firmly on her cigarette, and speaks sarcastically, her words emphasized by the curling movements of her lips. Kate is putting on a show for Cal: she is the best business woman in town, and she has no tender feelings. When Kazan frames her in front of her mirror, as she takes off her veiled hat and talks to her son of "motherly topics" (school, his relationship with his brother, plans for the future) communicating with Cal but only through the reflection in the glass, Kazan gives us a telling image of her character's refusal or inability to let her guard down. She cannot turn around and take the young man in her arms; she is in control as long as she shields herself behind her facade. Thus with Jo van Fleet's character, Kazan achieves a *trompe-l'oeil* (a Method actress building her character with non-Method characteristics) to better focus the viewer's attention on **one** character, Cal.

The same effect is achieved in the scenes between Cal and Aron; but with Richard Davalos' character, Kazan's conception follows the reverse trajectory. If, compared to Kate, Cal's brother is introduced innocuously (a long travelling shot of him walking with Abra as Cal accosts them, without any expressive emphasis on his character), a succession of troubling events and close shots of Aron soon appear. His front as a loving, healthy, normal, and untroubled youth is stripped to reveal a similarly uncomplicated, but contrasting persona, that of a mean-spirited boy.

We have already discussed Aron's shocking smile when Cal strikes him; but it's in the emotionally charged scene of Adam's birthday party that Kazan achieves the deconstruction of the Aron character. In this scene, Davalos' performance becomes the epitome of insensitivity and rigidity (in complete opposition to Dean).

While Aron had previously been clad in loose garments reminiscent of Dean's clothes, he is now dressed in a conservative fashion. Furthermore, the baggy suit he wears deforms and makes his muscular body somewhat ridiculous; he seems ill at ease. He is also framed in the dark background as he somberly watches the trio (Adam, Cal, Abra) celebrate in the lighted foreground. And finally, he is imprisoned in an unforgiving reaction-shot when Cal gives the long-awaited present to his father: Aron's blank face and heavily kholed eyes form an image evocative of many silent-era villains and their stylized rendering of emotion. Aron is jealous, calculating, and mean. It thus comes as no surprise to the spectator when, in the next instant, he announces to his father his intention of marrying Abra. He not only undermines the crucial moment of Cal's presentation (as only a true villain could), but also destroys, for the time being, the hope that Cal and Abra will be united.

Though Kazan has shown Aron's sweet and smiling face many times during the course of the film (in the ice-house as he flirts with Abra; at the gas station where he witnesses Adam's humorous driving lesson; near the train wagons dripping with melted ice, as he naively contemplates his father's brave countenance in the face of the refrigeration fiasco, etc.), it is the ominous close-ups which we remember. The Method actor chooses to use a **mask**—traditionally, a non-Method tool—to communicate his character's inner nature, a sharp contrast to Dean's graceful, transparent, and chameleon-like face.

## CONCLUSION

> [He] could not endure formlessness. He always strove for the most precise, rich, inwardly full and expressive external form for the ... dramatic work in question. He strove to eliminate triviality and to create new forms through the most imaginative means. His aim was the synthesis of imaginative sculptural form and inner truth.[14]

Though the preceding comment was in fact a critical assessment of Eugene Vakhtangov's style, it might well have been applied to Elia Kazan's and James Dean's relationship in interpreting the Method. Like the controversial Soviet actor and director before him, Kazan set out to disengage the Stanislavskian/Method performance from the "realist" yoke (naturalistic, low-key acting in an unobtrusive setting). In *East of Eden* he delivers it to the *risqué* world of "fantastic theatricality" by opposing caricatural and non-caricatural characters—playing in fact against the viewers' expectations of what Method acting is or what it should be. As for James Dean, he also achieves an analogous feat when he lets his "true to inner emotions" performance evolve in Kazan's expressionist (e.g. non-naturalistic, non-realist) *mise-en-scène.*

There is a scene, very early on in the film, which translates the aim of their particular work perfectly: the search for the poetry of emotions (an often forgotten Stanislavskian topic). After having been driven away from Kate's street without having met his mysterious mother, Cal soon returns and enters her house (a brothel). There, he coaxes a young waitress (Lois Smith, also of the Actor's Studio) to show him to Kate's office. They leave the smoke-filled barroom and tentatively enter a very narrow and dark corridor. As soon as there is a cut to a deep-focus long shot, framing the inside of the passage, the piano music and drunken laughter from the bar subside and ominous music fades out, even though we can still see the customers in the lighted, deep background. The young girl, afraid of Kate, doesn't dare go any further, her body "hanging" on to the wall, her supine figure silently imploring Cal as her silhouetted body separates him from the lighted barroom. But the young man chooses to advance inward, towards the camera and into the darkness, leaving the "safe" (and "realist") world behind. In silhouette, we see him tip-toeing in a feline manner to Kate's closed door, in the right foreground. When Cal bends down to the level of the doorknob, there is a cut to a closer shot of him opening the door, revealing Kate's room. He slowly walks in; the camera tilts up, revealing Kate asleep in her armchair under the glow of a lamp. The soft pastel light isolates her in the room's darkness. We cut to a reverse angle, taken from behind her chair; Cal, in full shot, looks at her and doesn't move. We cut back to the previous set-up; Kate wears a pink negligee, her long blond hair falls on her shoulders, and her arm and hand shield the light from her eyes. She looks very young and beautiful. Low music accompanies Cal's silent wait. We cut to the reverse-angle set-up; a shy Cal is seen bent down from the waist up, in the radius of the light (he doesn't use his arms, which he keeps tightened against his ribs and waist). He does not let his whole body enter the lighted area, as if still too much in awe of the apparition. Then abruptly, we go to an extreme close-up of Kate's deformed hands (she suffers from arthritis), taken from Cal's point of view. The music underscores her distressing moans: a telling image in sharp contrast to the previous vision. Next, we return to the set-up behind Kate's armchair and see Cal going down on his knees, sitting on his heels, patiently waiting for his mother to wake up (a studio light switches on, on top of him, casting a warmer light on his shoulders). His face beams, he moves his lips to say something but stays silent. When his mother finally does wake up, he softly asks her: "You let me talk to you?" He thrusts his body forward, hands on his knees: "Please? I gotta talk to you."

There is a cut to a full shot taken from behind Cal, near the open door of the room; we see Kate finally coming to her senses. She stops and stares at him, her features hard and uninviting. When she recognizes him, she shifts in her seat—the music rises—she throws her body back, grips the arms of the chair, and shouts for help, destroying the hypnotic atmosphere of the scene. From behind her armchair, we see her thrust her body forward, looming over the surprised and hurt Cal who is still waiting on his knees for some kind of "gift" from her; the frame suddenly becomes a claustrophobic space. Kate screams for Joe. From the doorway, we see her hide her face from Cal with her negligee-clad arm. She stands up in full shot, again shouting: "Get out of here … Joe!" Cal moves his hands, as if wanting to touch Kate to reassure her, but his small fluttering gesture goes unnoticed and only reinforces his fragility.

Joe and his associate soon rush in and violently pick up the boy while the mother sadistically shouts over and over again: "Punish him!" The nightmarish event is shown in a series of cramped and very short shots, contrasting with the contemplative shot-counter-shot exchange between the kneeling Cal and his sleeping mother. Cal is ejected from the room, out of the light and the illusion of warm motherly love, but his whole body fights back; his cries of "**No!** Let me talk to you!" try to break through Joe's insults. In the dark passage, seen in a deep-focus long shot, the boy frees himself from Joe's murderous grip and grasps a pipe across from Kate's door while the bodyguard tries to hold him back, pulling the young man along the sharp perspective lines that lead to the lighted barroom. We cut to a close shot of the pair fighting in the darkness near the floor; only Cal's hands are lit in the foreground holding on to the metal bar. Everyone is shouting; Cal is weeping and Joe tears his sweater. Kate opens her door; we cut to a close-up of her face: she winces as she witnesses the violent scene and Cal's pathetic cries. She hears Cal's plea, "I wanna talk to you...," but she closes the door, rejecting him, as she has before. The camera, back to a close shot of Cal hanging on to the pipe, shows us his deformed face. As the light coming from Kate's door disappears, he becomes hysterical and shouts: "Talk to me!" Darkness falls and Cal's hands release their grip, but he keeps pleading with her. At this point his voice—emerging from the unlit foreground—is deeper, coarser, more ominous. His, "Talk to me, please ..." has the sound of someone talking with his mouth full of blood (actually, the sound texture is so different at this point that one can safely advance the idea that the line was **post-dubbed** by Dean). The scene ends with Joe punching the young man in the stomach, his arm movement slashing the dissolving frame with red, even though he is fully dressed in black.

The use of chiaroscuro, expressionist art design, dramatic music, post-production intervention, and strong symbolic references in conjunction with Cal's innocent and tragic behavior (Dean's juxtaposition of low-key and then violently emphatic rendering of one line) have turned this scene into a dark Oedipal tale of rejection.

Truth in Art. The goal is the same for all performance philosophies and teachings; only the means differ.

Truth in Art, and not Reality or realism in Art. Stanislavsky often talked about the difference; some pupils of his and some critics have had a tendency to forget this nuance. Since by its nature

Fig. 11.10

Fig. 11.11

Fig. 11.12

Fig. 11.13

Fig. 11.14

Fig. 11.15

all that film can capture is the simulacra of reality and not reality itself, the ensuing confusion continues to defeat our understanding of the Method film performance. When Kazan gives us expressionist close-ups of Dean's suffering, love-hungry face, as in the rejection scene during the birthday party (figs. 11.10–11.15), one must abandon the issue of realism as one enters the domain of poetry.

## NOTES

1. Lee Strasberg, cited by David Garfield, *The Actors Studio* (New York: Macmillan Publishing Company, 1984), p. 16.
2. See Réné Château, *James Dean Story* (Paris: Editions Réné Château, 1975); David Dalton, Ron Cayen, *James Dean: American Icon* (New York: St. Martin's Press, 1984); Jean-Loup Bourget, *James Dean* (Paris: Henri Veyrier, 1983).
3. James Dean, quoted in Garfield, p. 97.
4. Stanislavsky, quoted in Garfield, p. 166.
5. Stanislavsky, quoted in Sonia Moore, *The Stanislavski System* (New York: Penguin Books, 1974, 1984), p. 42.
6. Garfield, p. 16.
7. Stanislavsky, quoted in Moore, pp. 44–45.
8. Garfield, p. 19.
9. Lee Strasberg citing Vakhtangov, cited by Garfield, p. 17.
10. Boleslavsky quoted in Garfield, p. 14.
11. Stanislavsky, quoted in Moore, p. 14.
12. The expression is Stanislavsky's. See Sonia Moore, p. 50.
13. See Kazan's discussion of Raymond Massey's performance in Michel Ciment, *Kazan par Kazan* (Paris: Stock, 1973), p. 205, [author's translation].
14. Moore, p. 87.

# 12. THE MAD AND THE BEAUTIFUL: A Look at Two Performances in the Films of Stanley Kubrick

Mario Falsetto

## I.

NOTWITHSTANDING THE COPIOUS AMOUNT of writing devoted to the work of Stanley Kubrick,[1] one area which has received and continues to receive little attention is Kubrick's work with actors. This is by no means the only area of Kubrick scholarship that deserves more attention. The literature for the most part emphasizes many of the same thematic discussions, neglecting Kubrick's formal achievements. It is also apparent, however, that film acting has been generally overlooked in most of the texts on Kubrick (as well as most other filmmakers, I might add). The present discussion is an attempt to partially fill this critical gap. We will limit our discussion to two major, though very different, performances that illustrate how an actor's performance works in concert with other elements to create a film's meanings. The two performances are Jack Nicholson's in *The Shining* (1980) and Ryan O'Neal's in *Barry Lyndon* (1975).

Ryan O'Neal is clearly an actor of limited range whose body of work is not particularly impressive. Known primarily for his television work of the 1960s (*Peyton Place*) and for several successful light comedies of the 1970s (*Paper Moon, What's Up Doc*), O'Neal's dramatic range is not very wide. And although *Barry Lyndon* elicited a fair amount of discussion when first released, most of it not very useful, Ryan O'Neal's performance, to my knowledge, has not been seriously analyzed.

By contrast, Jack Nicholson is one of the great film actors of his generation. Working with a range of directors as disparate as

Antonioni, Penn, Rafelson, Polanski, Huston, Forman, and many others, Nicholson has produced one of the most illustrious bodies of work of any contemporary film actor. His performance in *The Shining* contains some of his best work. It is also a performance that has generally been ignored by most film scholars. We will be concerned in the present discussion with exploring how these two performances work in concert with other filmic strategies to create meaning, and to illustrate how the internal logic and organization of the film depends to a great extent on how the performance is integrated into the film's overall design.

## II.

*Barry Lyndon* is Stanley Kubrick's complex and very ambitious adaptation of William Thackeray's 1844 novel, *The Luck of Barry Lyndon*. When the film was originally released in 1975 it was met with a decidedly mixed critical reaction. Many people admired the stunning visuals of the film but bemoaned its lack of dramatic intensity. Others complained that the film was merely an impressive art history slide show and decried the lack of conventional drama in the film. Few critics, whether positive or negative, attempted to deal with the complexities or richness of the film. Even critics who would normally be able to respond to the Brechtian/Bressonian de-dramatized stylization of the film failed to acknowledge that the film could possibly be as sophisticated as a Bresson or a Godard. Critics in general have not been able to deal with the achievement of the film with the rigor and sophistication it clearly deserves. Despite the shortsightedness of most critics, the film remains one of Kubrick's most important works and one of the most interesting films of the 1970s. Unfortunately, it will not be possible here to analyze in great detail the many layers of meaning in the film. Rather, I will focus my analysis on the performance of Ryan O'Neal in the central role; by doing this I hope to demonstrate some of the complexities and achievements of the film.

The role of Barry Lyndon would be considered difficult and demanding for even the best film actor. O'Neal is called upon to age from a youthful and spirited sixteen year-old to full middle age. He must also perform in nearly every scene of the film, which runs over three hours. The role is made more difficult because O'Neal's characterization of Barry is integral to other aesthetic strategies. O'Neal is frequently directed to give a stylized, non-naturalistic, mannequin-like performance. It's a performance that often lacks interiority or on the other hand has an impenetrable interiority with little external expression. O'Neal's work in his other films has generally been of a fairly conventional, naturalistic sort, and although he is possessed of a certain physical presence on camera and a mildly charming personality, very few people would argue that he has ever given a performance of great depth. Although it is rather subjective and difficult to substantiate, one can say that his strength seems to be in the area of comedy, rather than drama. And although his charm and physicality are in evidence in *Barry Lyndon*, the film more often than not demands that O'Neal be serious and invest his role with tragic rather than comic dimensions. A further complication is the way in which Kubrick places the actor in so many artificial poses; yet in other sequences he is called upon to act in a relatively naturalistic way. This combination of different styles of acting places a heavy burden on the actor.

Despite these difficulties and reservations, one must acknowledge and ultimately accept O'Neal's performance in the central role. In fact, I now cannot imagine another actor in the role. I have no doubt that a different actor might have invested the role with other qualities, but I am not at all sure he would have been appropriate to what Kubrick was trying to accomplish in the film.

The character of Barry Lyndon is created for the most part through presentation rather than through the carefully articulated character building more typical of mainstream narrative cinema. We come to know Barry through frozen gestures and immobile posing; his placement within the frame; and severe restriction and limitations of the frame edge, achieved in part through the use of the slow zoom, long takes, and limited though strategic use of camera movement. This is not to say that the dramatic situations in the film are unimportant in their revelation of Barry's character.

Rather, the visual presentation of Barry is as important as any other element in understanding his character.

The character of Barry is the agent or conduit through which the film articulates many of its thematic and aesthetic concerns. This articulation is made in many instances through the dialogue, but just as often it is made through pure visuals and the use of emotional music. It may be this nonverbal level of discourse (as it was in *2001: A Space Odyssey*, for example) that has been responsible for the difficulty many people have had with the film. Kubrick seems as intent on elaborating his many thematic, formal concerns as he is in building his main character.

*Barry Lyndon* is in many ways an elaborate and complex aesthetic/social investigation of the eighteenth century. The film explores notions of "art" and "beauty" and how this particular society sees itself through its artistic and architectural achievement. The film also examines the British class system and some of its rules of behavior. The analysis is restricted for the most part to the highest echelons of this society. It is also concerned with male-female interaction. And, as with most of Kubrick's work, these issues are examined with relation to our present moment in history: not overtly, of course, but all of Kubrick's work to some extent is about the present, even if it has a historical or futuristic setting. *Barry Lyndon* is without a doubt Kubrick's most elaborate statement on aesthetics and social mores, and it is no accident that he has chosen to analyze the Age of Enlightenment rather than a more contemporary period in history. After all, the eighteenth century was the apogee of cultural, social, and philosophical achievement and the crucial period leading to modernity. Even if now we have come to revise many of our notions about the period, it is still seen as crucial to the development of the modern age.

The character of Barry Lyndon is used primarily as a device to explore many of these issues. For this reason it is not only difficult, but almost irrelevant, to evaluate Ryan O'Neal's performance in isolation. The performance is simply too interconnected with other issues. How one feels about the film as a whole will determine to a great extent how one feels about O'Neal's performance. Conversely, because O'Neal's character is so central, how one feels about Barry will to a great extent determine the spectator's attitude to the film as a whole.

An elaboration of these claims is to some extent an examination of the concept of "authorial" point of view. The character of Barry is a central device through which Kubrick explores various questions. Barry becomes the invention through which Kubrick's "voice" or authorial presence is felt. He is as important as the more obvious traces of the filmmaker's presence, such as the slow zoom, editing patterns, careful compositions, and cinematography. *Barry Lyndon* clearly bears the mark of its maker in every shot. Ryan O'Neal's performance is another substantiation of the filmmaker's intervention. The way in which O'Neal's performance works in the film and the ways we read that performance are central to the way Kubrick inserts himself into the film.

## III.

*Barry Lyndon* is divided into two main sections. Part I chronicles Barry's more picaresque adventures. Barry is forced to leave home at a youthful age after a duel over the affections of his cousin Nora (Gay Hamilton). We see Barry's life as a soldier in both the British and Prussian army, his life as a Prussian spy, and finally his life as a gambler. The film does not dwell on these episodes; the narrative movement is insistent. In this part of the film we have the impression that Barry is simply swept along by events and circumstance. He does not actively plan many aspects of his life until near the end of Part I, when Barry meets Lady Lyndon (Marisa Berenson) and is about to take on the title and new life of Barry Lyndon. Part II of the film, noticeably darker in tone, is concerned with Barry's new-found station in life and his eventual downfall. This section of the film shows Barry as husband and father and his obsession with obtaining a peerage. Ultimately, he loses everything. The film as a whole is pessimistic in tone and presents a rather fatalistic vision.

Many scenes in Part I find O'Neal in situations where his physical movements are deliberately slow, artificial, and stylized, or completely immobile, locked in frozen gesture. Barry is most frequently seen in medium or long shot. Many times he is presented frontally, and Kubrick does not often resort to shot-counter-shot in these scenes. The film creates a pattern of distanciation strategies fairly early in the narrative and maintains this throughout the course of the film. We see Barry walking with his mother (Marie Kean) or his cousin Nora, or standing in a pose, arms folded behind his back, frequently with his head bent downward or looking straight ahead with a far off look in his eyes. In many of these scenes Barry does not speak, or if he does, he enunciates his words very slowly in quiet tones. Even in scenes where Barry is more active, such as the scene where he throws a wine glass at Captain Quin's (Leonard Rossiter) face upon hearing that Quin will marry Nora, Barry speaks in carefully modulated phrases. In this particular scene, although it is a heated moment for Barry, he is still fairly stiff as he calmly stands and throws the glass in the face of his "rival." It is in fact Quin who displays the most emotion in the scene, rather than Barry whose movements and actions are careful and tentative.

The strongest impression we have of Barry in these scenes is primarily physical. Barry is presented as passionate, stubborn, idealistic, and naive. This impression is formed essentially through our awareness of his body. We see its robustness and its beauty. What we admire about the young Redmond Barry is his youthful vitality. O'Neal is particularly successful in communicating these aspects of the character, perhaps because he is not expected to be especially thoughtful but more of a presence on the screen. Although we occasionally see Barry in reflective moments, these moments become fewer as the film progresses. O'Neal is particularly effective in portraying the hot-tempered, strong-willed side of Barry's character that will gradually be suppressed in the course of the film. It is a sad realization that, with a few exceptions, only in these early scenes is the character of Barry allowed to be genuinely emotional. The older and more experienced Barry gets, the more mannequin-like and unemotional he will become. The major exception in Part II is the sequence where Barry brutally attacks Lord Bullingdon, an action that will prove to be Barry's undoing.

Through the course of the film, Barry will take on a succession of roles. We see how various individuals and groups in society exploit Barry for their own ends. By the end of the film, what we admired in the original youthful character is no longer visible. The character of Barry Lyndon at film's end has little identity of his own, and what identity he has is in relation to others: his wife, his son, his mother, and the aristocratic society around him.

The pattern of role-playing and victimization is set early in the film. Barry is used by his cousins, who elaborately stage a duel to get Captain Quin into their family. Barry is forced to leave home and is immediately robbed by highwaymen on the road to Dublin. He becomes a British soldier and then a Prussian soldier, with no particular sense of why he is fighting. Of course, it makes no difference which side Barry fights on. It is true that Barry is forced by circumstances to join the Prussian army, but these episodes only reinforce the impression that Barry's will is not his own. It is slowly being drained from him, as is his energy and vitality. These "experiences," which might normally broaden Barry's outlook on life and enrich his character, in fact only serve to rob him of his youthful ideals and his naive belief in love. They are crucial in shaping the cynical, opportunistic individual we will see later in the film. Barry learns that to make his way in the world he must use deceit and trickery; he must pretend to be what he is not. At various points in the narrative, Barry pretends to be an English officer, a Prussian spy, a valet, and in one scene, the Chevalier, his gambling partner. This is the more obvious kind of role-playing. The other kind of role-playing in the film is less obvious, encompassing the roles that society forces on him. Barry will play the role of gambler, husband, lover, father, and the role he aspires to most, that of an English gentleman. There is sadly very little difference for Barry between the two types of role-playing. Both serve to gradually rob him of his identity and his innocence.

Barry spends much of the first half of the film "falling into" situations over which he has little control. His one ambition in life is to attain wealth and position. The years spent touring the European courts as a gambler with the Chevalier (Patrick Magee) instill in Barry the desire to be wealthy. That Barry should have these ambitions after years of close contact with nobility is surprising, since the picture the film paints of the aristocracy in these sequences is one of utter uselessness. They seem primarily concerned with a hedonistic pursuit of pleasure, style, fashion, and gambling. If Barry is made to strive for wealth and status, it is because he is convinced society values this way of life above all others. When the act of marrying into a great family fortune invariably proves unsatisfying, Barry foolishly believes he must direct all his energies and considerable wealth in the pursuit of a peerage. It does not occur to Barry that there could be something other than wealth, position, and the pursuit of pleasure in life. But then Barry can only reflect the values of the society that created him.

The idea that Barry must aspire to wealth, property, and title at the expense of his youthful ideals provides one of the film's harshest critiques. The text of the film seems to say that love, passion, and emotion may be appropriate responses for a young boy, but they have no place in the adult world. As the narrative unfolds, it is clear that little blame for this is placed on Barry. Barry is portrayed as a victim, and the film goes to great lengths to obtain sympathy for him. Barry plays one role after another and puts on one pose after another, until all that is left is the pose. Whatever was genuine and authentic in his original character is eventually lost. The film's fatalistic narrative argues that as we become more experienced we inevitably lose the innocence of our youth. The film goes further, however, in arguing that we also lose our energy, our will power, all that is vital, and even our sense of identity. There is never any notion that experience can enrich and make us wiser.

One of the most successful strategies of the film is the way Barry's character is created through his placement within the frame, frequently in frozen gesture with a blank expression on his face (fig. 12.1). These shots typically communicate the powerlessness of his character; the fact that Barry has little will or identity of his own. The artifice of the situation is further amplified by Kubrick's use of the slow zoom, which adds to the fatalistic quality of the narrative. The zoom only gives the illusion of movement, or, more precisely, an illusion of the illusion of movement. In genuine camera movement there is at least an indexical relationship between what we see on the screen and the actual physical movement

Fig. 12.1

of the camera through space. With the zoom we have no real movement through space. The zoom emphasizes the two-dimensionality and flatness of the image as much as camera movements with deep focus emphasize the three-dimensionality (albeit illusory) of the image. The zoom is mechanical and artificial in ways camera movement is not. The zoom flattens both physically and metaphorically. It is the perfect device to present the shallow character of Barry Lyndon. Coupled with the stiff, artificial, at times ceremonial, posing and arrangement of Barry within the frame, we have a brilliant portrait of a superficial character—and society—more concerned with surface beauty than substantive ideas and human emotion.

Barry/O'Neal is essentially a prisoner both of the frame and society. He has little will of his own. The two-dimensional, lifeless, orderly individual that Barry becomes is perfectly in keeping with, and to a large extent created by, his style of presentation. In sequence after sequence we see Barry in very similar poses. He often looks directly ahead but not at anyone. An example of this can be found in his role as a German spy. He stands in front of Captain Potzdorf (Hardy Kruger), who is seated with his uncle the Chief of Police. Barry speaks but does not speak *to* anyone: his gaze is not directed at either man. When he does speak it is in an unthinking manner, as if he were a machine or a mannequin. This scene is similar to others in the film where Barry stands erect, gazing straight ahead and speaking in a monotone, with little apparent thought. Another example is when Barry receives two Frederick D'or for saving Captain Potzdorf's life. Once again Barry is stiff, erect, and his gaze does not meet anyone's eyes.

There are many sequences in which we see Barry ceremoniously marching with his troops, rifle in hand, but once again there is a lifeless quality to his eyes. In one scene he may be leaning on his rifle in front of a bonfire, head lowered and expressionless. In another scene later in the film, he is with his mother on a small bridge as she speaks to him about his lack of position and wealth. It is not dissimilar to the army scene, only this time he leans on a cane instead of a rifle. But his head is once again lowered, and he has little expression on his face. In fact, he makes no comment throughout the entire scene: his mother does all the talking. All of these scenes are shot in similar ways; either long shot or medium shot and often employing a slow zoom into or out of the subject. Whether Barry is marching with his troops, or simply standing and watching, or playing at the gaming tables, he is being transformed into a lifeless individual before our eyes (fig. 12.2).

**Fig. 12.2**

There is a mechanical, robot or mannequin-like quality about him. He seems to be merely going through the motions and gives little thought to his actions. We rarely get a sense throughout the film that Barry thinks very much or has much of an interior life. The impression we get is that Barry is acting out his various assigned roles.

The blank facial expression and lack of interiority is apparent in the sequence where Barry contemplates escape from the British army (fig. 12.3). The sequence begins with Barry walking to a stream to collect water. He overhears two soldiers bathing in the water. Their conversation indicates that one of them must carry important papers to another army general and will thus afford Barry his chance for escape. The camera slowly zooms into Barry's face, and the voice-over narration explains the plot that Barry is supposedly hatching. The information conveyed by the narrator would be impossible to decipher from Barry's expression, which is essentially blank. We must take the narrator's word that this is what Barry is thinking. Barry carefully removes the clothing and horse of one of the officers in a matter-of-fact fashion. There is no drama to the scene. The plot has been advanced primarily through the device of the voice-over.

**Fig. 12.3**

What this shot and many others similar to it illustrates is that notions of character are frequently conveyed not by O'Neal's acting, but by other formal strategies. Through such devices as voice-over narration, blank facial expression and stiff presentation, slow zoom and other framing strategies, the film creates an essentially de-dramatized style of presentation. There is a clear relationship between Kubrick's formal strategies and flatness of presentation and the flat, shallow character of Barry. The limitations imposed on Barry through framing and other formal strategies echo the limitations and restrictions imposed on Barry by his society. What Kubrick has done is shift the weight of character development and narration away from the naturalistic/dramatic acting of the central character to other elements of the film. The result is a more complex and ironic film.

**Fig. 12.4**

Occasionally, the visual information conveyed by Barry's arrangement in the frame and the voice-over narration are in conflict. An example of this is a shot of Barry with a German woman. The scene prior to this shot showed Barry at this woman's table as she feeds her baby. The scene is gentle and touching; Barry is warm and loving, as is the woman. He seems desperately to want to love someone, even smiling in the scene perhaps for the first time in the film. It is clear Barry will spend a short, intimate time with this woman. When he leaves the woman, it begins as a touching farewell. But since Barry must now resume his life, he is once again in a frozen gesture. The arrangement of the two actors is interesting (fig. 12.4). They each have their heads slightly lowered, eyes partially closed; a side view in medium shot. They do not look anywhere, avoiding eye contact. With his head still lowered, Barry begins to speak. The couple is sad because they are parting, or perhaps a little embarrassed, but there is something artificial and posed about the composition. There is a distant, unreal, far-off quality about the shot. The framing and composition of the shot emphasize the emotional distance Barry must keep even in a tender moment. The shot emphasizes the disillusionment he begins to feel about life and love. As if to remind the spectator that true love is a childish illusion and has no place in this world, the narrator breaks in and adds a cynical note to the scene. He completely undermines the emotion of the moment as he intones about how this woman is like a neighboring town that "had been stormed and occupied several times before Barry came to invest it." The two lovers kiss passionately, but this is the last time Barry will engage in this kind of passion. The composition and the voice-over make it clear there is no place for these kinds of feelings of love in Barry's world. It is only a fleeting interlude to the "real" drama of his life. He cannot afford to hold on to these "childish" notions.

As the narrative unfolds Barry becomes more and more unfeeling and superficial. In his life as a gambler it is fine clothes, makeup, style, and fashion that are central. One senses very sharply in these scenes with the Chevalier (Patrick Magee) the emptiness of Barry's life. He increasingly abandons control of his own destiny. It is the Chevalier who decides what course their lives will take. And this life seems both precious and decidedly unhappy. Not only in the Chevalier sequences but throughout the film, Barry seems bereft of pleasure. The only exceptions are the scenes with his son Bryan.

In the scenes with the Chevalier, we have a sense that Barry has simply stumbled into another situation. Notions of happiness or satisfaction do not enter into what we comprehend of his thinking. Barry does not know what to expect out of life, but he gradually creates a set of expectations and ambitions centering around material concerns: title, wealth, property. This leads to Barry's courtship of Lady Lyndon and to his next role. (It is also significant that after Barry's seduction of Lady Lyndon, the narrator says, "To make a long story short, six hours after they met, her ladyship was in love." Not only is this admirable narrative compression, but the narrator pointedly does not mention Barry's feelings. It is clear that love is not a part of his scenario.) It is appropriate that at their wedding Barry is arrayed in the finest of clothes, thick makeup, lipstick, and coiffed and powdered hair (fig. 12.5). We have the impression that in addition to his new name, Barry is adopting a new identity. Although Barry is still a relatively young man at this point in the narrative, we have completely lost sight of the strapping youth of the early scenes. He has been replaced by an opportunistic, shallow, and lifeless dandy. Although there are scenes in the second half of the film filled with genuine feeling, where we can see traces of the young Barry, they are mere traces. Barry Lyndon is no longer Redmond Barry. He is an artificial creation of a decadent society.

**Fig. 12.5**

There are a few instances, however, when Barry attempts to break through the boundaries and limitations society has placed on him. When this happens, the limits of the frame edge are ruptured and Kubrick resorts to the hand-held camera and rapid montage. In Kubrick's work, the hand-held camera is most often used in moments of violence or unsettling, anxiety-provoking situations.

*Barry Lyndon* is no exception. In both sequences that I will discuss, the hand-held camera is used not only as a more interesting and exciting way to present the material, but also to communicate metaphorically the idea of freedom. In each instance we feel exhilarated when the restrictions of the frame have been transcended.

The first instance occurs in Part I, when Barry is taunted by a red-haired bully in the English army about a grease-laden water mug. Barry's first response is to attempt to fight the bully. However, what ensues is a carefully regulated fist-fight as Barry is forced to box his opponent within a square formed by the rest of the troops. Even here there are some limitations imposed on Barry: "No kickin', scratchin', the last man to remain standing is the winner." In contrast to his hulking and unrefined opponent, Barry is lithe, graceful, and intelligent as he easily defeats the bully. The sequence is rendered in a completely different style from the rest of the film: short shots, hand-held camera, and oblique angles. Barry's response to the situation is direct and immediate. He learns, however, that society has its own rules of behavior to which he must conform. In this case it is the army that imposes restrictions and limitations on Barry's responses and actions. Despite the rules, however, Barry is allowed to break free, if only momentarily, from the order imposed by his society. He also breaks free of the restrictions imposed on him by the frame edge. It is crucial that this sequence is organized around rapid montage, close-ups, and hand-held camera rather than the long take, long shot, and slow zoom of much of the rest of the film. Although Barry's victory is minor and partial, he is allowed a sense of freedom through this venting of his emotions.

The other incident is more interesting and significant. It comes later in the film in a sequence where Barry violently attacks Lord Bullingdon (Leon Vitali) at a music recital given by Lady Lyndon and Reverend Runt (Murray Melvin). The most significant aspect of Barry's loss of control in this sequence is that it is done in full view of Barry's guests and that it is so intense. This will be the last time in the film Barry will be allowed to express a direct emotional response to a situation.

The sequence begins innocently enough. A very slow, studied camera movement, left to right, reveals a small chamber orchestra playing a concerto. Lady Lyndon is at the piano, Reverend Runt plays the flute. All seems proper, stately, orderly, and civilized as the camera movement reveals about forty invited guests listening to the recital. Barry is seated in the front row with his mother by his side. The highly structured music perfectly reflects the ordered state of eighteenth-century society. A recital is the perfect event for Barry to stage in his quest for a peerage. It shows him to be cultured and the epitome of the "civilized" moneyed class he is trying so desperately to join. But the tranquility of the sequence is suddenly

**Fig. 12.6**

interrupted by the arrival of Barry's two sons.

Lord Bullingdon, Barry's antagonist since his marriage to Lady Lyndon, is in stockinged feet. Little Bryan wears his brother's oversized shoes. The boys walk in from the back of the room through the guests to the area where Lady Lyndon plays the piano. What is about to ensue is a family drama played out as if on stage. Lord Bullingdon kneels down to speak to little Bryan. He insults both Barry and Lady Lyndon. Lady Lyndon leaves the room in tears. What follows is an explosive sequence where Barry begins to beat Lord Bullingdon uncontrollably. It is the only liberating gesture Barry can make. He jumps on his son (fig. 12.6) and the sequence immediately reverts to hand-held camera and very rapid montage. The spectator is plunged into the event by the tactile physicality of the sequence. It is a vicious attack, yet there is an exhilaration about it. For one glorious moment Barry has thrown off his latest role. He abandons the pretense and artifice of his new station in life; he loses all sense of decorum. For one brief, fiery moment we see Redmond Barry with all his youthful passion and unbridled energy restored. Barry is no longer the mannequin, the lifeless character of earlier scenes. When he pummels Lord Bullingdon, he reacts not only to the immediate provocation, but to years of constraints and penalties of this society. There is an immediacy and physicality to the sequence, and to Ryan O'Neal's performance, that is absent from the rest of the film. All sense of order and control are abandoned by Barry; aesthetically, this is echoed in the violence of the montage, the hand-held camera, and the sound. Barry's rebellion is extreme but authentic.

**Fig. 12.7**

This is a very physical sequence that depends for much of its effect on the aggressive and ferocious way in which Ryan O'Neal uses his body (fig. 12.7). Barry has committed an unforgivable sin in this atrophied society: he has given himself over to his emotions.

Barry not only loses all hope of attaining his peerage, but will be completely shunned and ostracized by the very people he had sought to impress. Barry's real crime was not that he inflicted bodily injury on his son, but that he transgressed the rules of behavior and decorum of this society. For one brief moment Barry allowed himself to be alive, emotional—in short, to be human. These qualities of his youth, however, will not be tolerated by this society. It demands that Barry play by its rules, that he never show anger. Barry must always play the expected role.

The picture Kubrick paints of the eighteenth century in *Barry Lyndon*, beneath the surface beauty of the image, the exquisite fashions and architecture, is ultimately very negative. It is a society that values wealth, position, marriages of convenience, philosophy, art, music, fine clothes, grand architecture, and good breeding. But in the process of achieving what many consider an apogee of civilization, it has lost all its energy, passion, and intensity. It has been aestheticized into numbness and atrophy. Kubrick seems to be saying that it matters little what an era may produce if in the process we lose the essence of humanity: emotion and free will.

Barry loses all will to live after his attack on Lord Bullingdon. He resigns himself to his fate. In one final brilliant sequence, the duel with Lord Bullingdon, he almost begs his son to shoot him. Knowing that he can never be a part of this society again and knowing also that he can never regain the idealism of his youth, Barry has no place to go. Or, more properly, there is not place for Barry. Everything has been taken from him, including his humanity.

The film creates an intricate formal design to articulate many of its thematic concerns. The various strategies of long take, long shot, slow zoom, and character placement are only some of the elements in this formal design. The film, for the most part, creates Ryan O'Neal's "performance" through its visual design and the way it uses the actor's physical attributes. His placement within the frame and his relationship to the camera are two crucial ways this performance is created. Ryan O'Neal's performance is central to the overall strategy of *Barry Lyndon*, one of Stanley Kubrick's most ambitious and complete films.

## IV.

If Kubrick had set out to make a film as different as possible from *Barry Lyndon*, he could not have succeeded more spectacularly than with *The Shining* (1980). Where *Barry Lyndon* was all control and restriction, *The Shining* is in many ways the exact opposite. It is, of course, immensely controlled, but it is marked by a brilliant use of moving camera, insistent and expressive montage, and a steady pace that builds to an unforgettable climax. It differs as well in the wildly inventive and emotionally charged performance of Jack Nicholson in the leading role.

Jack Torrance (Nicholson) has contracted to be the winter caretaker of the Overlook, an elegant, rustic hotel located in the mountains of Colorado. Jack takes along his wife and son. The film is made up of a series of terrifying and funny episodes where Jack becomes emotionally unhinged and tries (unsuccessfully) to murder his family. It is a complex and very effective horror/ghost story. The film seems to fall neatly within its genre while consistently undermining genre conventions.

Nicholson gives a thoughtful, carefully orchestrated performance that could only have been worked out in its details during the actual shooting of the film, depending as it does on the ways Nicholson interacts with the camera and the other actors. The extensive use of the Steadicam no doubt facilitated a certain freedom of movement by the actors. This is evident in many scenes which are rarely static and almost always involve great orchestration of character movement. Nicholson's performance is absolutely crucial to the success of the film. The performance is wild and extreme, verging on the hysterical. At times Nicholson gives the impression of being out of control, and this may account for why the performance has been generally overlooked by critics (as well as a general critical neglect of the horror film). It may also have to do with the way Nicholson's performance relies so heavily on the physical as well as the comic for its effect. It's not a very "respectable" performance. It may strike some as overbearing, vulgar, and just plain "too-much." Clearly Nicholson is having too good a time for some critics to take his work here seriously. In fact, it is precisely these risky, over-the-edge aspects of his performance that make it so invigorating.

When we first encounter Jack, he is about to be interviewed for the caretaker job by Ullman (Barry Nelson), the hotel manager. As the camera follows Jack into Ullman's office, we get the immediate sensation that we are eavesdropping on the situation, that we are overhearing some rather private conversation. Perhaps it is the slight wavering of the Steadicam that contributes to this impression. There is a somewhat stiff and staged atmosphere about this initial sequence. The spectator feels like a silent presence in the room. It is an impression we will have many times in the film, and it comes from a feeling that the film, and Jack in particular, operates on several levels of discourse: the private and the more public. Characters obviously talk to one another, and the dialogue is certainly important in the film. But there seems to be a level of discourse in the film that does not depend on language but on gesture, reaction shots, glances, and symbolic imagery (e.g. "the elevator of blood" shots). If there are "evil" forces at work at the Overlook, they are not immediately apparent. If Jack has an evil side, it is not instantly visible, although it is hinted at from the very beginning of the film. We constantly get intimations of a dual plane of existence and dual natures.

In this early sequence with Ullman, we have the feeling that something is not quite right about Jack and his presentation of himself. We have the impression that he is putting on a pose or is "performing" for Ullman. There is a kind of "phony" exterior to his character. It is evident in the way Jack tries so hard to be affable and accommodating. It is also apparent in the grim reaction shots of Nicholson as Ullman describes the 1970 Grady axe murders. It becomes clear that the important elements in the scene are not the banal and clichéd information Ullman communicates to Nicholson. Although we expect a certain amount of exposition in the first part of the film, what is intriguing in this early scene is the interaction between Jack and Ullman. The intensity in Jack's expression as Ullman describes the axe murders clearly indicates that Jack is taken aback by the revelations. Although Ullman is rather lighthearted in describing the murders, Jack is genuinely stunned. In moments like these one senses the dark side of Jack's character lurking just below the surface.

There is a complexity and thoughtfulness in Nicholson's playing of the scene that is remarkably subtle. His characterization is complex and not easily read. Of course, it is also attributable to Kubrick's skill as a director and editor that these subtleties and nuances can be brought out so effectively in what appears to be a rather ordinary scene. There is a layer of deceptiveness in Jack's character that is not immediately apparent but nonetheless exists if one looks closely at the scene. It is a deceptiveness that operates on other narrative levels as well as in the performance of the main character. Things clearly are not what they seem in *The Shining*. We must dig below the surface of things to discern their meanings.

In the scene with Ullman, we sense that the stories told to Jack are not simply for his amusement or edification, but for some as yet unknown motive. Perhaps some part of Jack understands that he has a "role" to play in the upcoming drama/comedy; deep down, beneath the phony exterior, he understands who he is and what he must do at the hotel. There is a quality to Nicholson's acting that is at once exteriorized and interiorized, revealing and mysterious, obvious and subtle. The performance functions on many levels at the same time. Nicholson's skill as an actor is in the way he so effortlessly articulates the different aspects of his character, opening up many possible interpretations. Nicholson gives a very physical, highly comic and hammy performance. It reflexively ridicules itself and the conventions of the genre. His performance is at the same time somewhat interiorized, elusive, and thoughtful, and does not reveal itself quite so quickly or so obviously.

If I am right about the way Nicholson's performance functions and the way the film seems to be operating on different levels of meaning, then Nicholson's performance becomes even more central. His performance is carefully orchestrated to interact with other actors, the camera, the spectator, and the creator of the film. It is this fascinating set of potential relationships that makes the film and Nicholson's acting in it so intriguing.

One of the ways Nicholson elaborates his character is by giving the impression that he has a dual nature: a "normal" side and an "evil" side. We are presented with this duality many times throughout the film. One particularly forceful and amusing example comes in the early scene of Jack driving up to the Overlook with his wife (Shelley Duval) and son (Danny Lloyd). This sequence is interesting not only for what it reveals about Nicholson's character and performance, but also because it is the only time in the film we will see the entire Torrance family alone and together in the frame. This framing (fig. 12.8) reinforces the idea the Torrances are a typical American family; but, of course, this idea becomes subverted as the film proceeds. The semblance of normality begins to fall apart almost immediately. We will never see these characters together as a family unit—and sharing the frame—again. The sequence gives a hint of the duality operating both in Jack's nature and in the film's narrative.

**Fig. 12.8**

The intense expression on Jack's face as the shot in the car opens is in marked contrast to the effusive and happy exterior we saw in the earlier interview scene. Here Jack seems determined and preoccupied, disturbed about something. It's as if the closer he gets to the Overlook, the closer his other (darker) personality comes to the surface. When Danny innocently mentions that he is hungry, Jack's response has a cruel edge to it. When Danny asks about the

Donner party, Jack takes perverse glee in responding to his son's question. Nicholson rolls his eyes upward, arches his eyebrows—one of his more familiar facial expressions in this film—and gives a very knowing smile to the camera, as if he were sharing a secret or private moment with the spectator (figs. 12.9–12.10).

Fig. 12.9

Fig. 12.10

There are many scenes which continue this exploration of Jack's duality. One such scene has Wendy serving Jack his breakfast in bed. The scene begins as a mirror shot of Jack lying on the bed as he begins to eat his food. We know it is a mirror shot because the lettering on Jack's sweatshirt is reversed. Kubrick holds the shot in this manner throughout much of the scene, hinting in a formal way, through the organization of the frame, that a dual plane of existence may exist. This particular scene is interesting because it is the first time the strategy is introduced. The dialogue between Wendy and Jack is banal but revelatory. When Wendy tries to explain how simple the creative process is, Jack replies condescendingly. Wendy's reaction shots emphasize her role as a dutiful housewife. Her character is fearful and uncomprehending of Jack's reactions to her remarks; in general, she communicates a quality of submissiveness. Wendy's makeup, particularly the prominent red lipstick and Plain-Jane hairstyle, contribute to the idea that Wendy is little more than Jack's puppet or "kewpie" doll, with no will of her own. Halfway through their conversation, the scene shifts to a normal, un-mirrored shot. Jack discusses his feelings of *déjà-vu* and a feeling that he has been at the hotel before. The scene becomes more comic as Jack playfully dips his bacon into his eggs as he speaks. Jack makes light of his feelings, treating them as a joke. This is a small but effective example of how Nicholson uses a prop or creates a piece of business to add meaning to a scene. Coupled with the use of the mirror and the reversed framing, this adds layers of meaning to what could have been a very ordinary scene. The film creates more tension and a sense of uneasiness by the framing and use of long take. At the same time that we are amused by Nicholson's playing of the scene, we are bothered by Jack's treatment of his wife.

Another similar, though more complex scene later in the film has Danny discovering his father sitting on his bed looking at himself, trance-like, in the mirror (fig. 12.11). It is another example of how the framing reveals the dual nature of Jack's character. It is significant that both Jack and his mirror image are in the frame together, indicating perhaps that Jack's two personae are merging. Jack and his alter ego, the public and the private, are no longer distinguishable. By framing Jack's mirror image screen left and the real Jack screen right, Kubrick is formally indicating that both Jacks are equally present. They are no longer physically separated. Where in the earlier scene Kubrick holds the shot of Jack's mirror image, then shifts to a non-mirror shot, here both are in the same frame. Jack has noticeably deteriorated by this point; he seems dazed, detached from his surroundings.

**Fig. 12.11**

The conversation in the scene is also revealing. Danny asks his father if he likes the hotel. Jack responds that he loves it. In fact, Jack would like to stay at the Overlook "forever, and ever and ever" echoing the words of the Grady daughters of an earlier scene. Danny says, "Dad, you would never hurt Mommy and me, would you?" Jack responds in a lower, more gutteral tone, "What do ya' mean?" Jack continues, "I love you Danny. I would never do anything to hurt you." This time the inflection of his voice is almost like that of an old man. By taking on different voices in the scene, Nicholson not only communicates the breakdown of his personality, but perhaps the existence of multiple personalities. The idea of multiple personalities fits in perfectly with the larger, overall strategy of duality operating in Jack's character and other aspects of the film.

Occasionally Kubrick emphasizes the idea of duality by the order or sequencing of very different scenes, each contrasting with the other and each commenting on the other. An example of this begins with a close-up shot of Jack's typewriter on his writing table, surrounded by a few pencils and a burning cigarette in an ashtray. This shot is clearly metaphoric for Jack's creative stagnation. The meaning of the shot is intensified by a loud, pounding sound of Jack throwing a ball against a wall. The use of sound here amplifies what was only implied by the image. It adds an oppressive heaviness to the scene that perfectly complements the meaning of the props on Jack's writing table. It also carries additional metaphoric connotation of its own: that Jack is unable to break through his own "creative" wall. Also, Jack throws the ball against one of the many maze-motif wall murals of the hotel, adding another potential meaning: that the hotel itself is responsible for Jack's block. What is equally important in the scene is the way Nicholson uses his entire body. Nicholson's movements are viewed in long shot as he throws the ball with full force against the wall in long sweeping gestures. It is this "physicality" which is the most crucial aspect of Nicholson's performance and one which will be elaborated on in the remainder of this paper. Nicholson's performance is created through a subtle manipulation of every part of his body, frequently involving a prop of some kind.

This interior sequence is immediately followed by and contrasted with shots of Wendy and Danny running playfully in the snow and exploring the maze outside the hotel. They are having fun and releasing their energies in a healthy, liberating way in contrast to Jack's stagnation and repression inside the hotel. It is made clear that Jack's "reality" is very different than the world of his wife and son. A shot of Wendy outside dissolves into a shot of Jack inside, linking the two worlds. Jack's world is now exclusively the world of the hotel. He continues to play with the ball, throwing it down with great force. His energy is all wasted, uncreative. It is more and more his sheer physical presence, his body, that we are aware of as the film proceeds. Jack jumps as he throws the ball down with ever greater force. His hulking movements are slow, heavy, and brooding.

Almost every scene in the rest of the film illustrates the physicality of Nicholson's acting and how inventive he is in using his whole body to create a performance. A few examples will suffice to illustrate this point. Jack's first visit to the Gold Room comes immediately after his "nightmare" and Wendy's accusation that Jack was once responsible for beating up Danny. As Jack walks down the corridor to the room, we can see that Nicholson has momentarily taken on the persona of a crazy person, a bowery bum. Kubrick has mentioned in an interview that this was indeed Nicholson's inspiration for the scene, and it is superbly realized. Nicholson's movements, especially the way he flails his arms about and talks to himself, closely approximate the gestures of a mad derelict. Kubrick frames his actor in long shot so his entire body can be seen. The camera moves backward as Nicholson walks down the corridor. He punctuates the air with his fists, completely lost in his hermetic universe. Nicholson communicates the madness and the seething anger of the character by the insistent thrusting of his arms down the sides of his body and in the air as if striking at some unknown assailant.

This leads to Jack's first encounter with Lloyd, the bartender in the Gold Room. Jack sits in front of the bar. Mirrors line the wall behind the bar and directly in front of Jack's seated position. The sequence is notable for the way in which it humorously parodies the horror genre. (This level of parody will reach its climax later in the film as Jack, axe in hand, drags his injured leg in a clear hommage to several horror films of the 1930s.) In the scene with Lloyd, the parody is mostly, though not entirely, at the level of language. Jack begins by exclaiming, "God, I'd give anything for a drink. I'd give my goddam soul just for a glass of beer," clearly a jocular reference to the Faust legend. Lloyd himself undoubtedly conjures up vampire films by his dress and lack of expression. His slicked-back black hair and laconic facial expression, and the lighting which gives him a bloodless quality, all make reference to the undead. The sequence is filled with verbal clichés such as, "women ... can't live with 'em, can't live without 'em," "white man's burden," and "hair of the dog that bit me," all used with obvious irony. The sequence becomes particularly funny, albeit cruel, as Jack describes his problems with Wendy and the incident several years earlier when Jack dislocated Danny's shoulder. Nicholson plays the scene for comedy by the way he drinks his bourbon. He drinks his first drink as if it were some precious elixir, slowly savoring it and rolling his eyes in ecstasy. Nicholson shifts his body around, arches his eyebrows, and uses his fingers in playing the scene.

The scene illustrates one of the most important and surprising aspects of the film. In scenes like the one with Lloyd and many others later on, the film strikes a very delicate balance between the truly frightening and grotesque and the comic; between a genuine horror film and a comedy. It is especially noticeable in later scenes when Jack's mugging is inserted into the most violent and frightening scenes as he menaces Wendy and Danny. In scenes with Wendy, in particular, we are often torn between the enjoyment we derive from watching Nicholson perform and the comedy of the scene, and the cruelty he inflicts on his wife. It doesn't stop us from being fascinated by their scenes together, but the contrast is unsettling.

One scene in particular where Jack's cruelty and insensitivity to Wendy is especially harsh comes as Wendy casually interrupts Jack at his writing table. The scene begins with Jack intensely typing as Bartok plays ominously on the soundtrack. Wendy innocently walks in and says "Hi hon ... get a lot written today?" Jack is extremely upset by her interruption, and Wendy accuses Jack of being grouchy. Jack's response is extreme. He rolls his eyes upward, rips up the typing paper, pounds his forehead, arches his eyebrows, sweeps his hair back; all this as he screams and shouts insults and obscenities at Wendy (fig. 12.12). It is clear that Jack thinks this woman is quite stupid. He is condescending and insensitive to her feelings. And although Jack is very cruel to Wendy, it is a fascinating scene to watch. It is a good illustration of both the physicality of Nicholson's acting and the kind of ambivalent feelings we often have in scenes that are filled with complex and often contradictory elements.

Occasionally Nicholson's characterization is most effective when it is least agitated (perhaps to offer a contrast to most of the other scenes). One such moment is a remarkable shot of Jack that clearly indicates the character's descent into madness. The shot is a very slow zoom into Jack's unshaven face (fig. 12.13). He is frozen and immobile; completely lost in his own mental landscape. What is unusual about this shot is the lack of empathy the spectator feels with the character even though the close-up is so privileged. There is a disengagement and distance created by the shot that seems to be the opposite of what we would expect this kind of moment to reveal. The shot serves to objectify the character, negating any possibility of spectator identification. Kubrick zooms into a big close-up and holds the shot a long time. But rather than feeling closer to the character, we recognize how he is enclosed in his own universe. The animated gesticulating Jack of earlier scenes is well on his way to becoming the frozen statue we will see lying in the snow at the end of the film. Jack is now ready to do the hotel's bidding. He has shed his "normal" persona and can now allow his "evil" side to come to the surface. At the end of the shot (fig. 12.14), Jack smiles slightly. It is a curious moment. To whom is Jack smiling, and for what reason? Jack takes secret pleasure in some mental image, a feeling he cannot possibly share with the spectator. Yet, at the same time, the shot hints at the possibility of a complicity between Jack and the spectator; that we know and he knows what must be done. The drama (or comedy) must be allowed to play itself out to its bloody conclusion. The effectiveness and complexity of the shot is a result of both Kubrick's brilliant formal orchestration of the moment and Nicholson's underplaying of the scene. The elusive ambiguity in the shot creates reverberations of meaning that last long after the shot ends.

As the film proceeds, Nicholson's "physical" acting becomes more exaggerated, utilizing all parts of his body and different voices. He is alternately comic and terrifying. A scene where Jack wakes from a nightmare emphasizes and foregrounds the physicality of Nicholson's performance. The scene begins with Jack at his writing table, head lowered on his desk, screaming as he dreams of murdering Danny and Wendy. Jack seems genuinely frightened and horrified in the scene, indicating perhaps that he does not know the extent of the horrible crime he will attempt to commit. Nicholson uses his voice to good effect in the scene. After he wakes up and Wendy comes to comfort him, he crouches down on the floor. He

Fig. 12.12

Fig. 12.13

Fig. 12.14

huddles and shifts his body around almost as if he were a wounded animal, completely terrified and shaking (fig. 12.15).

**Fig. 12.15**

Nicholson uses his body in different ways depending on the kind of scene he is playing. For example, in a scene immediately after Jack, in a rage, leaves Wendy in the apartment and makes his way to the Gold Room for the second time, he passes through several aisles of kitchen implements. As he does this, Jack violently knocks over metallic kitchen utensils with wide sweeping movements of his arms. The abrasive sound in the shots adds to the intensity of the scene as the metallic objects hit the floor. The camera keeps all of this in frame by tracking back as Jack walks towards the camera in full frame. It is a short transitional scene leading directly to the major encounter between Jack and Delbert Grady in the Gold Room. The seething rage inside Jack is perfectly complemented by the violence in Jack's actions and movements, as well as the crashing metal on the soundtrack.

The second visit to the Gold Room begins with Jack predictably walking towards the bar and his pal Lloyd the bartender. In contrast to his previous visit, the room is filled with hundreds of ghostly hotel "guests." A dance band plays for the revellers as

Jack sits and orders his drink. As the 1920s dance music plays in the background, Jack moves rhythmically on his seat. Once again Nicholson does little bits of business. He takes a handful of peanuts and pops them into his mouth. He smiles broadly throughout the scene and frequently arches his eyebrows. Jack gets up from his seat, drink in hand, and sways to the music, doing a little dance of his own as he walks toward the main ballroom. It is here that Grady bumps into Jack (deliberately?), spilling a drink on him. The two actors then move to the washroom so that Grady can remove the stain. The narrative function of the scene is, of course, crucial. The scene in the washroom is unusual for many reasons. One of them is the vivid color scheme—striking reds and whites. It is also significant for the way in which Nicholson uses his body (principally the fingers of his left hand and his eyes and eyebrows) and manipulates his voice. When Jack asks Grady if he is "a married man," it is in a higher pitch with a slight nasal quality. When Jack mentions to Grady that "you were the caretaker" it is now in a lower voice. At times Nicholson rolls his eyes as if he were communicating secretly with the spectator. At other times Nicholson sounds like an old man. Throughout the scene there is a sense that Jack's character is fragmenting into different personalities or different aspects of his personality. This fragmentation or creation of multiple personalities is achieved primarily through Nicholson's acrobatics with his voice. Thematically, of course, it is a crucial step in Jack's disintegration and descent into madness.

Nicholson is almost completely immobile through this scene as Grady cleans the stain from his clothes. The sequence begins in long shot with both actors in full figure. The only noticeable movement Jack makes is the constant manipulation of the fingers of his left hand. Presumably Jack has a stain from a drink on his fingers. But Nicholson foregrounds the motion to such an extent that the movements also communicate his anxiety. When Grady mentions that Jack has "always been the caretaker," there is a cut to a medium close-up of Jack in stunned silence. Nicholson holds this expression as Grady vulgarly mentions that Danny is attempting to contact "the nigger" Halloran (Scatman Crothers). As the conversation continues, Nicholson continues to use his voice to communicate his disbelief.

As the film's narrative proceeds, the physical quality of Nicholson's performance becomes more pronounced and insistent, and the dramatic intensity of the film builds. After the brilliant sequence of Wendy discovering Jack's manuscript, Jack's physical attacks on Wendy become more threatening and overt. In the shots immediately leading up to the violence on the staircase between Jack and Wendy, Jack discusses what to do about Danny. As he recites the following lines in a rhythmical sing-song fashion, emphasizing the final word in each line, Jack slowly moves in on his wife and it now becomes clear he is trying to murder her:

> "Maybe it was about *Danny*.
> Maybe it was about *him*.
> I *think* we should discuss *Danny*.
> I think we should discuss what should be *done*."

In addition to the obvious rhythmical ordering and emphasis of the lines of dialogue, there is an added aural manipulation that sounds vaguely electronic or metallic. Jack's lines have clearly been mechanically distorted, adding an artificial, non-human or other-worldly quality to the character of his voice. It is a very subtle addition to the soundtrack and not immediately apparent in a casual viewing. The shots are noteworthy for Jack's particularly cruel treatment of Wendy. It goes far beyond the sarcasm of earlier scenes. Jack harps on "his responsibilities," and it is quite clear just how over the edge he is. Jack mocks Wendy and cruelly imitates her voice while flailing his arm out at her. This leads directly to shots of Jack and Wendy (with baseball bat) on the staircase (figs. 12.16–12.17), one of the most exciting and vicious sequences in the film. The scenes are categorized by a performance aspect more apparent than earlier scenes. Jack seems to be giving a performance for Wendy and the spectator. His characterization is extreme and exaggerated. His manipulation of the various parts of his body and voice here seem grotesque yet farcical. Both performers emphasize the physical quality of the scene, and the contrast between Wendy's desperate fear and sense of physical exhaustion and Jack's humor and playacting is sharply drawn.

As Wendy swings the bat at Jack, he responds by taunting her

Fig. 12.16

Fig. 12.17

with his hands, fingers, and voice. He even wags his tongue diabolically at her several times. Again, Nicholson's constant changes of vocal inflection emphasize the shifting personalities that were hinted at in the earlier scene with Grady. Jack is turning into a monster before our very eyes. This impression is strengthened in later scenes, such as Jack's comic impersonation of the "Big Bad Wolf" as he attacks Wendy with the axe. It culminates most forcefully in the final maze sequence as Jack chases Danny, the father turning into a pure evil force incapable of any human utterance.

In the sequence on the stairs with Wendy, Kubrick purposefully abandons all subtlety, and Nicholson's "hammy" performance is foregrounded. It signals the level at which the rest of the film will be played out. It also indicates the degree to which Nicholson will use his face, hands, and voice to create the grotesque creature his character becomes. At this point in the film, Jack's transformation into an evil, animal-like being is not yet complete but well underway. As Wendy knocks out Jack with the bat, the moment is heightened by the piercing chords of music on the soundtrack. Jack's last human capability, the power of speech, has effectively been eliminated. Although Jack continues to speak for some time in the film, he gradually loses more and more of his capacity for speech because of this initial blow to the head.

The wounded Jack is dragged and locked in a kitchen cooler and uses his powers of trickery and evil deception as he pleads with Wendy to let him out (fig. 12.18). There is a vague allusion to fairy tales and to other horror films as he tries to talk his way out of the cooler. He switches personalities often in this scene. At one time he changes his voice to sound like a hurt little boy, playing on Wendy's sympathy. Other times, Jack screams at Wendy, attempting to bully her into letting him out. Nicholson again uses his tongue and fingers to add to his characterization. Yet the more horrifying and menacing Jack becomes, the funnier the film. Even though Jack is about to axe his son and wife to death, the film is easily as funny as it is horrifying. We have no way of knowing how much of the tension created by mixing the horrific with the comic was contributed by Nicholson's presence in the role; it is a fair guess that it was substantial.

The film's narrative is played out on such a level of abstraction

Fig. 12.18

and "unreality" that the notion of character empathy is virtually impossible. The spectator is at once distanced from the proceedings because of the level of parody and irony, while at the same time the film's momentum and intensity are totally absorbing. And although the spectator may in no way empathize with Jack, we are taken up with enjoying the performance. We don't particularly want Jack to stop his performance because it would put an end to the pleasure we derive from it. This is not to say we want Jack to murder his family; rather, the last hour of the film is played out on such an absurd level that it precludes any kind of sympathy for the characters or moralizing by the spectator. The film is non-naturalistic, extreme, grotesque, and very funny.

There are many instances of verbal humor in the last half of the film that add to the overall effect. When Jack crashes through a door with his axe, he exclaims with mocking humor, "Wendy, I'm home," saying the line like a "dad." Nicholson is also very funny in his impersonation of the Big Bad Wolf, wheedling, "Little pigs, little pigs." Jack mugs and limps his way through many of the scenes in contrast to the genuine terror and piercing screams emanating from Wendy. (There are, of course, many psychosexual inferences that resonate throughout these scenes. Jack's use of the axe is not arbitrary. Its phallic implications are obvious as it rips through various doors behind which cowers the terrified and helpless Wendy, mouth wide open (fig. 12.19). The symbolic rape of Wendy clearly stands in for Jack's repressed sexuality and creative stagnation.) Not only is there an interesting mix of moods in the film, but also a real contrast in acting styles. Shelley Duvall plays her scenes here in a very convincing and naturalistic way. She seems to be performing, or is directed to perform, as if she were in a genuinely scary, more conventional horror film. She seems truly terrified and physically exhausted. Nicholson of course, plays his role in a very different way. He is a non-naturalistic comic, a self-knowing parodist of the menacing figure in horror films. The mix of acting styles and shifts between comedy and horror are genuinely surprising and unconventional. As a consequence, the spectator must shift his or her response from one moment to the next. Are we to take the film seriously? Are we meant to laugh? How can we laugh at what Jack is trying to do, yet how can we not laugh?

As the film nears its climax, Jack's limp becomes more

**Fig. 12.19**

pronounced and his mugging—"Here's Johnny"—becomes more outrageous. The film often seems on the verge of becoming so comic that any horrific moments will be dissipated. But this does not happen. Whenever we feel as if the film cannot possibly be scary, Kubrick creates a genuinely frightening moment. An example of this is Halloran's murder, which is quite gruesome and comes in the middle of Nicholson's mugging. What is most audacious about the film is precisely the way it keeps shifting tone without losing its bearings, giving Jack laugh lines just at those points when he is most murderous. Jack is quite "clever" in his use of language, even though he is being transformed into a monster and will shortly be unable to utter a single word. Very few filmmakers and actors could have carried this off so successfully. Nicholson's great comic *and* dramatic talent is the key to the film's success. I cannot imagine another actor who can so effortlessly shift from comedy to drama. Nicholson's particular history as an actor for many years outside the Hollywood System but now so very much a star of that System also invests the role with additional meaning. The role demands a recognizable star who can parody not only the genre but also himself.

The film culminates with the technically brilliant sequence of Jack pursuing Danny through the maze, axe in left hand and holding

**Fig. 12.20**

his jacket with his right (fig. 12.20). Jack becomes the personification of every child's nightmare: a nameless, inarticulate evil force;

even more terrifying because it is Danny's "Daddy." As Jack shouts and slurs his words, he becomes less and less capable of verbal articulation. He skulks and howls and finally collapses in exhaustion. The transformation is now complete: Jack has become a deformed maniac incapable of uttering an intelligible word, barely capable of making any sound at all. This final sequence is no longer comic; rather, it recalls the nightmare quality of fairy tale or dream imagery. Nicholson's physicality and use of his voice, coupled with the intensity of the montage, the brilliant use of the Steadicam, music, and harsh blue lighting, all combine to create one of the most unforgettable sequences in contemporary film.

## V.

The performances of Jack Nicholson in *The Shining* and Ryan O'Neal in *Barry Lyndon* represent two very different and extreme approaches to film acting. They both illustrate how a performance can be integrated into the fabric of a film. They illustrate how a performance contributes, in sometimes surprising ways, to the overall aesthetic of a finished film. They are good examples of how Kubrick takes real risks with his actors. Even when the results seem less than ideal, as in the case of *Barry Lyndon*, there is a sense in which the ambition of the film transcends the limitations of the performance. In the case of Jack Nicholson's work, it is a towering performance by one of the best actors currently at work in film. It is a risky, surprising, unique, and very effective performance that pushes screen acting to the very limits of what is acceptable in a serious film. In fact, Nicholson's performance is important precisely because it helps redefine what "serious" film acting is. And although the two performances are very different and the two actors have very different skills, they have another thing in common: they both could exist only in a film. As such, they are important in the continuing movement of film away from literature and theater, still one of narrative cinema's most urgent projects.

## NOTES

I would like to acknowledge the superb editorial assistance and many valuable and perceptive suggestions made to the author by Dr. Carole Zucker, editor of this volume. I am grateful for her generosity and patience.

1. See especially Wallace Coyle, *Stanley Kubrick: A Guide to References and Resources* (Boston: G. K. Hall, 1980). Though by no means a complete listing, it does give some idea of the extent of the pre-1980 Kubrick bibliography.

# 13. PERFORMANCE IN THE FILMS OF ROBERT BRESSON: The Aesthetics of Denial

**Doug Tomlinson**

IF RENOIR'S AESTHETIC IS THAT OF complexity and Hitchcock's is of complicity, Bresson's is that of denial. Where Renoir's characters are complex within an ambivalent moral system and Hitchcock's are guilty within a Manichean schema, Bresson's are near-reclusive within asceticism.

In Bresson's cinema, this ascetic philosophy is in evidence from his invention through visualization of character.[1] Not only are his characters denied the pleasures of existence, his performers (whom he refers to as models) are denied purposeful expression, his collaborators denied artistic input, his spectators denied access to character psychology traditionally communicated through systems of projection and identification. In his *Notes on Cinematography*, he quotes Pascal: "They want to find the solution where all is enigma only."[2]

Bresson's conviction that cinema must be unique unto itself and unlike any other form of artistic communication means that performance, traditionally the main element of narrative cinema, is presented in a radically altered form. In order to understand his radical use and presentation of performance, one must understand his conception of character as well as his theory of performance, his editing strategies as well as his placement of the performer within individual compositions.

## THE BRESSONIAN CHARACTER

Each of Bresson's characters is imprisoned in this life. For some this involves physical incarceration, for most, spiritual. *The Diary of a Country Priest* (1950), *A Man Escaped* (1956), and *Pickpocket* (1959), form a trilogy examining male alienation: religious, political, sexual. The three protagonists, the country priest, Fontaine (*A Man Escaped*), and Michel (*Pickpocket*) share certain characteristics: they are all outsiders, all somewhat wary of the society which surrounds them. This creates a sense of restraint, a guarded or shy appearance as if avoiding direct confrontation. All three are amateurs: at profession (priest), project (Fontaine), and craft (Michel). All three have a ritualistic obsession which effaces their physical personality: the priest's devotion to an ascetic existence, Fontaine's to his project of escape, Michel's to perfecting his prestidigital technique. All three are alienated: the priest from his community by his asceticism; Fontaine from his nuclear family, his political family (the Resistance), and prison mates by his incarceration in a jail cell; Michel by his homosexuality and its emergence in criminal behavior. Each of these male protagonists takes refuge in an hermetic posture; all seem prone to despondency. And yet in privation there is release.

Many adjectives have been used to describe these examples of the typical Bressonian character: alienated, despondent, stubborn, hermetic, effaced. While such adjectives are indeed apt, they need to be augmented by a series with a more positive connotation: modest, shy, introspective, focused, guarded, even noble. In retrospect, Bresson's characters are more complex than they appear at first. The perceived stubbornness is often merely hiding the more sensitive and intelligent aspects of a character who has been, to use Bresson's term, "flattened" by the experience of life and thus forced to seek refuge in seemingly antisocial behavior.[3]

The hermetic posture in these males is, however, temporarily ameliorated by a catalyst, the protagonist's release into communication facilitated by a cathartic encounter. The country priest's acceptance of his imminent death is facilitated by his encounter with the countess, her acceptance of his counsel giving him a fulfilled sense of purpose; Fontaine's acceptance of Jost is a positive force in his escape plan; Michel's acceptance of himself is facilitated by Jeanne's acceptance of him. Communication aids resolution and release.

There is, however, in Bresson's films, an inconclusive nature to that release, no sense that the new situation will be any less alienating. That Bresson's characters remain imprisoned even after their narrative release is indicated by his denial of any sense of release through psychological projection. At the end of *Pickpocket*, Michel and Jeanne communicate through a screen, Michel's face unendowed with a purposeful expression. In *A Man Escaped*, Fontaine and Jost walk away from the prison into a dark void; we are not allowed access to their faces in this moment of release, for freedom is but a temporary reality (fig. 13.1).

**Fig. 13.1**

Bresson denies access to easy solutions, thus reiterating Pascal. He denies his models any expression of resolution, insisting that a level of ambiguity be maintained beyond the final image; he denies the spectator psychological closure, positing that ultimately the question of character is unresolvable.

## PERFORMANCE THEORY

> No actors.
> (No directing of actors.)
> No parts.
> (No learning of parts.)
> No staging.
> (But the use of working models, taken from life.)
> *Being* (models) instead of *Seeming* (actors).[4]

> Choose your models well, so they lead you where you want to go.[5]

Bresson has discussed at length and in detail the inaptness of traditional modes of performance for the film medium. Accordingly, he developed a visual strategy for the presentation of performance which involved the denial of both the actor's and spectator's habitual access to emotional and psychological properties of a character.

His basic mistrust of traditional performance involves the psychological obviousness of "pretending," his belief being that "the actor's obligation to his art is to be somebody else." This notion is anathema to Bresson; his desire is to reveal character rather than construct it. His process involves a reduction rather than an increment in strategies; his desired result being an increase in the spiritual value obtained by his "models." He feels that human beings are complex and that what actors are trained to do is to simplify that complexity.

> Habit is too strong. The actor is an actor. You have before you an actor. Who effects a projection. That is his movement: he projects himself outside. While your non-actor character must be absolutely closed, like a container with a lid. Closed. And that, the actor cannot do, or, if he does it, at that moment he is no longer anything.[6]

> For there are actors who try, yes. But when the actor simplifies himself, he is even more false than when he is the actor, when he plays. For we are not simple. We are extremely complex. And it is this complexity that you find with the non-actor.
>
> We are complex. And what the actor projects is not complex.[7]

While Bresson does not disavow its validity for the stage, he finds this theatrical approach inappropriate for the cinema, particularly his own. Bresson's desire is not to document the art of performance and thus pay tribute to the double nature of character and performer, but to present uniquely conceived models of human character. The public, he claims, has been wrongly "schooled to cherish the alternate presence of 'him and the other,'"[8] his most damning statement in this regard being from *Notes on Cinematography*: "Failure of *Cinema*. Ludicrous disproportion between immense possibilities and the result: the Star-system."[9]

An avoidance of that duplicity has informed his casting strategy since 1950,[10] his refusal to hire those with acting experience extending to his own models. Bresson claimed that knowledge of his process and its results on the screen would ultimately jeopardize his control.[11]

Initially, this approach involved casting for moral resemblance, a process wherein he attempted to find someone whose moral outlook approximated that of the character.[12] Bresson believed that from such a person he would get an unconscious honesty and thus erase the line between character and performer. The camera—which he regularly referred to as "that extraordinary instrument"—would then reveal that honesty.[13]

Having secured a level of authenticity through this approach to casting, Bresson then moved to ensure its continued effect through a very rigorous style of rehearsal.

Bresson's antitheatrical approach to performance includes a disavowal of the process of character building and the exploration of psychological motivation. His preference has been to have his models execute simple actions removed from narrative or emotional context, in an unknowing void. As he has said:

> I may have my character walk to a desk and place a book on it for as many as 10, 20, 30, 40 times. When I see what I want, when he gives me what I want—this tiny glimpse of him—I take it.[14]

The desired effect is a level of automatism, of moving in a fashion in which there is no exteriorizing of emotion or psychology, no form of purposeful expression. The repetition of movement in rehearsal is meant to suppress intentionality and thus free authenticity.

> Model. Reduce to the minimum the share his consciousness has. Tighten the meshing within which he cannot any longer not be him and where he can now do nothing that is not *useful*.[15]

Bresson either adopted this theory from Montaigne or found confirmation of it in that writer's work. As he said to Charles Thomas Samuels:

> Anyway, mechanics are essential. Our gestures, nine times out of ten, are automatic. The way you are crossing your legs and holding your head are not voluntary gestures. Montaigne has a marvelous chapter on hands in which he says that hands go where their owner does not send them. I don't want my non-actors to think of what they do. Years ago, without realizing any program, I told my non-actors, "Don't think of what you are saying or doing," and that moment was the beginning of my style.[16]

What Bresson attempted to do was recover the automatism of everyday life, those unconscious moments which he felt were the true indicators of personality. What he sought was the revelation of instinct.[17]

Bresson's approach to achieving this unconscious automatism involved the flattening of both external elements of performance: the physical and the vocal. By denying the intentionality of these exterior aspects, Bresson believed he was moving his models closer to being in a state to reveal authentic character.

It has been suggested that the key to Bresson's physical presentation exemplifies the *tabula rasa*, Locke's theory that all ideas and rational experience are empirically built up from sense impressions (as opposed to the doctrine of innate ideas). It has also been suggested that Bresson renders the face expressionless so as to impute expression through the principles Kuleshov derived from his Mozhukhin experiment. I would argue that neither assumption is correct, the two being somewhat interconnected by the implication of construction. While it is true that Bresson denies his models overt expression, it is not for the purpose of construction but rather for the possibility of revelation. For Bresson, the expression is not on the face, it is *in* the face, his aim being a presentation of physiognomy rather a *re*presentation of psychology.

Bresson strives for the same ironed out quality for the vocal track. Here Bresson insists again that overt expression be removed, that the words simply be read with proper attention to their rhythmic structure. Inflection and projection are not necessary, as individual timbre is what embodies authentic character. Bresson instructs his models to speak all their lines as if in monologue, thus removing any level of expression which might be engendered in the attempt to communicate ideas to another person. As he has stressed, monotone is not synonymous with monotonous, and authentic meaning will erupt only when intentionality has been eradicated.

The purpose of these strategies is to serve Bresson's overall conception of a cinema free of artificiality. Because Bresson perceives the performance code as the most prone to artificiality, he works to delimit its traditionally communicative powers.

## NARRATIVE STYLE AND STRUCTURE

An understanding of the third level of Bresson's utilization of the performance code involves examining his narrative style and structure so as to determine the place accorded performance in his compositional strategies and editing patterns. In his compositions, Bresson systematically downplays the importance of the human figure, generally rendering it the equal of environment; in his editing, he avoids traditional narrative systems which are used to clarify and focalize. He removes the emphasis from performance values, as would be consistent with his approach to the casting and rehearsal of his models.

His compositional strategies include: a reduction in purposeful facial close-ups; attention to nonfacial gestural synecdoche; a use of setting and lighting to maintain the balance in compositional effect of figure and environment; a reduction of character-related camera movements.

As Bresson has noted: "Shooting is not making something definite, it is making preparations."[18] While he takes enormous care to ensure that his *mise-en-scène* has a very specific hieratic quality, ultimately he is more concerned with his montage.

His editing strategies as they relate to performance include: an avoidance of traditional figurations for projection and identification; an elliptical style by which he avoids the on-screen representation of cathartic or paroxysmal acts, including moments of heightened emotion; a style of juxtaposition which is used to effect the communication of ideas and information rather than Kuleshovian derived emotions; a reliance on repetitive rhythmic editing structures.

Beyond the compositional and editing strategies, one must also take note of Bresson's unique use in this trilogy of first-person voice-over narration. Where most first-person narrators are generally talkative and informative, Bresson's are shy and guarded. Where most speak of emotional trauma and mystery and embroider their *récit* with editorial comments, Bresson's impart factual information. Where most speak with first-person egocentricity, Bresson's present themselves as both subject and object. Where most examine a situation in a series of flashbacks to lend a sense of psychological investigation, Bresson's narrate a straight or near-linear chronology.

Most importantly, Bresson's use of voice-over divorces the two performance aspects of face and voice, thereby downplaying the effect of their simultaneity. Delivered in monotone and generally without an accompanying facial close-up, Bresson's voice-overs give primacy to the word over the speaker. The voice, thus removed, reinforces the overall environment of isolation and alienation.

Communicative powers in the cinema are largely embodied by systems of projection and identification. As outlined, Bresson rehearses his models so as to avoid the former; in his style and structure, he works to avoid the latter.[19] Where Hitchcock essentially encourages both projection and identification, and Renoir generally encourages projection but avoids identification, Bresson denies both. In the case study of *A Man Escaped*, I will examine some of the methods by which he denies these systems.

## *A MAN ESCAPED*

*A Man Escaped*, like other Bresson films, is the story of a struggle, in this case against both the self and the physical confines of a prison. Fontaine will be free physically only when he is free spiritually; he will be free only when he gives himself up to grace.

The film is set in Lyon in 1943 during the Nazi occupation. Based on the actual account of French Resistance member André Devigny, the film details the planning and execution of an escape. In an attempt to indicate both the factual nature of the story and his devotion to an ascetic style, Bresson prefaces the film with the title: "This story actually happened. I set it down without any embellishment."

In the course of the narrative, Fontaine (who is in every scene) encounters both encouragement and discouragement from his fellow inmates, some anxious for him to succeed, others fearful of repercussions for all if he fails. Throughout, Fontaine remains committed to the idea of escape, but—being human—allows himself to procrastinate. Even after his sentencing (he is to be shot), he hesitates. It is not until he overcomes his fear and allows fate to intervene (hence the film's alternate title, "The Spirit Breathes Where It Will," from St. John's gospel), that Fontaine is released from both his physical and mental imprisonment.

Bresson cast the film using his moral resemblance principle, choosing François Leterrier, a 27-year-old philosophy graduate who had recently completed his military service, for the role of Fontaine. (Leterrier was also the same age and rank as Devigny.) The role of the skeptical prisoner Blanchet was played by an elderly Belgian man of letters. German students played Gestapo officers.

Roland Monod, a former theology student, was cast as Pastor de Leiris. In the November 1956 issue of *Cahiers du Cinéma*, Monod published an article entitled, "Working with Bresson." In that article he confirmed Bresson's theoretical approach to characterization:

> Bresson told me that since the pastor's strength lay in the intensity of his inner life, the more I turned in upon myself, the less I seemed outwardly to give, the more this depth of being would impose its strength and authority on the screen....
>
> "Forget about tone and meaning," Bresson told me. "Don't think about what you're saying; just speak the words automatically.... The film actor should content himself with *saying* his lines. He should not allow himself to show that he already understands them. Play nothing, explain nothing. A text should be spoken as Dinu Lipatti plays Bach. His wonderful technique simply *releases* the notes; understanding and emotion come later...."
>
> The dialogue directly recorded at the studio ... [Bresson found] *still too human*, too anecdotal. We had to go back and re-record our lines in a sound studio. There, phrase by phrase, word by word almost, we spoke our lines after their author—ten, twenty, thirty times over, trying to match as exactly as possible the intonations, *the rhythm*, that in the end Bresson played every part ...[20] (emphases two, three and four, mine)

In *A Man Escaped*, Bresson involves us exclusively with the activities of Fontaine. We meet other characters only as their activities intersect with his, notably in the communal washroom. Fontaine's contact with others outside this communal space is limited by his solitary incarceration. He does manage to communicate with others, but under conditions in which they are physically separated, their communication illegal. Mostly we witness Fontaine alone in his cell, fashioning the tools of his escape.

Of the four characters he speaks to surreptitiously outside the washroom, only Terry, an inmate who is inexplicably allowed to walk the courtyard, is visible to him. The others are in their cells. He speaks with Orsini through the peephole in his door, to Blanchet while both are at their exterior windows. His communication with a fourth prisoner is limited to tapping messages through their shared wall. Late in the film, after his imminent execution has been announced, Fontaine receives a roommate. While the boy, Jost, is at first perceived as an obstacle, his true function is soon revealed.

Forced to include or kill him, Fontaine opts for the former and finally discusses his plan. It is under such dire circumstances that Bresson generally structures and examines the difficulties of communication.

Fontaine's central preoccupation during the first part of the film is with releasing the panels of his cell door. It is in the structure of these scenes that we most clearly witness Bresson's avoidance of systems of projection and identification.

An analysis of a typical sequence is instructive:

shot 1: close-up of two hands holding a spoon wedged in the door panel (fig. 13.2)

this shot is taken from an oblique angle without an establishing shot; the vertically panning camera traces the push of the spoon down, up, then back down

shot 2: close-up of Fontaine, in profile, the face somewhat obscured in shadow (fig. 13.3)

VOICE-OVER: I made slow progress because I was afraid to make noise.

shot 3: close-up of hands (fig. 13.4)

the camera is positioned as in shot 1

hands move downward with the spoon wedged in the door panel; the camera pans vertically with the hands as they put the spoon on the floor

VOICE-OVER: I had to sweep up my shavings with a straw plucked from my broom

shot 4: long shot of the hallway, with Fontaine's door in the mid-ground (fig. 13.5)

a straw sweeps up shavings, pulling them under the door

shot 5: close-up of hands sweeping the shavings into the cell, then picking them up (fig. 13.6)

the camera is positioned as in shots 1 and 3

> one hand then picks up the spoon, puts it in the door panel, withdraws it to a pocket, pulls it out again and gets it part way back to the door panel before withdrawing it completely. Fontaine then retreats to a seated position on the bed, eyes pulled to the extreme screen left. He then looks down and off right for a few seconds until he hears: "Is that you Fontaine?" (fig. 13.7)

In this five-shot sequence we see four key aspects of Bresson's style of projection and identification avoidance: (a) the absence of a clear traditional close-up of the protagonist for means of gaining reaction to the visualized proceedings, (b) the camera placed at an angle oblique to the action so that literal point of view is clearly not intended, and moving the camera in a panning motion to reinforce the presence of the camera as the agent of narrative, (c) the use of gestural synecdoche to communicate Fontaine's caution, and (d) most radically, cutting to the other side of the door, a space Fontaine is unable to see.

The scenes of Fontaine working on his door are not completely devoid of facial close-ups, but is is generally at moments of achievement or frustration that Bresson tends to remove them completely, deny clear access, or locate the reaction in a nonfacial gesture. Projection in a close-up would generally be anticipated in such intense scenes; a director like Hitchcock would heighten the suspense by employing figurations which would induce or enforce identification with the character's cognitive processes.

The following sequence exemplifies aspects of that strategy:

shot 1: close-up of hands working on the door with spoon blade

> the camera, positioned at an oblique angle to the action, pans upward with hands and spoon
>
> VOICE-OVER: After three weeks, trying to be noiseless, I managed to loosen three boards.

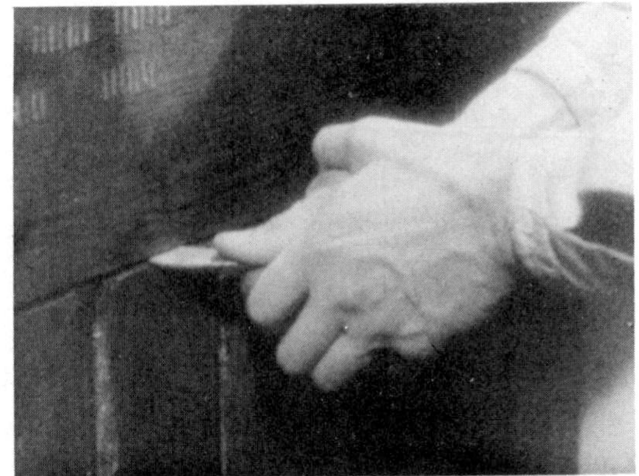

Fig. 13.2

Fig. 13.3

Fig. 13.4

Fig. 13.5

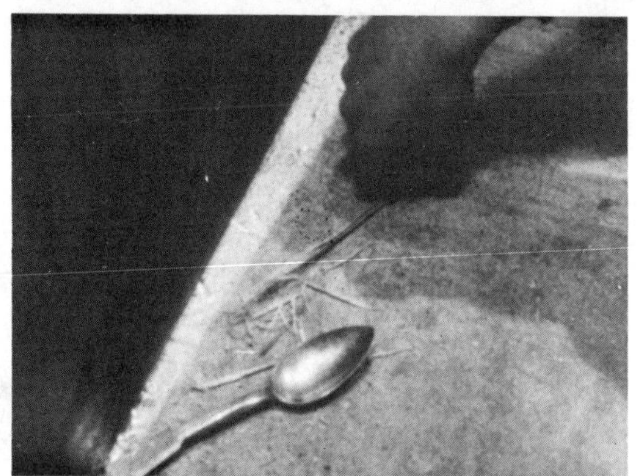

Fig. 13.6

Fig. 13.7

shot 2: brief close-up of Fontaine, eyelids down, no access to pupils (fig. 13.8)

shot 3: close-up of hands pushing down on the spoon wedged horizontally in the door frame (fig. 13.9)

VOICE-OVER: But their ends were held by tenons too strong for my spoon.

shot 4: close-up of Fontaine, as in shot 3

sound of snapping

no facial reaction, very minimal body jerk

shot 5: close-up of hand, palm up holding the bowl of the broken spoon (fig. 13.10)

the hand then exits screen right, leaving as the image just the spoon handle still wedged horizontally in the door

an excruciating sound is heard as he attempts to free the panel

Fontaine withdraws his hands, cut on movement to shot 6

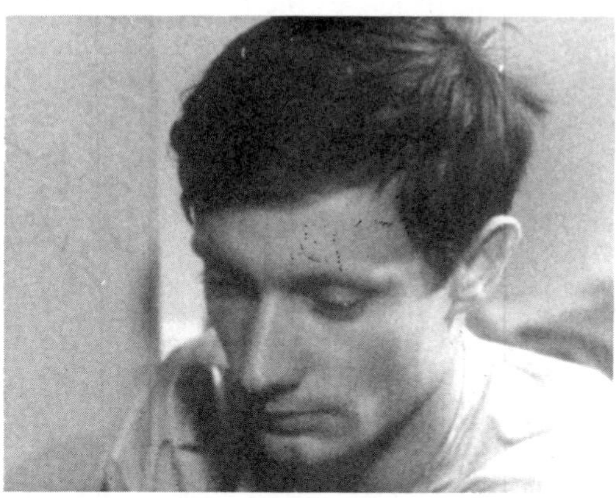

**Fig. 13.8**

shot 6: continued movement of hand withdrawing

Fontaine backs up until his body is seen from the ribs down (fig. 13.11)

VOICE-OVER: To split the frame (as he sits), I needed another spoon to use as a lever.

sitting on the edge of the bed, Fontaine is seen in profile hunched over with his left elbow on his left knee, eyes downcast at the end of the shot as he begins to raise his head toward the door (and away from the camera)

fade to black

In this six shot sequence, Bresson uses two close-ups of Fontaine's face, neither having a particular function vis-à-vis the action, neither functioning as a purposeful reaction component or to anchor a voice-over or figuration for visual identification.

In shot 4, the main catharsis occurs when the spoon handle breaks. Curiously, there is neither a facial nor overt body movement to correspond to the breaking action. Bresson uses only the sound of the spoon snapping to convey their occurrence. Importantly, the next shot is to a close-up of Fontaine's hand with the severed spoon and then the spoon blade alone, their reactions to the disaster being far more significant in the Bressonian system than any facial gesture.

Shot 5 covers a significant period of time, Bresson never cutting or panning to Fontaine's face. It is not until he has completed the activity and moves to sit on his bed that Bresson deigns to give us a shot of Fontaine which includes the face. That shot, however, like the previous one, involves a nonfacial reaction to the disaster, Bresson detailing Fontaine's frustration through posture rather than facial gesture. A facial close-up at this point would have been within the standard cinematic presentation, affording the performer an opportunity to project frustration and providing the spectator the

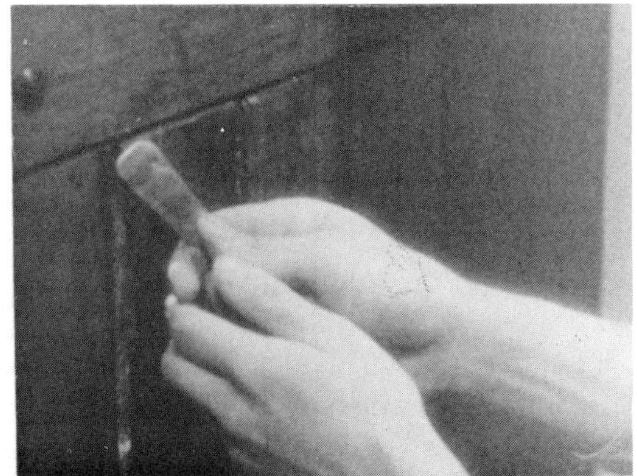

Fig. 13.9

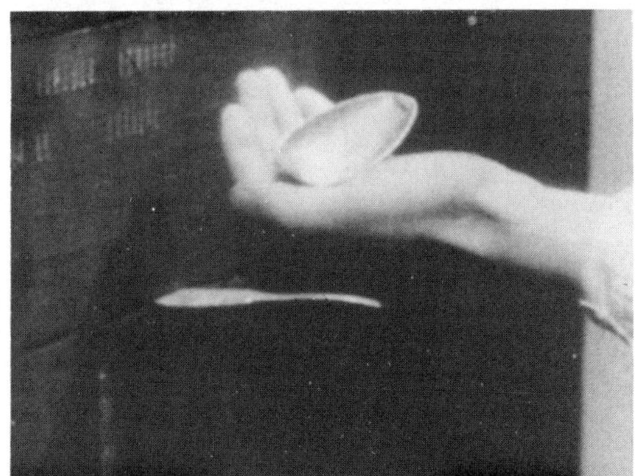

Fig. 13.10

Fig. 13.11

occasion to strongly identify with this moment of crisis. Bresson purposely eschews the obviousness of such easy resolution.

Another sequence where traditional close-up reaction shot editing is elliptically denied is when Fontaine successfully removes the panels of his door, walks around the corridor, and speaks briefly with Orsini. In this extended (62 foot) two shot scene, Bresson not only denies us visual access to Orsini, but also refuses a clear facial close-up of Fontaine, downplaying completely any sense of traditional projection or identification as structured through facial indicators.[21] Hence, Bresson counteracts what we might intuit as Fontaine's joy and sense of freedom by keeping him obscured, for the most part, in darkness and/or long shot, reducing his body to a vague element in a severely darkened composition. A close-up would not only have removed the possible ambiguity of dual emotion (free, but not free) but foregrounded psychology over ambiance. Bresson avoids such standard formulation here, preferring to convey emotion only at the end of the scene, and then by voice-over as Fontaine walks away from the camera and into darkness. Continuing to deny tradition, he situates the content of Fontaine's monotone voiceover as his perception of Orsini's reaction: "His surprise pleased me."

In this scene, Bresson does not attempt to build emotional impact through a shot-reaction-shot structure of alternating close-ups or to impute cognition through specific psychologically endowed figurations. He simply inserts it. As such, we are encouraged to respond to words communicated *through* the model, not verbal or visual expression communicated *by* the model.

Fontaine effects this release from a cell on the upper level of the prison, having been moved there after his first meeting with the prison official and after his series of conversations with Terry.

When Fontaine is moved to this new cell he encounters, as one of his neighbors, an old man named Blanchet. Resistant at first to communicating or even acknowledging his presence, Blanchet is eventually moved by Fontaine's dedication to escape and sacrifices his blanket to help make the necessary ropes.

On ten separate occasions Fontaine and Blanchet converse,

each man situated at his exterior window. In visualizing these conversations, Bresson used only two camera setups, repeating them in each scene: a two-shot in which Blanchet is deeper in the frame, and a close-up of Fontaine. Throughout, the physical set-up forbids them eye contact, the bars impede our access to their faces.

Repetition of the same camera set-up is one aspect of Bresson's style of rhythmic editing (the first two scenes analyzed in this case study were marked by this structure: the inexorability of returning to the same spot). A second involves the structure of dialogue. For example, the rhythmic structure of the first three conversations is that of question and answer. In all, Blanchet asks six questions, two in the two-shot configuration, the other four off-screen while Fontaine is shown in close-up. The two most penetrating questions are those posed in two-shot, the first being the opening question of the second conversation: "Why do you do it?" (referring to Fontaine's plan to escape), the second being the last of the third conversation: "How will you escape?" The response to Blanchet's first question: "To fight ... to fight against myself," is rendered in two-shot. Similarly, Bresson chose this set-up for Blanchet's two most poignant statements: "Then stop scraping, we'll all be punished," at the end of the first conversation, and, "I need courage to kill myself. I tried a shoelace. It broke,"during the second. These question-and-answer dialogues, rendered in isolated close-ups, would have increased the potential for systems of projection and identification to intensify the drama. Bresson, however, is particularly careful to avoid the psychological and emotional ramifications of a close-up of either man during these key moments, preferring to place the accent on the inexorability of fate through rhythm and setting, rather than the projection of character through performance.

All close-ups of Fontaine during these conversations involve seemingly less significant moments, save one; appropriately it is his most ambiguous response. When Blanchet asks "How will you escape?" Fontaine answers, "I haven't the slightest idea." Bresson, who generally refuses the close-up for pointed responses, here renders visually significant his protagonist's most confused statement. Not surprisingly, Bresson saves this moment for the end of the scene, then has Fontaine climb down from his window, leaving us to contemplate those words while looking at the barred window. Bresson does not keep Fontaine on screen long enough to have him relay the importance of that statement through facial gesture. Rather, we come to understand the ramifications of his words through a sustained visual reiteration of the environment of the prison.

The communal washroom is the main location for visual as well as verbal contact. Bresson never once gives us a sense of how large the space is, how many inmates are there at any given time, how many guards are present, where they are located, or how they oversee the space. He, does, however, establish an environment of necessary caution: in the first washroom scene in which Fontaine meets other inmates, conversation has barely begun when from off-screen comes the command of "Silence!" Not only does this effectively establish an atmosphere which pervades further scenes in this location, but it activates a seminal figure of Bresson's choreographic style: eyes darting in and out of eyeline matches with extreme precision.

These scenes are emblematic of conversation in Bresson's work: the frustration of communication signalled by a precise choreography which inhibits projection by and identification with character.

Of these washroom scenes, twelve focus on the encounters of Fontaine and the Pastor de Leiris, while three focus on Fontaine and Orsini, the will of God and the mistakes of Orsini being the two factors which enable Fontaine to escape successfully at the film's end. The scenes with the pastor are rife with hesitation on the part of Fontaine, his choreographed eye movements connoting uneasiness and/or embarrassment as well as the necessary caution. Typical is the following section of the washroom scene immediately following the night when Fontaine climbs through his door and walks around the corridor:

shot 1: group shot of Fontaine, the pastor, and three other inmates

Pastor (handing a note to Fontaine): Read and pray. God will help you.

Fontaine moves to put the note in his pocket, the camera moving with him to the coat rack.

shot 2: FONTAINE (as he passes behind the pastor): We must help ourselves too. (fig. 13.12)

PASTOR: Do you pray?

shot 3: FONTAINE (in close-up at the trough): Sometimes. (fig. 13.13)

PASTOR (off-screen): When things look bad?

FONTAINE (looking off-screen in the opposite direction to where the pastor is): Yes.

shot 4: PASTOR (in close-up): That's easy. (fig. 13.14)

shot 5: FONTAINE (in close-up): Too easy (fig. 13.15)

shot 6: PASTOR (in close-up as he turns to look at Fontaine, without speaking)

shot 7: FONTAINE (in a close-up): God can't do everything for you. (fig. 13.16)

Fontaine looks left to the pastor, quickly disengaging his glance by returning his eyes to the downward position, then up to look off-screen right.

Bresson reinforces the religious/philosophical differences between these two men by filming this discussion about prayer as a series of close-ups, rather than the two-shots they had previously cohabited. This strategy not only emphasizes the fragmentation of this particular conversation, but more effectively communicates the awkwardness this level of personal interaction obtains for Fontaine. Note particularly shot 3, when Fontaine turns away from the pastor, and shot 7, when he quickly disengages his glance. The choreography of turning away is ultimately more effective than the verbal admission of guilt.

## CONCLUSION

In traditional narrative cinema, as in most theater, characters are developed and performance created for the most part through the visualization of conversation. In such situations, a director can extend the projection of character through performance to effect a system of spectatorial identification, encouraging it through any number of configurations involving characters in purposeful or sustained action or reaction, or enforcing it through sustained point-of-view editing. These strategies form a dominant aesthetic but are not the only approach to the presentation of character.

In Bresson's cinema, conversation is severely limited and generally cryptic, reflecting the director's belief that communication between humans is fraught with difficulty. Extended conversations are rare, the uneasy quality of the exchanges typified by the avoidance of eye contact between conversants. Bresson's characters are denied the explication of actions and reactions on any psychological or emotional level as such explication is an affront, marked by disingenuousness and a lack of authenticity.

Performance in Bresson's films is a product of the aesthetics of denial, notably a denial of all traditional rhetorical approaches. In his films, he attempts to defocalize performance by removing the immediacy of its effect. His central approach involves a denial of systems of projection and identification.

If asceticism is the pathway to a greater spiritual awareness, then Bresson's cinema is an exemplification of that doctrine. Therein lies his unique contribution: he forces us to reassess our cinematic aesthetic, specifically our spectatorial needs; he forces us to forestall our habitual reliance on performance.

Fig. 13.12

Fig. 13.13

Fig. 13.14

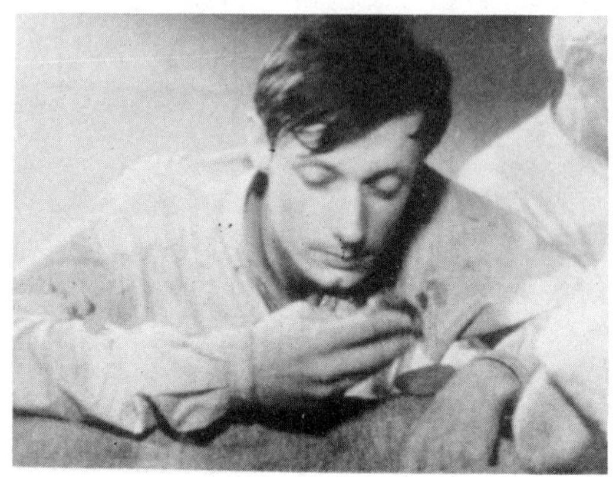

Fig. 13.15

Fig. 13.16

## NOTES

1. Bresson has written all his scripts since his third feature, *The Diary of a Country Priest*, in 1950. (He collaborated on the first two.) Having complete control meant writing his scripts by himself.
2. Robert Bresson, *Notes on Cinematography* (Paris: Editions Gallimard, 1975), p. 40. Typically ambiguous, this note could refer to his characters, models, and/or audience.
3. Bresson, interviewed by Jean-Luc Godard and Michel Delahaye, *Cahiers du Cinéma*, no. 178, 1966; trans. in *Cahiers in English* no. 8, p. 17. Bresson has consistently used a 50mm lens to flatten the image and thus further visualize this concept.
4. *Notes on Cinematography*, p. 1.
5. *Notes on Cinematography*, p. 41.
6. Bresson, interviewed by Ronald Hayman, *Transatlantic Review*, Summer 1973, p. 21.
7. Godard and Delahaye interview, p. 16.
8. *Notes on Cinematography*, p. 53. The actual wording is, "The actor is double. The alternate presence of him and of *the other* is what the public has been schooled to cherish."
9. *Notes on Cinematography*, p. 47.
10. The genesis of this dictum apparently began when problems arose on the set of his second feature, *Les Dames du Bois de Boulogne* (1944), due to his inability to suppress performance virtuosity to suit his aims. The case of Bresson vs. Maria Casares is well documented, his difficulty stemming from her inability to satisfy his needs, hers from a feeling of being reduced to a prop. See particularly Casares in *World Theatre* 8, 1959, repr. *Voices of Film Experience*, ed. by Jay Leyda (New York: McMillan, 1977).
11. Bresson did break this rule once, when he cast Jean-Claude Guilbert as both Arnold in *Au Hasard, Balthazar*, and Mathieu in *Mouchette*. Filmed in the same year, Bresson was able to keep Guilbert from having access to his screen image until both films were shot.
12. Later he would redefine that strategy, claiming that vocal quality was the more important aspect and admitting to a procedure of casting his nonprofessionals by telephone. By the 1970s, he had further refined that strategy to a point where casting was a matter of what he called "luck and intuition." See particularly Carlos Clarens' interview with Bresson in *Sight & Sound*, Winter 1971/2, and Michel Ciment's in *American Film*, October 1983, for Bresson's comments on these changes in strategy.
13. Whether schematized or not, there is also a physiognomic dimension to his casting. The facial and physical similarities of Claude Laydu (the priest), Francois Leterrier (Fontaine), and Martin Lassalle (Michel), for example, can be seen easily.
14. Bresson, interviewed by Marjorie Greene, *Film Quarterly*, Spring 1960.
15. *Notes on Cinematography*, p. 26.
16. Bresson, interviewed by Charles Thomas Samuels, *Encountering Directors* (New York: G.P. Putman's, 1972), p. 60.

17. The key passage from Montaigne is the following from his *Essays*:
    We cannot command our haire to stand on end;
    nor our skinne to startle for desire or feare.
    Our hands are often carried where we direct
    them not.
18. *Notes on Cinematography*, p. 53.
19. While projection is a function of performance, the method of its presentation is controlled by the director; while identification can be *enforced* (through sustained point-of-view editing), it can also be suggested by the director (through sustained use or repetition of purposeful image) or suggested through the projection of character psychology or actor persona. (Hitchcock, for example, cast many of his leads for the benefits of habitual identification with the star persona.)
20. Roland Monod, "Working with Bresson," *Cahiers du Cinéma*, Nov. 1956, trans. in *Sight & Sound*, Summer 1957.
21. If eye contact had been desired, Orsini could have opened his peephole; if Bresson had wanted to visualize him, he could have cut to the inside of his cell, having committed a similar act when he visualized the hallway and door shavings outside Fontaine's cell. Bresson denies our visual access to Orsini, preferring to have us imagine him through the sound of his voice. A two-shot does not negate systems of projection and identification. It can, however, de-emphasize them.

# 14. REPRESENTATION, SPECTACLE, PERFORMANCE IN BERNARDO BERTOLUCCI'S *THE CONFORMIST*

**Angela Dalle Vacche**

## I.

BERNARDO BERTOLUCCI'S *The Conformist* (1970), based on the novel by Alberto Moravia,[1] has often been considered a self-reflexive, modernist text because it explores how representation, spectacle, and performance function when cinema looks at the fascist past. The culture of the regime becomes the testing ground of Louis Althusser's theses as developed from his reading of Antonio Gramsci's *Notebooks*.[2] In particular, Gramsci's concept of "hegemony" acquires a seminal value in Althusser's work. By hegemony Gramsci meant:

> The "spontaneous" consent given by the great masses of the population to the general direction imposed on social life by the dominant fundamental group; this consent is "historically" caused by prestige (consequent confidence) which the dominant group enjoys because of its position and function in the world of production.[3]

In my analysis, I wish to suggest that Bertolucci's exploration of representation, spectacle, and performance in cinema can be better understood in the light of post-structuralist and neo-marxist categories, such as the positing of imaginary relations, the construction of consent, and the interpellation of the subject. In *Language and Materialism* (1977), Rosalind Coward and John Ellis explain that in borrowing from Jacques Lacan the concepts of the imaginary and interpellation, "Althusser only acknowledges the inadequacy of the terms available in Marxism, rather than us[ing] the full implications of the psychoanalytic ..."[4] Lacanian terminology. For Coward and Ellis, Althusser's imaginary means "that which is not real,"[5] and interpellation indicates "the calling on the individual as a homogeneous, non-contradictory whole—or subject—which is then the coherent support for ideological representations."[6]

I shall ground my reading of *The Conformist* in parallels between Althusser's and Bertolucci's views because they raise similar questions about the constitution of subjectivity in culture and history. Bertolucci's critique of Crocean thought echoes Althusser's anti-humanist contention that idealism postulates a transcendental subject. As Andrew Britton explains, the French theorist denies "... the primacy of the self-conscious subject as a theoretical category and suggests that the subject is an ideological construct whose conviction of self-determination is illusory."[7] By arguing that self-determination is only an illusion, Althusser challenges the hegemonic status enjoyed in Western thought by Descartes' dictum, "Cognito ergo sum." Within the narrower boundaries of Italian culture, Bertolucci's views on the function of subjectivity in history spring from a struggle against the idealism which informs Croce's interpretation of fascism. For Croce, the regime is not based on the problems of the middle-class, but is instead comparable to a disease which suddenly attacks a healthy organism. By contrast, Bertolucci finds fascism not an evil parenthesis, but the extreme degeneration of ongoing bourgeois practice.

Representation is a broader term than spectacle and performance because it includes all sorts of *mise-en-scène*, behavior, image, and artifacts—in short, a whole range of signs engaged in producing a vision of the past. As Hayden White remarks, this vision of the past is never definitive because "... history is in no sense a science and its generalizations are products of a historical or poetical imagination in no way capable of being 'refuted' or 'disconfirmed' by evidence."[8]

Although history is not a science, its generalizations take on the form of powerful narrative constructs, capable of making a claim of truth about the past. The representation of the past on the screen draws its power from a comparable paradox. On the one hand, this representation is always misleading; on the other hand, it is fascinating to the point that the viewer is willing to believe in the truth of what he sees, even if only for a moment. The images on the screen are at the same time lies and lures. This tension between simulation and fascination becomes the driving principle of a game of disclosures and concealments, light and darkness. Representation produces the appearance of a lifelike reality. Its movement is at once an *illusion* and an *elusion.* From the Latin *ludere*, that is to say, to play, the etymology of these words confirms the metaphor.[9] Cinema plays a game of conformism. It constructs a surrogate world whose function is to satisfy our desire for truth through the representation of either different, unrelated, or conflicting elements which are made to appear congruous with each other, as if they were all fit neatly within a larger, coherent, and intelligible scheme of narration.

Representation is conformist because it relies on the meshing of sounds and images, of looks and movements, to construct beautiful but misleading pictures. Spectacle is one of the most conformist forms of representation because it gains the consent of the viewers by giving them images which are pleasurable to look at. Spectacle defines a very special kind of representation; behind a pleasurable facade it conceals a lack, an intrinsic inadequacy. The term spectacle comes from the Latin verb *spectare*, to look at. The noun designates a region accessible to the public gaze, with a display of animate or inanimate elements, or a combination of both. A spectacle is a *mise-en-scène* with superlative features, which declares its endurance regardless of the audience.

By contrast, a performance is a particular kind of spectacle which assumes the work of individuals whose voices, gestures, and actions form an object of consumption for either a potential or actual audience. Performance "gives life" to a *mise-en-scène* which, until that moment, was frozen into a spectacle. Although the discourse of spectacle is one of passivity comparable to a monologue, there is in any performance a degree of dialogical exchange between actors and spectators. Since the days of its invention, cinema has fulfilled the dream of representing life in motion. In the passage from the stage to the screen, performance does not "give life" but "is" life. This juxtaposition of the inertia of spectacle with the dynamism of performance suggests that the technology of cinema is based on an equivalent tension between stillness and mobility. The mechanical projection of images on the screen is possible as long as the actual stillness of each individual frame allows for the illusion of movement, through the projector, of these very frames.

This metaphorical definition of performance in film means that the actors' words, movements, and expressions are executed by bodies capable of moving, speaking, and looking. As Jean-François Lyotard explains, the performance of these bodies "is intended for other living bodies—the spectators—who are capable of being moved"[10] by these words, movements, and expressions. Lyotard's definition of performance as "giver of life" leads him to the formulation of an anthropomorphic model, whose "… elementary unit is polyesthetic like the human body: capacity to see, to hear, to touch, to move, … the idea of performance seems linked to the idea of inscription of the body."[11]

For Lyotard, the body is the main site where this exchange takes place. His emphasis on the body is consonant with Bertolucci's use of actors' performance to depict the constitution of subjectivity required by interpellation in fascist ideology. These definitions of spectacle and performance respectively describe the condition of passivity generated by consent and the desire to see one's own identity represented as an acting subject rather than a passive object afloat in the vast sea of subjection.

Through his major character, Marcello Clerici (Jean-Louis Trintignant), Bertolucci describes how a whole social class hides its shallow way of life under a facade of respectability. Marcello takes on the behavior of the conformist, so that his private, homosexual identity may disappear behind a public, heterosexual image. With Marcello, performance is an act of simulation whose reward is the pleasure of conforming to a system of authority. Regardless of their political beliefs and sexual inclinations, nearly all the characters in *The Conformist* practice the art of deception. Lino (Pierre Clementi), the chauffeur, masquerades as Butterfly, a beautiful woman with long hair. Marcello's fiancée, Giulia (Stefania Sandrelli), feigns virginity until her honeymoon. In Paris, Clerici approaches his former mentor at the University of Rome, the anti-fascist Professor Quadri (Enzo Tarascio), with the secret intention of murdering him. Anna Quadri (Dominique Sanda), the professor's wife, flirts with both Marcello and Giulia. Even Prof. Quadri, whose name evokes a clear, geometric figure, has a shady side; he is willing to tolerate his wife's flirtations with his most dangerous enemy. Manganiello (Gastone Moschin), Marcello's brutal assistant, is the only character who does not dissimulate. As his name indicates,[12] Manganiello represents the most aggressive and mindless version of fascism. With Manganiello, the regime lifts its appealing mask to show its crude and violent nature. All these different characters inhabit a Freudian scenario whose director is the unconscious. Bertolucci empowers his characters with disguised desire; they can then perform on the stage of Fascist public life. In assuming the position of the unconscious, Bertolucci's direction of actors takes on a double strategy: to disguise and to recover repressed desires. Bertolucci's interest in politics and in sexuality emerges in his vision of the past and in his direction of actors and of camera movement. These two representational strategies suggest a theory of fascism which can accommodate both a psychoanalytic and a Marxist model.

## II.

With a profusion of details evocative of the period, Bertolucci highlights the seductive power of the fascist style in fashion, architecture, industrial design, and painting.[13] The regime tried to impose the cultural myths of advanced capitalism on a society still plagued by backwardness. This project—to construct illusions for the masses—corresponds word for word to Althusser's definition of ideology. In *Lenin and Philosophy* (1971), he equates ideology with illusion, arguing: "Ideology represents the imaginary relationship of individuals to their real conditions of existence."[14] For Althusser, ideology is a sort of representation through which men do not represent the system of real relations which regulates their existence, but their imaginary relationship to that system. As soon as culture internalizes and perpetuates this relationship, the latter is no longer "imaginary," but is perceived as "real." This Althusserian notion of ideology emerges from Bertolucci's critique of the bourgeois lifestyle. He argues that the value system of this social class, based on religious traditions, moral obligations, and social codes, does not correspond to a set of universal and natural rules. Rather, it is a series of strategies of control developed by a social class to maintain hegemony.

In his *Prison Notebooks*, Antonio Gramsci explains that a ruling class maintains its hegemony by using consent to legitimize the use of coercive powers. Gramsci writes:

> The normal exercise of hegemony on the now classical terrain of the parliamentary regime is characterized by the combination of force and consent, which balance each other reciprocally, without force predominating excessively over consent. Indeed, the attempt is always made to ensure that force will appear to be based on the consent of the majority.[15]

Gramsci's definition of hegemony as a combination of force and consent leads to Althusser's argument that it is not a reality of coercion that men represent to themselves in ideology, but a relationship based on a consent which is wholly imaginary. The staging of athletic events and military parades proved to be a very effective way to build up the consent for the regime.[16] This relationship of consent between the governed and the governing was perceived as real rather than as imaginary because the spectators were under the illusion of performing spontaneous roles in these spectacles. In Gramsci's words, behind the "... spontaneous consent of the masses who must 'live' those directives, modifying their own habits, their own will, their own convictions to conform ... there was a perfect preparation."[17]

This exploitation of consent to disguise force is comparable to the strategy of cinematic spectacles which encourage the spectator to enjoy a condition of passivity. In *The Conformist*, Bertolucci reconstructs the climate of the thirties by imposing a polished *mise-en-scène* over situations of disruptive violence. The sleek images which Bertolucci creates for this horrifying tale exemplify one of the regime's typical strategies: the staging of spectacles to hide the signs of disturbance which lie beneath the surface of a regimented society. Piacentini's series of identical windows and the Art Deco lintels which frame Marcello, the muted colors of the women's clothing, and Marcello's military gait are all icons of regimentation. These visuals amount to conformism. They express the individual's desire to project one's own self in "the imaginary relations" which constitute the ideology of fascism.

This tension between regimentation and loss of control becomes explicit in the sequence where Giulia dances in front of Marcello. To a syncopated tune from America, she attempts to seduce her composed fiance. Her provocative movements contrast with the black-and-white striped pattern of her dress. The reoccurrence throughout the film of stripes, bars, and shadowy lines creates a visual network of control which serves to block all threats to the established order. Dance is an appropriate vehicle for the release of Giulia's repressed sexuality. Whenever it is associated either with spontaneity or tribal rituals or entertainment, dance evokes the emotions and calls attention to the energy stored in the body, in opposition to control and ratiocination. While dancing, Giulia becomes an emblem of femininity which, by definition, is associated with the pleasure of the senses and silliness. Although it never upsets her apartment's orderly decor, her performance increases the sensuousness of the *mise-en-scène*; it's more on the order of a tease than a rebellion. Dance, instead of teasing Marcello, threatens him in a Parisian ballroom, when he finds himself trapped in the coils of a snake-like procession of dancers. Their spiraling movement renders him immobile. Although Giulia's dance at the beginning of the film is a manifestation of desire, the choreography of Marcello's entrapment spins out of his obsession to be "the same as everybody else." In this later case, recreational dance is a figure of consent whose price is the loss of individuality.

Consent, however, rests on the illusion of individuality, one of the imaginary relations constructed by men in ideology. Thus, performance is the way in which the individual subject plays out the role of his or her own self in the spectacle staged by the regime. In Althusser's words, since consent rather than force constitutes the ground of this playing out of the self, the individual "is interpellated as a (free) subject in order that he shall submit freely to the commandments of the Subject; i.e. in order that he shall (freely) accept his subjection, and the actions of his subjection 'all by himself.'"[18]

In *The Conformist*, the actors' performances cover a range of styles meant to convey different ways in which the characters construct themselves as individuals in the representation system of fascist ideology. This sketch of interpellation through the performance styles of Bertolucci's actors assumes that "the ideas of a human subject exist in his or in her actions."[19] In other words, conformism is functional to a subjectivity which believes it is free so long as its actions conform to its ideas. Conformism, then, is not an evil of fascism, but the product of an "idealist scheme"[20] which perpetuates a belief in the possibility of a "free" consciousness and of moral "truths."

Fascism makes this strategy of interpellation most apparent through "hailing." For Althusser, ideology hails "subjects among individuals."[21] He means that the function of hailing is to single individuals out and so confer on them the status of "subjects." Hailing, however, marks a closed circuit where the subjection of individuals is the *condicio sine qua non* for a subjectivity they perceive as their own. The gesture of hailing is an appropriate sign of subjection before a leader. It also brings to mind the inquisitive attitude of a policeman hailing suspects. Hailing means both subjection to and subjection of. In hailing one sees how interpellation operates under fascism. It permits the individual to hail his fellow citizens as subjects once he has received authority from one leader he himself has hailed.

In *The Conformist*, Bertolucci defines interpellation in terms of the myth of the cave, recounted by Marcello during his first conversation with Prof. Quadri. Interpellation is an inescapable condition experienced by individuals who, like Plato's slaves, do not realize that their subjectivity is not real but only a construction within ideology. By volunteering his services to Mussolini's secret police, Marcello Clerici has access to an heterosexual subjectivity which gives him the right to hail homosexuals, Jews, and anti-fascists. After the fall of the regime, he hails his friend Italo Montanari as a fascist in the attempt to remain a "subject" whose position conforms to the political consciousness of a new historical phase. In the dark study of Prof. Quadri, Marcello's hailing does not betray him in front of his victim. It is rather a gesture of acknowledgement between the disciple and the mentor who can thus recognize each other. Marcello hails Prof. Quadri as the Subject, the Father whose Humanist Culture[22] has put the son in the position to be a subject who freely accepts his subjection. Albeit he is an anti-fascist, Prof. Quadri's physical deformity suggests that the germ of fascism lies in the body politic of the Liberal state and is not, as Croce would have it, an evil from the outside.[23] Quadri's wavering from a paternal to a defensive attitude toward Marcello suggests that the victim and his murderer share a common ground in terms of moral values and social class. This bond between the professor and his former student challenges the distinction between fascism and anti-fascism, between the responsibilities of the fathers and the actions of the sons.

Bertolucci turns to the thirties to tell the story of his generation's struggle in 1968 against the legacy of a bourgeois humanist culture. His vision of the thirties is marked by an underlying awareness of the explosive tensions between fathers and sons marked by the students' barricades in Paris, during May '68. The extensive use of chiaroscuro alternates glowing tones of light with sharply defined schemes of color. The heavy curtains in the dressing room of Anna Quadri and the hanging bed sheets in the deserted corridors of Lino's house hide the secret of erotic encounters followed by violent confrontations. These regions of cool darkness, muffled whispers, and echoing footsteps clash with the blinding sunlight cast on the surreal dock of Ventimiglia or against the dazzling whiteness of the snow in the murder scene. The "fascinating fascism"[24] of the time of Bertolucci's fathers—Croce, Attilio (Bertolucci), Moravia, to name a few—[25]casts a romantic overtone on their sons who, in the late sixties, yearned for emancipation from authority and from tradition. In *The Conformist*, Bertolucci is unable to completely free himself of the binding power of his fathers' cultural tradition. He can only acknowledge his inability to reconstitute his subjectivity outside bourgeois idealism. He sets a Crocean model of a "history of liberty" against a history of the bourgeois desire for order. (This awareness of a standstill is exemplified by the director's involvement with Paramount: his alliance with American capitalists is congruous with the interests of the social class he represents and rejects at the same time.)

The performance styles of Bertolucci's actors describe how, underneath different personae, there is at work a continuity of interpellation of an idealist subject. Prof. Quadri's tolerance of his wife's lesbian inclination, Anna's contradictory behavior, Marcello's need for approval, and Giulia's brainless drive for pleasure indicate only different positions in the construction of the same idealist subject. Whether this subjectivity perceives itself as "free" in the realm of normality or of perversion, it always assumes the conformity of the ideas it "freely" recognizes as its own and its actions. All the characters of *The Conformist*, from the fascist Marcello to the anti-fascist Prof. Quadri, have been hailed by ideology, which has rewarded them with the illusion of a coherent, independent, and organic subjectivity, regardless of the political camp to which these characters belong. The multiple roles performed by Dominique Sanda do not situate the character of Anna Quadri outside the interpellation of either fascist or any other kind of ideology. These shifting roles only voice the insatiable desire to be oneself and the other, to be an individual and to be many at the same time. In the specific case of fascism, the project of ideology is to sublimate this desire by turning the overlapping of interests of the single citizen and the state into an ideal. Bertolt Brecht denounces precisely this strategy of the regime as mystifying when he says, "The continuity of the ego is a myth. Man is an atom that perpetually breaks up and forms anew."[26] Just like the rest of his characters, the director is a "conformist," simply because his construction of characters and his direction of camera movement do not take place outside ideology. Even the enigmatic, unconventional character of Anna Quadri does not constitute any real alternative to the way in which fascist ideology turns Marcello into a slave who lives with the illusion of being a master. As a modernist filmmaker, Bertolucci's direction of Sanda only makes more explicit these constant breaks and formation of new wholes—which the viewer might otherwise dismiss—in his desire for a coherent and intelligible narrative.

This recognition of conformity between ideas and actions is comparable to the need for congruity between private values and public behavior. The individual subject thinks that he is "free" to the extent that his actions fit within the body politic of the national subject which represents him. By turning the actors' bodies into emblems of the national body politic, Bertolucci never really leaves an idealist tradition. He merely updates a concept of subjectivity which goes back to Giambattista Vico[27] by adding the flavoring of psychoanalytical preoccupations. From Vico's theory of history, to Croce's rereading of the Neapolitan philosopher, to Bertolucci's view of fascism, the body politic takes on a psychoanalytic twist which brings to mind Norman O. Brown's popularization of Freudian thought rather than Jacques Lacan's theories. Vico argued that the unfolding of the historical process undergoes different stages marked by generational transformations. After rediscovering Vico's argument cited by Brown in *Closing Time*, that the body is an "historical variable,"[28] Bertolucci concludes that under different ideologies the image of the body politic is subject to change. Yet this changing appearance of the national body politic only reveals different modes of representation which have the function of positing the same ideal subject in different historical periods. This emblematic use of the body as a locus for the representation of the subjectivity of an ideal nation is the result of a strange blend between popular Freud and vulgar idealism. Trintignant and Sanda act out the struggle between the death instinct (Thanatos) and the pleasure principle (Eros), which Freud locates in the body. The former's performance recalls the granitic look of fascism made of unequivocal visual emblems, while the latter's is a fleeting appearance of ambivalent images. Marcello's postures are comparable to fascist sculptures and Anna's to a dance of ever-shifting roles. Marcello as the statue and Anna as the dancer exemplify the two extreme poles of Bertolucci's representation of the body: from the hypnotic stillness of a crowd in front of a leader to the shimmering fluidity of the shadows on the walls of Plato's cave.

Their performances, however, are also complementary because the passage from Marcello's monolithic to Anna's proteiform persona signals the crisis of ideals and morals. Their movements exemplify the ways in which stillness and mobility, normality and perversion, duty and pleasure, are not "absolute" and opposed categories, but sets of relational and mutually exclusive pairs. Bertolucci employs dance and sculpture metaphorically throughout his film. One of the aims of sculpture is to create the illusion of motion by locking this effect within a still mass. Classical dance, on the other hand, consists of highly controlled steps moving towards a condition of illusory stillness which signifies the reaching of an ideal pose. This relation of complementarity between sculpture and dance signals the blurring of boundaries between homosexual and heterosexual, private and public. All these distinctions remain always "internal to bourgeois law,"[29] meaning that they function to perpetuate the authority of the ideal subject.

Bertolucci's direction of camera movement calls attention to this juxtaposition of rigid poses and flowing motions which characterizes the relation of love and hate between Anna and Marcello. In conforming to his actors' performances, Bertolucci acknowledges that his camera does not signify outside interpellation. His tracking shots toward huge, altar-like desks, across enormous marble halls, under black-bordered lintels, exhibit a highly directional and controlled quality. Likewise, his pans along the glittering shop windows and the fashionable streets of Paris flow with an easy, soothing tempo, thanks to George Delerue's musical score. As if it were a third site of performance, Bertolucci's camera enacts, on a formal level, the movement from hostility back to attraction between Marcello and Anna.

Bertolucci's emphasis on how gestures function on the screen demands the transformation of the camera into an acting subject. Bertolucci comments:

> ... and I move the camera as if I was gesturing with it. I feel that the cinema is always a cinema of gestures—very direct, even if there are fifty people in the crew. But imperialism is an enemy of these 'gestures'... This is why...one cuts out all that was direct and 'gesticular' in the rushes;.... I employed the editing to underline the gesticulation of the film.[30]

Here Bertolucci explains how he managed not to be entirely subject to the demands of "imperialism." On the set, Bertolucci's direction of actors owes more to the hand-held cameras of Neorealism and of Jean-Luc Godard's *nouvelle vague* than to the classical Hollywood style. There is, however, very little room left for improvisation in his direction of camera movement, which is always carefully keyed to the actors' performances. This redundancy between the camera movement and the actors' behavior is as pleasurable as the smooth rhythm and clarity of meaning sought by Hollywood narrative cinema. The editing, by contrast, maintains the erratic and unpredictable quality of a sudden "gesticulation." For example, the editing of flashbacks in Marcello's past is a convoluted *mise-en-abyme* of episodes whose narrative organization reveals affinities between viewing a film and dreaming, both of which are based on condensation and displacement. There is a tension between the gesture of redundancy performed by the camera and the editing of past episodes in Marcello's life which resembles an uncontrollable gesture. The moving camera matches the polished look of the *mise-en-scène* with the *mise-en-exécution* of the actors. The visceral quality of the editing however, seems to emerge from those dark regions of the subconscious where the desire to recover the repressed identity of a private self resists against the deceptive surface of a public subjectivity constructed in the mirror image of the ideal citizen, interpellated by fascist ideology.

In the context of the fascist past, Bertolucci reduces Freud's concepts of repression and sublimation to two major symbolic movements: pulling in and flowing out; the self-absorbed look of a sculpture and the spinning away of a dancer. By constantly intersecting each other, these two movements signal the dialectic quality of the relationship between Marcello and Anna. Because Marcello's character is an embodiment of conformism, Trintignant's appropriately restrained acting style eschews open gestures and reveals no emotion. His public image fits Susan Sontag's description of fascist aesthetics, which are based on "the containment of vital forces; movements are confined, held tight, held in."[31] The statuelike Marcello wears an impenetrable expression on his rarely smiling face. Unlike Giulia and Anna, he never lies down or sprawls on a comfortable chair. When he sits on the bed or on the backseat of the car, he is always straight-backed and stiff, his hat low over his eyes. Anna and Marcello speak many languages. Anna's poised Italian, unlike her exasperated French, signals an aristocratic, aggressive sensuality. Marcello in the car, instead, mumbles lines from a Latin poem, a sign of his classical, humanist education—a prerogative of his class. Yet his words are incomprehensible enough to cast a veil on his thoughts. In her dance studio, Anna's black cane underlines her cold, sophisticated charm. The cane is a sign of sexual independence which usually activates the code of masculinity as domination. Marcello is associated with a bouquet of flowers rather than a cane, which he stiffly carries to Giulia's house.

This oscillation between Marcello's constrained conformity and Anna's decadent behavior climaxes when their personae are reversed. Statue becomes dancer and dancer becomes statue. After a dance routine in her studio, Anna, her leg bent, leans against the wall. When Marcello appears unexpectedly, she maintains her lithe and provocative posture. As he bends down, Marcello mimics the graceful bow of children after a performance. He now violently jerks Anna into the next room. He turns the ritual greeting at the end of a dance lesson into a challenge to Anna's pedagogical role. For a moment, Marcello pretends to be a dancer to force Anna into a partnership and, thus, assert his control over her. In the ballroom sequence, however, while she dances with Giulia, Marcello's wife, Anna replaces the latter's husband. The two women, clothed respectively in black and white, form a plastic image of balanced volumes in motion. Their arms stretch out as they execute a sensuous tango. The male's traditional stiffness in the tango is softened by Anna's careful lead—her swift, sinuous turns blending with Giulia's mindless flexibility. When Anna allows Giulia to step outward and dance around her, she takes on a statue-like immobility with which she controls her partner from a distance (fig.14.1).

Despite his attempts towards a conformist behavior, Marcello is strongly attracted to Anna's deviant sexuality. This attraction re-

**Fig. 14.1**

sults in Marcello's temporary psychological dependence on Anna. By appealing at the same time to Marcello's private, homosexual self and to his heterosexual public image, she endows her character with a bisexual identity which becomes his alter ego. As soon as Anna undresses in front of Marcello, his aggressiveness gives way to an attitude of insecurity and withdrawal. The spectacle of Anna's white skin glaring in darkness paralyzes him, forcing the truth of his homosexuality to surface. Anna's glistening body becomes the mirror of Marcello's repressed identity. The latter pulls a blanket on top of Giulia's nude back while she is asleep. He is annoyed when he sees his mother's decaying body on display. He instinctively perceives that the unveiling of the human figure can illumine his sexual truth, hitherto disguised under the clothing of conformity. Sanda's performance style evokes a traditional view of femininity as moodiness and unreliability. This stereotype beautifully summarizes the famous operatic "La donna è mobile qual piuma al vento...."[32] Anna's lesbianism teases out Marcello's repressed homosexual fantasies. Anna's sexuality is comparable to the sirens' voices promising happiness to the sailors. Her promiscuous life-style glows with the lure of the very same freedom which the subject thinks he will find in the siren call of ideology: interpellation.

Amid changing disguises, Anna's physical features obsess Marcello's memory because her image links together the contradictory facets of his sexual identity. As mistress to a Fascist cabinet member, Anna becomes a mother figure to Marcello. Spying upon their encounter, Marcello hides behind a curtain and so assumes the role of the child who surprises the parents in the bedroom. The zoom underlines the drive of Marcello's voyeuristic gaze. After traversing the empty space of the room, his eyes light upon Sanda's leg swinging under a huge, marble tabletop. He then focuses on her profile hidden under a short, black veil (figs. 14.2–14.4). The fragmentation of Sanda's body into a few highly eroticized components suggests the power of the visual associations at work in Marcello's memory. Anna's traits of motherhood are compatible with her role of mentally deranged prostitute in the whorehouse of Ventimiglia. After rejecting his guilt-ridden and corrupt parents, Marcello protectively hugs Sanda. He rests his cheek against hers, as child or parent would do, but not a lover.

Anna's clothing style is a strange blend of seduction and sobriety. By wearing pants she projects an image of self-confidence, yet the silky, shiny textures and the drooping cut of her shirts strengthens her appeal as a well-heeled *femme fatale*. In her living room, Sanda's soft feminine silhouette clashes with one of her legs as it arrogantly dangles from the arm of a chair, or with the palm of her hand decisively resting on her hip (figs. 14.5–14.6). Sanda's performance incorporates the masculine postures of Marlene Dietrich's cabaret routines. Likewise, in the construction of Giulia's character, Sandrelli exploits the whining voice, the childish pouting, and gullible expression of Hollywood starlets in early sound comedies and melodramas. Sanda's and Sandrelli's performance styles illumine Bertolucci's strategy of evoking the atmosphere of the period. His cinema of gestures is based on a careful

Fig. 14.2

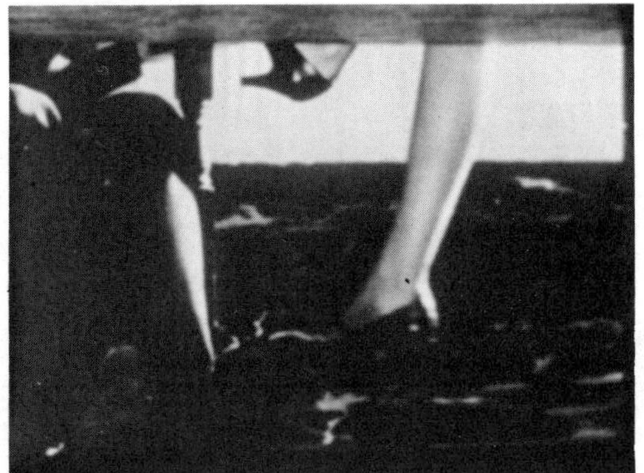

Fig. 14.3

Fig. 14.4

Fig. 14.5

Fig. 14.6

collage of all those movements which the popular imagination associates with the stars of thirties genre films.

Marcello's wavering between emphatic exhibitions of fascist virility and infantile frailty corresponds to Anna's ambivalence. Anna's oscillation between a heterosexual and a lesbian identity is comparable to Marcello's inability to overcome childlike insecurities through his exhibition of authority. His rigid postures are a clear attempt to deny sexual duplicity. In the office of a Fascist official at Ventimiglia, Marcello holds a gun with his arm rigidly stretched across a door-frame: a posture of aggression with a sculptural quality (fig. 14.7). On the steps of his mother's house, with his arms crossed on his chest, Marcello exhibits his attitude of inwardness and signals his need for a public image of control. In the radio studio, Marcello describes his financée's unrestrained manifestations of desire. In front of his friend Italo, he performs a gesture of embrace, once again crossing his arms over his chest. In his imagination, Marcello relates to his body as to Giulia's. This embrace reveals the narcissistic nature of his undeclared homosexuality. Yet, despite his play at transforming himself into a feminine counterpart, this is not a sensuous embrace. Rather it resembles the straight-jacket position assumed by Marcello's father in the scene set in the asylum (figs. 14.8–14.9).

Trintignant's indecipherable expression masks a fragile and impressionable sensitivity. During an eerie blackout, after the announcement of Mussolini's resignation, some motor vehicles drag huge Fascist sculptures of heads, busts, and eagles across a bridge on the Tiber. With these haunting images of the fall of a regime, Bertolucci stages the spectacle of the dismantling of a value system. He dramatizes the collapse of that ideal statue through which Marcello tried to sublimate his deviant sexuality. As Susan Sontag remarks, the absolute physical perfection of the fascist body is fascinating, while it conceals the violence of its repressed sexuality.[33] The proteiform traits of Sanda's body echo the crumbling of this perfect statue. By extending this interpretation of Sanda's performance from a sexual to a political level, her metamorphoses signal the disintegration of the national body politic, constructed by the regime as a guarantee of conformity. The very term "corporativism," used to describe the organization of labor in the fascist state, indicates the privileged status granted to the image of the body. The majestic and virile look of neoclassical, fascist sculptures powerfully conveyed the desire to construct oneself as an individual in the image of an ideal, transcendent subject. According to Bertolucci, the body is a privileged site used by the regime to stage the construction of consent. Through this

Fig. 14.7

Fig. 14.8

Fig. 14.9

image of the body as a body politic, the individual's awareness of self may conform to an idealized representation of public subjectivity as it is interpellated by fascist ideology.

Through a series of opposite yet complementary pairs—such as consent and interpellation, spectacle and performance, stillness and mobility, tracking shots and fluid pans, sculpture and dance—in *The Conformist*, Bertolucci represents the way in which ideology in the fascist period constructs subjectivity. Under Mussolini's regime, subjectivity finds in the idealized image of the body politic an illusory ground for the self-realization of the individual as long as he is a happily integrated member in the body of the fascist state. But, for Bertolucci, the body politic is one of the images fascist ideology can most successfully exploit to validate itself through the same effects of coherence and intelligibility sought by cinematic representation in dominant narrative cinema. *The Conformist* is a spectacle-film, a Paramount production, where Bertolucci plays the game of enticing the viewer with exactly the same representational strategies used by fascism to fascinate a whole nation. As Robert Philip Kolker remarks in his essay on *The Conformist*,[34] at the very end of the film, Marcello's gaze toward the camera is meant for the viewer. The latter is now trapped inside Marcello's field of vision and, inevitably, implicated in all his secrets. This gaze is the gesture through which the cinematic apparatus can hail a viewer and place him in a position comparable to that assumed by the slaves in Plato's cave, the archetypal movie theater. In gazing at the camera, Marcello can afford to break the cinematic illusion and call attention to the enslavement of the viewers, who, by the end of the film, have been subjected to the fascination of Bertolucci's images of fascism.

## NOTES

1. Alberto Moravia, *Il Conformista* (Milano: Bompiani, 1951).
2. Antonio Gramsci (1891–1939), major Italian intellectual, member of the central committee of the newly born Italian Communist Party (Livorno Congress 1921), arrested in 1926 by the Fascist police. Gramsci began writing his notes (published as *Prison Notebooks*) in 1929 and continued working on

them until 1935, when his ill health made sustained concentration impossible. In all there were 32 notebooks consisting of 2,848 pages covering a wide range of topics—Italian history, education, culture, philosophy, the role of intellectuals, theory of the state, catholicism, etc. The central and guiding theme of the *Notebooks*, a combination of fragmentary notes and more sustained analysis, is the development of a "new" Marxist theory applicable to the conditions of advanced capitalism.

3. Antonio Gramsci, *Selections from the Prison Notebooks*, ed. and trans. by Quintin Hoare and Geoffrey Nowell-Smith (New York: International Publishers, 1971), p. 12.
4. Rosalind Coward and John Ellis, *Language and Materialism* (London: Routledge & Kegan Paul, 1977), p. 75.
5. Coward & Ellis, p. 75.
6. Coward & Ellis, p. 75.
7. Andrew Britton, "The Ideology of *Screen*: Althusser, Lacan, Barthes" *Movie* 26 (Winter 78/79), pp. 2–3.
8. George G. Iggers, *New Directions in European Historiography* (Middletown, Connecticut: Wesleyan University Press, 1975), p. 175.
9. For this etymological remark, see: Ulrick Wicks, "Borges, Bertolucci and Metafiction" *Narrative Strategies* (Macomb: Western Illinois University Press, 1980), p. 22.
10. Jean-Francois Lyotard, "The Unconscious as Mise-en-Scène" *Performance in Post-Modern Culture*, ed. by Michael Benamou and Charles Caramello (Madison, Wisconsin: Coda Press, 1977), p. 88.
11. Lyotard, p. 88.
12. The surname Maganiello is quite close to "manganello": the baton used by Fascists during their raids.
13. Susan Sontag remarks: "Art Nouveau could never be a fascist style; it is, rather, the prototype of that art which fascism defines as decadent; the fascist style at its best is Art Deco, with its sharp lines and blunt massing of material, its petrified eroticism." see: "Fascinating Fascism," *Under the Sign of Saturn* (New York: Farrar, Straus and Giroux, 1980), p. 94.
14. Louis Althusser, *Lenin and Philosophy and Other Essays* (New York and London: Monthly Review Press, 1971), p. 162.
15. Gramsci, p. 80, n. 49.
16. Gramsci, p. 266.
17. Sontag comments on how totalitarian regimes choreograph the masses for demagogical purposes: "The masses are made to take form, be design. Hence mass athletic demonstrations, a choreographed display of bodies, are valued activities in all totalitarian countries; and the art of the gymnast, so popular now in Eastern Europe, also evokes recurrent features of fascist aesthetics; the holding in or the confining of force; military precision." See "Fascinating Fascism," p. 92.
18. Althusser, p. 182.
19. Althusser, p. 168.
20. Althusser, p. 168.
21. Althusser, p. 174.

22. With "Humanist Culture," I am referring to all these values and traditions which constitute the cultural make-up transmitted by the state educational system in Italy.
23. Different historians and critics (Peter Bondanella, Mira Liehm, Robert Philip Kolker, Richard Witcombe, and Francesco Casetti) have proposed different interpretations of Quadri's character. Some argue that the anti-fascist politics and the deformity of this character are meant to evoke the figure of Antonio Gramsci; some associate Quadri with two anti-fascists brothers, Carlo and Nello Resselli, assassinated in France; some feel that Quadri's ambiguous position is comparable to Bertolucci's predicament as a bourgeois intellectual with a membership in the Italian Communist Party; Quadri is a hunchback, a "gobbetto," in Italian. This term recalls the surname of Piero Gobetti, a non-Marxist anti-fascist.
24. Sontag, op. cit.
25. I am mentioning here only the Italian father figures whose authority Bertolucci's work questions as a result of their association with bourgeois culture. In the opposite camp of left-wing politics, Jean-Luc Godard and Pier Paolo Pasolini can also be seen as father figures for the Italian director.
26. Coward and Ellis, p. 75.
27. Giambattista Vico (1668–1774), philosopher, historian, and social scientist. Among his major works: *La Scienza Nuova* (The New Science) in 1725, which was translated in an abridged version by Jules Michelet in 1824 and received European recognition. In the twentieth century, Benedetto Croce has been the most eloquent interpreter and champion of Vico's thought. The basic theme of *La Scienza Nuova* is the establishment of a consistent eternal pattern in the origin and development of human institutions. (Freely adapted from Peter Bondanella and Julia Conway Bondanella, *Dictionary of Italian Literature* [Westport, Connecticut: Greenwood Press, 1979], pp. 539–42.)
28. Norman O. Brown, *Closing Time* (New York: Vintage Books, 1974), p. 21.
29. Althusser, p. 144.
30. Amos Vogel, "Bernardo Bertolucci: An Interview," *Film Comment*, VIII, 3 (Fall 1971), p. 26.
31. Sontag, p. 93.
32. This line appears at the beginning of a very famous aria from Guiseppe Verdi's *Rigoletto*, Atto I, Scena I. In English: "Woman is as fickle as a feather in the wind...."
33. For a more specific discussion of the representation of the body in Leni Riefenstahl's work, see Susan Sontag, "Fascinating Fascism," op. cit.
34. Robert Philip Kolker, *Bernardo Bertolucci* (New York: Oxford University Press, 1985), pp. 87–104.

## NOTES ON CONTRIBUTORS

**Noël Carroll** is Associate Professor of Philosophy and Associate Professor of Theater at Cornell University in Ithaca. He has written articles for *Daedalus, Artforum*, October, *The Drama Review, Film Quarterly* and *the Journal of Aesthetics and Art Criticism.* Carroll has recently published *Philosophical Problems of Classical Film Theory* and *Mystifying Movies.*

**Angela Dalle Vacche** has a Ph.D. from the Film Studies program at the University of Iowa. She teaches Film and Italian at Vassar College and is working on a book dealing with the representation of history in Italian cinema, entitled *The Body in the Mirror.*

**Jerome Delamater** is Associate Professor and Film Track coordinator in the Department of Communication Arts, Hofstra University. He is the author of *Dance in the Hollywood Musical.*

**Mario Falsetto** is Associate Professor of Film Studies at Concordia University in Montreal. Past President of the Film Studies Association of Canada, Falsetto is currently Associate Dean of Fine Arts. He is working on a book-length study of Stanley Kubrick's films.

**Lucy Fischer** is an Associate Professor of Film and Director of the Film Studies Program at the University of Pittsburgh. She is the author of *The Film Career of Jacques Tati* and *Shot/Counter-Shot: Film Tradition and Women's Cinema.* She has published articles on film in: *Film Quarterly, Screen, Cinema Journal, Quarterly Review of Film Studies, Millenium Film Journal, Sight and Sound.*

**Sylvie Gendron** is doing graduate work in film studies at Paris III, France.

**Marian Keane** is a Ph.D. candidate in Cinema Studies at New York University, completing her dissertation on film acting. She is currently teaching film at the University of Colorado.

**Johanne Larue** teaches Film Studies at Concordia University while doing graduate work at L'Université de Montréal. She collaborates on the journal *Séquences.*

**Roberta Pearson** is an Assistant Professor at the School of Communications, Pennsylvania State University, and is co-authoring a book with William Uricchio entitled, *Invisible Viewers, Inaudible Voices: Reception and Intertextuality in the Early Cinema.*

**William Rothman** has taught film studies at Harvard and New York University. He is the author of *The Films of Alfred Hitchcock: The Murderous Gaze* and *The "I" of the Camera.*

**Bart Testa** teaches cinema studies and semiotics at the University of Toronto. His publications include a catalogue monograph, *Spirit in the Landscape* (The Art Gallery of Ontario), along with articles for *The Canadian Journal of Social and Political Theory* and in the anthologies *Words and Moving Images* and *Dialogue.*

**Doug Tomlinson** teaches film studies at Montclair State College. He recently published *Filmmakers Speak.*

**Thomas Waugh**, Associate Professor of Film Studies at Concordia University, is editor of the anthology *Show Us Life: Towards a History and Aesthetics of the Committed Documentary* and is currently working on *Hard to Imagine: An Illustrated History of Homoerotic Photography and Cinema.* He is also a regular contributor to such journals as *Jump Cut, The Body Politic* and *Cinema Canada.*

# INDEX